THIRD EDITION

45 Techniques
Every Counselor Should Know

Bradley T. Erford
Peabody College at Vanderbilt University

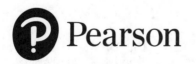 Pearson

Director and Publisher: Kevin M. Davis
Portfolio Manager: Rebecca Fox-Gieg
Content Producer: Pamela D. Bennett
Portfolio Management Assistant: Maria Feliberty
Executive Field Marketing Manager: Krista Clark
Executive Product Marketing Manager: Christopher Barry
Procurement Specialist: Deidra Headlee
Cover Designer: Pearson CSC, Carie Keller
Cover Photo: Shutterstock/optimarc
Full-Service Project Management: Pearson CSC, Shiela A. Quisel and Prince John William Carey
Composition: Pearson CSC
Printer/Binder: LSC Communications, Inc./Crawfordsville
Cover Printer: Phoenix Color/Hagerstown
Text Font: Times LT Pro

This text was previously published under the title *40 Techniques Every Counselor Should Know*.

Library of Congress Cataloging-in-Publication Data

Names: Erford, Bradley T., author.
Title: 45 techniques every counselor should know / Bradley T. Erford.
    Other titles: Forty five techniques every counselor should know
Description: Third edition. | Hoboken : Pearson Education, Inc., [2020]
Identifiers: LCCN 2018051928 | ISBN 9780134694894 | ISBN 0134694899
Subjects: LCSH: Counseling. | Counseling psychology.
Classification: LCC BF636.6 .E74 2020 | DDC 158.3--dc23 LC record available at https://lccn.loc.gov/2018051928

1   19

ISBN 13: 978-0-13-469489-4
ISBN 10:   0-13-469489-9

This effort is dedicated to The One:
the Giver of energy, passion, and understanding;
Who makes life worth living and endeavors worth pursuing and accomplishing;
the Teacher of love and forgiveness.

About the Author

Bradley T. Erford, Ph.D., LCPC, NCC, LPC, LP, LSP, is a professor in the school counseling program of the Department of Human and Organizational Development in the Peabody College of Education at Vanderbilt University. Previously, he was a faculty member at Loyola University Maryland. He was the 61st president of the American Counseling Association (ACA) for 2012–2013 and ACA treasurer for 2017–2018.

He is the recipient of the ACA Research Award, ACA Extended Research Award, ACA Arthur A. Hitchcock Distinguished Professional Service Award, ACA Professional Development Award, Thomas J. Sweeney Award for Visionary Leadership and Advocacy, and ACA Carl D. Perkins Government Relations Award. He was also inducted as an ACA Fellow. In addition, he has received the Association for Assessment in Counseling and Education (AACE) AACE/MECD Research Award, AACE Exemplary Practices Award, AACE President's Merit Award, the Association for Counselor Education and Supervision (ACES) Robert O. Stripling Award for Excellence in Standards, Maryland Association for Counseling and Development (MACD) Maryland Counselor of the Year, MACD Counselor Advocacy Award, MACD Professional Development Award, and MACD Counselor Visibility Award.

He is the editor of numerous texts including *Orientation to the Counseling Profession* (Pearson Merrill, 2010, 2014, 2018), *Crisis Intervention and Prevention* (Pearson Merrill, 2010, 2014, 2018), *Group Work in the Schools* (Pearson Merrill, 2010; Routledge, 2016), *Clinical Experiences in Counseling* (Pearson Merrill, 2015), *Group Work: Process and Applications* (Pearson Merrill, 2011, 2019), *Transforming the School Counseling Profession* (Merrill/Prentice-Hall, 2003, 2007, 2011, 2015, 2019), *Professional School Counseling:*
A Handbook of Principles, Programs and Practices (pro-ed, 2004, 2010, 2016), *Assessment for Counselors* (Cengage, 2007, 2013), *Research and Evaluation in Counseling* (Cengage, 2008, 2015), and *The Counselor's Guide to Clinical, Personality and Behavioral Assessment* (Cengage, 2006), as well as co-author of seven more books: *Mastering the NCE and CPCE* (Pearson Merrill, 2011, 2015, 2020), *45 Techniques Every Counselor Should Know* (Merrill/Prentice-Hall, 2010, 2015, 2020), *Free Access Assessment Instruments for Common Mental Health and Addiction Issues* (Routledge, 2013), *Educational Applications of the WISC-IV* (Western Psychological Services, 2006) and *Group Activities: Firing Up for Performance* (Pearson Merrill, 2007). He is also the general editor of *The American Counseling Association Encyclopedia of Counseling* (ACA, 2009).

His research specialization falls primarily in development and technical analysis of psychoeducational tests and has resulted in the publication of more than seventy-five refereed journal articles, a hundred book chapters, and a dozen published tests. He is editor of *Measurement and Evaluation in Counseling and Development* (MECD) and senior associate editor of *Journal of Counseling & Development* (JCD).

He was a representative to the ACA Governing Council and the ACA 20/20 Visioning Committee. He is a past president and past treasurer of AACE, past chair and parliamentarian of the American Counseling Association–Southern (US) Region; past-chair of ACA's Task Force on High Stakes Testing; past chair of ACA's Standards for Test Users Task Force; past chair of ACA's Interprofessional Committee; past chair of the ACA Public Awareness and Support Committee (co-chair of the National Awards Sub-committee); chair of the Convention and past chair of the Screening

Assessment Instruments Committees for AACE; past president of the Maryland Association for Counseling and Development (MACD); past president of Maryland Association for Measurement and Evaluation (MAME); past president of Maryland Association for Counselor Education and Supervision (MACES); and past president of the Maryland Association for Mental Health Counselors (MAMHC). He was an associate editor of the *Journal of Counseling & Development*.

Dr. Erford is a licensed clinical professional counselor, licensed professional counselor, nationally certified counselor, licensed psychologist, and licensed school psychologist. Early in his career, Dr. Erford was a school psychologist/counselor in the Chesterfield County (VA) Public Schools. He maintains a private practice specializing in assessment and treatment of children and adolescents. A graduate of the University of Virginia (Ph.D.), Bucknell University (M.A.), and Grove City College (B.S.), he teaches courses in assessment, research and evaluation in counseling, ethics and professional issues, school counseling, and stress management.

Introduction

To some, a text specifically featuring counseling techniques is an anathema, an abomination even. From their perspective, counseling is a process and an art. It should be a relationship built between client and professional counselor that is undergirded by the core conditions of genuineness, empathy, and respect as espoused by Carl Rogers; best conducted using effective communication skills, such as those delineated by Ivey and Ivey's Microskills approach; and facilitated using theoretical counseling processes, such as those championed by Glasser, Ellis, Adler, or Perls. I agree! Counselor education programs all over the world do an excellent job of preparing counselors to do all of the above with a high degree of skill.

But what led to the composition of this text was the pragmatic realization that even professional counselors who are highly skilled communicators, grounded in a rich theoretical approach, and truly living the core facilitative conditions sometimes have difficulty moving the client toward the agreed-to objectives of the counseling experience. Counselors-in-training experience these difficulties very frequently and often desire specific, direct guidance on what to do in these situations to create movement. Specialized techniques, arising from important counseling theories, can provide this movement when they are judiciously applied.

This specific training need is the true motivation behind this text. The techniques are presented one at a time in a deconstructed manner, and each has a theoretical genesis and a rich, extant literature base that informs professional counselors about its appropriate and effective use. The techniques presented are clustered within the theoretical domain with which it is most closely associated (see Table I.1). I believe that all techniques are integrative in nature and will eventually be categorized as such because the future of counseling will entail becoming more integrative. For the time being, various theoretical camps claim certain procedures and techniques within their domains, and Table I.1 illustrates this artificial partitioning.

Each technique in this text is presented in a standardized manner. First, the origins of the technique are presented. Some have a rich history steeped in a single theoretical orientation. Others are more integrated or claimed by several theoretical approaches. Next, each chapter covers the basic steps or procedures for implementing each technique, followed by common variations of these procedures documented in the literature. To demonstrate real-life applications of how each technique can be used in counseling, case examples are presented. Most of the case examples include actual transcripts from an actual session. Yes, the transcripts were edited for brevity and clarity, and to remove distracting affectations and mitigated speech that clients and professional counselors present in real life (e.g., divergent thoughts, digressions). In addition, each technique is evaluated for usefulness and effectiveness using sources from the extant literature. The literature provides a rich source of ideas regarding what each technique has been (or could be) used to address, as well as how effective it was in addressing those issues. This information allows the reader to make empirically based decisions to benefit clients and maximize client outcomes. Finally, the reader will be invited to consider how the technique could be applied in real life. Several case studies are presented at the end of this introduction and the reader is challenged to construct a couple more cases from current, previous, or even anticipated future clients and students. Considering how to apply each technique helps to prepare you for the challenges ahead and remind you that these 45 techniques can and should be used in real life to help clients and students accomplish objectives!

TABLE I.1 The 45 Techniques Described in This Text, Categorized by Primary Theoretical Approach	
Theoretical Approach	**Techniques**
Section 1: Solution-focused brief counseling	Scaling; exceptions; problem-free talk; miracle question; flagging the minefield
Section 2: Adlerian or psychodynamic	I-messages; acting as if; spitting in the soup; mutual storytelling; paradoxical intention
Section 3: Gestalt and psychodrama	Empty chair; body movement and exaggeration; role reversal
Section 4: Mindfulness	Visual/guided imagery; deep breathing; progressive muscle relaxation technique (PMRT); meditation
Section 5: Humanistic-phenomenological	Self-disclosure; confrontation; motivational interviewing; strength bombardment
Section 6: Cognitive-behavioral	Self-talk; reframing; thought stopping; cognitive restructuring; rational-emotive behavior therapy (REBT); systematic desensitization; stress inoculation training
Section 7: Cognitive-behavioral for use within and between sessions	Assigning homework; bibliotherapy; journaling
Section 8: Social learning	Modeling; behavioral rehearsal; role play
Section 9: Behavioral approaches using positive reinforcement	Premack principle; behavior chart; token economy; behavioral contract
Section 10: Behavioral approaches using punishment	Extinction; time out; response cost; overcorrection
Section 11: Emerging approaches	Narrative therapy; strengths-based counseling; client advocacy

Each of the techniques in this text has been selected because of its usefulness and effectiveness in creating client movement toward agreed-upon objectives. Of course, writing a measurable behavioral objective is an important issue in itself and will be addressed here at the outset, in this Introduction.

COUNSELING OBJECTIVES

Erford (2016, 2019a) provided an easy-to-implement, nuts-and-bolts procedure for writing measurable objectives using the ABCD model: (A) audience, (B) behavior, (C) conditions, and (D) description of the expected performance criterion. In individual counseling, audience (A) refers to the individual client. In other types of counseling, the audience could be a couple, family, group, or some other system or configuration, like a class-room of students. Behavior (B) usually refers to the changes that the client and counselor will observe as a result of the intervention—that is, the actual behaviors, thoughts, or feelings that one will observe to be altered. Conditions (C) refer to the specific contextual applications or actions that will occur. In counseling sessions, this usually refers to the intervention that will be implemented and the context or circumstances surrounding its implementation. The description of the expected performance criterion (D) is usually the quantitative portion of the objective: how much the behavior will increase or decrease.

Counseling goals are differentiated from counseling objectives by the degree of specificity and measurability. A counseling goal is broad and not amenable to direct measurement. A counseling objective, on the other hand, is both specific and measurable. A reasonable goal of counseling may be "to increase a client's ability to manage stress and anxiety." Notice how the wording of a goal is nebulous and not amenable to measurement as stated. In developing a counseling objective related to this goal, particular emphasis is given to specific actions that are measurable. For example, a possible objective stemming from this goal could be "After learning thought stopping procedures, the client will experience a 50% reduction in episodes of obsessive thinking after a one-week period." Another possible objective might be "After learning deep breathing procedures, the client will practice deep breathing for at least five minutes, three times a day, every day of the week." A third example might be "After implementing time out with contingency delay procedures, the client's display of noncompliant behaviors will decrease from the current average of 25 episodes per week to no more than 5 episodes per week." Notice how the objectives designate the audience, the stated behavior, how the behavior will be addressed, and the level of expected performance (Erford, 2016, 2019a).

Establishing counseling objectives early in a counseling relationship is important for at least five reasons. First, classic studies indicated, and there is an emerging consensus in the research literature (Erford, 2019b), that about half of the progress in counseling ordinarily occurs within the first eight sessions and one of the best indicators of counseling outcome is whether the counselor and client were able to come to a quick agreement on counseling goals, ordinarily defined as occurring during the first two sessions.

As one can easily see, establishing counseling objectives early in the counseling relationship is vital to successful client outcomes. This doesn't mean that clients will always immediately know or understand the true nature of the issues that bring them to counseling. It does mean that those clients who can immediately establish counseling objectives are more likely to experience successful outcomes. By extension, it also means that professional counselors skilled at getting clients to develop counseling objectives quickly will be more successful in helping clients reach desired outcomes. It also does not assume that the "real problem" will be identified early in counseling. Many times,

making progress toward obvious, surface-level problems will facilitate the client–counselor trust needed to tackle those deeper psychological issues that the client is less likely to reveal early in a counseling relationship.

Second, counseling objectives provide a concrete, operationalized target of where the counseling process is headed and how both the client and professional counselor will know that progress is being made. As such, objectives allow periodic updates of progress and concrete displays of whether the counseling interventions are having the desired outcomes. In program evaluation, we refer to this as formative evaluation because periodic checks reveal whether the professional counselor should stay the course and continue the current counseling approach or modify the approach to improve client outcomes.

Third, objectives present targets that initiate movement. Targets are essential in counseling because they motivate clients and thus create movement. Indeed, at its core, counseling is all about motivating clients to move in the direction of counseling goals and objectives in a way that empowers clients to be able to continue making progress toward life goals independently after counseling has ended.

Fourth, a well-crafted objective allows the professional counselor to glean effective approaches, interventions, and techniques from the extant counseling literature shown to be useful in helping clients with similar issues. Counseling has a rich outcome research literature, and this literature informs professional counselors of best practices for resolving client issues. Each chapter, each technique featured in this text, includes a section entitled "Usefulness and Evaluation of [the Technique]." This chapter section features outcome research from the counseling literature to guide professional counselors in the effective application of each technique, including the issues each technique has been demonstrated to address and its effectiveness in doing so. Such information informs professional counselors of the appropriate use of each counseling technique.

Finally, a measurable objective lets the client and professional counselor know when counseling has been successful, when new objectives can be crafted and pursued, or when counseling can be terminated. Objectives serve as the target for success in counseling. It is important to note that each of these five purposes for objectives serves to motivate both the client and the counselor and to energize the counseling process. Having gained an understanding of the purpose of this text and having discussed the development and effective use of counseling objectives, readers are now ready to consider important multicultural applications.

MULTICULTURAL COUNSELING AND TECHNIQUES

It has been said that all counseling is multicultural counseling. Each client comes to a session with a unique worldview shaped by various cultural experiences, such as through race, ethnicity, gender, sexual orientation, socioeconomic status, age, and spirituality, among others. Such client worldviews will affect a client's receptiveness to certain theoretical approaches and the resulting techniques or interventions. Multiculturally competent counselors recognize that counseling theories help answer *why* questions—for example, Why is the client seeking counseling? Why is the difficulty occurring? Why now? Interrelated with this realization, multiculturally competent counselors realize that the experience of a human being may have some finite limitations, but the perceptions and interpretations of these experiences are infinite. Explained another way (Orr, 2018), "There is a specific range of emotions that humans are capable of expressing; however, the meaning that is assigned to those emotions is dynamic and based on the ever-evolving variables of culture and context" (p. 487). Orr proposed that counselors must constantly strive to adapt counseling theory to meet the diverse client needs stemming from this dynamic interplay, all the while realizing that, where culture is involved, within-group differences are almost always larger than between-group differences. Adapting theories to the individual client context allows counselors to frame client problems in unique ways, creating new challenges—and opportunities—for the application of techniques to problem resolution. In this

way, counselors can choose to stay grounded in a primary theoretical orientation while simultaneously integrating techniques into the approach that help to create movement for clients of diverse backgrounds.

So how does a multiculturally competent counselor adapt a theory to fit the unique worldview of a client? The detailed answer to this question is rooted in the context of each client's dynamic situation, and four general guidelines were offered by Orr (2018):

1. *Illuminate assumptions:* All theories are predicated on certain assumptions about mental health and worldview. Before using your chosen theory with any client, you need to familiarize yourself with the associated underlying assumptions.
2. *Identify limitations:* All theories do not fit all people, so explore the limitations of your chosen theory even before you begin working with clients. Pinpoint the gaps or gray areas in your theoretical orientation and strategize ways to compensate for them.
3. *Simplify concepts:* Theories are notorious contributors to jargon. Quite often various theories use multiple terms to refer to similar phenomena. Consider the concept of the therapeutic alliance as first described by Freud. Subsequent theorists have used any number of terms, such as partnering, rapport building, and so on, to describe the same process. Develop a layperson's explanation for your chosen theory that contains easily recognizable concepts in place of jargon.
4. *Diversify interventions:* Many theories are accompanied by a particular set of interventions. These interventions may be primary to the theory, but they are by no means the only way to apply that theory. Consider the commonly recognized empty chair technique, which involves clients imagining and role-playing a conversation with someone with whom they are in conflict as if that person were actually present. This technique is typically attributed to psychodrama and Gestalt theory, but it can be adapted for use with a

wide range of theoretical orientations. This technique can be especially useful with clients who have a more collectivist worldview, regardless of counselors' primary theoretical orientation. In those situations, the empty chair can be occupied by imagined family or community members, elders, or other supporters who might be needed to endorse the particular treatment.

APPLYING TECHNIQUES TO CASES AND CLIENTS

At the end of each chapter, you will be invited to apply the techniques to several cases outlined below, but you are also strongly encouraged to construct case studies of clients or students you have seen, are currently working with, or are likely to encounter in the future. Think deeply and creatively about how each technique or a variation of the technique could apply to one or more of these cases. Remember, the purpose of the technique is to create movement in the session and help the client to accomplish a therapeutic objective.

Right now, think about three to five challenging cases from your past or currently on your case load. Reflect on these challenging cases as you read about the 45 techniques you encounter throughout the remainder of the book and try to apply the techniques as applicable. In addition, consider the follow five diverse cases and apply the techniques as applicable. For a multicultural twist, imagine how the techniques might be differentially applied to each case if the clients were from diverse racial or ethnic backgrounds, were male or female, or had diverse affective orientations.

Case A: Ali is a youngster with behavior problems. In school Ali does not follow instructions, gets out of the chair without permission, calls out without raising a hand, and invades the personal space of other students. At home, Ali does not comply with parent directions, is oppositional, has an incredibly messy bedroom, and fights with older siblings. Lately Ali appears more sad, is sullen, and complains, "Everybody is always yelling at me!"

Case B: Bailey is an anxious and depressed teenager who is very moody and broody! Bailey also presents with a couple of specific phobias: test anxiety and fear of heights. Lately, Bailey has been fighting night and day with the parents and usually ends up running to the bedroom in tears and slamming the door. Bailey has historically been an excellent student, but grades have been slipping. Oh, and the love interest is described by friends as "bad news." "Even my friends don't like my date!"

Case C: Corey is a stressed-out college student who has harnessed newfound freedom to develop a love for parties and a taste for alcohol and other drugs. Passing out several times has been a wake-up call, especially because of not remembering whether or not sex had occurred. The grades are slipping and weight accumulating. "In the doldrums" would be a good description of the current mood state. "If I fail out of college, this amazing party will end! I have to turn things around."

Case D: Dakota is a young adult confused about what direction life should take. Sure, there is the whole career thing; a lot of good that degree in XXXX did! "I have been going from one dead end job to another; I need to figure this out." There is also that whole partner-for-the-rest-of-my-life thing, complicated by the same-sex attraction urges evident since adolescence but never acted upon, as well as complicated by religion and traditional parents-waiting-to-become-grandparents. "Ugh. My parents would kill me if they knew.… " All of this confusion is leading to a lot of depression, anxiety, and substance use to kill the pain.

Case E: Ellery is a mature adult approaching seasoned citizenhood and grieving the loss of a partner of 25 years. With no kids, Ellery is questioning not only the meaning of life but also whether life will or even should go on. Ellery and her partner had caring family and social networks, but Ellery has lost touch and ignored these during her grieving.

SOME FINAL REMARKS BEFORE YOU GET STARTED

Successful counseling involves moving clients from situation or problem identification to successful attainment of their goals and objectives. The operational word in the previous sentence is *moving*. All professional counselors know how to establish counseling objectives and how to tell when those objectives have been met. All professional counselors are skilled in implementation of a counseling process, whether it stems from a single theoretical orientation or from an integrative approach. But what happens when the counseling process stagnates, the client becomes frustrated with little or no progress, and the counseling relationship is in danger of premature termination?

In this book, I have advocated for a flexible approach to counseling that allows professional counselors to choose techniques shown in the outcome literature to address specific counseling objectives effectively and create the movement in counseling that is vital to success. I have *not* advocated for the nonjudicious or haphazard application of the techniques contained herein; such an approach is unprofessional and unethical. But when you are in session with a client whose progress has halted, I hope you will recall enough of the knowledge and procedures contained within this book to help move that client forward in the counseling process and ever closer to the counseling objective that both you and the client committed to reaching.

Counseling is indeed an art, but technical know-how allows the artist to create an exceptional work. Now it is time to begin a whirlwind tour of *45 Techniques Every Counselor Should Know*. Enjoy!

NEW TO THIS EDITION

A number of features have been added to this third edition:

- Meditation was added to the section on mindfulness-based procedures. Mindfulness is an important emerging approach to counseling and has been coming into greater prominence recently.
- A new section on the additional emerging approaches to counseling was added, including narrative therapy, strengths-based counseling, and client advocacy.
- A subsection within cognitive–behavioral therapy (CBT) presents a new chapter on assigning homework that joins journaling and bibliotherapy as techniques that bolster work between counseling sessions and focus on counseling objectives.
- A number of transcripts have been added, edited, or expanded to more clearly exemplify each chapter technique.
- Sources were updated and added so that this third edition contains more than 50% of the references from 2010 or later—yet it maintains the classic sources.

Acknowledgments

I wish to express my gratitude to Susan (H. Eaves) Carmichael, Emily Bryant, and Katie Young for their contributions to the first edition. As always, Rebecca Fox-Gieg and Kevin Davis of Pearson have been wonderfully responsive and supportive. Special thanks go to the reviewers whose comments helped to provide substantive improvement to the previous edition manuscript: Keely Hope, Eastern Washington University; Kimberly Langrehr, University of Missouri-Kansas City; Ian Lertora, Texas Tech University; Mary Mayorga, Texas A&M University-San Antonio; and Tiffany Stoner-Harris, Western Illinois University.

Brief Contents

Contents

Techniques Based on Solution-Focused Brief Counseling Approaches

Solution-focused brief counseling approaches have become increasingly popular since the 1980s due to managed care and other accountability initiatives, which place a premium on cost and time effectiveness. Solution-focused brief counseling approaches go by many names, but currently the most prominent orientation in counseling circles is solution-focused brief counseling (SFBC). SFBC is a social constructivist model built on the observation that clients derive personal meaning from the events of their lives as explained through personal narratives. SFBC counselors value a therapeutic alliance that stresses empathy, collaboration, curiosity, and respectful understanding but not expertness. Many pioneering authors and classic studies have made contributions to our understanding of the SFBC approach. De Shazer (1988, 1991) and O'Hanlon and Weiner-Davis (2004) are often credited as scholarly and theoretical forces behind the prominence of SFBC, which deemphasizes the traditional therapeutic focus on a client's problems and instead focuses on what works for the client (i.e., successes and solutions) and exceptions in the client's life, during which the problems are not occurring. Berg and Miller (1992, p. 17) summed up the SFBC approach succinctly by proposing three basic rules on which SFBC counselors operate: (1) "If it ain't broke, don't fix it;" (2) "Once you know what works, do more of it;" and (3) "If it doesn't work, don't do it again." It is easy to see the basic appeal of this commonsense approach to counseling.

Walter and Peller (1992) proposed five underlying assumptions of SFBC that expand on these three basic rules: (1) Concentrating on successes leads to constructive change; (2) clients can realize that exceptions for every problem that exists can be found, during which the problem does not exist, effectively giving clients the solutions to their problems; (3) small, positive changes lead to bigger, positive changes; (4) all clients can solve their own problems by exposing, detailing, and replicating successes during exceptions; and (5) goals need to be stated in positive, measurable, active terms. Murphy (2015) and Sklare (2014) successfully applied SFBC to children and adolescents, using the rules and assumptions cited above, to focus on changing client actions rather than developing insights. Sklare concluded that insights do not lead to solutions; successful actions lead to solutions.

The five techniques covered in this section include scaling, exceptions, problem-free talk, miracle question, and flagging the minefield. Each is not exclusive to SFBC; indeed, all can be used in an integrative counseling approach (see Erford, 2018).

Scaling is a commonly used technique when counseling individuals of nearly any age and from any theoretical perspective. Basically, scaling presents clients with a 10-point (or 100-point) continuum and asks them to rate where they currently are with regard to, for example, sadness (1) or happiness (10), extreme anger (1) or tranquility (10), hate (1) or love (10), totally unmotivated (1) or totally motivated (10). Scaling is helpful in gauging a client's current status on a wide range of issues. It is even more helpful when it is reused periodically to gauge the progress of a client. Scaling is a very quick and helpful assessment technique with wide applicability in counseling.

Exceptions are essential to the SFBC approach because exceptions provide the solutions to the client's "problems." Counselors probe and question the client's background for times when the problem wasn't a problem, determining exceptions and providing the client with alternative solutions to act on.

Problem-free talk is a technique that allows the counselor to turn the counseling intervention from a problem-focused environment to a solution-focused environment. SFBC counselors hold the core belief that when clients focus on problems, they become discouraged and disempowered, and any insight they might gain into the origin and sustenance of the problem is not therapeutically valuable. A complementary belief is that finding exceptions and solutions to problematic circumstances encourages and empowers clients, leading to actions and successes.

The miracle question helps to reconstruct the way a client perceives a problematic circumstance into a vision for success that motivates the client to pursue the actions that will lead to successes.

The final technique is a treatment adherence technique called *flagging the minefield*. Treatment adherence is critical in any field in which clients or patients seek and receive help. Many, even most, clients receive the help they seek but then do not follow the treatment regimen, for whatever reason, basically guaranteeing that the treatment will not be effective over the long term. For example, a patient may go to a doctor to address a medical condition but then not follow the doctor's advice. If medication is prescribed, the patient may not have

the prescription filled or may not take the medication according to the doctor's directions. Flagging the minefield is a technique ordinarily implemented during termination that facilitates clients' thinking about situations during which the positive outcomes and strategies learned during counseling may not work, and it gets clients thinking ahead of time about what should be done in those circumstances to persevere and succeed. Treatment adherence is a critical issue in counseling; what good is all that hard work and effort to alter problematic thoughts, feelings, and behaviors if the client will return to problematic functioning shortly after counseling is terminated?

MULTICULTURAL IMPLICATIONS OF SOLUTION-FOCUSED BRIEF COUNSELING APPROACHES

SFBC is a culturally respectful approach to working with clients of diverse backgrounds because it discourages diagnoses, focuses on the client's personal frame of reference, and encourages clients to integrate and increase actions that have already been shown to be a successful fit for that personal frame of reference. The SFBC approach proposes that the client is the leading expert on what works for the client, and the counselor's role is to help the client recognize what already works for the client. The counselor then encourages the client to alter his or her actions and cheerleads the client's successes. SFBC approaches are particularly appreciated by clients who prefer action-oriented, directive interventions and concrete goals—for example, most men, Arab Americans, Asian Americans, and Latinos and Latinas (Hays & Erford, 2018). Meyer and Cottone (2013) also indicated that many Native Americans respond well to solution-focused approaches and scaling questions. SFBC is one of the more effective cross-cultural approaches because it empowers clients' personal values, beliefs, and behaviors and does not try to dispute or alter these values, beliefs, and behaviors (Orr, 2018).

CHAPTER 1

Scaling

ORIGINS OF THE SCALING TECHNIQUE

Scaling is a technique that helps both counselors and clients make complex problems seem more concrete and tangible (Murphy, 2015). Scaling originated within behavioral approaches to counseling, and today, it is largely used in solution-focused brief counseling (SFBC), which was started by de Shazer and arose out of strategic family therapy (Lethem, 2002).

Because client thoughts, feelings, and behaviors are not always realistic or concrete, scaling questions provide a way to move from these more abstract concepts toward an achievable goal (Sklare, 2014). For instance, the counselor can say, "On a scale of 1 to 10, where 1 represents the worst that things could be and 10 represents the best that things could be, where are you today?" Scaling questions can also help clients to set tasks that will allow them to move to the next rank-order number. In this way, scaling can help measure client progress over time. Scaling techniques give clients a sense of control and responsibility over their counseling because scaling techniques help clients specify goals for change as well as measure their progress toward accomplishing those goals.

HOW TO IMPLEMENT THE SCALING TECHNIQUE

Scaling questions usually involve asking the client to give a number between 1 and 10 that indicates where the client is at some specified point (Murphy, 2015). The counselor usually designates 10 as the more positive end of the scale (thus higher numbers equal a more positive outcome or experience).

Scaling can be used to identify goals or to help the client progress toward an already established goal. Clients can identify goals by identifying specific behavioral indicators that signify they have reached a higher number (7, 8, 9, 10) on the scale.

Once a goal has been established, scaling techniques can be used to help the client move toward reaching the goal. After the client has identified where he is on the scale (with 10 meaning that he has reached the goal), the counselor can ask questions to discover what small steps the client could take to reach the next rank-order number (Corcoran, 1999). Questions include "What would you take as an indication that you have moved to a number 6?" and "What would you be doing then?" (Lethem, 2002). Scaling also provides an opportunity for counselors to compliment clients' progress by using questions such as "How did you get from a 1 to a 5?"

VARIATIONS OF THE SCALING TECHNIQUE

Instead of using a scale of 1 to 10 for small children, scaling can be shown pictorially (Lethem, 2002). For instance, professional counselors can use a range of facial expressions, from frowning to smiling, or numbered steps leading to the desired change. When using scaling in a group, it is important to ask each person for a rating. Differences should be explored to discover the reasons behind the differences. In addition, relationship scaling questions can be used to help clients identify the perspectives of other people in their lives (Corcoran, 1999). Clients can be asked "How do you think your parents (or teachers) would rank you?" These answers can then be compared to the client's self-rating, which often forces clients to realize what actions they need to take in order to show others the improvements they've made (Corcoran, 1997).

EXAMPLES OF THE SCALING TECHNIQUE

Following are several short scenarios for which scaling would be appropriate and useful in order to assist both the client and professional counselor in viewing or assessing the problem in a more tangible way.

EXAMPLE 1: Scaling used to reduce catastrophic thinking

Maria (M):   I'm completely panicked. Thinking about my first day of school, and not as a student, but actually as a teacher . . . me, a teacher . . . is sending me right over the edge.

Counselor (C):   Right over the edge?

M: (Speaking rapidly) Right over the edge. Like, just thinking about it makes me want to throw up. I really don't think I can do it.

C: I can see how nervous you seem even now, just from talking about it.

M: I am! Thinking about it, talking about it . . . If I can't handle that, how am I going to handle it when I actually get to that moment? You know? I'm a basket case.

C: Okay. All right. I'd like you to close your eyes for a second and picture your first day of school, okay? You're in front of your class. (Pause) You're getting ready to teach a new lesson that you've never taught before. (Pause) Your new classroom is full of your new students. (Pause) They are sitting in their seats, looking at you. (Pause) Now, go ahead and feel the emotions that come up. Don't try to prevent them or hold them back. (Speaking very slowly) Feel the anxiety, and the fear, and the dread. Feel any emotion that may come up. Okay, now can you describe to me how you're feeling?

M: Um, I have this nauseous feeling in my stomach. Um, my palms are kind of sticky or sweaty or something. Um, I'm kind of concerned about the students and what they're thinking and making sure that, um, you know, they're gonna like my lesson. There's a lot of thoughts going through my head about what's gonna happen in the next few minutes or whenever I get started. I'm just really anxious . . . my feelings and thoughts.

C: Okay, on a scale from 1 to 10, with 1 being really, really extremely anxious—like you probably wouldn't even be able to stand up there—and 10 being very confident and comfortable, where do you think you'd be on that scale?

M: Um . . . I guess maybe like a 4.

C: Okay, so that doesn't sound quite so terrible. You could probably get through the lesson at a 4, right?

M: Yeah, I guess I could. It wouldn't be the most comfortable or enjoyable experience, but you're right, I could definitely get through it. It just feels so much worse sometimes though . . . like dreading it is the worst part, maybe.

C: Uh-huh. That could be true.

M: I just feel like something will go terribly wrong, and I get myself so worked up.

C: All right, then. Let's try this. Tell me—and I bet you've already thought about it—tell me what the worst thing is that could realistically happen on that first day of you being the teacher.

M: Hmm. (Chuckles) I have actually thought about it. . . . Sometimes I visualize that the students, just a few at first, lose interest in the lesson. More and more they become disinterested, and a few of them begin talking to one another. Then more students begin to follow their lead, and they begin to giggle and talk louder so that it is very obvious they are not paying attention to me. Pretty soon, the entire class is chaotic and doing what they please, and not one student is attending to the lesson.

C: Okay, so you have thought about that! On a scale of 1 to 10 again, with a 1 being a catastrophic, career-ending, mortifying event that you absolutely could not get through, and a 10 being no big deal at all, where would this scenario that you've visualized fall?

M: A 5.

C: Now, not to say that your anxiety is not justified, but to help you view it more objectively, let's scale it against another event. Okay, so thinking about the worst thing that could ever happen to you in life in general . . . the very worst thing in life—someone you love being murdered, your child being kidnapped, something that horrific—with that in mind, now rescale the visualized classroom event. With 1 being catastrophic and 10 being no big deal, where would you place the classroom event?

M: Like an 8 or 9. In the big scheme of things, it's not a big deal at all. It would be a little embarrassing if the other teachers saw I couldn't handle my own class, but other than that, really not that big a deal after all.

C: Okay. And if the worst-case scenario of that day is actually only a 8 or 9, then how will that change where your anxiety level would be on that scale of 1 to 10?

M: Way lower. Way, way lower. Really nothing beyond a few first-day jitters.

EXAMPLE 2: Scaling used to assess motivation for change

Counselor (C): So, Amy, so far Mollie has been sort of reporting on her progress and how she's doing in moving toward her goals . . . which is a necessary condition to her living with you . . . that she make movement toward her goals and keep her life, you know, going in a positive direction.

Amy (A): Yes, she is making some progress.

C: Okay. You know, to really make sure and to monitor your sister's progress, let's set up some kind of monitoring system to help you make sure that she's following through—that she wants to, so that your confidence will increase as well as your seeing her meet these goals.

A: Okay.

C: So, thinking about your perception of Mollie's motivation to change and follow through with her goals, currently, in comparison to when you two first came in to see me, on a scale from 0 to 100, with 100 being extremely confident that Mollie is moving in a positive direction and definitely going to follow through with and accomplish her goals, and 0 meaning you have no confidence at all and see no real progress being made, or even any effort on her part—where do you think you lie on that scale?

A: Um. . . . (Thinking) I would say probably about a 65.

C: 65?

A: Yeah.

C: Okay, well that's 35%, you know, 35 points to go before we get to 100. That's not bad at all! What is it that makes her progress a 65? Tell me a little bit about that 65.

A: Um, well, the reason I'm not higher than 65 is that she hasn't started saving any money for the courses that are starting really soon, and I don't know that she's going to have much financial help, so that kind of worries me. But at the same time, um, this past weekend, she was studying for her GED. So I think she's serious about that. She's registered for her classes at this college, so that's why it's a little bit higher, but the money thing kind of worries me.

C: Okay, so the 65 comes from the studying for the GED and the registering for classes. But the other 35 points comes from the lack of money or effort toward saving?

A: Yes. And I think that sounds fair (Looking over at Mollie).

C: Mollie, what do you think about this 65? Is this where you would place your progress and motivation?

Mollie (M):   Well, when you were first asking Amy that question, I was thinking around 80 or 85, even. But then listening to her explain how she came up with that number . . . well, I guess a 65 makes sense. (Thinking) I don't know, maybe a little higher than a 65, just because I know my motivation for change is high, but I can't expect anybody else to know that because it's inside me.

C: Everyone else gauges your motivation by looking at your actions?

M: Uh-huh.

EXAMPLE 3: Scaling in personal relationships

Counselor (C):   Well, what I believe I'm hearing from both of you is that you "can't" talk to the other. Kevin, you said that Tamara "can't have a conversation without picking a fight." Tamara, you said that Kevin "ignores me and says almost nothing" when you try to talk to him. (Pauses) But you both feel that you are the better communicator in the relationship?

Kevin (K):   Yes.

Tamara (T):   I at least try. He doesn't even bother. And I don't see how we are going to get through some of our issues if we can't even communicate with each other about them.

C: I agree that communication is going to be very important to working through these other dilemmas and feelings. So perhaps we should focus some of our attention on improving communication. Kevin, what are your thoughts on this?

K: We've never been really good at talking things through. But everything just seemed to work itself out anyway—until now. So I'd love for you to help Tamara have a conversation without making it into something more.

C: Well, what I'd like to do is help you both improve *yourselves* and the way *you* communicate.

Okay. Here is a sheet of paper for each of you. On the bottom half of the paper, I'd like you to give yourself a score from 1 to 10 based on how well you think you communicate, with 1 being a terrible communicator and 10 being a great communicator. (Both Kevin and Tamara were able to do this very quickly with little thought.) Now, on the other half of the paper, on the top half, I want you to each think for a moment about the way your partner communicates with you. After this, we will change the focus to yourselves, but for this last moment, you get to focus on your partner and his or her shortcomings. All right. So for now, thinking about how your spouse communicates with you, I want you to give him or her a score from 1 to 10, with 1 being the worst communicator ever . . . everything he or she does leads to problems and miscommunications rather than effective communication. Now a 10 would indicate that you find your spouse to be a very effective communicator and find that the end result of a conversation is satisfying and the reason it was begun was accomplished. (Gives them both a few moments to write down a number) Okay, I would like to hear what each of you has.

T: I'll go first. Do you want to know what we put for ourselves or just for the other person?

C: Um, however you want to do it is fine.

T: Okay. Well, I gave myself an 8 because there are probably one or two minor things I could do a little better, but for the most part, I am an effective communicator, just based on what I do.

C: Uh-huh.

T: Okay, and so I gave Kevin a 4. . . .

K: (Interrupting) A 4?!

T: Yes, a 4, because if he's involved, it's just bound to go badly.

C: And what about you, Kevin? What did you write down?

K: Well, I gave myself a 9 because I'm not the problem here. And I gave Tamara a 6.

C: The great news is neither of you scored the other as a 1, so you both agree that the other does some things right with regard to communication. Okay. I want to ask you both if you would now be willing to completely scratch out the score you gave for yourself. ✓

T: Why?

C: Well, if we assumed, Tamara, that you really were an 8 on a scale of 1 to 10, and you, Kevin, really were a 9, we wouldn't have a lot to work on. You would both be nearly perfect communicators. Instead, I'd like to help you both to let go of your self-perceived communication skills and focus on how your partner perceives you. If we are going to improve, we have to really consider how our partner sees us. Tamara, the way Kevin perceives you is as important as the way you perceive him. And the same is true for you, Kevin. And as long as we feel we are near perfect at this, we won't improve. So, if you're willing, I'd like for you to each scribble over the number you gave yourself and trade papers, and now let's operate from the assumption that you, Tamara, are a 6, and you, Kevin, are a 4.

T: I'll change his to a 5.

C: Okay, Kevin, you are a 5.

K: Can I change hers to a 5 so we're the same?

T: No! (Laughing)

K: (Laughs)

C: Now, with your new numbers, I'd like you to both consider what's keeping you from being a 10.

K: (After some thought) Well, I can be pretty defensive sometimes when she tries to talk to me, and I'm bad about tuning her out.

C: That's certainly a good start. Tamara? What about your new score? What do you suppose keeps it from being a 10?

T: Well, I suppose I don't always pick the best time to start a discussion and, um, I tend to dominate the conversation and get angry.

EXAMPLE 4: Scaling to recognize old baggage and personal reactions

Anthony (A):   I just get so angry. I really lose my cool and I don't even know why I get that mad. She just makes me so . . . I could just . . . scream . . . well, I do, I mean, I do scream. Not at her, of course. But as soon as I hang up the phone, I just scream as loud as I can to get it all out. Like, the other day, she called to tell me happy birthday, and it wasn't my birthday, it was my sister's. And I just kidded with her about getting older and forgetful, but then I couldn't wait to get off the phone because I was just boiling inside. And as soon as I hung up, I screamed . . . and cried. I really don't get it . . . why I let her push my buttons like that . . . over something so silly that she probably really can't even help because she really is getting older.

Counselor (C):   This phone call with your mother is a good example for us to work with to maybe help you gain some insight into your reactions.

A: Okay. How?

C: Your reaction the other day, after you hung up the phone, on a scale of 1 to 100, with 1 being no reaction at all, no emotional reaction whatsoever, and 100 being this huge, overwhelming, uncontrollable emotional reaction, what would you say your reaction the other day was on this scale?

A: (Looking down and fidgeting) Um, well, let's see. . . . I guess it would have been about a 90. It felt very uncontrollable and overwhelming . . . it just swallowed me up.

C: Okay. Now, realistically, what your mom said on the phone, about the birthday when it wasn't your birthday, but your sister's, on a scale of 1 to 100, with 1 being no big deal and 100 being just this terrible thing for a person to do to you, what was your mother's comment?

A: Give her comment a number, too?

C: Yes, from 1 to 100, if you can.

A: Well, because I know she didn't do it intentionally, I would say like a 15, I guess.

C: Okay, Anthony. We have a comment at a 15 and a reaction at a 90.

A: Yeah, yeah, we, uh, we do, don't we? How does that happen? (Smiles)

C: Let's think for a moment about what the numbers 16 through 89 represent. Usually when we get a 15 and we react with a 90, there is much more there that accounts for our reaction. What are all those other numbers about, do you suppose? What button did your mother's comment push?

A: (Thinks for a moment while still looking down and begins to cry) I feel so bad for even saying this, and I know I should be past it by now, and I try so hard to be grateful for her *pathetic* attempts at being a mother now, but she *still* can't get it right, and I just want to *scream* because every time I talk to her it's this *ridiculous* reminder that she still sucks! (Crying harder) She walked out on us when we were kids because her boyfriend was more important and he didn't like kids, so she chose him over us and we didn't for the life of us understand why she had left us or what we had done wrong, and God that was so long ago, and she's apologized a hundred times, but she still is not . . . she'll *never* be the mother I need her to be. I'll *never* get over what she did to us. (Angrily) We weren't important enough for her to stay with us then, and we're not important enough for her to know when our damn birthdays are now!

EXAMPLE 5: Scaling in suicide assessments with an adolescent in a school setting

Counselor (C): So, Juan, your life right now, how you feel about your life, on a scale of 1 to 10, with a 10 being satisfied and happy and a 1 being unbearable, where would you say your life falls on this continuum?

Juan (J): Like a 1 or something.

C: Okay, and the likelihood of you harming yourself, even killing yourself, as you've been considering lately, on a scale of 1 to 10, with 10 being totally no intention to hurt yourself and a 1 being definitely going to commit suicide, where would you say you are right now?

J: Probably a 2 or maybe even 1 again.

C: (Pauses for a moment) Juan, I don't know if this is true for you, but I've noticed that when I've worked with other students who feel as you do at this moment, I've noticed something very interesting. I've noticed that almost always, they don't necessarily *really* want to die . . . they just don't want to keep living at a 1. (Pauses) Might that be true for you also, Juan?

J: I never thought about it like that. I mean . . . (Thinking out loud) "I don't really want to die, I just don't want to keep living at a 1." (Thinking again) You know, I can see where that fits . . . but if I don't know how *not* to live at a 1, then I feel like I only have one choice.

C: Yes, yes, I can see that. So, if you'd be willing, I'd like for us to work together right now to consider how we can get you from a 1 to a . . .

J: Anything would be better than a 1.

C: Okay, then, let's work together to see how we can get you to anything better than a 1. What are some things that you need to be different in order for life to be better than a 1? They could be things related to classes, personal relationships, parents . . . whatever you can think of.

USEFULNESS AND EVALUATION OF THE SCALING TECHNIQUE

Scaling techniques tend to measure progress toward concrete goals; consequently, they lend themselves to outcomes research (Lethem, 2002). Scaling can be used in a wide variety of situations. Some examples include assessment of progress toward a solution, confidence about finding a solution, motivation, severity of a problem, the likelihood of hurting oneself or others, and self-esteem (De Jong & Miller, 1995). Scaling has also been used with youth involved with the juvenile justice system and their families (Corcoran, 1997), as well as with families involved with child welfare services (Corcoran, 1999). Juveniles from multiproblem families, low socioeconomic status (SES), or diverse backgrounds improved on their treatment goals.

The scaling technique has been embedded in a comprehensive SFBC approach and used in at least three school-based outcome studies with middle school students. Franklin, Biever, Moore, Demons, and Scamardo (2001) indicated that 71% of middle school student behavior cases improved when using scaling as part of a solution-focused approach in a middle school setting. In a study showing no difference due to treatment, Newsome (2004) used an SFBC groupwork model with at-risk junior high school students who showed no improvement in attendance or grade point average (GPA) when pretreatment GPA was used as a covariate. Finally, Springer, Lynch, and Rubin (2000) studied the effects of a solution-focused mutual aid group for Hispanic children of incarcerated parents that embedded scaling into a more comprehensive SFBC approach. Teachers reported that the middle school student participants reduced presenting concerns to below the clinical significance criterion for both internalizing (effect size [ES] = 1.40) and externalizing (ES = .61) difficulties. At the same time, the teenage participants' self-report resulted in an ES of .86 for externalizing problems, but no differences were noted in youth self-report for internalizing problems (ES = .08).

In studies of adults, Lindforss and Magnusson (1997) reported that Swedish criminals participating in an SFBC procedure that used scaling as one component experienced less recidivism and fewer serious crimes at 12- and 16-month follow-ups. Meyer and Cottone (2013) found that modifications of the scaling technique can be used effectively with Native Americans to reduce the perception of boasting. Lee (1997) reported that a solution-focused brief family therapy approach resulted in 65% of families successfully reaching diverse goals.

Finally, in a systematic review, Beyebach (2014) reported that scaling was used to efficiently rate treatment effectiveness from session one through termination and follow-up. This review included clinical trials by Beyebach et al. (2000); Cortés, Peralta, and Machado (2007); and De Jong and Hopwood (1996), which all used progress scaling questions as outcome measures. Richmond, Jordan, Bischof, and Sauer (2014) found that SFBC that included scaling to make goals more concrete actually reduced patient symptoms between intake and session 1 compared to problem-focused approaches.

APPLICATION OF THE SCALING TECHNIQUE

Now apply the scaling technique to a current client or student you are working with or revisit the brief case studies presented at the beginning of this book. How can you use the scaling technique to address concerns and create movement in the counseling session?

CHAPTER 2

Exceptions

ORIGINS OF THE EXCEPTIONS TECHNIQUE

According to Presbury, Echterling, and McKee (2002), "Finding exceptions is the quintessential technique of resolution counseling. The exception—a time when the problem is not happening—is a resolution that the client has already achieved, however temporarily" (p. 75). The origin of the exceptions technique lies in the assumption that all problems have exclusions that can be used to facilitate solutions. As humans, we sometimes view our problems as having always occurred, as constant, and as unrelenting, even for brief moments. If we do recognize exceptions to the problem, we tend to deny their significance. This is most likely due to the way the brain filters, processes, and stores information. However, almost every situation has a time period, however brief, where the problem was not a problem at all. Professional counselors must listen closely for these exceptions, point them out, and use them to facilitate solutions. In this way, clients gain hope and are empowered by their own ability to affect their environment.

HOW TO IMPLEMENT THE EXCEPTIONS TECHNIQUE

The exceptions technique can be used in a nondirective way, in which the professional counselor is constantly listening for an instance of when the problem was either improved, even if only slightly, or did not exist at all (e.g., "She never listens. The only person who can get through to her is her grandmother."). This complaint, or description of the problem, contains an exception that is going unnoticed and unutilized (Linton, 2005).

"Problems never always happen. Exceptions always do" (Presbury et al., 2002, p. 74). But because clients often do not recognize their own exceptions or give credence to them, the professional counselor must notice them and use them effectively. After all, it is rare to find clients who seek counseling to communicate about the times they were trouble free. They are far more likely to tell you about and expect you to solve their problems. In addition, professional counselors have been trained historically to listen for the details of the problem. For the exceptions technique to be of use, counselors must retrain their ears to listen for the potential solutions, sources of strength, and personal resources.

For example, consider the case in which a 16-year-old female complains weekly of the conflict in her home. She and her twin brother in particular have vicious battles on a daily basis; they are almost unable to tolerate each other's presence in the same room. One week she comes in for her session and briefly mentions the past week's happenings and in so doing states, "Me and Tony went to the mall. He drove us there so I could hang out with my friends while he shopped for a present for his girlfriend." This is an exception and one that could easily go unnoticed by the counselor. Instead, it should be pursued and elaborated upon in a way that enables the client to identify what was different about this day that she and her brother not only refrained from fighting but actually had a positive collaborative encounter. If the counselor points out this instance and the client responds with "I guess he just decided to stop being such a jerk for a day," continue to facilitate a personal focus. The counselor might respond "Perhaps. But let's pretend that it was more than that . . . that maybe there was something *you* did differently that helped lead to that exception."

The exceptions technique can also be used directly by asking questions like these: "Tell me about a time when . . . " or "How close have you come . . . ?" These questions are also helpful after the answer to the miracle question (see Chapter 4) is formulated. The professional counselor can ask if any part of the miracle is already occurring or if the client can recall a time when it did occur. The counselor then listens for what the client did differently that led to the absence or improvement of the problem.

VARIATIONS OF THE EXCEPTIONS TECHNIQUE

Exceptions can be listened for and pointed out. They can be asked for directly. As a technique, it can be combined with the miracle question (see Chapter 4). The exceptions technique can also be combined with scaling (see Chapter 1). When expected exceptions do not immediately make themselves known, the client can be given a task designed to illuminate exceptions to the problem. The task variation entails giving the client a homework assignment between sessions that generally takes this form: "Between now and our next session, pay attention to (take note of, list times) when you experience part of the miracle (notice less of the problem, respond in a way that is helpful) . . . . "

When directly asking for exceptions, the professional counselor must use caution because certain phrasings of the technique could lead a client to feel patronized or that the concern is trivialized. Make certain that pointing out exceptions heard through the telling of the problem is done in a way that is hopeful and reminiscent of cheerleading (e.g., "Wow, how'd you manage to get through that? Most people couldn't have done it!" [Sklare, 2014]). When directly asking for exceptions, make sure to validate client concerns and perspectives before respectfully inquiring (e.g., "Your situation seems especially difficult. Can you recall a time when you remember feeling better than you do right now?").

In addition to delicate phrasing, the exceptions question can also be asked in a way that focuses on the circumstances or environment (e.g., "What is going on around you at that time that is different than at other times?" or "Who is around during the times the problem seems less noticeable?") or with follow-up questions that emphasize client resources (e.g., "What are you doing differently that could be leading to this exception in the problem?" or "What have you been able to do since our last session to cause an exception to occur?"). Regardless of the variation or follow-up, always ask in a way that presumes exceptions—in fact, that they exist—and always have the client elaborate on the exception with enough detail to assist in formulating a solution.

EXAMPLE OF THE EXCEPTIONS TECHNIQUE

Stan is a 16-year-old boy who has been missing school more and more frequently, stating physical illness as his most common reason for his absences. After a thorough physical examination by his medical doctor, it was recommended to Stan's mother that she seek counseling services for Stan because the root of his somatic complaints was presumed to be something other than medical in nature. Stan comes across as both emotionally mature and intelligent, though lacking in social skills and confidence. He immediately begins talking about his strong dislike of his new school and the difficulty he has had making friends and getting through the day without being teased relentlessly.

Stan (S):   I wish I never had to go back there. I just don't seem to fit in. It's real clique-ish. It's like if you didn't grow up here or you don't have lots of money . . . they just . . . they're just brutal.

Counselor (C):   The other students?

S: Yeah, it's bad. Really bad. It's like they targeted me from day one and haven't let up since.

C: Really bad how?

S: Really bad as in there's nothing about me that seems to please anybody around there. They find fault with everything about me. And it's constant. It's like I can't get a moment of peace around there. It starts as soon as I set foot on campus and doesn't let up until I leave. It's never ending.

C: I can see why you don't like going.

S: Seriously, right? Who wants to go through that every single day of their life? They invaded my locker the first week of school. I don't know how they got in it . . . I can't even get in it half the time . . . which is something else I get made fun of for. Anyway, they went through it and found some song lyrics I had written in one of my notebooks and photocopied them and posted them all over the place. That's when it began, and it hasn't stopped.

C: Wow. That would feel like an invasion of privacy.

S: Yeah. Those were personal to me. You know? A lot of it was about how I missed my old girlfriend and my old hometown and stuff. I got labeled a crybaby because of it. That's where the nicknames came from—"Stan's Not the Man," "Stan the Man . . . Not!," "Stanny Wanny Wants to Be a Manny." It's ridiculous. It's awful is what it is. And nothing I do will change it. I swear some days I think I'm gonna lose it. For real.

Up to this point, the professional counselor has facilitated Stan's telling of the story and has provided support and validation. The counselor will now ask a form of the exceptions question in a supportive way to avoid the client feeling trivialized.

C: It really does sound like a very difficult situation for you. And yet you've almost made it through the entire school year. Most people would've already "lost it." Yet you haven't. How have you been so strong?

S: I don't think I have. I've obviously not been able to stop it from happening. And I keep missing school to avoid it.

C: But you've not "lost it," so you're doing something right.

S: I try to tell myself that it doesn't matter . . . that these people don't matter to me . . . or won't in the future . . . that this is all temporary and it will be different one day.

C: So you try to put it into perspective, realize that it's just a small part of your life and that it won't feel this terrible down the road, not as terrible as it feels now when you're in the middle of it.

S: Yeah. I try. It helps. I also think about how, when I get real down on myself and feel like I'm worthless, I also think about how many friends I had at my old school and that people really did like me. That helps too . . . helps me feel less like a loser.

C: Good. So putting it in perspective and thinking about a time when you were well liked and treated fairly help you keep from "losing it."

S: Exactly. But it doesn't make the problem go away. It just keeps me from making it a lot worse.

C: Fair enough. So tell me, Stan, can you think of a time since you started your new school when the problem didn't seem quite so bad?

S: It always seems bad.

C: I bet. I bet. (Pauses) But maybe there was a break in the teasing or an incident where they were nice to you?

S: They've never been nice, but sometimes I do get a break . . . usually around fourth period.

C: What's fourth period?

S: History. They don't seem to be as bad around the time of my history class.

C: What is so different about history class?

The counselor wants to assess for situational or environmental exceptions.

S: Oh, it's just because of Jason being around at that time.

C: Who's Jason?

S: He's this really cool guy. Everybody respects him and he's nice to me so none of those jerks give me a hard time when he's around.

C: Good! That's great news! Right? That one of the well-respected cool guys likes you and takes up for you?

S: Yeah. Thank goodness for him, or it would really be unbearable!

C: Okay, so we're really glad about Jason. But tell me, Stan, how are you different when Jason's around?

Now the counselor wants to bring the exception back to being influenced by something Stan is doing.

S: What do you mean?

C: Well, I'd be willing to bet that you come across a little differently around fourth period. What do you think?

S: I'm probably breathing a sigh of relief, that's for sure.

C: I bet you're right. What does that look like?

S: I'm probably a little calmer, more relaxed, less nervous and tense. I know I'm about to have some positive interaction instead of all the negative.

C: Good. What else?

S: You mean what else am I like?

C: Yes. What else are you doing differently around fourth period?

S: Well, I probably don't look so down and out. Probably don't walk with my head down, staring at my feet.

C: Good. So that would mean you look and walk how?

S: Well . . . hmm, I've never thought about this . . . I mean, I guess I would have to say that if I'm not looking down and out and I'm not staring at the ground then I'm probably looking a little more upbeat and holding my head up.

C: Exactly. Do you think you might look a little more confident around fourth period?

S: Sure.

C: Less like a target of bullying?

S: Definitely.

C: Do you think that has anything to do with why they leave you alone around that time? Not just because of Jason?

S: I never thought about it that way . . . maybe, I guess . . . yeah, maybe . . . sure.

C: Do you think you could do more of that? Even when Jason is not around? Just try it . . . oh,

let's say, during second period each day this week . . . and see what happens?

S: Okay . . . it might be worth a try!

Stan is now enthused because he's been validated; he's realized there is an exception to his misery; and, even more important, he's realized he may play some part in that exception, meaning he may have some control over this situation.

USEFULNESS AND EVALUATION OF THE EXCEPTIONS TECHNIQUE

In general, finding exceptions to problems is a basic tenet of solution-focused brief counseling (SFBC) approaches and is beneficial for identifying strengths and resources within the client that are already being used to create instances where the problem is no longer a problem. In this way clients begin to view their situations with an internal locus of control, thereby increasing their responsibility for events. Asking clients to recall even one exception to a moderate problem can help increase a client's positive mood and initiate the benefits of the solution-focused approach. The exceptions technique is also useful in helping clients view brief moments of relief as keys to solving problems.

The literature shows beneficial results with various populations and settings when using solution-focused methods, including the exceptions technique. In family counseling settings, two outcome studies showed the promise of the exceptions technique within an SFBC process. Zimmerman, Prest, and Wetzel (1997) used the exceptions technique in a solution-focused couples counseling process to improve dyadic adjustment significantly. Lee (1997) reported that an SFBC process that included the use of the exceptions technique led to a 65% success rate in reaching diverse family goals.

Several studies demonstrated the effectiveness of exceptions embedded in the SFBC process for school-age youth. Littrell, Malia, and Vanderwood (1995) explored the use of three variations of brief counseling approaches with high school students and found that the use of exceptions in each process helped to diminish the uncomfortable feelings clients had about problems. They also found that the short-term (single-session) approach achieved the same result as longer-term solution-focused approaches. Corcoran (1998) used a solution-focused approach focused on exceptions to problems to work effectively with middle and high school at-risk youths. Corcoran (1999) then continued by demonstrating the utility of exceptions and other solution-focused methods while working with child protective services clients. Both of these populations are noted as resistant to treatment, and they are often involved in involuntary treatment. In another study with middle school students, Newsome (2004) noted a differential effect in outcomes because the SFBC group with at-risk students yielded no improvement in attendance but significant improvements in grades. Additional studies have documented the effectiveness of the exceptions technique in combination with other solution-focused approaches in working to produce positive change with behavioral problems in an inclusive classroom (Quigney & Studer, 1999), with violence in a psychiatric inpatient facility (Oxman & Chambliss, 2003), with families (Reiter, 2004), and with juvenile offenders (Corcoran, 1997).

APPLICATION OF THE EXCEPTIONS TECHNIQUE

Now apply the exceptions technique to a current client or student you are working with or revisit the brief case studies presented at the beginning of this book. How can you use the exceptions technique to address concerns and create movement in the counseling session?

CHAPTER 3

Problem-Free Talk

ORIGINS OF THE PROBLEM-FREE TALK TECHNIQUE

George, Iveson, and Ratner (1999) established problem-free talk as an important solution-focused technique useful for establishing a connection with clients. Through this tool, the professional counselor engages the client and/or the client's family in discussion of the positives in life and what is currently going well and working for them—and thus getting to know them as people first. As with other solution-focused techniques, problem-free talk is a purposeful tool to elicit conversation that reveals strengths and resources. It has been realized that the presence of abilities, interests, resources, and strengths is as important as the absence of complaints, illness, stress, and symptoms.

Problem-free talk serves several purposes. First, it is useful in the beginning of a helping relationship to develop rapport with the individual, couple, or family seeking counseling services because it demonstrates interest in clients as people. Second, it is helpful in abating nervousness about the counseling process, which many people new to counseling services can feel is mysterious. Third, it can undo the power imbalance that is assumed by many clients to exist, so that the professional counselor seems like a person rather than an all-knowing expert. Most important to solution-focused brief counseling (SFBC), however, engaging in problem-free talk can provide an opportunity for the counselor to see the client defined by something other than the presenting problem and, in doing so, allows for identification of strengths and resources that should be noted for future use in solutions.

HOW TO IMPLEMENT THE PROBLEM-FREE TALK TECHNIQUE

Problem-free talk is to be used intentionally at the beginning of the counseling process, at any time throughout the session or range of services, and any time a new family member is introduced into the counseling setting. Problem-free talk often occurs naturally at the onset of the first session and at the beginning of subsequent sessions as a result of socialization. As naturally as it may come, however, the professional counselor should be intentionally listening during this time specifically for the client's competencies and potentials. These competencies and potentials should then be noted and used later as exceptions to problems, as material for the preferred future, and as part of the solution.

When problem-free talk does not occur naturally at the beginning of counseling, the professional counselor can ask specific questions to elicit it. Typically, these questions take the form of "Before discussing your problem further, I'd like to hear more about you. What is it you enjoy doing and feel especially good at?" Other tag-on questions could include "What do you feel you have handled well?" "How have you coped in the past?" and "What good things might others say about you?" Another version of this could be "Tell me what your life was like before all this began. What were you like as a person?" The professional counselor should join this conversation so that it has a light and natural feel to it. During this two-way conversation, the counselor should listen for times when the client has had better experiences and for the client's positive attributes.

The professional counselor must be careful to engage in this talk either at the beginning, prior to the discussion of client concerns, or after a respectful amount of time has passed and the client has been given the opportunity to discuss the problem as fully as necessary. Otherwise, switching the focus to problem-free talk may appear insensitive, disrespectful, annoying, or patronizing (Lowe, 2004). Lowe warns that clients may not benefit from lengthy problem-free talk, may simply want to discuss the problem at hand, or may be hostile so that talking about positives would be counterproductive.

VARIATIONS OF THE PROBLEM-FREE TALK TECHNIQUE

Problem-free talk can be initiated at the beginning of counseling to get to know the client, at any time during the counseling session to take a break from heavy problematic storytelling, or throughout the course of counseling specifically to elicit resources for a solution. When new members enter the counseling relationship, it is important to engage in problem-free talk to put the new member at ease and also to catch a glimpse of the interactions and relationships among members outside the problem situation. Questions or statements used to facilitate this talk can range from "Tell me more about yourself as a person" to "What positive things do you have going for you in your life at this time?" Essentially, the timing, intention, and form of problem-free talk can vary. Sharry (2004) also suggested variations of this technique by using it as a game or exercise in family counseling with the members of the family pretending to be one another and stating their greatest asset, naming their favorite family trip or times together, or developing and drawing pictures of their family motto.

EXAMPLE OF THE PROBLEM-FREE TALK TECHNIQUE

Jaylen, age 17 years, and her mom, age 35 years, frequently engage in extremely volatile conflicts during which they scream obscenities at one another, throw items occasionally, and make threats such as "Maybe I'll just die, and then you'll be sorry." Jaylen is what most would define as a "good kid," working part-time at the same job for over a year, staying out of trouble in school, obeying most rules at home with the exception of curfew violations from time to time, and maintaining well above passing grades. However, she and her mom are very similar in their conflict style and "do battle," as they call it, far too often. Up to this point in counseling, Mom has been in only one time and Jaylen has insisted on coming to counseling alone to work on issues unrelated to Mom. Today, Mom is coming in with Jaylen as requested to begin focusing on their relationship now that other concerns have abated. On first entering the counselor's office, the following takes place.

Counselor (C):   Hi, Mom! So glad you're with us today!

Mom (M):   Yeah, I didn't think Jaylen was ever going to ask me to come. I was just trying to give her space . . . you know how she is . . . all particular and stuff!

Jaylen (J):   Whatever! (Playfully said)

C: So what good things have been happening for you two this week?

M: God, we've had a crazy week! I was so proud of Jaylen. This other mom came in the mall where she works and started going off on her because Jaylen and her daughter are in an argument over a boy right now. Normally, I wouldn't put it past Jaylen to go off on some woman that came up to her like that. I mean, Lord, her daughter isn't four! She can take up for herself! But Jaylen didn't. She just smiled and nodded.

The counselor notes this as an exception and praises Jaylen.

C: Wow, Jaylen. Impressive. How'd you manage to hold your tongue so well?

The counselor is briefly cheerleading and asking for details to this exception.

J: I didn't want to get in trouble at work. I really respect my boss.

This is important information to use to decrease conflicts between Jaylen and her mom: Respect for another equals ability to respond appropriately and avoid conflict.

C: Good, good. What else? What else has been good this week . . . what about with you two?

M: Jaylen stayed home Friday night with me, and we ordered pizza and watched a movie. I couldn't believe she actually ditched her plans to hang out with me!

J: Oh, Mom . . . I'm gonna get all emotional! (Stated in a playful manner, grabbing Mom's arm and leaning over to her at the same time)

The counselor is a bit surprised to see Jaylen and her mom interacting in such a playful manner because previous information about their relationship has centered only on its destructiveness. This interaction has provided the counselor with important information for preferred future details as well as exceptions. Most helpful, however, has been the observation of their loving and playful interaction, which helps the counselor consider this mother/ daughter pair as perhaps having a very distinct interaction pattern that works for them, though not typical and in need of some modification.

USEFULNESS AND EVALUATION OF THE PROBLEM-FREE TALK TECHNIQUE

As with other solution-focused techniques, problem-free talk is useful in providing information about client strengths and abilities that may have gone unnoticed or undervalued in importance. Realization of these hidden strengths, times of coping, and potential resources can serve to decrease hopelessness and instead increase motivation. Some have worried that it may interfere with engagement; however, it has been found instead to be a relief for clients and informative for counselors (Hogg & Wheeler, 2004).

In addition, Bowles, Mackintosh, and Torn (2001) found the use of problem-free talk to be a useful tool for nurses to use consistently at the beginning of an interaction with a patient in order for the nurses to show they were interested in the patient and not simply in the patient's medical condition. Smith (2005) discussed a client situation in which problem-free talk was helpful. "Dave was seen at his request together with his support worker. He appeared deeply ashamed of his behavior and reluctant to discuss it when we first met. Much of our first two sessions [was] spent in *problem-free talk*" (p. 103). In this example, Smith went on to say that because of the use of problem-free talk, positive attributes about Dave were discovered. It also seems fair to surmise that this technique is helpful when working with clients who are ashamed, reluctant to talk, noncompliant, or involuntary.

The problem-free talk technique has also been incorporated into a number of studies evaluating the usefulness of solution-focused methods. Among them, Bucknell (2000) cited the incorporation of problem-free talk when training future teachers in the classroom. Lynch (2006) documented its use with drug offenders, stating "Instead problem-free talk is encouraged illustrating how the drug user does in fact cope with many aspects of [his or her] life successfully" (p. 42). Finally, Zimmerman, Prest, and Wetzel (1997) found that problem-free talk embedded within a solution-focused approach improved dyadic adjustment in couples counseling.

APPLICATION OF THE PROBLEM-FREE TALK TECHNIQUE

Now apply the problem-free talk technique to a current client or student you are working with or revisit the brief case studies presented at the beginning of this book. How can you use the problem-free talk technique to address concerns and create movement in the counseling session?

CHAPTER 4

Miracle Question

ORIGINS OF THE MIRACLE QUESTION TECHNIQUE

Erickson's crystal ball technique encourages clients to imagine a future with no problems and then to identify how they resolved the problems to create such a future. This technique originally served as the foundation for the miracle question because knowledge of the crystal ball technique, coupled with de Shazer's frustration with clients' inability to formulate goals, resulted in what has now become known as a key strategy in solution-focused counseling.

Historically, counseling has entailed a problem-focused direction. The miracle question forces clients to consider what it is they really want, rather than simply what they do not want, thereby shifting from a problem-focused perspective to one that is generating solutions. It is obvious that a client wants to stop feeling depressed, that a parent wants his or her child to stop misbehaving, or that a partner wants a husband or wife to stop taking the partner for granted. What this question requires, however, is the consideration of what that change looks like. If these things were to stop, what would that entail? What would be different? How would you know?

In exploring this idea, clients often find their own solutions or at least brainstorm possibilities that had previously gone unrecognized. Progress is often made in counseling unbeknownst to, or at least unacknowledged by, the client. In other words, if a client never considers what "better" looks like, how will she recognize it once it is achieved? By detailing tangible evidence of the absence of the problem, the miracle question sets criteria for evaluating improvement. In addition to defining improvement with details, the miracle question, in its very process, achieves a solution-focused course, emphasizes the hope of a better future, places responsibility on the client, and triggers the client's inner resources in an effort to define what it is she wants.

HOW TO IMPLEMENT THE MIRACLE QUESTION TECHNIQUE

The miracle question is especially helpful in goal setting, though it can be used at any time throughout the counseling process. When used for goal setting, it can help to develop clear and concrete descriptions of what the client hopes to gain from counseling. In addition, it emphasizes the presence, rather than the absence, of something, thereby helping to create a positive goal rather than a negative one. The miracle question is of greater value when the counselor allows it to develop naturally within the session (Stith et al., 2012). When using this technique, it is important that the counselor avoid problem solving for the client, is patient, and helps the client understand how to bridge the gap between the miracle question and the belief that change is actually possible.

Asking the miracle question typically takes the following form: "Suppose that, one night, while you were asleep, there was a miracle and this problem was solved. How would you know? What would be different?" (de Shazer, 1988, p. 5). It is important, however, for the professional counselor to assist clients in making their proposed solutions tangible, reasonable, and focused on themselves.

If a client were to say that she would know a miracle had occurred because she would wake to find her husband cleaning the house and bringing her breakfast in bed, the professional counselor would need to refocus the client to examine how the client would be different, not necessarily how others would be different unless that other person is also in counseling. For instance, if a client states that her miracle would entail a behavior change in others, the counselor should help her understand reciprocity and the ripple effect of our own—and her own—behavior by asking "If your husband were cleaning the house and bringing you breakfast in bed, how would you be behaving differently toward him?" Helping a client understand that even small changes in her behavior can elicit more changes in others' behavior is empowering.

Other useful ways to ask the miracle question suggested by Murphy (2015) include the following:

- If this problem suddenly vanished, what would you be doing tomorrow at school that would be different from what you usually do? What would be the very first sign of this miracle? Then what?
- Pretend there are two movies about your life. Movie 1 is about your life with this problem, and Movie 2 is about your life without the problem. I already know a lot about Movie 1. Tell me what Movie 2 would look like. Who would be in it? What would they be doing? What would you be doing differently in Movie 2?
- If someone waved a magic wand and made this problem disappear, how would you be able to tell things were different?

Magic wand, magic pill, and magic lamp questions seem best used with children, who often have difficulty understanding the concept of a miracle. Regardless of how the question is asked, it is important to facilitate the client in expanding on the solution, following up in a way that explores more deeply the idea of resolution and a problem-free future. It is also useful to ask for imagined third-party observations in a way that will further clarify what the change looks like.

VARIATIONS OF THE MIRACLE QUESTION TECHNIQUE

The miracle question can be used to identify and examine exceptions to the problem. After a client answers the miracle question, she can then be queried to consider if any of those signs of improvement are currently occurring or have occurred at various times. If so, what was different, or, better yet, what was she doing that was different, and can she do more of it? This technique essentially emphasizes the need for behavioral changes rather than cognitive or affective changes. It is assumed that if one acts differently, one will subsequently feel and think differently.

The miracle question can be combined with the scaling technique (see Chapter 1) so that the client, after describing a symptom-free scenario, then can be asked to consider what a small improvement might look like or what a moderate improvement would look like. For example, the counselor might ask "If that is how your optimal outcome would look, life without this problem, how might it look with some improvement? In other words, if the scenario you just described is a 10 on a scale of 1 to 10, 10 being the best outcome, how might a 5 look?" The miracle question can also be combined with the "acting as if" technique (see Chapter 7), resulting in a challenge to the client to begin behaving as if the miracle has already occurred.

EXAMPLE OF THE MIRACLE QUESTION TECHNIQUE

Jesse is a 14-year-old male who has been referred because of his so-called bad attitude, which often results in disagreements with his parents and disruption of the home environment. Over the past six months, he has had many disagreements with his parents, conflicts with his siblings, non-compliance with chores and other requests, and dropping grades. He takes no responsibility for these issues and is sick and tired of everyone else blaming him.

Jesse (J):   Seriously, I don't see what the big deal is. I'm tired of everybody being in my business.

Counselor (C):   So you don't know what all the fuss is about?

J: Nope. If everybody would just leave me the hell alone . . .

C: You'd be fine.

J: Totally fine. But that don't seem to be happening now, does it?

C: Doesn't seem to be, no. (Pauses) So what do you think everybody else sees as such a big deal?

J: My "bad attitude." Whatever. God they get on my nerves.

C: Your bad attitude?

J: Yeah, everybody says I have a chip on my shoulder or something.

C: You disagree.

J: Yeah. I disagree. I don't need to be here.

C: So what could we do to prove that?

J: What do you mean?

C: Well, how can you and I show them that you don't need to be here in counseling?

J: Just tell them I don't need it.

C: Let's suppose it's not that simple . . . me just saying so. Let's assume that it will also take us *showing* them that you don't need to be here. How might we do that?

J: No ideas here.

C: Well, let's pretend for a minute that you can travel in time. And let's say that you travel into the future a few months from now, and during that time we had worked together to solve your problem . . . the one that brings you here today. So you travel in time to a few months from now, and you wake and everything is better. What would you notice that would be different in your life that would let you know you no longer needed counseling?

J: Well, I'd notice that everybody wouldn't be on my case anymore.

The client gives a negative goal (e.g., the absence of something) as well as a goal that is focused on others.

The professional counselor's task is to move the client in the direction of a positive goal focused on himself.

C: What would they be doing instead?

J: They'd be nice to me.

C: Okay. And if they were being nice to you, what would you be doing?

J: I'd be happy.

The client gives an emotional state. The counselor's job is again to attempt to move the client toward behavioral and action-oriented goals.

C: Okay. And if they were being nice to you and that made you happy, what would you be *doing*?

J: I'd be smiling. And being nice.

C: Okay. And what does "being nice" look like?

J: I'd probably be playing with my brother, getting along with him, and letting him hang out with me.

C: Okay. So you'd be getting along well with your brother and letting him hang out with you. What else?

J: I wouldn't be arguing with my parents.

C: What would you be doing instead? Instead of arguing with your parents?

Again, attempts are being made to change the absence of something into the presence of something.

J: I'd be saying "Yes, ma'am" and "No, ma'am" and being respectful. I'd probably be telling them about my day and stuff.

C: So you'd be getting along well with them and using respectful language with them and telling them things about yourself and your life.

J: Yeah. And if we were getting along like that, I'd be doing my chores too, and they'd be all proud of me and junk.

C: How would you know they were proud of you?

J: 'Cause they'd tell me so. They'd be all shocked and happy.

C: And if they told you they were proud and were happy, what would that look like for you?

J: That'd just make me want to do more. Probably even my school work.

C: So you see how you doing something differently causes them to do something differently, which then makes you want to do even more things differently?

It is important to help clients see that by focusing on their own behavior, rather than insisting others change, they can create changes in others through the ripple effect.

J: Yeah, I see that.

C: And you see that if you traveled in time and this problem were solved, it might look something like you getting along well with your brother, being respectful to your parents, telling them things about yourself, doing your chores, them being proud of you, all of you being happier, and you maybe even doing more of your schoolwork?

J: Yeah, I can see that too. Guess we have some things to work on, huh?

USEFULNESS AND EVALUATION OF THE MIRACLE QUESTION TECHNIQUE

The miracle question technique is especially useful in identifying solutions and forming concrete goals, and it is also beneficial for use with clients who seem to have lost optimism or hope for a better future. Clients often become emotionally hardened and resigned to their current way of feeling, thinking, and behaving. By using this technique, the professional counselor is tapping into and reviving the client's sense of hope and promise for improvement. This inspiration and motivation are necessary for effective change to occur.

The miracle question also forces the focus to shift from problem oriented to solution oriented. It identifies what specifically will be different, often leading to improved goal setting because the goal

setting is more concrete and tangible. Finally, it serves as a tool to measure progress in counseling because it gives very specific goals that need to be achieved rather than vague and overgeneralized complaints.

To date, the literature does not show the effectiveness of the miracle question technique as an independent tool used alone. However, the effectiveness of solution-focused tools (e.g., exceptions, scaling, problem-free talk) that include use of the miracle question specifically has been documented with a variety of populations and issues. In particular, the miracle question has been used in combination with other solution-focused brief counseling (SFBC) techniques to produce favorable results (de Shazer et al., 2007). For instance, Atkinson (2007) used the technique along with other solution-focused tools to assess the motivation level of those who used tobacco, alcohol, and other drugs. Burwell and Chen (2006) used these same tools with clients seeking career counseling to assist them in becoming their own change agents and problem solvers. Franklin, Streeter, Kim, and Tripodi (2007) evaluated the effectiveness of an alternative school incorporating solution-focused techniques and found it to be useful in reducing dropout rates for at-risk teens. Additional studies focused on the effectiveness of the miracle question and solution-focused tools when working with couples (Treyger, Ehlers, Zajicek, & Trepper, 2008) and addictions (Emlyn-Jones, 2007).

Several studies focused on the use of the miracle question embedded within an SFBC approach with middle school students. Franklin, Biever, Moore, Demons, and Scamardo (2001) reported that 71% of middle school student behavior cases improved (by teacher report) after using the miracle question in an SFBC approach. Springer, Lynch, and Rubin (2000) used the miracle question embedded in a solution-focused mutual aid group for Hispanic children of incarcerated parents and found that teachers reported middle school students reduced concerns to below the clinical significance criterion for both internalizing (effect size [ES] = 1.4) and externalizing

(ES = .61) difficulties. In addition, youth self-report resulted in an ES = .86 for externalizing problems, but no differences noted in youth self-report for internalizing problems (ES = .08). Finally, Newsome (2004) used the miracle question embedded within SFBC group work with at-risk junior high school students who showed no improvement in attendance but significant improvements in grade point average (GPA).

APPLICATION OF THE MIRACLE QUESTION TECHNIQUE

Now apply the miracle question technique to a current client or student you are working with or revisit the brief case studies presented at the beginning of this book. How can you use the miracle question technique to address concerns and create movement in the counseling session?

CHAPTER 5

Flagging the Minefield

ORIGINS OF THE FLAGGING THE MINEFIELD TECHNIQUE

We have all gone to a medical doctor and received prescription medications or advice that we were asked to follow. But did you always follow the doctor's orders—to the letter? Likewise, counselors assign homework for clients to work on between sessions, but do clients always do it? Flagging the minefield (Sklare, 2014) is a technique that is a form of treatment adherence and relapse prevention that was created to help clients generalize what they learned in counseling to future situations that they may encounter. Many clients go through numerous counseling sessions and have difficulty applying what they learn in the sessions to their real-life experiences. Using the flagging the minefield technique at various therapeutic transition points, such as when shifting from working on one goal to another or from the use of one technique or strategy to another, and especially at termination, helps clients identify situations in which they may encounter difficulties coping or adjusting, times when what was learned in counseling sessions may not seem helpful enough. By considering these potential problem situations in the safety of the counseling relationship, the counselor can help the client consider how to cope and adapt in the real world. Flagging the minefield is a generalization and relapse prevention technique: It helps the client transfer counseling insights and compensatory behaviors, thoughts, and feelings into the world the client encounters every day.

HOW TO IMPLEMENT THE FLAGGING THE MINEFIELD TECHNIQUE

Flagging the minefield is typically used at the end of the counseling process (i.e., at termination). This technique got its name because the counselor and client mark future situations in which the client can use what has been learned to avoid setbacks, just like miners mark mines in the fields when they are working to avoid explosions. The counselor and client create situations that may occur in the future that have not yet been discussed. The counselor asks the client to problem-solve the situation using what the client has learned in previous sessions and then to predict what he would do in the given situation. Once the client has given a prediction, the counselor helps the client process the situation, drawing on what they have discussed and learned throughout the counseling process. In this way, the counselor helps the client transfer learning to the external world and future events.

EXAMPLE OF THE FLAGGING THE MINEFIELD TECHNIQUE

For the changes made in counseling to generalize to future issues, it is imperative that potential pitfalls and obstacles to optimal functioning be identified. Some professional counselors worry that discussion of such events will cause the client to place less value on counseling by feeling that its effectiveness can easily be undermined. However, identification of such issues is a necessary part of the counseling process and can be viewed as empowering the client to address future concerns independently. Increasing client confidence is part of empowerment; therefore, it is especially important for the professional counselor to praise the progress made and to encourage the continuation of meaningful gains. In flagging the minefield, recognizing warning signs and potential pitfalls is crucial to the process. Proactive problem identification and plan development are also critical components to lasting changes.

Counselor (C):   The important thing is not to need a system. The important thing is to behave responsibly and respectfully without needing to have all of this intervention. Right? And you'll be good at it—you've already shown that. Look at all the progress that's been made. Okay, so now we're ready to do the culminating activity called flagging the minefield, which is basically kind of looking into the future and preparing yourself for situations that will really test the progress you've made as a family. Flagging the minefield is a way for you to identify obstacles to success and ways to overcome those obstacles. You know that Damon has been challenging—well, that might be an understatement. There are times when that gets very frustrating, and that may be the case for some time into the future. So we need to think into the future about those times that are bound to happen, no matter how good you are with the techniques and skills that you have learned. You know, no matter how well they've worked in the past, whether it's time out or a token economy or these response-cost systems or overcorrection or positive reinforcement procedures, there are going to be times when they're just not working. There are going to be times where he's going to be what we call "emotionally labile" and really kind of upset and emotional, and it just seems like nothing is going to work. So it can help for us to know that up front, and discuss them together, and perhaps consider when those moments are most likely and how we might handle them. Okay? So, when are some of those times when you know he's going to be particularly challenging?

Mom (M):   There are times when we are there with the whole family, and we're doing things that are not particularly interesting to him, but he needs to be with us because it's a family situation. There are moments when he is not happy about doing something, and he will make sure he lets us know that he isn't happy.

C: Yeah . . . so family events that must include him but that he doesn't necessarily want to be a part of.

M: Yes. And it can be a very difficult situation because a lot of times you might be out at a restaurant or you're in a place where you really . . .

C: Public places, right.

M: Public places are very difficult.

C: Okay, so you've already identified two situations that are naturally going to occur in the future, and you realize even now that these are going to be more difficult times than others. And by difficult I mean not only that he will be more likely to act out but also that you may find it more difficult to follow through with the skills you've learned in counseling . . . mainly due to the scenario and the surrounding circumstances of being forced to go along with a family event or being in a public place.

M: I agree with that. Definitely those are going to be the more difficult situations.

C: Right . . . so imagining yourself in either of these situations, how might you deal with it?

Dad (D): Well, the first thing that comes to mind for me when I think of a family event is that Damon is often expected to support his older siblings in their activities because we as a family support them and Damon is part of that. Um . . . for instance, his older brother plays golf, and we, as a family, often watch his golf matches. Anticipating and being realistic in my expectations for Damon would probably help. I think we have to be realistic enough to know that he can only take so much of a certain thing.

C: Exactly. Okay. So, reminding yourself ahead of time that Damon will only want to watch his older brother golf for so long, and being realistic with your expectations for his attention span . . .

D: Yes, and you know, it's even difficult for some adults to want to watch an entire game of golf. And, of course, some matches are particularly painful to watch! And then I think back to this one day that we were all out shopping for like 4 hours or something, and this was quite enjoyable for my wife and daughter, and Damon did really well for 3 hours, but then that was it. He reached his limit. And I think we can be very conscious of that and take that into consideration when planning our day, rather than assuming that since he's done well for 3 hours, we can continue on for 3 more. That's not rewarding his good behavior at all. In fact, he might view it as punishment. I think we must respect his opinion and feelings to a certain degree and be able to separate "taking his feelings into consideration" from "giving in to his demands."

C: Okay. So what I'm hearing you say so far is that being realistic in your expectations of his behavior and feelings can certainly help these potential minefields. Also, knowing what his limits are and trying, within reason, not to push beyond those limits. And then also anticipating which family events are going to pose a problem for Damon would be beneficial.

M: Right. Also, it might help to talk to him ahead of time, instead of simply hoping he doesn't notice he is spending all day doing something he doesn't want to do. Maybe instead, I could tell him up front that for this amount of time today, we are all going to do this certain activity as a family, and that you know everybody gets their time. Perhaps I could even use the Premack principle with the delayed rewards to help with these situations—for instance, saying ahead of time "Damon, we are going to watch your brother's golf game this morning, but as soon as it is over, you can spend the afternoon playing with your remote-control cars."

C: Absolutely. Seems you two are both strategizing a good offense. Let me ask, what are some things you have tried in the past, and have these things worked?

M: Sometimes what we do works, and sometimes it doesn't. And a lot of it has to do with something you said earlier about his emotional . . . what did you call it?

C: Lability.

M: Uh-huh. And sometimes you can't predict it.

C: Yes, and just knowing that can be helpful.

D: Well, I think the main thing that we've done in a lot of those instances where we want to do something that we know he doesn't want to do is to find an alternative something for him to do. For instance, when we know he's not going to like the plans that day, we may work something out with another parent or friend to say, "So and so has a lacrosse game, and we know Damon doesn't want to sit through another one of those," and so he may go to a friend's house and play, and then we'll pick him up when the game is over. The problem I think we both have with this is that we sometimes feel like we are giving in to him and he is training us rather than the other way around.

C: Right. I understand that. Certainly there will be events that do not require his presence and that any child his age would have difficulty sitting through, and in these cases I certainly see where finding another option for what he does during that time would be appropriate.

M: I like that you sort of qualify it as certain instances that neither require his presence nor are easy for any child to enjoy. That feels more like we are making an informed and intentional decision that makes sense, rather than giving in to him to make it easier on us.

C: Good. Good. So, although these family events are probably more often than not public events, let's talk about public places as a potential minefield in general. Let's think of ways to be proactive with Damon's behavior in public places. What do you find difficult for yourselves or for Damon in these circumstances?

D: I think he knows he is more likely to get his way when he misbehaves in public because we are more likely to give in to make it easier on us just for that brief moment.

C: Ah, good point. So if he knows this ahead of time, I'm willing to bet that public places are more often the setting for his misbehavior.

M: These days, yes. He has gotten so much better at home and in private. But in public, he's still . . . um . . . he is still the old Damon.

C: Hmm . . . could this in any way be a result of Damon's parents being the "old mom and dad" in public? Children catch on very quickly.

M: You know, I hadn't thought about that, but absolutely. We are very much the way we always were when others are staring or whispering or giving that judgmental glance.

C: Uh-huh. And what is it about those judgmental glances that makes you more likely to be the old mom and dad?

D: Well, we live in a society where we care what others think of us. And if it comes down to a stranger thinking I have a spoiled child or I am a mean parent, well, I'd just rather them think Damon is spoiled.

C: Okay. So are there any exceptions to this general example?

M: Well, I can remember one time that all the glances in the world didn't matter, and I followed through with my instructions to Damon, even though he proceeded to have a very embarrassing temper tantrum in the middle of a store.

C: And what made this time different?

M: Well . . . um . . . I remember we were out of town, and I remember thinking that I didn't really care what those people thought of me or my child because none of them knew me and I would never see any of them again.

C: Ah, yes, I see. So perhaps we could apply that same thinking to situations that are not out of town. Okay, what are some other things that you can do? What are some resources that you can bring to bear on the situation to make it a lot easier, without having to abandon the skills you have already shown to work?

The professional counselor moves on to identify two to three more specific potential mines, problem-solve general solutions, and identify resources to use to address these issues should they occur. This type of intervention makes it more likely that clients will think creatively when problem situations do occur. Rather than giving up, clients are more likely to demonstrate treatment adherence, persevering through challenging situations.

USEFULNESS AND EVALUATION OF THE FLAGGING THE MINEFIELD TECHNIQUE

Flagging the minefield is used to help clients understand how they can use what they learned in counseling to overcome problems they may have in the future. This technique can be used with clients who were brought to counseling for a variety of different reasons, including "smoking cessation, dietary change, increasing physical activity, stress reduction, and alcohol use reduction" (Ockene, 2001, p. 43), cocaine dependency (Barber, Liese, & Abrams, 2003), social skills training (Piccinin, 1992), academic problems (Fearrington, McCallum, & Skinner, 2011), depression (Akerblad, Bengtsson, von Knorring, & Ekselius, 2006), mood disorders and medication (Byrne, Regan, & Livingston, 2006), and improvement of dyadic adjustment in couples (Zimmerman, Prest, & Wetzel, 1997).

Several factors contribute to the efficacy of flagging the minefield. Miller, Kelly, Tobacyk, Thomas, and Cowger (2001) suggest that the counselor should expect some noncompliance on the part of the client and throughout the counseling process should explain to the client the importance of the client's actions. If the client has a positive perception of the alliance with the counselor, the client will be more likely to adhere to the treatment (Patton & Kivlighan, 1997). The client's beliefs about the issues and whether or not the client thinks he needs treatment also contribute to the efficacy of this technique (Davidson & Fristad, 2006). When working with children, this technique is more effective when the parents play a role in the child's participation and adherence (Nock & Kazdin, 2005).

APPLICATION OF THE FLAGGING THE MINEFIELD TECHNIQUE

Now apply the flagging the minefield technique to a current client or student you are working with or revisit the brief case studies presented at the beginning of this book. How can you use the flagging the minefield technique to address concerns and create movement in the counseling session?

SECTION 2

Techniques Based on Adlerian or Psychodynamic Approaches

Section 2 represents a group of techniques that have psychodynamic origins, and several were specifically introduced by Alfred Adler, a colleague of Freud and the originator of individual psychology. Adler was a highly respected theorist; Albert Ellis (1993) stated, "Alfred Adler, more than even Freud, is probably the true father of modern psychotherapy" (p. 11). Adler was an early constructivist who believed that clients construct and narrate the realities to which they respond, which he called fictions, and then take these fictions as truth or fact. His social interest theory proposed that, from an early age, people develop interest in others according to how they are raised. But some individuals experience conditions and circumstances that prevent them from developing normal degrees of social interest, leading to psychological and mental disorders and problems of adjustment.

Adler contributed several theoretical constructs. *Lifestyle* refers to a person's unique goals, beliefs, and ideas for coping with the challenges life brings. Birth order pertains to psychological reactions to the order in which one is born into a family, which can shape perceptions, experiences, and personality. For example, first-born children are often described to be high achieving and responsible, whereas youngest children are often described as spoiled and continue to be treated as less responsible or capable. Adler also believed that feelings of superiority or inferiority arise in individuals' personalities, sometimes leading to a superiority complex or an inferiority complex. Early recollections are also important because they show how clients place an importance on and attribute meaning to memories from early childhood events. The primary goal of Adlerian and psychodynamic counseling approaches is to recognize and assimilate explanations for events and occurrences that may vary from the client's fictions so that the client experiences growth and develops alternative ways of compensating for challenging episodes in life.

Adlerian counselors use a variety of experiential, behavioral, and cognitive techniques in order to enhance interpersonal relationships and intrapersonal understanding. The techniques explained in this section include I-messages, acting as if, spitting in the soup, mutual storytelling, and paradoxical intention. I-messages help clients take responsibility for their own thoughts, feelings, and behaviors while encouraging others to do the same. Clients can be taught a simple way to structure their comments so that the clients communicate their needs and desires to others without blaming or criticizing. Acting as if is a technique that allows the client either to act purposely according to her fiction or to alter an assumed fiction by behaving in a different manner (e.g., assuming an alternative to the fiction). Spitting in the soup is an expression used to name a commonly used paradoxical technique in Adlerian counseling. In this technique, the professional counselor encourages the client to increase the use of the problematic thought, feeling, or behavior in order to help the client learn that she is actually in control of the symptom, thus empowering change.

Mutual storytelling is primarily a psychodynamic technique; it was developed by Richard A. Gardner (1974) to help elicit therapeutic content from children and adolescents who are not able or willing to address therapeutic content through direct verbal discussion. Clients tell a story, which the counselor analyzes for themes and metaphors. Then the counselor retells the story using the same or similar characters, but with a more pro-therapeutic message, often including various alternative scenarios for the characters to resolve conflicts they encounter.

Paradoxical intention is also claimed by numerous theoretical orientations and should be undertaken with caution. Paradox ordinarily involves reframing the client's problem behavior and asking the client to engage in the behavior she is trying to stop but restraining the expression of that behavior to certain circumstances (e.g., place, time). Paradox is quite effective in eliminating problematic behaviors because clients realize they actually have control over when they do and do not display the behaviors, thus breaking the cycle of expression.

MULTICULTURAL IMPLICATIONS OF THE ADLERIAN AND PSYCHODYNAMIC APPROACHES

The Adlerian approach focuses on social interest and is quite respectful of individual clients, their worldviews, and various cultural heritages, primarily because Adlerian counselors understand the importance of feelings of inferiority and superiority and directly relate to feelings and issues presented by clients from disenfranchised or historically oppressed groups who may feel discouraged or alienated. Adlerian views of egalitarianism help to counteract feelings of inferiority and stigmatization and may be particularly useful with clients from diverse cultures, ethnicities, genders, and sexual orientations. Adlerians offer a cooperative approach rather than the competitive approach common in U.S. society.

The Adlerian approach may be particularly appropriate for clients of African descent because of the inherent principles of collectivism, social interest, collaborative goal setting and intervention development, and exploration of multigenerational family issues. These emphases on family and community building are appealing to individuals from many cultures (Hays & Erford, 2018).

Clients from some cultures (e.g., Latino/ Latina, Native American) may feel particularly comfortable with storytelling techniques, and psychodynamic approaches have been particularly effective with Latinos and Latinas. The emotive aspects of psychodynamic approaches may be particularly appealing to women more than to men. Conversely, emotionally laden psychodynamic approaches, particularly interactions that are highly intense and require self-disclosure of feelings and personal and family information, may not be appropriate for individuals of Arab or Asian descent because individuals from these cultures may not feel comfortable expressing strong emotions. On the other hand, the authoritative style of some psychodynamic counselors may be appealing to these same individuals. In addition, analysts tend to ask probing questions, which may be interpreted as insensitive. Thus, counselors using this approach must take additional care to gauge a client's comfort level with commonly used techniques.

Psychodynamic approaches have some additional potential limitations when they are used across cultures (Hays & Erford, 2018). For example, not all cultures emphasize or even acknowledge the unconscious processes that analysts assume underlie motivation and behavior, and psychodynamic approaches tend to diagnose and view some culture-specific behaviors as pathological (e.g., child-rearing practices that foster dependence over independence, perceived unequal treatment of genders). In addition, the slower speed of these approaches may be problematic for some individuals, especially those who may be unable to afford a long-term therapeutic approach. Finally, these approaches often do not pursue concrete outcomes, making some clients uncomfortable expending the investment of time required for changes to occur.

CHAPTER 6

I-Messages

ORIGINS OF THE I-MESSAGES TECHNIQUE

The use of personal pronouns is important in a number of theoretical counseling orientations, including Adlerian and Gestalt, person-centered, and existential therapy. For example, Perls and other Gestalt therapists encouraged clients to use *I* instead of *it*, *you*, or *we* when talking about themselves (Corey, 2016). Using I-messages, sometimes called I-statements, forces the client to take responsibility for her feelings, behaviors, or attitudes without placing blame on another. I-messages also help the client to realize that she is required to take action in order to change the situation.

In the 1970s, Thomas Gordon introduced the idea of I-statements to the area of family studies. Gordon, who focused on the individualistic and autonomous aspects of relationships, believed that I-statements were an effective way of relating to others. I-messages contain minimal negative evaluation, usually promote a willingness to change, and do not harm the relationship between the speaker and the receiver of the message (Gordon, 1975).

I-messages express feelings in a way that minimizes counterattacks and is less likely to cause resistance or rebellion (Corey, 2016). Unlike you-statements, which are often judgmental and accusing, I-messages convey neither judgment nor directives. Instead, I-messages identify feelings inside the speaker and communicate the speaker's recognition that her view of the situation is subjective. This acknowledgment leaves room for other perspectives to be expressed, thus initiating dialogue between the two people in conflict and helping to solve problems through open, respectful communication (Hopp, Horn, McGraw, & Meyer, 2000; Warnemuende, 2000).

I-messages are sometimes called responsibility messages (Gordon, 1975). People are often unaware of the effect their behavior has on others. When using an I-message, however, the speaker takes responsibility for her feelings and shares them with the receiver. The speaker also communicates the impact of the problematic behavior, leaving the recipient aware and therefore responsible for modifying her behavior.

HOW TO IMPLEMENT THE I-MESSAGES TECHNIQUE

Individuals can be encouraged to substitute personal pronouns in any situation where they are avoiding responsibility for their actions or feelings. For example, if the individual says, "It will not happen again," he can be asked to change this statement to "I will not let that happen again."

Simple I-messages acknowledge the existence of a problem, feeling, or idea. They involve only the person making the statement and therefore are relatively nonthreatening. Simple I-messages can be used when a person wants to identify a problem but fears that others will become defensive. On the other hand, compound I-messages are helpful when simple changes in behavior will solve a problem or when the speaker wishes to start a dialogue about a more complex problem. Compound I-messages involve three parts: a description of the problem (usually a behavior), the effect the problem or behavior has on the speaker, and the feeling experienced by the speaker. Gordon recommends that I-messages follow this sequence: behavior, effect, then feeling (Gordon, 1975). This sequence communicates that the feeling is caused by the effect, not the person's behavior.

More recently, professional counselors using I-messages have been taught to follow the structure: I feel _____ (feeling) when you _____ (behavior) because _____ (consequence). I-messages should be specific and focus on behaviors rather than personalities. The consequence part of the I-message can be either consequential or interpretive (Remer, 1984). Whereas consequential confrontations focus on concrete results, interpretive confrontations deal with the reasons for the behavior. For example, an interpretive confrontation would be "When you leave dirty dishes in the sink, I feel angry because I think you're doing it to irritate me" (p. 58).

Many people of all ages confuse emotions with behaviors. It can be helpful to discuss emotions and act out a few example emotions before teaching about I-messages. Demonstrating the difference between I-messages and you-messages also can be especially useful. After the demonstration, children can process the different reactions the two produce and why I-messages are more effective.

VARIATIONS OF THE I-MESSAGES TECHNIQUE

Sometimes I-messages contain a fourth part, in which the speaker communicates what she would like to happen (Frey & Doyle, 2001). After the traditional I-message, the speaker adds "And I want _____." The speaker is therefore responsible for taking a proactive role in finding a solution to the problem. Another variation is the use of we-statements, which communicate that the speaker thinks a group or relationship has a problem. For example, a group leader may comment "We seem to be more interested in staying on the surface of this issue." Unlike I-messages, we-statements neither identify the source of the problem nor imply or suggest individual responsibility or solutions. Consequently, we-statements identify a problem in a

way that does not create defensiveness or resistance. We-statements suggest that the people involved are connected and need to work together to find a solution. We-statements are useful when someone wants to emphasize the togetherness of the group and initiate a problem-solving process in the group. We-statements are inappropriate, however, when the speaker is trying to avoid taking responsibility for an individual problem by defining it as a group problem or when the speaker is using the message to coerce or control others.

EXAMPLE OF THE I-MESSAGES TECHNIQUE

As you will recall, an excerpt from a counseling session with Tamara and Kevin was incorporated into Example 3 of Chapter 1, on scaling. In their example dialogue, they both agreed to accept the other's scaled perspective of themselves and their communication abilities. They also agreed that the ability to communicate effectively would influence the course of their marriage as they attempted to cope together with more difficult issues. Building on their previous progress, the professional counselor now begins educating Tamara and Kevin about the importance of I-messages and begins teaching them to use these messages in place of less productive means of communication.

Counselor (C):   So we all agree that there are some needed improvements in the way we communicate. And that it is necessary and important to make these improvements for the well-being of your relationship.

Tamara (T):   Yes, and I like that we both agree now that neither of us talks to the other in a productive and healthy way.

C: That's right. What I've gathered is that Kevin feels like you are picking fights with him, and so he tunes you out and becomes defensive. And, Tamara, it seems you feel that Kevin ignores you, and so you dominate the conversation and become angry.

Kevin (K):   That sounds like a cycle.

C: A cycle is exactly what it is.

T: It's like I'm thinking "If he would pay attention to me, I wouldn't have to keep on and get angry!" but he is probably thinking "If she would talk less and lower, I wouldn't have to tune her out or feel the need to defend myself!"

C: Exactly. Now that you know that, is that enough for you to communicate differently?

T: (After a pause) Um . . . well, hmm . . . I don't know.

K: It helps. But when we are in that moment, I don't know that that is going to be enough.

C: Okay. So I know I've heard one of you say in the past that a common source of tension is the division of household and family responsibilities . . .

The professional counselor intentionally brings up a topic that will likely lead Tamara and Kevin to initiate a heated discussion so that he can observe their typical style of communication.

K: That's a nice way to put it . . . though not exactly how I would say it.

C: And how would you put it?

K: Um, let's see . . . nothing is ever enough to satisfy her. She is never happy with what I do.

T: That's because you don't do enough. You think that just because you lift a finger I should be *so* grateful and appreciative when your "exceptional contribution" to the running of our household is just one of a hundred things I do every day!

K: (Takes a deep breath and contorts his face)

T: Do you not have anything to say to that?

K: What good would it do?

T: None. That's because you know you have no defense. Because what I'm saying is the truth.

C: Okay, if you don't mind, I am going to interrupt now simply because you have provided me with an excellent example of how you typically communicate, and that will help us know where to begin. What I heard as I listened to you just now is a lot of focus on the other person, which tends to set the stage for an argument. When we do this, we are

avoiding responsibility for our own feelings and behaviors, and instead putting the other person on the defense . . . hence their need to either defend themselves, attack, blame, or emotionally run away from the other person. What I want us to begin with, then, is a very basic communication skill that stresses your own personal feelings, behaviors, and attitudes, rather than pointing the finger at the other person. Staying with the same topic that you two just discussed, I want you to complete the statement "I feel _____." Tamara, would you like to start? "*I feel . . .*"

T: I feel . . . taken for granted.

C: Good. "I feel taken for granted *when you . . .*"

T: I feel taken for granted when you expect me to take on most of the household responsibility.

C: Good, and a little more. "I feel taken for granted when you expect me to take on most of the household responsibility *because . . .*"

T: Okay. Let's see . . . I feel taken for granted when you expect me to take on most of the household responsibility because I think you are capable of doing more to help me.

C: Great, Tamara. And now, Kevin, I would like for you to respond to Tamara with "I feel . . ."

K: Ugh . . . okay . . . I feel . . . I don't know . . . I feel irritated.

C: Uh-huh. "I feel irritated when you . . ."

K: I feel irritated when you point out everything that I don't do.

C: Good, and "I feel irritated when you point out everything that I don't do because . . ."

K: Because . . .

C: Start at the beginning, if you don't mind, because we are learning this. "I feel irritated . . ."

K: I feel irritated when you point out everything that I don't do because it's like the times I do help are completely overlooked.

C: All right. For each of you, what are your reactions to the statements you just heard from your spouse?

K: I'm feeling all mature and respectful for saying it like that. I'm pretty proud of myself.

T: (Laughs) Yeah, I'm kind of feeling bad for not complimenting him more for what he does do to help.

C: Ah, both good points. What you'll find with this style of communication—it's called an I-message—is that not only will you feel better about yourself for communicating this way, but you'll also be more likely to see your partner's point of view, understand where he or she is coming from and, in turn, feel empathy for your spouse's position.

T: I can see that.

C: Good. Okay, I want you to continue with your conversation now, and I will interject to help you practice until you get very good at it.

T: So just keep talking?

C: Sure. Keep expressing yourselves with the "I feel . . . when you . . . because . . ." We'll keep it very specific like this until you feel it comes more naturally.

T: Okay. I guess it's my turn, unless you want to go, Kevin?

K: You can go ahead.

T: Well, I'll respond to your last statement. I tend to overlook the good you do because I feel so angry because . . .

C: "When you . . ."

T: Oh yeah. Kevin, I tend to overlook the good you do because I feel so angry when you don't do more because I think you don't care that I'm already overwhelmed with responsibilities as it is. It's hard to be appreciative when you're pissed, you know?

K: Believe me, I know. Okay, okay, my turn. Hmm, honestly, I sometimes don't care that you have more responsibilities when you are fussing because I feel like whatever I do is not enough and it won't be noticed anyway.

USEFULNESS AND EVALUATION OF THE I-MESSAGES TECHNIQUE

I-messages can be used in many situations. Gordon (1975) believed that I-messages work especially well with children, both in parenting and in school disciplinary situations. The technique is also used commonly in couples counseling to good effect. I-messages are commonly used in a variety of conflict situations and may help those involved to reach an effective resolution (Kammerer, 1998). I-messages are frequently taught to help people manage their anger in positive, nonviolent ways (Phillips-Hershey & Kanagy, 1996), and they are applied in assertiveness training to help those who are overly aggressive or too passive (Hollandsworth, 1977). Martinez (1986) found I-messages to be effective in handling general classroom behavior problems, as did Cohen and Fish (1993), who also found the technique useful with specific problem behaviors such as laughing, arguing, burping, and other off-task behaviors.

Considerable research has been conducted on the effectiveness of I-messages, in both disciplinary and conflict situations. In a study examining the use of I-statements to influence student behavior in the classroom, Peterson et al. (1979) found that using I-messages produced a decrease in disruptions, although not in all participants. Remer (1984) studied reactions to I-messages in recorded confrontation situations. He found that, in response to I-messages containing all three components (behavior-feeling-consequence), participants rated themselves as more willing to change their behavior and more likely to be open to negotiation. They also rated this method of confrontation as more effective than any one component alone or any combination of two components.

Two other studies explored the effectiveness of I-messages in conflict situations. Both examined the difference in self-reported reactions produced by assertive and aggressive/accusatory statements. Assertive statements were defined as I-messages, and aggressive/accusatory statements were composed of you-messages (Kubany & Richard, 1992). Kubany, Richard, Bauer, and Muraoka (1992) found that female participants rated assertive statements as less aversive, less likely to evoke antagonistic emotions, more likely to evoke compassion, less likely to evoke antagonistic behaviors, and more likely to evoke conciliatory behaviors. They concluded that using accusatory statements to express anger in close personal relationships may antagonize, alienate, and/or impede conflict resolution. When Kubany and Richard (1992) extended this research to the adolescent population, they found nearly identical results. Both male and female adolescents rated themselves as more likely to express anger and respond antagonistically to you-statements than to I-messages. Although much of this research is based on self-reports and not on actual behavioral observations, the results suggested that I-messages were more effective at promoting conflict resolution than you-messages or other methods of dealing with

conflict. Finally, cultural sensitivity and specificity are required when using I-messages. For example, Cheung and Kwok (2003) concluded that parents in Chinese culture avoided and actively resisted using I-messages when communicating feelings of anger but readily used the techniques to convey feelings of worry and frustration. Likewise, Kim (2014) adapted I-messages among Korean couples to help with marital communication problems.

APPLICATION OF THE I-MESSAGES TECHNIQUE

Now apply the I-messages technique to a current client or student you are working with or revisit the brief case studies presented at the beginning of this book. How can you use the I-messages technique to address concerns and create movement in the counseling session?

CHAPTER 7

Acting as If

ORIGINS OF THE ACTING AS IF TECHNIQUE

Acting as if is a technique based on the Adlerian approach. The goal of Adlerian therapy is to increase clients' social interest and community feelings (Carlson, Watts, & Maniacci, 2006) as measured according to four criteria: (1) decreasing symptoms, (2) increasing functioning, (3) increasing the client's sense of humor, and (4) producing a change in the client's perspective. Acting as if helps the client change not only perspective but also behavior, which in turn leads to increased functioning. It is not enough for clients to see things differently; they must also act differently.

Adler believed that all people created cognitive maps of their lives and that these maps served as a guide for how to lead their lives (Carlson et al., 2006). These cognitive maps were fictitious. However, Adler believed that people act "as if" these maps were real and therefore live accordingly. But Adler also believed that these maps could be changed to help the client behave in a more productive manner. The acting as if technique has clients assume roles and behave as though they can accomplish what they believe they cannot accomplish.

HOW TO IMPLEMENT THE ACTING AS IF TECHNIQUE

Acting as if is a technique in which the professional counselor asks the client to act as if he had the skills to handle a difficult situation effectively (Seligman & Reichenberg, 2013). Many clients use the excuse "If only I could . . . ." At this point, the counselor instructs the client to act out the role as if he could

do whatever he was hoping. The client may find it useful to think of someone who has these skills and then envision how this person would handle the situation at hand (Carlson et al., 2006). By trying out a new role, clients often learn that they can carry out the part and also become a new person in the process.

Acting as if one is the person one wants to be can challenge self-limiting assumptions that a person holds (Corey, 2016). Clients are asked to try and catch themselves repeating their old patterns of behavior. Commitment is a very important part of the acting as if technique. If clients truly wish to change, they must be willing to do something about their problems.

VARIATIONS OF THE ACTING AS IF TECHNIQUE

Some professional counselors segue into the actual implementation of the acting as if technique by using a reflective questioning process. The counselor asks the client questions meant to get the client thinking about what he would do differently (thoughts, feelings, and actions) if he were actually in the situation and already behaving differently. This allows the client to imagine how he would act before he is actually asked to do it in real life, which prepares the client ahead of time. It also allows the professional counselor to flag the minefield (see Chapter 5) by exploring times when acting as if in real life might be challenging.

Watts developed a variation of the acting as if technique called reflecting as if (Watts, 2003; Watts & Garza, 2008; Watts, Peluso, & Lewis, 2005; Watts & Trusty, 2003). This three-phase adaptation encourages clients to take their time and think through how they would act, feel, and think differently if they behaved in a manner consistent with their goals. First, the professional counselor asks reflective questions to help the client construct an understanding of what the change in actions might look like. Second, as if behaviors consistent with client goals are constructed collaboratively by the client and counselor. Finally, the client selects the least challenging behavior to try out in real-life circumstances. After experiencing success and modifying the approach, the client tries more and more challenging behaviors over time. The counselor and client process the experiences in subsequent sessions to celebrate the successes and modify use for future encounters.

Watts and Garza (2008) also suggested that professional counselors could help children express themselves by drawing the differences one might see if they would act as if their problems did not exist. Then the counselor would follow up with a detailed discussion to facilitate the client's understanding of the path to change and development of the capacity for change. This could then be followed by in-session practice acting as if, experimentation outside counseling sessions, and finally implementation during key time periods.

EXAMPLE OF THE ACTING AS IF TECHNIQUE

Laney is a 16-year-old girl whose boyfriend of one year broke up with her eight months ago. She was so distraught at that time that she refused to return to school where he also attended. Mom is emotionally reactive and inconsistent but also overly indulgent with poor parental boundaries, and she allowed Laney to withdraw from public school to be homeschooled. After four months at home, Laney had yet to complete any of her schoolwork. In addition, other troublesome behaviors had developed, and at the onset of counseling four months ago, Laney was engaging in starvation and self-injury and was described as emotionally erratic and destructive. After four months of weekly sessions, she exhibits no self-injury or starvation and has begun to catch up on her schoolwork. She has improved emotional stability, with reduced destructiveness and explosiveness, but she continues to struggle with becoming overly somatic and distraught. She has recently made the decision to return to school when the new academic year begins in a few weeks.

Laney (L):   I just want to be normal. I just want to be like other girls my age.

Counselor (C):   And that would mean returning to school?

L: Yeah. I'm tired of being at home all the time . . . like some hermit . . . what if I'm a hermit . . . you know my dad has schizo-something . . . he's like that. He's a hermit. Oh, God, what if I'm like him? What if that's why I quit school? What if I'm crazy? (Becomes physically affected by her thinking, pulls her knees up to her chest, places her head between her knees, and begins running her hands through her hair too harshly)

C: Laney, we've worked on this. You know how to stop that.

L: (Stops moving her arms but stays with her head between her knees, takes a deep breath and is silent for several moments) I am not a hermit. I am not like my dad. I do not have to be like my mom. I am my own person. I'm not a freak. I'm not crazy. I'm really not crazy. I'm getting better. I'm okay. I am okay. I am okay. (Another deep breath, raises her head, gives a half-hearted smile with eyebrows raised)

C: You are okay.

L: Yeah. I'm gonna be.

C: Good. You were wanting to be "normal" like other girls your age?

L: Yes. Normal. Like, not crazy. My old friends think I'm a freak for staying home. They know I'm not really being homeschooled. I shouldn't be home anymore. I should be a normal 16-year-old.

C: And what do you think that would look like?

L: For one, I'd be in school. I would be at the mall. I would be at the pool this summer. I've been avoiding all these places because of Matthew. I really lost it when he broke up with me. Really lost it. I know I'll lose it again if I see him and that all this progress I've made will be for nothing.

C: So you believe that if you're put back in the same old situation, you'll go back to being the same old Laney.

L: That's what I'm afraid of, yeah, pretty much. I can't go back to that. I mean, I know I still have a ways to go even now, and I'm okay with that. But I really can't go back to that. But he just has that effect on me, you know? I mean, not as much as he did. It killed me when he broke up with me though. It felt like my life was over. I didn't know who I was anymore. I had been Matthew's girlfriend. I didn't know who Laney was anymore. And I totally lost it. I felt like everyone was staring at me . . . talking about me. And he was talking to other girls. I felt so abandoned . . . so alone. And I freaked out. I lost it. I cut his tires. I threatened to kill myself. Then I cried my eyes out, refused to leave his house, begged him back. Was on the ground crying. It was ridiculous. I just couldn't go back to school and face that. I refused to go back for two straight weeks, but I just kept getting worse instead of better, so Mom didn't make me go back. She said it would be too much for me. (Pause) But I want to go back now. I don't want it to control my life anymore. I'm just terrified it will.

C: You control that, you know.

L: How? I don't know how I'll react. What if I can't control it?

C: If you script it ahead of time, learn the art of pretense . . . charades . . . make-believe . . .

L: What do you mean? (Looks very interested and amused, even eager)

C: Well, you've talked before about wanting to be an actress, and you certainly have a flair for the dramatic. (Laney and the counselor grin at each other) What if we create a character for you, create a new persona and act as if you are someone else?

L: I like the way this sounds.

C: What do you wish you could be like when you return to school?

L: Wow . . . (thinks seriously, showing how invested she is in this idea) . . . I want to be normal . . . and healthy . . . I want to be the epitome of cool, calm, and collected. I want to appear confident, unaffected by ridiculous high school drama. I want to be happy, with myself, but not in a giddy immature way, but in a mature, self-assured way. I want to be the girl who would never be so ridiculously emotional that she would grovel in the dirt, slice up tires, or cut herself. I want to be poised. I want to be unaffected. Because it won't just be facing Matthew that will be difficult. Everyone will be whispering about where I've been and why I'm back. I've got to be able to handle all of that. But that's not me. I'm not that together and strong.

C: Then let's develop your new character.

L: Like a movie character?

C: Exactly like a movie character. And you can base it on one you already know. If you can think of a character in a movie that exhibits these traits and skills you are talking about . . .

L: (Suddenly her enthusiasm is deflated) But isn't that like asking me to be something that I'm not?

C: Or maybe I'm just asking you to be different than you were. Because it wasn't working too well for you. You aren't quite sure how to be different yet. But you do know what you want to be like. So you act as if you are . . . what it is you want to be. Because sometimes the easiest way to change is to act like you already have.

L: Acting! I love it. I can totally do this. (Enthusiasm obviously returning) Okay, so don't laugh, but the person that comes to mind is Scarlett O'Hara in *Gone with the Wind*. Honestly, she is exactly what I'm describing. Nothing got to her. Nothing.

C: Well, maybe she had one or two weak moments. Remember when Ashley left for war? And what about at the end when Rhett left her? Let's think about how she handled rejection and losing the two men she loved the most.

L: You know she did have a few moments where she groveled too. But she dusted herself off way quicker than I did. It was like it never happened.

C: Exactly.

L: And usually she would wait until after the storm was over to fall apart . . . and she would usually do it in private. It was rare that anyone saw her weaknesses.

C: How could you tell she was strong?

L: The way she walked in a room. The expression on her face. The calmness in her voice. The way she handled situations.

C: And even when she fell apart, she got it together quickly. Scarlett was a master at "resetting" herself. It's like she herself was playing a character and had a restart button she would press if she ever came out of character. Could you act as if you were Scarlett when you return to school? Could you give more thought this week to how she would handle various situations that you might face when you return?

L: Absolutely. I think I'll watch the movie again this week and pay very close attention to the traits she has that I want to possess.

USEFULNESS AND EVALUATION OF THE ACTING AS IF TECHNIQUE

Acting as if can be used in a variety of situations where the client does not believe he possesses the necessary skills to confront a challenging situation. A man struggling with shyness can act as if he is assertive (Carlson et al., 2006). A woman who is intimidated by her domineering or chauvinistic husband can act as if she were brave enough to stand up to him (Seligman & Reichenberg, 2013). In addition, children undergoing medical treatments have handled the treatments more successfully when they have pretended to be their favorite superhero.

APPLICATION OF THE ACTING AS IF TECHNIQUE

Now apply the acting as if technique to a current client or student you are working with or revisit the brief case studies presented at the beginning of this book. How can you use the acting as if technique to address concerns and create movement in the counseling session?

CHAPTER 8

Spitting in the Soup

ORIGINS OF THE SPITTING IN THE SOUP TECHNIQUE

Stemming from an old German proverb and credited to Ansbacher and Ansbacher (1956), spitting in the soup is a paradoxical Adlerian technique that is used to decrease client symptoms by first determining the underlying purpose for them and then pointing out this purpose to the client. In this way, Adler believed that, even if the client chose to maintain her symptomatic behavior, she could do so only with the realization that she was somehow benefiting from it. For most clients, this knowledge renders the symptoms less attractive or, to continue the metaphor, less palatable. If symptoms are less attractive and do not seem as beneficial in some way, clients are typically less likely to continue them.

Although the professional counselor does not necessarily encourage the continuation of symptoms, he does not request that they stop either. Instead, the counselor acknowledges that behavior has a purpose. The purpose is validated as useful, and the counselor works with the client to develop the skills needed to meet this purpose in a different, more prosocial way. According to Rasmussen and Dover (2006), "By understanding that it is the client's desire to feel as good as possible, the counselor can work with the client to find better ways to obtain that sought-after goal" (p. 387). If newer, more adaptive ways of obtaining the goal are not taught, the client will engage in symptom substitution rather than adopt a behavior replacement. Adler believed that, to maintain symptoms, clients must fight against them. Paradoxical techniques

demonstrate how clients create their own symptoms, unconsciously but for a purpose.

HOW TO IMPLEMENT THE SPITTING IN THE SOUP TECHNIQUE

An established rapport and trusting relationship must be in place before a counselor uses this technique. Otherwise, the client's likelihood of rejecting the use of the technique is increased. Prior to spitting in the soup of the client, useful questions the counselor might ask to formulate a hypothesis about the purpose of symptoms might include "How do you gain from this behavior/emotion?" "Does anything positive come as a result of your behavior/emotion?" "If you were to give up this behavior/emotion tomorrow, what would you be losing?"

To use this technique effectively, it is important to understand its full purpose and capacity to bring about change. When implementing this technique, keep in mind that Adler believed most maladaptive behavior to be a result of poor social interest, feelings of inferiority, or relational issues. Oberst and Stewart (2003) maintained that unhealthy behaviors or symptoms typically result from avoidance of life's demands and tasks, or from an effort to gain power, attention, or love.

According to Rasmussen and Dover (2006), "a client has developed a way of life that enables him or her to reach a desired goal, but his or her methods are flawed" (p. 387). Typical motivations and maladaptive symptoms may include the use of anger outbursts to gain power, respect, and control; depressive symptoms to gain nurturing and support from others; feigned helplessness to avoid responsibilities and tasks; or lack of self-care to gain displays of love and affection from significant others. Just as a 3-year-old will use a maladaptive behavior, such as a temper tantrum, to gain a tangible item or avoid a task, older children, adolescents, and even adults continuously engage in similar versions of this same behavior.

By spitting in the soup, the professional counselor shows the client what she is gaining from her symptoms (Carlson, Watts, & Maniacci, 2006). Then the counselor acknowledges that the client may continue using her symptoms, although now she will have increased knowledge of why. Although the client may continue to display symptoms, the symptoms have now lost their "good taste." In other words, the counselor identifies the motives behind the client's self-defeating behaviors and ruins the client's supposed payoff by making it unappealing (Seligman & Reichenberg, 2013). The client may still try to eat the soup (i.e., continue the behavior), but it is no longer enjoyable. The counselor has spoiled the soup (i.e., the game) of the client.

When encountering resistance to change despite use of this technique, the professional counselor must examine the reasons for the resistance. Typically, when clients resist change despite having their soup spoiled, it may be because they have different goals than the counselor has surmised; feel the counselor is not sympathetic, understanding, or supportive enough; find the counselor disagreeable, too direct, or unlikable; and/or lack the necessary motivation for change (Rasmussen, 2002). In each of these instances, the counselor should redefine goals, employ methods to increase client motivation, and focus efforts on establishing a deeper level of rapport.

VARIATIONS OF THE SPITTING IN THE SOUP TECHNIQUE

No variations of this technique were identified in the extant literature, although it certainly takes various forms, depending on the counselor, client, presenting symptoms, and identified motivators.

EXAMPLE OF THE SPITTING IN THE SOUP TECHNIQUE

Dianne is a 46-year-old female who has been referred from a medical clinic designed to treat chronic pain. Dianne describes symptoms consistent with depression and emphasizes her complaints of physical pain, which leave her feeling unable to function regularly. To date, these physical complaints have no medical explanation, therefore resulting in her referral for counseling.

Counselor (C):   So you've felt this way for some time now, though you're not sure exactly when it began. Can you recall what life was like before?

Dianne (D):   I come from a large family, and I'm the oldest out of my other four siblings. My mom died when I was really young . . . I was eleven . . . Dad started drinking a lot after she died. He really never was the same. So it was almost like we lost both our parents at the same time, just in different ways.

C: That must have been extremely hard for you.

D: I almost didn't notice at the time how hard it was. I was too busy picking up the extra slack. With Mom gone and Dad passed out all the time, there was no one to take care of the others. It all fell on me. I was the one who had to take care of everyone else, including Dad. I don't remember stopping long enough to feel sad. (Long pause as she thinks about this . . . short deep breath) And then one day, I decided to get married. Part of it was just so I could get out of the house and pass the responsibilities on to my younger sister. But soon I got pregnant and had my first daughter . . . then another . . . and I was at it again . . . taking care of everybody else. I just got so tired. So . . . so very tired.

C: Sounds like you never really had a break.

D: Never. And then Charles left . . . that was my husband . . . that was years ago. We're still married, I guess. He calls every now and then. He moved upstate somewhere . . . sends money every so often. My girls were angry at me for him leaving. They started running all over me too. And my younger brothers still need taking care of, even as grown men. One's constantly in and out of jail. He's always needing help getting back on his feet. One is alcoholic and is always needing to be rescued. My sister is on disability, and I have to keep her kids sometimes. And my dad . . . his health is really bad now. I've tried my best to take care of him as well. I would go get his groceries every week and try to keep his house clean. (Drifted off into her thoughts, begins to shake her head back and forth and puts her forehead down into her hand) And now to top it all off, I'm having all this physical pain that the doctors can't seem to find a reason for.

C: Seems to never end.

D: Exactly. And why is this happening to me of all people?

C: Doesn't seem fair.

Thus far, the counselor has made only supportive statements intended to validate the client's feelings and experience. This is especially important because her physical complaints have not been validated from a medical perspective thus far and because the counselor is soon going to ask her a difficult question that has the potential to create defensiveness. A client's defensiveness is less likely if the client feels validated beforehand.

D: Not fair at all. My life has been hard enough. Filled with unfairness already . . . enough to last a lifetime. I'm sick of it.

C: Exactly. Sick of it indeed. Sick of your life. Because of your life.

D: What do you mean?

C: Is there any part of you that wants to be sick?

D: No! I don't want to feel this way! Why would I want to be sick? I'm the victim in all of this.

C: Let me ask it differently. Do you benefit . . . at all . . . in any small way . . . from being sick?

D: No.

C: So if suddenly you were well tomorrow, you wouldn't be giving anything up?

D: Well, yes. (Speaking very rapidly) I'd lose this wonderful break I'm currently getting . . . my family would expect me to take care of all of them again . . . my brothers would constantly be wanting money . . . my sister needing constant help . . . my daughters angry and hateful to me all the time . . . (Stops) . . . Oh, dear . . . um . . . seems that maybe I do benefit some from being sick.

C: It seems that the only way you've figured out to give yourself a break from taking care of everyone else is to be the one that needs taking care of. It's okay. It's okay to continue being sick. If it makes you feel better. If it gets your needs met. It's okay for now.

The client may continue to eat the same soup, but it will not taste as good now that she knows what the ingredients are. In other words, the client may continue not feeling well, being a victim, but it will not have the same effect for her, and so she will be motivated to find alternative ways, more healthy ways, to get her needs met.

USEFULNESS AND EVALUATION OF THE SPITTING IN THE SOUP TECHNIQUE

No empirical evidence was located to validate the effectiveness of the spitting in the soup technique independently, although it has been used in conjunction with other Adlerian techniques (e.g., I-messages, acting as if, lifestyle assessment) in several studies. Doyle and Bauer (1989) suggested the use of this technique while treating children with post-traumatic stress in order to help them alter their distorted view of themselves. Herring and Runion (1994) used Adlerian techniques, including spitting in the soup, with ethnically diverse children and youth to increase social interest and improve lifestyles. Harrison (2001) advocated the use of this technique and other Adlerian principles to work specifically with survivors of sexual abuse, who so often present with resulting symptoms of self-injury, depression, and eating disorders. For additional empirical evidence of the effectiveness of paradoxical techniques used to address a wide range of presenting problems, see Chapter 10.

APPLICATION OF THE SPITTING IN THE SOUP TECHNIQUE

Now apply the spitting in the soup technique to a current client or student you are working with or revisit the brief case studies presented at the beginning of this book. How can you use the spitting in the soup technique to address concerns and create movement in the counseling session?

CHAPTER 9

Mutual Storytelling

ORIGINS OF THE MUTUAL STORYTELLING TECHNIQUE

Storytelling has a rich tradition among humans, and these stories, including the Bible, fables, and fairy tales, influence human behavior. Stories reflect cultural laws, ethics, and the day-to-day rules that govern behavior and guide decision making. It stands to reason that storytelling can play a helpful role in counseling.

The early roots of the mutual storytelling technique can be found in play therapy, which included the use of stories and was first used with children by Hug-Hellmuth in 1913 (Gardner, 1986). In the 1920s, Anna Freud and Melanie Klein, both influenced by Hug-Hellmuth, incorporated play therapy into their analytic sessions with children. Anna Freud used play to develop a therapeutic alliance with her clients before moving into verbalizations. In contrast, Melanie Klein believed that play was a child's primary means of communication. Beginning in the 1930s, Conn and Solomon began to notice that many children were unable to analyze self-created stories. Conn and Solomon discussed the story on a symbolic level with the client and used this communication to bring about therapeutic change. From the work of Conn and Solomon, Richard A. Gardner, a psychodynamic therapist, developed the technique called mutual storytelling in the early 1960s.

Due to his experience with resistance to analysis, Gardner disagreed with the psychodynamic idea that the unconscious needed to be brought into conscious awareness (Allanson, 2002) for therapeutic progress to be made. He believed instead that allegories or metaphors could bypass the conscious and be directly received by the unconscious (Gardner, 1974). He also thought that clients' resistance to hearing about their wrongdoings could be avoided by discussing the inappropriate behavior of others (e.g., fictional characters) and the lessons they learned as a result of these mistakes (Gardner, 1986). By using a story that is individually relevant to a specific person at a particular time, the lessons conveyed in the mutual storytelling technique are more likely to be received and incorporated into the listener's psychic structure. Gardner used the level of engagement and the anxiety experienced while listening to his story to determine how accurate his interpretation had been and how well his lesson was understood (Allanson, 2002). The more the counselor knows about the client's background and presenting concerns, the better the counselor is able to use this technique.

HOW TO IMPLEMENT THE MUTUAL STORYTELLING TECHNIQUE

Before using the mutual storytelling technique, it is important to develop a therapeutic relationship with the client and understand as much about the client's background and current issues as possible. This will help the counselor understand the client's metaphors and use them effectively in the retelling of the client's story.

The first step in the mutual storytelling technique is to elicit a fictional self-created story from the client. The client is given broad range to create the story, but as with any good story, it must contain a beginning, middle, and end, with interesting characters and some action (Arad, 2004). Although this can be done in many ways, Gardner preferred to tell the client that he was the guest of honor on a make-believe radio or television program. The program involved inviting clients on the show to see how good they were at making up stories. The story had to be from their own imagination, and it was against the rules to tell a story about anything that really happened, anything they had read or heard about, or anything they had seen on television or in a movie (Smith & Celano, 2000). The story must also include a moral or lesson.

Most clients have little difficulty telling a good story, and even get better and more expansive with repeated attempts. If the client has difficulty beginning a story, however, offer to help the client. For example, say very slowly, and with substantial pauses, "Once upon a time . . . a long time ago . . . in a very distant land . . . far, far away . . . far beyond the mountains . . . far beyond the deserts . . . far beyond the oceans . . . there lived a . . ." (Gardner, 1986, p. 411). Gardner would periodically point his finger at the client, indicating that the client should say whatever was on his mind at the time. Continue to prompt the client with "And then . . ." or "The next thing that happened was . . ." until the client is able to continue the story on his own. This method of prompting is successful in eliciting a story from nearly all clients except the overly resistive.

While the client tells his story, the counselor should take notes to help analyze the story content as well as formulate the counselor's own story variation. When the client has finished telling a story, it is important for the counselor to ask about the moral or lesson of the story. The counselor may also ask for a title to the story or which characters the client relates to, even who the client would or would not like to be (Gitlin-Weiner, Sandgrund, & Schaefer, 2000).

While silently interpreting the client's story, Gardner suggested considering the following guidelines:

1. Identify which figure or figures represent the client and which figures symbolize significant people in his life. Keep in mind that two or more figures may represent different parts of the same person.

2. Gain an overall sense of the atmosphere and setting for the story.
   a. Was it pleasant, neutral, horrifying, aggressive?
   b. Where did it take place? (There is a big difference in the interpretation of a story when the setting is one's home, school, neighborhood, the jungle, or a desolate landscape.)
   c. What feeling words were expressed by the client?
   d. What were the client's emotions and/or expressions while telling the story (e.g., animated, aggressive, depressed, stoic)?
   e. What is typical content, and what is stereotypical content?

3. Although numerous interpretations may be possible, select the one that is most pertinent at this point in time, often cued by the content of the client's moral or lesson.

4. Ask yourself "What would be a healthier, more mature adaptation than the one provided by the client?"
   a. Sometimes presenting several options provides the client with future alternatives in resolving difficulties. Counseling should open up new avenues of thoughts, feelings, and behaviors not typically considered.
   b. Offer multiple, empowering options, rather than narrow, self-defeating options.
   c. The counselor's moral or lesson should reflect the healthier resolution.

5. Watch the client's reaction as you retell the story. Intense interest or marked anxiety, among other responses, may indicate that you are close to the mark.

Kottman (1990) added that counselors should also focus on how the client views self, others, and the world, as well as what patterns and themes emerged. Because the story may be subject to several different interpretations, it is important for the counselor to consider the client's own moral or lesson (Gardner, 1986). This will aid in selecting a theme that is most applicable to the client at that moment in time. Based on this information, the counselor should ask himself "What is the primary inappropriate resolution to the conflicts presented here?" (p. 414).

After identifying a more mature or healthier mode of adaptation, the counselor uses the client's characters, setting, and initial situation to tell a somewhat different story, usually incorporating many similar characters and actions but offering a healthier resolution to the conflict presented in the client's story. The goal is to provide the client with more and better alternatives to solve problems, gain insight into problems, and develop an awareness of new perspectives and possibilities.

After the counselor finishes telling a story, the client is asked to identify the lesson or moral of the counselor's story. It is preferable that the client figure out the lesson on his own. If the client cannot do so, however, the counselor may present the moral for him. Note that stories often present more than one lesson, and each lesson should emphasize a healthier resolution to the problem.

Recording (e.g., audio, video) the client while telling the story is encouraged. Unlike other objects around which stories can be formed, such as drawings, dolls, or puppets, a recording device does not restrict or channel the client's story. In addition, recording allows the client to view stories (both client and counselor versions) a number of times in order to provide multiple exposures to the messages the counselor is trying to express. Listening to or viewing the recording is often assigned as homework.

VARIATIONS OF THE MUTUAL STORYTELLING TECHNIQUE

The mutual storytelling technique can be helpful for addressing many situations involving unconscious or subconscious processes, and it is particularly helpful for engaging clients who are resistant to so-called talk therapy. As with many projective techniques, the clients unknowingly provide important information to the counselor. This technique is ordinarily used with children and adolescents, but it can be adapted for use with adults and families.

The mutual storytelling technique has been used as a basis for several ancillary games or modes of presentation. Gardner developed *The Storytelling Card Game* (Gardner, 1986), which allows clients to choose cutout characters and background scenes that act to stimulate storytelling. Erford (2000) developed a CD-ROM for PC called *The Mutual Storytelling Game*, which provides background and character graphics (human and animal) to stimulate storytelling. The CD-ROM has the advantage of allowing the printing of hard copies of the scenes for the note taking, tracking, and evaluating process. It also provides multicultural (i.e., White, African American, Asian American, Hispanic American) and animal character sets. *The Mutual Storytelling Game* is available for purchase from the American Counseling Association, which benefits from all proceeds (www.counseling.org/publications).

Gardner developed another set of games that can be useful with clients who are less receptive to telling stories on their own. The *Pick-and-Tell Game* (Gardner, 1986) allows the client to pick a toy, a word, or a picture of a person from the Bag of Toys, the Bag of Words, or the Bag of Faces, respectively. The client then uses the object picked to create a story and tell the moral or lesson of that story. In addition, Winnicott developed the *Scribble Game*, in which storytelling is based on drawings (Scorzelli & Gold, 1999). The counselor begins by closing his eyes and drawing on a piece of paper. The client then turns the scribble into something and tells a story about it. The game continues as the client then draws something for the counselor to complete and interpret.

Other variations on the mutual storytelling technique include doll play, the use of puppets, and writing a story. Webb (2007) described combining storytelling with doll play in order to encourage clients to act out family situations. Gitlin-Weiner et al. (2000) believed that puppets could be interviewed to allow the client to convey the motivation of the characters and hence discover solutions to problems. After interviewing the puppets, the counselor can talk directly to the client about the story in order to assess the client's defenses, coping styles, and capacity for self-observation.

Finally, the mutual storytelling writing game, developed by Scorzelli and Gold (1999), involves the counselor and client creating a story together. The counselor begins the story with "Once upon a time . . ." and asks the child to complete the statement. The story continues back and forth between the counselor and client until the child ends the story. Depending on the client's preference or limitations, either the client or the counselor can write down the story. Webb (2007) suggested writing down all of the stories told by the client and creating a journal.

EXAMPLE OF THE MUTUAL STORYTELLING TECHNIQUE

Justin, age 7 years and in grade 2, was referred for anger control issues and moderate classroom disruption. He frequently became angry in peer interactions. Other students' parents had complained to the teacher and principal. He was also quite resistant to traditional talk therapy, so I used the mutual storytelling approach. The general goal of counseling was to help him to express his anger in a more prosocial manner and to develop alternative reactions to frustrating and stressful interpersonal interactions.

But Justin didn't believe he had an anger issue and refused to talk about it—or much else. So we went to plan B—an indirect approach. Justin composed a picture using the *Mutual Storytelling Game CD-ROM* (Erford, 2000) of a forest background, a fox, turtle, owl, and tiger cub (see Figure 9.1).

Counselor (C): All right, Justin. I want you to tell a really good story about this picture that you just did on the computer, and we printed out—and it's a beautiful picture. What I want you to do is to tell a great story, have the characters talk with each other any way you want them to. You want to tell what they're thinking and what they're feeling and certainly what they're doing. And if they want to talk to each other, they can talk to each other. Remember that every great story has a beginning and lots of good details and also a really good ending. And at the end of it, I'm going to ask you to tell a lesson or a moral for the story, kind of what some of the characters in the story learned. Then I will retell your story, and I might tell it a little bit differently during my turn. But your job right now is to tell a really good story about that picture. You ready?

FIGURE 9.1 Justin's mutual storytelling baby tiger picture.

Justin (J):   Uh-huh. One day, a baby tiger got lost in the woods . . . and um . . . and um . . . a fox was in the woods and was hungry. He kept on eating, eating all the animals in the forest. And the tiger didn't know about that. But one day, the owl . . . the owl told him that, and then he looked over to where the fox was at prowl and saw a . . . um . . . turtle, and the fox ate him. And . . . um . . . the fox liked it. Okay . . . and then the tiger . . . um . . . went up the tree to live with the owl. And that's the end.

C: That's the end?

J: Uh-huh.

C: Okay . . . so the tiger is living up in the tree with the owl?

J: Uh-huh.

C: Okay . . . and what is the lesson of the story or the moral of the story?

J: How to warn . . . warn people.

C: Okay. Tell me more. How would you warn people?

J: By telling them about the danger and finding a safe place to hide.

"Intermission"

Justin's story was unusually short, lacking details, thoughts, and feelings. It also presented with some content related to his presenting problem: aggression. The counselor's response could address many issues, but the primary purposes of the retelling that follows were to (1) model more extensive, detailed storytelling, (2) give alternative solutions to anger and aggression, and (3) reinforce several themes applicable to his presenting problem. In addition, the metaphorical use of the owl and turtle were irresistible, so the retelling cast the owl in a wise, friendly role while the protective features of the turtle were revealed.

C: Okay. All right. Justin, I'm going to go ahead and retell the story, and I might add some details and might subtract some details. But that was a really good story. That had a lot of exciting adventure in it. I'm going to be really hard pressed to tell a better story, but I'll try my best.

J: (Nods and laughs)

C: One day, there was a tiger—it was actually a tiger cub, a small tiger, a little baby tiger—and it got lost in the woods. And it was kind of walking through the woods, looking around, going, "Wow, this doesn't look familiar. I'm lost, and I don't know where my mom is, I don't know where my dad is, and I'm just kind of walking around trying to find my way home." And he was all alone because, as you can imagine, tigers don't have a whole lot of friends, because they're the kind of folks that kind of run around eating people. A lot of people wouldn't want to be a tiger's friend, and that goes for tiger cubs too, because they're afraid, you know, if they get too close to him, he might eat them.

J: Yeah. (Laughs)

C: So he was feeling kind of lonely and a little bit depressed because nobody would talk to him or give advice. He went by a chimpanzee and he said, "Hey, can you help me find my mom?" The chimpanzee headed for the tree because he didn't want to get too close to the tiger. The baby chimpanzee said to the mother chimpanzee, "Hey, why can't we help out the little tiger cub?" And his mom said, "Because he'll eat you up. You just stay away from people like that 'cause he's a tiger and tigers are mean and eat people." So the tiger cub felt kind of lonely and upset because no one would help him find his way back to his parents. But up in the tree, watching all the action, was an owl. That's what owls do—sit way up high and check out what's going on, and they see a lot of things the other people might not notice. That's why owls are often looked at as being very wise creatures. Owls are kind of all knowing and very wise.

J: (Nods and laughs)

C: The owl was checking things out, looking at the situation, and the owl had a pretty big heart. So the owl said, "Maybe I should help out the tiger cub. He's not really hurting anybody, and he's probably getting pretty hungry, but he's really in need of a friend right now to help him find his way back to his parents." So the owl swooped down and said, "Hey, what's going on, little tiger cub?" The tiger cub was crying by this time, and if you've ever seen a tiger cub cry, it's really kind of a sad thing because his fur gets all matted and messed up—really a sad sight.

J: Sure is (laughing).

C: So the owl, of course, saw that the tiger cub was crying, "Boohoo, I'm lost, I can't find my mom, I can't find my dad. I don't know what to do." The owl said, "Hey, maybe I can help you out." "Oh, could you please, sir? I'd appreciate it so much," said the tiger cub. And the owl thought, *Hey, the tiger cub has some pretty good manners, and if the tiger cub has pretty good manners, then maybe I'll take him under my wing, so to speak, help him along, help him find his parents.* So while he was talking to the tiger cub—you know, owls have extraordinarily good hearing and eyesight— he spotted a fox . . . uh . . . coming along, and this fox was actually kind of hungry—he was out looking for a meal. So the owl said, "I'll tell you what. Let's go up into the tree over here because this fox is coming along and you don't want to be around when the fox comes through because he'll eat little tiger cubs like you."

J: (Laughs)

C: So the tiger cub climbed the tree—because tigers can do that—and they sat on the branch together. Then the owl said, "Oh my goodness, watch this," and they saw that fox spying on the little turtle. And the turtle had this nice hard shell on. The fox was going to have turtle soup—without the soup, if you know what I mean!

J: Yeah (Laughing). He was gonna eat him up!

C: Right. He was going to eat this turtle, clean him right out of his shell, and have him for dinner. So he went over to the turtle, and, of course, the turtle saw the fox coming. So what did the turtle do immediately?

J: Um . . . hide in his shell?

C: That's right . . . he hid in his shell. And there's a reason why he hid in his shell: He was protected in there. And turtles, any time they feel threatened or scared, they will often pull their feet and all four legs and their head into their shell, and inside they can think, *What should I do?* And a lot of times, the best thing to do is just to wait and to think until the fox gives up. The fox came over and moved the shell around, and you know, was trying to get in there, trying to get at some of that good old turtle meat, 'cause he was trying to make a good dinner. And eventually, the fox, after about 15 minutes, gave up. He said, "This is just ridiculous. I can't get any dinner from this turtle. I'm just wasting my energy. I'm gonna go find something a little bit easier or maybe a little bit tastier. I don't even like turtle meat to begin with. It's a little bit tough; it's not real tender like tiger cubs and stuff like that."

J: (Roaring with laughter)

C: So off he went. He walked under the tree and didn't even notice the owl and tiger up there watching this whole thing. He just kind of went off to find something else to eat for dinner. They kept watching the turtle and saw the turtle poke his head out and look around real carefully to see if the fox was still there. And then eventually, when the turtle felt it was safe, he went walking along to find some water or someplace where he could relax a little bit because he'd done his job—he'd protected himself, and he'd live to see another day. The turtle was going on to see his family and friends, to see what they were doing. And so the tiger cub looked at the turtle and said, "Wow, that was really great. I mean, here was the mean old fox that was gonna make him his dinner, and all he did was just protect himself, go in his shell, and he didn't seem to be scared or nothing at all." And the owl said, "Well, that's the way it is, you know, when you're a turtle and you carry your home around on your back like that. If something threatens, you go right in and figure out what it is you should do and you wait for a safer time." And then the tiger cub said, "You know, that's really what we did, wasn't it?" The owl said, "Absolutely. We saw the fox coming because we had good hearing and vision and we went ahead and climbed up into the tree to a safer place—to a place where we wouldn't get hurt."

And the tiger cub said, "Wow, what a really important lesson." "Oh really?" the owl said. "What kind of lessons did you learn?" "Well, I learned first of all the one thing you do whenever you feel threatened and scared is to go find a safe place so that you don't get hurt and so you can think about what you should be doing." "Oh really? And what have you been thinking about?" asked the owl. "Well, I've been thinking about how to find my mom and dad." And the owl said, "Oh, really? How would you find your mom and dad?" "Well, you have such great vision and such great hearing. Would you mind flying up above the canopy of the forest here to see if you can locate my mother and my father?" And the owl said, "You know, because you've been so good and such a good friend to me today, I think I'll do just that."

So the owl took off way above the trees and flew just a couple miles and already heard the tiger cub's mom calling. His mom was just worried sick because the little tiger cub wasn't anywhere to be found. And so he swooped down onto the tree and said, "Hey, mama tiger, I know where your little boy is. He's right up the road. You can go right ahead up the trail and just follow me." So the mama tiger said, "Thank you so much, I've been worried to death about my little tiger cub." And the owl just flew away and the tiger kept running along, as fast as she could and let out a big tiger roar. The father tiger heard this too, and so they basically came at the same time and found the little

baby tiger still safe up on the tree branch where the owl left him. The owl landed right beside him, and the mommy and daddy tigers looked up and saw the little tiger cub meowing, sitting right there on the tree branch. And the tiger club was so excited, he just climbed down the tree, went over, and, of course, his mom—you know how moms are—started licking him and stuff like that. "Oh, I missed you so much, I love you," kissy, kissy, kissy, and having such a good time. But that's how tiger moms show how much they love their little tiger cub.

J: (Laughing hysterically)

C: And so the little tiger cub looked up and said, "Thank you so much for helping me out today. I've learned so much today with you. Would you mind if I came back sometime so we can play again?" And the owl said, "Sure, any time. That's fantastic." And, of course, the mommy and the daddy tiger said, "Oh, thank you so much! If there's anything that we can do for you, you just let us know, and we'll be there to help you out because you are a fantastic owl, and you did this very nice thing for us." The end.

J: Wow. That was way better than mine.

C: Sometimes longer stories are more entertaining. And you'll have more chances to tell other stories next time. So, there are a couple of lessons they actually learned: the one the tiger cub already shared about finding a safe place to think and calm down when you feel scared or threatened. But both of them also learned some lessons too, didn't they? Can you think of any of the other lessons that the owl and tiger cub might have learned?

J: (Thinks for about 15 seconds, then shakes his head no)

C: Well, the tiger cub also learned that if people think you are mean or nasty—even if on the inside you really are not—then they will avoid you, or even might not help you if you really need it. He also learned that friendliness and good manners are a great way to get people to like and help you, right?

J: He sure did!

C: Now the owl learned that if you show kindness to someone, you are often rewarded, and so now his best friends in the whole jungle are whom?

J: Uh . . . the tigers.

C: Right, the tiger family. And they are a good group of folks to have on your side because if anyone's ever picking on you, all you have to do is go get your tiger family friends. Okay . . . so the tiger cub learned some really good lessons about how you go inside your shell, you relax, you try to figure out what to do and so forth. And the tiger cub and owl learned some good lessons about what it's like to be a good friend, okay?

J: That was a great story—I like tigers!

C: Great. Now I want you to take this recording home with you and listen to it again every night until the next time I see you. Okay?

J: No problem! Can my mom and little brother listen too?

Brief Analysis

In this retelling, the counselor sought to reveal several helpful alternative coping strategies that people (or tiger cubs) can use in anxiety-producing situations—alternatives that do not involve aggression. The counselor also sought to reinforce a couple of themes that were applicable to his client's presenting problem: (1) Alienation occurs when you are mean to people, or even if they just think you are mean, and (2) good manners impress people and make it more likely that they will want to be friendly or helpful toward you. Finally, because this was Justin's first time telling a story, the counselor wanted to model more extensive, detailed storytelling so that Justin would be more expansive the next time the technique was used in the following session.

USEFULNESS AND EVALUATION OF THE MUTUAL STORYTELLING TECHNIQUE

Originally developed to overcome clients' resistance to analysis of unconscious material, the mutual storytelling technique can be used both as a diagnostic tool and as a therapeutic technique. When used diagnostically, the professional counselor does not respond with a story of his own but instead prompts the child to provide more stories in order to develop an idea of the client's unconscious drives, needs, or conflicts. To allow sufficient themes to emerge, the client should provide at least a dozen different stories before the counselor forms a diagnostic opinion. When the technique is used therapeutically, the counselor responds with a story involving an appropriate resolution to the conflict in the story, as described above.

The mutual storytelling technique can be used to facilitate the development of a therapeutic relationship with clients who have difficulty talking about themselves or who are resistant to counseling. It is not recommended for use with individuals with poor verbal skills or subaverage cognitive abilities. It can also be applied to the group counseling context (e.g., group members take turns contributing to a story).

According to Gardner (1986), the mutual storytelling technique is most useful with clients between the ages of 5 and 11 years. Clients younger than 5 are usually incapable of telling an organized story, and clients older than 11 begin to realize that they are revealing themselves in their stories and may become resistant to this technique. Stiles and Kottman (1990) suggested, however, that the prime ages of use were 9 to 14 years because of older clients' more advanced verbal skill, imaginations, and life experiences. Gardner used the technique with clients with post-traumatic stress, hyperactivity and distractibility, learning disabilities, disinterest in school, withdrawal from peers, shyness, acting-out behavior, and manifestations of the Oedipus complex (Gardner, 1974, 1986; Schaefer, 2011).

O'Brien (2000) described the use of this technique for children with attention-deficit/hyperactivity disorder (ADHD) in order to transmit insight, values, and standards of behavior. For example, the counselor can use a metaphor of trains and motors to explain to the child that his brain is like a motor that is going too fast. The people on the train cannot see anything out the windows when the train is traveling very fast. But if the train could slow down, the people would be able to see the scenery. Likewise, Kottman and Stiles (1990) believed that the mutual storytelling technique could be used to help correct client misbehavior. By listening to a client's story, the professional counselor can discover the client's motivation to misbehave: attention, power, revenge, or inadequacy. The counselor can then use a story to help the client to redirect his mistaken goal or faulty beliefs or to develop the client's social interest. Iskander and Rosales (2013) found that mutual storytelling as an intervention affected the target classroom behaviors of students on the milder end of the autism spectrum and with ADHD. Finally, the mutual storytelling technique can be used with clients who are depressed or suicidal (Stiles & Kottman, 1990). Telling stories can help clients come to terms with their sense of loss, desire for rescue, or feelings of helplessness or hopelessness. The counselor can also use stories to teach clients new ways to express anger or cope with the world.

Little empirical research has been conducted on the efficacy of the mutual storytelling technique (Stiles & Kottman, 1990). Anecdotally, Gardner successfully treated a child with post-traumatic stress disorder by repeated use of the technique (a sort of storytelling desensitization). Gardner cautions that the technique should be used only by counselors adequately trained in psychodynamics, dream analysis, and the interpretation of projective material (Gardner, 1974), but I have not found this to be the case. When using the technique simply for pointing out and increasing problem resolution strategies and choices, psychodynamic training becomes far less consequential. Gardner (1986) also mentioned that it is unrealistic to expect a single story or confrontation to bring about permanent change in a client. Some counselors will engage the client in one or two stories per counseling session for multiple sessions, devoting the remainder of the session time to other counseling strategies and processes. In this way, the mutual storytelling technique is used in conjunction with several other methods of treatment.

APPLICATION OF THE MUTUAL STORYTELLING TECHNIQUE

Now apply the mutual storytelling technique to a current client or student you are working with or revisit the brief case studies presented at the beginning of this book. How can you use the mutual storytelling technique to address concerns and create movement in the counseling session?

CHAPTER 10

Paradoxical Intention

ORIGINS OF THE PARADOXICAL INTENTION TECHNIQUE

In paradoxical intention, the professional counselor directs the client to perform in a way that seems incompatible with the therapeutic goal. Victor Frankl (2004, 2006), credited with developing this technique, described paradoxical intention as encouraging clients to seek what they are avoiding, to embrace what they have been fighting, and to replace their fears with a wish. Milton Erickson and Jay Haley are also widely credited with development and applications of the paradoxical intention technique, particularly as used in strategic family therapy. With this technique, clients are told to exaggerate their symptoms. For instance, a client who experiences panic attacks and fears that she may die suddenly might be told to just let go and let the panic engulf her. Instead of being told to try to get better, clients are encouraged to try to get worse. When people consciously try to get better, their symptoms sometimes increase. Often, however, the harder clients try to produce their symptoms intentionally, the more they find they are unable to do so. As such, the "wind is taken out of the sails of anticipatory anxiety" (Frankl, 2006, p. 83).

Paradoxical intention is a truly eclectic technique because it is not tied to any one theoretical approach. It is used by a variety of theoretical orientations, including systemic family therapy, existential therapy, reality therapy, transactional analysis, and individual or Adlerian psychology (Young, 2017). There are several different types of paradoxical intentions, including symptom prescription (or symptom scheduling), restraining, and reframing.

Symptom prescription involves a therapeutic directive for the client to continue her symptomatic behavior. Sometimes the client is also given specific instructions on when to perform the symptom; this is called *symptom scheduling*. In *restraining*, the professional counselor directs the client to prevent change or to stop trying to change the symptoms (Swoboda, Dowd, & Wise, 1990). Essentially, the client is given the message that the client must stay the same in order to change. The professional counselor may point out the negative consequences of change in order to encourage the client to resist feeling better. An example of a paradoxical restraining directive is "if your depression lifted, people would react to you more favorably and would put greater demands upon you" (Swoboda et al., 1990, p. 256). In *reframing*, the problem is explained in a way that alters the client's point of view and, therefore, the meaning of the situation (see Chapter 23 on reframing).

The rationale behind paradoxical intention is that most problems are more emotional than logical (Hackney & Cormier, 2017). Clients become involved in a cycle with fears evoking symptoms, which in turn increase the fears (Seligman & Reichenberg, 2013). By encouraging clients to do or wish for the thing they fear most, clients may undergo a change of attitude toward the symptom. For instance, when a client who struggled with stuttering is encouraged to try to stutter, the client was attempting a task that she did well. Therefore, the client no longer feared failure, and she was free of anxiety. Consequently, relaxed speech may proceed. On the other hand, another client, who was afraid to leave her house because she feared that she might faint, was instructed to try to make herself faint

(Seligman & Reichenberg, 2013). Despite her best effort, she was unable to do so. Thus, the client had to change her attitude about fainting, and her fear of fainting diminished.

Paradoxical intention helps clients become aware of how they are behaving in certain situations and their responsibility for their behavior (Corey, 2016). Paradoxical techniques often put the client in a double-bind situation when asked to exaggerate the problematic behavior. If the client accepts the professional counselor's directive, she demonstrates control over the symptom. On the other hand, if the client chooses to resist the directive and to decrease the symptomatic behavior, it is not merely under control but eliminated. The goal of paradoxical intention is to help clients reach a point where they no longer fight their symptoms but instead exaggerate them. As a result, the symptoms will continue to decrease until clients are no longer bothered by them.

HOW TO IMPLEMENT THE PARADOXICAL INTENTION TECHNIQUE

Paradoxical intention is not usually used until more conventional counseling methods have been tried. This procedure should be used with caution and under supervision until the professional counselor becomes proficient in its use. The illogical nature and the novelty of the paradoxical intention technique can be used to create motivation in a discouraged client (Young, 2017). Before using a paradoxical directive, the professional counselor should ask herself the following questions to determine if the technique is appropriate:

1. Have I established a strong bond of trust between myself and the client?
2. Might the use of paradox have a boomerang effect, so that the client feels tricked and thus becomes even more resistant?
3. How has the client responded to the use of other techniques?
4. Am I clear on what I expect to accomplish, and do I have an educated sense of how my client might react to this procedure? (Corey, 2016, p. 386)

After determining that paradoxical intention may be used, the professional counselor should ensure that the specific inappropriate behavior is identified. Then the professional counselor should persuade the client to produce the behavior in an exaggerated manner. Finally, the professional counselor may inject humor into the situation as the client engages in the behavior. This allows the client to detach from the problem by laughing at it. These steps should be repeated until the inappropriate behavior is minimized. In addition, it is sometimes helpful to restrain the expression of the symptom to certain days, times, or situations.

Jay Haley, who used paradox in his famous strategic family therapy approach, outlined eight specific facets of paradoxical intention: (1) establish a relationship with the client, (2) define the problem, (3) establish goals, (4) offer a plan, (5) disqualify the current authority on the problem, (6) give a paradoxical intention directive, (7) observe the client's response to the directive and continue encouragement, and (8) avoid taking credit for the improvement.

VARIATIONS OF THE PARADOXICAL INTENTION TECHNIQUE

The *relapse technique* is similar to another paradoxical intention: symptom prescription. In this variation of the technique, the professional counselor asks the client to return to her former behavior after the problem is solved (Corsini, 1982). The relapse technique can help clients realize the inefficiency or silliness of their prior behavior. It also prevents unintentional relapse because the clients are often unable to re-create their old behavior without laughing or feeling silly.

EXAMPLE OF THE PARADOXICAL INTENTION TECHNIQUE

An exceptional example of paradoxical intention can be viewed in the video *A Family with a Little Fire* (Montalvo & Lincoln, 1973), featuring Braulio Montalvo, an associate of Salvador Minuchin at the Philadelphia Child Guidance Clinic. In this video,

Montalvo encounters a single mother and her children. The eldest daughter (about 7 years old) has set furniture in the apartment on fire a couple of times. After hearing the mother and daughter explain the circumstances, Montalvo asks the daughter to show him how she lights the fires (he just happened to have everything she needed under the table in the counseling room!). After observing her mightily botch the fire setting, he critiques her performance, at one point excoriating her for being "the worst fire setter I have ever seen!" Then he says, "Watch how I do it" and he walks her through appropriate fire-starting and safety procedures as the mother looks on. This is followed by practice in which the mother and Montalvo critique and refine the daughter's emerging fire-setting skills. Montalvo then assigns homework by prescribing the symptom and then restraining its expression. Every evening for a half hour, the daughter and her mother are to practice fire setting in the apartment (prescribing the symptom); however, the daughter is not to touch the matches or practice outside that mother–daughter practice period (restraining the expression of the symptom). The daughter never lights the apartment on fire again. Of course, under the surface, it is quite likely that the underlying dynamic was a striving for maternal attention, and this intervention certainly provided some mother–daughter quality time. But the intervention eliminated the problematic behavior by having the client *engage in the problematic behavior*.

I provide two additional case examples. The first case illustrates several principles of paradoxical intention. First, the problematic symptoms are reframed as positive behavior. They are defined not only as positive but also as positive in a way that is contradictory to the client's value system and view of himself. Second, the will of the professional counselor is reversed as soon as it is discovered that this very will for the client to improve may be a predominant part of the problem, preventing a full recovery from symptoms and a completely healthy level of functioning. Third, the symptom that had recently shown vast improvement is prescribed. This symptom is prescribed in a way that bounds the client to make progress regardless of prescription outcome.

Michael is a 19-year-old male with a long history of social anxiety and a more recent history of panic disorder with agoraphobia. On graduation from high school, Michael accepted a scholarship to a university in a neighboring state where he experienced his first panic attack prior to an examination during his second semester. He found himself unable to complete the semester as the panic attacks worsened, and he returned home to live with his family, dropping out of college and losing his scholarship. Once home, he returned to the part-time job he held while in high school, but he soon found he was unable to maintain this position due to the panic attacks and the mounting fears of leaving the family house. Soon these fears generalized to any activity outside the home, with the exception of church-related functions and counseling sessions. In general, Michael had a fear of fear, with church, home, and counseling being the only three places he found safe.

At the outset of counseling, which began approximately seven weeks prior to the current session, Michael was "unable" to drive and insisted that his mother drive him to church and counseling. He experienced panic attacks several times daily, most notably in his mother's presence. When this was pointed out to Michael, he stated it was because "she makes me so anxious and upsets me with her constant nagging." Though it soon became clear to the professional counselor that Michael's behavior was beneficial to him in a number of ways, he sincerely had no awareness of this and found it impossible to take any responsibility for his symptoms. Various mindfulness, social learning, and cognitive-behavioral interventions were employed (e.g., progressive muscle relaxation technique, deep breathing, thought stopping, cognitive restructuring, positive reinforcement, role playing) during the course of the last seven weeks of counseling, resulting in vast improvement.

Up to this point, Michael had made great strides toward improving his quality of life and level of functioning. He had maintained a very positive and determined attitude and always complied with work outside counseling sessions. First, Michael began *allowing* his mother to drive him places other than church and counseling, as long as it was within a five-mile radius of the home. He had also begun to venture from the car and stand outside the supermarket while his mother picked up an item or two inside. In addition, he even began driving himself at times, though he required a passenger "just in case." He was now able to go as far as 10 miles away from home. Finally, he had begun to ride and train his horses again and felt a great sense of accomplishment from this. Overall, he had experienced a reduction in panic attacks from approximately two to four a day to only one to two a week.

Quite unexpectedly, the improvements stopped. Over the course of the last two sessions, no improvements were made. Michael seemed unable to progress any further, or he was reluctant to do so. He continued to find it impossible to accept any responsibility for his remaining symptoms. He did admit to enjoying the sympathy and attention he received, and in general he was still able to control the lives of family members by his special needs. It was then that the professional counselor realized that this very control Michael wished to maintain and exert over his family was also being generalized to the therapeutic relationship. Suddenly, the resistance to improve became clear. The pressure to completely abandon the symptomatic behavior became the very reason it continued.

Following is an attempt by the professional counselor to alter the way the client perceives the problem. This is termed paradoxical reframe. The counselor is redefining the problematic behavior as positive. This is especially useful if the professional counselor is planning to prescribe the symptomatic behavior.

Michael (M):   I just can't seem to be the way they want me to be. I just can't seem to be completely healthy.

Counselor (C):   Then don't be.

M: I don't understand.

C: I can see how you are reluctant to give up this last bit.

M: What do you mean?

C: Well, I can understand how you can think you have no other means for getting your needs met, or having any power in your family. It probably just seems easier to remain needy and sick than to be strong and assertive. It's actually quite smart of you. And really, you aren't doing all that poorly anymore. In fact, the initial reasons that brought you here aren't all that troublesome anymore. Sure, they're still there, but they're not really that bothersome, and if they continue to get your needs met, well then, why not? In fact, you may even want to step it up a bit.

Paradoxes are actually quite logical when considering the family system in which they are to function. With that in mind, the professional counselor offers the following.

M: I'm confused.

C: Well, you mentioned earlier that your mom is so pleased with your progress that she's beginning to require more of you again. Even though you are not 100% better, you are certainly improved. Apparently, that improvement is enough to convince her that you are a healthy adult again. It also seems to me that, since you and I have worked very hard together and have used every method proven to work with these situations, yet you still have a few lingering symptoms . . . well . . . it seems to me that they may very well be a part of who you are. We may as well embrace them. And while we're at it, perhaps even increase them to get your mom off your back.

M: How will I do that?

C: Just do exactly the opposite of everything we've been doing. When you initially came in, you were having anywhere from two to four panic episodes a day. Now, you are down to one or two a week. Is that right?

M: Yes.

C: Well, perhaps we moved too quickly. Yes, now that I think of it . . . yes, I think it might be best to have at least one panic attack a day.

M: But how?

C: Oh, easy enough. You are still having difficulty driving yourself farther than 10 miles beyond your house . . . and with crossing bridges . . . you are still taking alternate routes to avoid bridges, aren't you?

M: Yes.

C: Well, just push the envelope a bit, and when you hit that 10-mile mark, keep driving a little farther than 10 miles and pull over to the side of the road, turn the ignition off, and then tell yourself "I can't do this. I can't breathe. If I go farther, I will surely die!" Repeat that until you have an episode, complete with hyperventilation and heart palpitations.

The pressure that is likely leading Michael to be resistant is now gone. He is no longer being pressured to be completely healthy.

M: But this seems so different from what we've been doing.

C: This is a new situation we have here. A new situation calls for a new plan. Before, we wanted to make you as healthy as possible. Now we realize that you should embrace your fearfulness because not only is this a part of who you are but it also gets your mom to ease up.

Either way, Michael will see an improvement. If he is able to have a panic attack as prescribed, he will see that he is able to cause them. And if he is able to cause them, then he is able to prevent them. If the symptom prescription is not successful, and Michael resists the professional counselor's attempts in order to maintain control of counseling, he will have driven beyond the 10-mile mark without a panic episode, thus still making progress. Michael now has also been given a paradoxical reframe that goes against his view of himself. The professional counselor now has painted the picture that his symptoms are manipulative or are useful for getting what he wants. This is generally disagreeable to Michael's value set and presents him with a choice. He will either refuse to continue his symptomatic behavior to manipulate his family, or he will continue his behavior but refuse the inherent benefits of control and sympathy. If he refuses the benefits of his behavior, he will eventually give up the behavior as well because his behavior is, in fact, motivated by this benefit.

The second case example is one of my all-time favorite (and entertaining) interventions with squabbling and oppositional siblings. In the following scenario, Isabella and Jorge are the parents of Alejandro and Santiago, 14- and 12-year-old siblings who are "always at each other's throats." This session occurred near the end of a 10-week couples and family treatment sequence.

Jorge (J):   It is just so frustrating that we have made so much progress on these other issues, and then we go home and they are always at each other.

Isabella (I):   It takes us out of our happy zone and, oh, how the steam comes out of my ears!

Counselor (C):   So the progress we have made in communicating as a couple and a family has not taken root in the relationship between Alejandro and Santiago? Is that how you see it?

Alejandro (A):   Typical little brother—bratty little dork!

Santiago (S):   Typical big brother—smelly dweeb!

C: I see! And this usually takes the form of . . .?

I: Arguing, shouting, name calling, physical fighting . . . you name it.

A: Not so much fighting. He's easy to beat up on!

S: Am not. (Santiago launches himself at Alejandro and is caught midair by Jorge and returned to his chair.)

J: Stay in your chair, son. No fighting in Dr. Erford's office.

A: Saved again, you wimpy little fart face!

S: @$$ĥ0£€!

I: Santiago!

C: Okay. I think I get some of the picture. Is this pretty typical?

I: Usually way worse. Seems like we are breaking up fights more and more. We just want it to stop. We are *exhausted*!

C: As we have discussed on a number of occasions, the kids are moving into the teenage years and demanding more autonomy and independence—a challenging stage in the changing family life cycle—and it is important for teenagers to express themselves and their emotions and frustrations. But we also want them to vent the frustrations in socially appropriate ways that comply with the household rules and that are not exhausting.

I: Amen!

C: Guys, each of you, please grab a book from my shelf. Any book will do. And now come to the center of the room. (The counselor stands and moves to the center of the room with Santiago and Alejandro.) Now stand back to back . . . take three steps . . . drop the book on the floor . . . and stand on it. Now during the remainder of this activity both feet need to touch the book; you cannot leave the book. Understand? (Both boys nod.)

I (the counselor) move a chair so that I can sit by the parents, and all of us have a good view of the boys. It is important to constrain the boys' movements in this activity so that they do not physically fight with each other, and I have found standing on a magazine or piece of paper to be a valuable restraint mechanism.

C: Okay, guys, now what I want you to do is argue with each other. Show us what you've got.

A: Huh?

C: Just argue with each other like you do at home.

I: But keep it clean, please. We don't want Father José to have to install a revolving door on the church confessional! Is that okay?

C: Sure. Mom wants no cussing.

S: Are *jerk* and *moron* and other stuff like that okay?

C: (Turns to mom and dad, who nod agreement)

A: What a stupid question, idiot! You have a brain as bright as dog crap—and twice as stinking!

S: Then lick my brains, turd-breath . . .

I will spare the reader the remainder of the interchange, which was quite colorful, perhaps even humorous if you like preadolescent put-downs related to human and animal body parts and elimination functions. While the boys were winding up,

I discussed with the parents whether this was typical arguing (it was) and whether they were ready to attack this problem with an effective and humorous, albeit time-consuming, approach. They indicated that they would try anything to get them to stop arguing. Two to three minutes have passed and the children have fallen quiet after a final foray that ended with something about an "anal-brained @$$ wipe."

C: Keep going, guys.

A: How much longer do we have?

C: (Looks at the wall clock) Um . . . 25 more minutes.

S: What?

A: Are you crazy—25 more minutes?

C: Yep. It is important for you to establish independence from each other and your parents, and to express your emotions and frustrations. So this is your chance. (Turning to the parents) Would you like some popcorn or a drink for the rest of the show?

J: Sure, I'll take a soda.

I: None for me, thanks.

We continue to sit and chat about the boys and their arguing and fighting habits. Into the activity 10 to 15 minutes, the boys have stopped arguing altogether and are listening to us talk, totally bored with the activity.

A: Can we *pleeeeease* stop? We're done arguing.

S: This is *soooo* boring.

C: Hard to believe that fighting with your brother could be boring, but I'll take your word on it. I suppose we can end early if you promise to do your homework for next week.

S: Homework? You are giving us homework?

A: Shut up, San. (Gives Santiago one of those "Shut up and just do it" glances) Sure. What's for homework?

I ask the boys to take their seats, and I assign the homework—a paradoxical intention intervention that both prescribes the symptom (instructs them to fight) and restrains the expression of the symptom (but only under the following conditions). I also retrieve two small notepads from my desk.

C: Every night from 7:30 p.m. to 8:00 p.m., I want you to repeat this exercise. (The boys groan audibly, eliciting a smile from each parent.) Grab a magazine, take three to four steps apart, drop the magazine, plant yourself on it, and have at it for exactly 30 minutes. Argue about anything you want—that is your time. But for the *other* 23 and a half hours, no arguing or fighting or name calling. Here is a notepad, one for each of you, to write down everything you are mad about during the rest of the day. If you want to argue or insult your brother, write it down and save it for the activity. But no physical fighting. If you think of a particularly hurtful comment, write it down and save it for later. Understand? (Both boys groan again and roll their eyes.)

S: But what if we get bored and finish early? Can we just stop early if we promise not to argue?

C: (To the parents) It is very important that they do this activity for at least 30 minutes each evening until our appointment next week.

I: We will. I can see the reasoning in this, and I hope it works!

This family significantly reduced the amount of sibling arguing in the first week of implementing paradoxical intention, and the rates stayed reduced through termination and follow-up. During the next session, we worked on implementing more socially appropriate forms of conflict resolution—methods that did not involve bruises and swearing. Without realizing it, the boys learned that they could control the expression of the symptom, and once the symptom abated, they were able to substitute a more appropriate communication style. Often, prescribing the symptom makes no sense initially. Why should the client be instructed to perform the behavior the client came to counseling to stop? But doing so and, at the same time, constraining the expression of the symptom to specific circumstances of time and place give the client control over the expression of the symptom—control that the client never thought she had!

USEFULNESS AND EVALUATION OF THE PARADOXICAL INTENTION TECHNIQUE

Paradoxical intention can be used with a variety of presenting problems, but it should be used with caution and under supervision until the professional counselor becomes proficient in its usage. It may be especially useful with clients who are involved in repetitive behavior patterns that seem involuntary or automatic (Young, 2017). Paradoxical intention may also be useful with clients whose problematic behavior is a means of getting attention from others (Doyle, 1998). Paradoxical intention has been used to treat anxiety disorders, agoraphobia, insomnia, juvenile delinquency, stress, depression, procrastination, disruptive behavior, temper tantrums, obsessions, compulsions, phobic reactions, behavioral tics, urinary retention, and stammering (Corey, 2016; DeBord, 1989; Kraft, Claiborn, & Dowd, 1985; Lamb, 1980).

Paradoxical intention has been particularly well studied as an application in the treatment of insomnia and has been repeatedly verified as an effective treatment approach. Wu, Appleman, Salazar, and Ong (2015) conducted a meta-analysis of CBT techniques, which included paradoxical intention and showed moderate to large effects in the treatment of insomnia. Indeed, the American Academy of Sleep Medicine (AASM, 2014) included paradoxical intention among its list of effective and recommended treatments for chronic primary insomnia. A randomized controlled trial (RCT; Ataoglu, Ozcetin, Icmeli, & Ozbulut, 2003) used paradoxical intention on patients with psychogenic nonepileptic seizures in which patients with conversion disorder were asked daily to reexperience their anxiety-provoking situations/experiences; the researchers found that experimental group participants outperformed control group participants at both termination and follow-up.

Paradoxical intention has been credited with inducing rapid reduction and frequent elimination of symptoms (Lamb, 1980). Most clients respond within 4 to 12 sessions. According to a literature review conducted by DeBord (1989), paradoxical intention is an effective treatment strategy for agoraphobia, insomnia, and problem blushing. Indeed,

92% of studies on paradoxical intention reviewed by DeBord resulted in positive outcomes. DeBord also found that symptom prescription resulted in at least some degree of improvement in 14 out of the 15 studies reviewed. Finally, DeBord discovered that in all four studies examined, paradoxical reframing was more effective in treating negative emotions than were other forms of treatment. Likewise, Swoboda et al. (1990) looked at the effectiveness of restraining, reframing, and a pseudo-therapy control in treating depression and determined that paradoxical reframing was the most effective treatment, followed by restraining.

A review conducted by Fabry (2010) found positive results in 18 out of 19 studies involving paradoxical intention, all with no adverse effects reported by study participants. Ameli and Dattilio (2013) proposed that paradoxical intention could enhance the efficacy of counseling interventions, and Dattilio (2013) reported effective use of paradoxical intention in family approaches to counseling. Paradoxical intention should not be used when exaggerating the symptom may cause a real danger to the client, such as suicidal symptoms.

APPLICATION OF THE PARADOXICAL INTENTION TECHNIQUE

Now apply the paradoxical intention technique to a current client or student you are working with or revisit the brief case studies presented at the beginning of this book. How can you use the paradoxical intention technique to address concerns and create movement in the counseling session?

Techniques Based on Gestalt and Psychodrama Principles

The word *gestalt* means "a structured, meaningful unity that stands out against a background in the organism/environment field" (Wolfert & Cook, 1999, pp. 3–4). Gestalt therapists focus on the organism being whole and believe that people find and make meaning of their experiences by forming gestalts. Gestalt and psychodrama approaches provide an interesting combination of existential, phenomenological, and behavioral techniques that rely heavily on present-moment experiences, existential meaning, interpersonal relationships, and holistic integration.

Some other approaches to counseling may appear reductionistic, but Gestalt therapy helps clients construct meaning and purpose through heightening their awareness and perceptions of what is happening in the present moment. Change is viewed as a perpetual state, and counselors using Gestalt and psychodrama approaches frequently attempt to discern environmental, interpersonal, and intrapersonal challenges and barriers to change, thus helping the client to adapt and accommodate to internal and external environments. Counselors help clients complete *unfinished business* that prevents healthy contact and adaptation to the environment and satisfy needs through development of clear and flexible relational boundaries. Gestalt and psychodrama techniques tend to create intense emotions and can be viewed as contrived or silly by some clients expecting a more traditional talk therapy approach.

Three classic Gestalt and psychodrama techniques are presented in the following chapters: empty chair, body movement and exaggeration, and role reversal. Role reversal and the empty chair techniques originated in psychodrama, and Gestalt therapists frequently use these procedures, and exaggeration, to create therapeutic movement. The empty chair is used to elicit powerful emotion-laden dialogue with important, albeit absent, individuals in the client's life, or two sides or dimensions of a single client, such as when a client is conflicted about how to deal with an issue and could benefit from acting out and discussing the internal dialogue in an externalized manner with a supportive counselor. Body movement and exaggeration are used to help clients understand meanings underlying their nonverbal communications, often bringing hidden meanings and communications to the conscious level. For example, a client who shakes a finger to emphasize a point, or says something that the counselor thinks is more meaningful than the client perceives, is asked to repeat the action or the phrase, sometimes a half dozen times, while the counselor and client discuss possible implications and hidden meanings in those actions or verbalizations. Role reversal is a technique that has the client take on the opposite perspective, argument, or role in order to explore meanings from various perspectives. For example, a teenage client who believes her autonomy is being quashed by a controlling father is encouraged to take on the father role and process her feelings and complaints from that perspective. All of these techniques aim to expand the client's awareness of circumstances and create and construct new or revised meanings in order to better adapt and accommodate to the environment.

MULTICULTURAL IMPLICATIONS OF THE TECHNIQUES BASED ON GESTALT AND PSYCHODRAMA PRINCIPLES

An advantage of the Gestalt and psychodrama approaches is the importance of the therapeutic relationship and underlying philosophy that each client should be approached openly and without preconception in order to help understand present-moment perceptions. It stands to reason that Gestalt therapy could be particularly effective in helping bicultural clients reconcile and integrate conflicting or confusing culturally based values and beliefs presented by the cultural contexts within which one exists. For example, many individuals whose culture of origin values collectivistic practices struggle in a competitive, individualistic American business world (Hays & Erford, 2018). Gestalt and psychodrama approaches are meant to address such conflicts.

Gestalt techniques often create intense emotional reactions in clients, and some clients from some cultures may be unaccustomed to expressing strong emotions to others or to non–family members (e.g., Arab Americans, Asian Americans). In addition, some clients may be more emotive and appreciate the insights and existential orientation of a Gestalt approach. For example, some clients may appreciate the encouragement to express suppressed or even denied emotions and discussions of healthy boundaries in interpersonal relationships. At any

rate, professional counselors must exercise caution and good judgment when using techniques based on the Gestalt approach because interventions must always be timed appropriately and implemented with sensitivity to individuals with diverse cultural characteristics, especially those who are emotionally reserved, because these clients may resist such approaches and terminate counseling prematurely (Hays & Erford, 2018).

Some clients are more comfortable expressing themselves nonverbally rather than verbally or may say one thing but communicate conflicting information through nonverbal means. A Gestalt counselor's focus on facial expressions and gestures can help these clients understand internal conflicts and construct a more integrated environmental connection. It is almost common sense, but it is essential to remember to focus on the client and the client's needs rather than on the use of a Gestalt technique in a mechanistic manner.

Gestalt and psychodrama techniques empower both men and women by emphasizing self-awareness, the legitimacy of feelings, and autonomy of action, as well as by integrating sometimes disconnected elements of thoughts, feelings, values, and behaviors. Gestalt and psychodrama techniques are adaptable to effective work with diverse populations, such as some African Americans (Plummer & Tukufu, 2001) and some Asian Americans (Cheung & Nguyen, 2013). But it is important to understand that some clients from diverse racial, ethnic, or socioeconomic cultures may resist a Gestalt approach because of emotional intensity or perceived artificiality (e.g., talking to your hand or an empty chair, repeatedly sticking out your tongue), which may make the counseling appear contrived and silly to them. In addition, some clients from non-Western cultures may perceive Gestalt counselors to be confrontational because of the nature of the directed physical interventions employed, may feel threatened, and may terminate prematurely (Hays & Erford, 2018).

CHAPTER 11

Empty Chair

ORIGINS OF THE EMPTY CHAIR TECHNIQUE

The empty chair technique originated from psychodrama and was readily imported into Fritz Perls's Gestalt therapy. Gestalt therapy aims to prevent the dichotomy that leads to a disconnect between the individual and his environment. Perls first used the empty chair to help individuals role-play what they would like to say to, or how they would like to act toward, another person. It allows for cathartic experiences and expressions to help clients deepen interpersonal and intrapersonal emotional connections. By definition, Gestalt includes both the creation and deconstruction of the whole, and the empty chair technique reflects the integration of polarities—that is, by expressing both sides of the issue at once, a person can work out conflicts among values, thoughts, feelings, and actions (Young, 2017).

To promote an understanding of this theory, and in turn the empty chair technique, the basic concepts of Gestalt therapy follow (Coker, 2010):

1. A person exists within his or her environmental context; no individual person is completely self-supporting.
2. People either have contact with their environment or withdraw from it.
3. If a person has contact with the environment, that person connects with people and things that are reinforcing or desired.
4. If a person withdraws from the environment, that person tries to eliminate people and things that are believed to cause harm.
5. It is not always healthy to have contact and is not always unhealthy to withdraw.

6. The main purposes of the personality are the contacts and withdrawals one has with the environment.
7. A person is both an individual and a function of the environmental context.
8. In Gestalt counseling, the focal point is how (not why) the person perceives troubles in the here and now.
9. The goal is for the professional counselor to provide the individual with what is needed to solve present and future issues.
10. Gestalt therapy places great importance on the experiential aspect of the here and now.
11. By becoming aware of the here and now, as well as contact and withdrawal attempts and interpretations, one can gain insight into living effectively in her or his environment.

HOW TO IMPLEMENT THE EMPTY CHAIR TECHNIQUE

After establishing the therapeutic relationship and building trust with the client, the professional counselor can use the empty chair technique during a session with the client. Implementing this method involves six steps (Young, 2017). To warm up, the professional counselor should request that the client think about polar opposites in his life and a specific example in which the client has felt both ways, or ambivalent, about the issue. In the first step, the professional counselor explains why this technique will be used in an effort to quell any resistance the client may have. The professional counselor should set up two chairs directly facing each other; the chairs represent either side of the polarity. For the client, becoming aware of his feelings surrounding this polarity is important before moving on to the next step. In the steps that follow, the client will sit in one chair representing one side of the polarity and face an empty chair representing the other side. As the client expresses his feelings surrounding either side of the polarity, the client switches to the corresponding chair.

In the second step, the professional counselor works with the client to deepen the experience (Young, 2017). The professional counselor begins by having the client choose the side of the polarity for which the client has the strongest feelings. The client is then given time to become familiar with and even more aware of how he is feeling. The professional counselor needs to help the client stay in the here and now by asking questions that bring the client back to the present. For example, if a client says, "I really could have punched him," the counselor can question, "Are you aware of that anger now?"

In the third step, the goal for the client is to express the most prominent side of the polarity. During the expression, the professional counselor cannot be judgmental. By staying in the here and now, the client should act out his experience rather than describe it. The professional counselor can encourage this by instructing the client to use exaggerated gestures or vocal expressions. To deepen the experience, the counselor can request that the client repeat phrases or words several times. In this step, the professional counselor can also take time to summarize what she sees as the client's situation. The professional counselor should ask *what* and *how* questions rather than *why* questions to continue deepening the experience. Once the client has come to a point which the professional counselor sees as an appropriate place to stop, the counselor asks the client to switch chairs. A stopping point can be determined only by the professional counselor and occurs when the client has gotten stuck or seems to have fully expressed himself.

The fourth step in using the empty chair technique is counterexpression. As the client sits in the opposite chair, he replies to the first expression. Once more, the professional counselor helps deepen the experience for the client by encouraging him

to express the reverse argument and by evoking an emotional response.

In the fifth step, the professional counselor has the client switch roles until it is determined (by the professional counselor or the client) that each side of the issue has been completely articulated. This allows the client to become aware of both sides of the polarity. Sometimes during this step, a resolution between each side of the issue occurs, but a solution is not always an outcome of this technique.

The sixth and final step of the empty chair technique focuses on getting the client to agree to an action plan. The professional counselor may assign homework as a way to get the client to investigate both sides of the dichotomy.

VARIATIONS OF THE EMPTY CHAIR TECHNIQUE

Vernon and Clemente (2004) illustrated a less involved variation of this technique for use with children. In this method, the professional counselor asks the child to play his side of the conflict. If the conflict is intrapersonal, the professional counselor asks the child to choose one side to begin. After the child expresses himself, the professional counselor should request that the child move to the empty chair and express the other side of the issue. Have the child switch chairs as necessary until both sides are adequately expressed. If the child has difficulty talking to a chair, use a recorder instead of a chair.

Another variation of the empty chair is the fantasy dialogue. For example, if a client has many somatic complaints, the professional counselor can ask the client to have a conversation with the body part in an effort to find out if the ailment has any benefits for the client. By becoming aware of the benefits, the client may be able to resolve the issue (Young, 2017). Forced catastrophes is an additional variation of the empty chair technique, but this variation should be used cautiously, especially if working with anxious individuals. It can be used with clients who are always expecting the worst. The professional counselor works with the client and insists that the client face the worst scenario possible, even if it is unlikely to occur. The professional counselor helps the client express the emotions that go along with the nightmare situation.

EXAMPLE OF THE EMPTY CHAIR TECHNIQUE

Sasha is a 19-year-old college student who has been in individual counseling for approximately seven weeks. She first sought services due to relationship issues with her current on-again/off-again boyfriend. It quickly became evident that these issues were a pattern in nearly all relationships with Sasha, who oscillated between damaging, anger-driven strength and fear-based helpless dependency. Establishing a trusting relationship with Sasha proved especially difficult, although once established the relationship seemed particularly strong. Soon, issues of past sexual and physical abuse were brought to the fore-front, and Sasha felt confused by the dichotomy that she seemed to experience, represent, and express session after session.

Sasha (S):   (Slightly lethargic) Sometimes, I just . . . I just get so tired, you know? It wears me out to be me sometimes. And that sounds so ridiculous. I mean, if being me is so tiresome, on me and everybody else, why not just be different? I mean really . . . why not? Why not just be different?

Counselor (C):   If being the way you are now is so tiring . . .

S: Yeah. If this is so bad, change it! And now I feel irritable. I feel aggravated and I don't even know why.

C: Sasha, I see you experiencing just now, what it is that has been sort of happening all along . . . your emotions . . . the way you are feeling . . . it shifts suddenly, which leaves you feeling drained and bewildered.

S: And angry.

C: And angry.

S: You know, part of me wants so badly to be like, I don't know, like Scarlett O'Hara's sister-in-law in *Gone with the Wind* . . . what's her name?

C: Melanie, wasn't it? Ms. Melanie.

S: Yes! Melanie. Sometimes I want to be like Melanie.

It can often be very helpful to identify with a character in an effort to recognize intrapersonal characteristics, discuss complex feelings more easily, or use as a figure to strive toward.

C: And other times?

S: Oh, well, other times, like Scarlett, of course.

C: And what do these two characters represent to you?

S: Well, Scarlett is obvious. She is strong. She doesn't let anything stop her from getting what she wants. She can be hurtful to others. But it keeps others from hurting her, you know? And I really respect her. And, well, Melanie . . . well, I could never be Melanie. She was so self-sacrificing, soft-spoken, and kind, but sometimes she seemed so sad. Scarlett walked all over her because she was weak compared to Scarlett. Very weak.

C: And it seems like I've heard you express a wish to be like Melanie, but then you also say that you could never be like her.

The professional counselor offers a very tentative confrontation to help Sasha see a very concrete example of the dichotomy she presents.

S: See? It makes no sense. I don't think I know what I want. Or who I am. Or why I'm one way one minute and another way the next.

C: Sasha, I think that you, like most of us, have several selves that make up who you are. The difference with you is that you haven't always been very aware of these selves or their usefulness or purpose. Because of this, they often oppose one another rather than work together. Does that make sense to you?

S: Yeah. I think so.

C: I'd like to try something with you now to help you express both of these aspects of yourself.

S: Okay.

C: And it may feel silly at first, but because I believe in your ability to get past that and because I believe in the effectiveness of this technique, I think it will prove very beneficial.

S: I trust that.

C: Okay. What I want you to do is called an empty chair technique, and it will actually involve the use of two chairs. (Pulls another chair up to face Sasha's directly)

S: (Laughs nervously)

C: It's okay to feel nervous or unsure at first. But I really think you can do this. Okay, so previous relationships have shown, and I've observed, and you've begun to realize, that you seem to act and feel in completely opposing ways sometimes. In fact, just now, you related your opposing sides to the characters of Melanie and Scarlett, who are very opposite one another. (Pauses) If you could, Sasha, what emotional labels might you give these opposing selves?

S: Well, one is the obvious angry part of me. The other . . . um . . . hmm . . . well . . . the other part of me would be the scared part.

C: Okay. And which of these two do you feel most now?

S: Actually, I'm feeling more scared and vulnerable today.

C: Okay. So imagine for a moment if I were able to pull two separate persons from you . . . one angry and the other scared. And think about how they might look different . . . one of them might have her shoulders raised and squared off, with a glare in her eyes and a tightly clenched jaw. The other, well, she might have her shoulders slightly sunken, her hands clasped together, maybe looking downward to avoid others' gazes. Imagine that they are both able to sit in these chairs now and speak to one another. But you are the only one who can give them a voice. Only you know what they need to say to one another. So starting with the vulnerable you, what I'd like to have you do is express that part of yourself that feels vulnerable and afraid. And tell the "angry you" what

the "vulnerable you" feels. Don't be "strong Sasha" right now. Just concentrate on feeling what "afraid Sasha" feels.

The professional counselor is empowering Sasha.

S: Right now?

C: Yes, whenever you are ready. You can do this, and I will help you if you need me.

S: (Takes a long deep breath and clasps her hands in her lap; looks down at her hands and speaks softly, almost in a whisper) I feel afraid—all of the time. All of the time, I feel afraid. And it is a miserable feeling. (Pauses for several moments, but is still looking down at her hands, which are still clasped) I feel so helpless (Pauses) and weak (Pauses) and pathetic. (Takes another deep breath) I let others trample all over me. I let others get away with anything because I want them to love me. Or just like me. Just be nice to me. And I know it's so pathetic. (Whispers) It's so pathetic. (A little louder) But I also feel kind . . . and trusting. And that feels nice. It feels good to be good. I don't like not being good. You aren't supposed to hurt others just because they hurt you, and you should be ashamed of yourself if you do. (Looking up from her hands and looking directly at the empty chair) You hurting others is no better than what he was. You remind me so much of him sometimes. No, I shouldn't say that. God, sometimes I hate him.

C: What about right now?

S: Right now . . . right now, I wish he liked me enough to . . . to not hurt me. I still wish he liked me. He so obviously didn't like me. And I don't know why. (Silence)

C: Okay, Sasha, I'd like for you to move to angry Sasha's chair and give her a voice.

S: (Moving to the other chair) Yeah, now I'm feeling more comfortable! You *are* pathetic! (In a whining voice) "I want them to love me. Or just like me. Just be nice to me." Good Lord! Can you get any more disgusting? You make me sick. You do. You make me sick. If you'd been stronger to begin with, *we* wouldn't be here! You need me. You can just admit that. If it wasn't for me, you wouldn't have made it. And you can be "ashamed" of me all you want. But don't you dare say I'm just like him. I am what I have to be to get you through your pathetic life. You, my dear, are a liability. (Stops to take a breath)

C: Repeat that please. "You are a liability."

S: You are a liability.

C: Again.

S: You are a liability.

C: Again.

S: You are a liability!

C: And what you're feeling right now.

S: I'm exhausted, and yet I cannot *afford* to be any different than what I am or she will cost us our life. We won't make it if I'm not strong. And I am so tired of being strong.

C: Because being strong is the same as being angry for you.

S: Anger is what makes me strong. But it is also so tiring.

C: Tell her.

S: If you would be a little stronger, I wouldn't have to be so angry. If you could be a little less pathetic, I could be a little less cruel. I don't want to be cruel or angry. It's too much work, and I'm tired. I want to be more like you. But not exactly like you. You are just still far too weak. (Sasha seems to have exhausted this side of herself and seems to be at a stopping point.)

C: I'd like you to switch chairs once more and express anything that vulnerable Sasha has left to say.

S: (Switches chairs, clasps her hands in her lap once more but doesn't stare down at them) I am sorry that you have to be a part of me. It is a constant reminder of what we've been through. I do not like you or what you do or how you feel or how you treat others. But for now, you are a necessary part of me. (Sasha pauses for several moments and then looks over to the professional counselor, indicating she is done.)

C: Excellent! (Turns unoccupied chair back forward, and Sasha follows the same)

S: It helps . . . thinking of them like that . . . it helps me to see that I do have opposing selves but that they are both part of me. I feel more accepting of that.

C: And both necessary parts of you . . . maybe just to a lesser degree than you think.

S: So maybe if they could become a little less intense or learn to blend or compromise a little.

C: Exactly. There are positives to each of them, you know. They both represent incredible characteristics that you have and show how you have coped in the past. I tell you what. I'd like for you to continue to think on this over the next week, and I'd like for you to make a list of the positives associated with each of these parts of you, as well as circumstances where each of these aspects of yourself might prove very helpful. In other words, let's get an idea of their strengths and their usefulness, at least when used appropriately and in moderation.

USEFULNESS AND EVALUATION OF THE EMPTY CHAIR TECHNIQUE

The empty chair technique gets individuals to externalize the dichotomies of their feelings (Corey, 2016). The technique can be used with both interpersonal and intrapersonal issues. Professional counselors can use this technique to help individuals become aware of feelings that are below the surface but can still have an effect on the client's well-being (Hackney & Cormier, 2017). Kramer and Pascual-Leone (2013) discussed the outcome studies using the empty chair technique and found it to be effective for resolving a range of intrapsychic conflicts.

Crose (1990) found the empty chair technique to be useful in working with clients who have unfinished business. By bringing the past into the here and now, professional counselors can help clients resolve issues they may have with people who are deceased or who are no longer part of their lives. The professional counselor presents a safe and comfortable place for the client to express feelings of love or anger for the chosen person or people.

Coker (2010) supported the use of the empty chair technique by professional school counselors. If the professional school counselor wishes to use this technique with a student having a conflict with another person, the counselor first asks the student to give a vivid description of the person. The student sits in one of the chairs and needs to imagine that person in the empty chair. The professional counselor then asks the student to describe the conflict and to say whatever the student would like to the person with whom the student is having the conflict. The professional counselor can use the six steps of the empty chair process to continue with the session. The professional school counselor can also use the empty chair technique when a student is having a conflict within himself. Coker suggested that this technique is very useful with adolescents and in particular with those who feel one thing in their head and another in their heart.

Clance, Thompson, Simerly, and Weiss (1993) conducted a research study investigating whether Gestalt techniques were effective in changing the participants' body images. Of the 30 participants, 15 each were in the control group and the experimental group exposed to the Gestalt techniques. Clance et al. concluded, "Gestalt therapy and awareness training do effect measurable and significant change in group participants' attitudes toward body and self" (p. 108). They also found that the Gestalt techniques were more effective with male than female participants. The empty chair technique can also be adapted for work with diverse populations, such as African Americans (Plummer & Tukufu, 2001) and Asian Americans (Cheung & Nguyen, 2013).

Greenberg and Higgins (1980) compared the effects of two treatments, focusing and empty chair, when clients experienced a dichotomy. They measured the clients' depth of experience and reported change of awareness. The study had 42 participants, with equal numbers in the empty chair, focusing, and control groups. Results of the study showed that the participants in the empty chair group made significant gains in awareness and depth of experience when compared with the focusing and control groups.

Several studies explored the use of the empty chair technique in facilitating emotional arousal, unfinished business, and forgiveness. Diamond, Rochman, and Amir (2010) exposed 29 women with unresolved anger to a single-session intervention comprised of empathy, relational frame, and empty chair, significantly increasing average client emotional arousal (sadness). They found that the empty chair technique also increased clients' fear/anxiety levels, probably due to the potential for interpersonal rejection or attack by the person who was the focus of their anger. In a controlled trial, Greenberg, Warwar, and Malcolm (2008) found that the empty chair technique promoted significantly higher levels of forgiveness, letting go, and global indicators than a psychoeducational intervention aimed at addressing emotional injury. Hayward, Overton, Dorey, and Denney (2009) found significant changes in relational patterning (control and distressed voice) in four of five cases when clients were exposed to a relating therapy process that included assertiveness training and empty chair. Paivio and Greenberg (1995) conducted a study investigating the efficacy of the empty chair technique in resolving unfinished business. Thirty-four participants were divided into two groups: the psychoeducational group and the empty chair group. Each group received 12 weeks of therapy, and at post-treatment 81% of the empty chair group participants reported unfinished business resolution compared to 29% of the psychoeducational group participants. The researchers concluded that at the one-year follow-up, empty chair therapy "was significantly more effective in reducing symptom and interpersonal distress, reducing discomfort and increasing change on target complaints, and achieving unfinished business resolution" (p. 425).

Powell, Rosner, and Butollo (2015) studied 119 women whose husbands were killed or missing during the war in Bosnia-Herzegovina who were assigned to either a supportive control condition or a seven-session dialogical exposure group treatment using the empty chair technique, yielding a medium effect size ($d = .56$) at termination, and significant effect sizes at one-year follow-up ($d = .37$ for traumatic grief, and $d = .73$ for post-traumatic avoidance). Thus, a short-term Gestaltian exposure approach featuring the empty chair technique was effective in treatment of traumatically bereaved women, purportedly through supporting clients as they gained awareness and expressed inner dialogues related to trauma.

Young (2017) also provided a critique of the empty chair technique. He cautioned that clients may be resistant to engage in this strategy out of fear of appearing foolish. Also, he believed that some professional counselors are too quick to move their clients from chair to chair, before either polarity is fully expressed. He warned professional counselors not to use this technique with clients who have problems controlling their emotions because this technique can bring out a person's extremely strong feelings. Because of the possibility of clients' strong emotional response, professional counselors need to make sure to follow up with clients soon after using this technique. Young also suggested that professional counselors who are inexperienced with this technique be under the supervision of a more experienced and knowledgeable professional counselor. Young also cautioned against using this technique with individuals experiencing serious emotional distress, such as those with a psychotic disorder.

APPLICATION OF THE EMPTY CHAIR TECHNIQUE

Now apply the empty chair technique to a current client or student you are working with or revisit the brief case studies presented at the beginning of this book. How can you use the empty chair technique to address concerns and create movement in the counseling session?

CHAPTER 12

Body Movement and Exaggeration

ORIGINS OF THE BODY MOVEMENT AND EXAGGERATION TECHNIQUE

Body movement and exaggeration is a technique that emerged from Gestalt therapy. Perls believed that a client's verbal and nonverbal communication revealed cues that could be focused on and exaggerated to deepen a client's understanding of the thoughts and feelings that underlie experiences and emotional responses. In Gestalt therapy, the counselor uses a holistic approach and an assortment of techniques intended to increase the client's self-awareness. Professional counselors typically use body movement and exaggeration with clients who need to become aware of the verbal and nonverbal signals that they are sending to others (Corey, 2016).

HOW TO IMPLEMENT THE BODY MOVEMENT AND EXAGGERATION TECHNIQUE

When implementing body movement and exaggeration, the counselor first needs to observe the client's verbal and nonverbal cues. Paying close attention to the client's nonverbal behavior, the professional counselor should pick out what may seem like an unimportant gesture. This gesture could be "trembling (shaking hands, legs), slouched posture and bent shoulders, clenched fists, tight frowning, facial grimacing, crossed arms" (Corey, 2016, p. 212). Once the counselor identifies this gesture, he asks the client to exaggerate it with the hope that the

meaning of the gesture may become apparent. As the client is exaggerating the movement, the client is asked to give a voice to the movement.

VARIATIONS OF THE BODY MOVEMENT AND EXAGGERATION TECHNIQUE

Exaggeration can be used in counseling sessions during which the client says something important but does not realize that the statement is important. In this case, the counselor asks the client to repeat the statement, increasing the emotional intensity each time the statement is said, until the client is able to realize the full impact of the statement (Harman, 1974). This variation was demonstrated in the Chapter 11 example when Sasha was asked to repeat "You are a liability!"

EXAMPLE OF THE BODY MOVEMENT AND EXAGGERATION TECHNIQUE

Thomas is a 56-year-old man who has no prior history of receiving any type of counseling services. He experienced the passing of his 81-year-old mother just over a year ago but has been unable to deal with her death and feels stuck. He has requested help with sorting out his resulting emotions related to her and stemming from her death.

Thomas (T):   I don't understand. I just don't quite understand why I'm having such difficulty . . . feeling what I know I feel.

Counselor (C):   The sadness . . . loss . . . .

T: Yes. It's there. It won't go away. Yet it won't come out either.

C: It seems stuck?

T: Trapped. I feel stuck because it feels trapped.

C: Uh-huh.

T: I want to stop being so preoccupied by her. By her death. Her life. I want to move forward. It's like she's still got hold of me.

The counselor notices the subtle yet important use of the word still, *implying that this is not new and that in life, the client's mother also had hold of him.*

C: Still?

T: (Thomas looks up now, raising his head, and giving full eye contact.) Yes, *still*.

C: She still has hold of you.

T: She still has hold of me.

C: Say that again.

T: She *still* has hold of me.

C: And again, a little louder.

T: She STILL has hold of me.

C: Again.

T: She STILL has hold of me! She STILL has hold of ME! She won't let me GO!

T: (After a pause, a purposeful silence) I don't know where that came from. Or what that was . . . (Pauses as he thinks)

C: What did it feel like?

T: Panic. Anger.

C: Uh-huh. Yes, to me too.

T: But I'm not angry.

C: Maybe not all of you . . .

The counselor now notices a clenched fist Thomas almost seems to be hiding between his knees. It is very common to notice a discrepancy between verbal words and nonverbal behaviors when someone is denying a real emotion.

C: Your fist seems angry.

T: My fist? (He looks down, notices his clenched fist, and immediately unclenches it and moves it to the side.)

C: I'd like for you to clench it again. This time harder. And place it back between your knees. (Thomas clenches his fist, places it between his knees and begins shaking his legs now.) Your legs are shaking. Make them shake more. (Thomas begins moving his legs more rapidly.) Give your legs a voice. What would they say now if they could talk?

T: They're nervous.

C: Nervous?

T: Yeah, they don't like what the fist is doing.

C: What is the fist doing?

T: Getting angry.

C: And that makes the legs nervous?

T: Yes.

C: Clench your fist a little harder and keep it pinned down with your knees . . .

T: Very angry.

C: So part of you is very angry. And the legs want to hide it . . . the fist. But the fist wants to . . .

T: Hit something.

C: Which is why the legs want to pin it down . . . to keep it from hitting.

T: Anger is no good. It just makes a mess. It should be contained.

C: Trapped? (There is a pause in body movement as Thomas looks back up, realizing the connection between denying his anger and feeling stuck.)

In this dialogue, body movement and exaggeration were used to highlight an important keyword that held meaning and then to acknowledge a denied emotion. The technique could also be used to further express that emotion and pinpoint its root.

USEFULNESS AND EVALUATION OF THE BODY MOVEMENT AND EXAGGERATION TECHNIQUE

Flexibility is one of the reasons why Gestalt techniques are popular among counselors. Because there are no rigid guidelines for using these techniques, they can be altered and modified for many different issues. The techniques from Gestalt therapy can be modified to work with many different clients and presenting problems, but some clients will most likely not benefit from the Gestalt approach (Wolfert & Cook, 1999). For example, professional counselors should consider using techniques from other theoretical approaches when working with clients who are severely disturbed or who are not aware of their own experiences (Harman, 1974). Still, Strumpfel and Goldman (2002) reviewed the research on Gestalt techniques and found that techniques such as body movement and exaggeration can be used with a variety of emotional disturbances, such as depression, phobias, personality disorders, psychosomatic disturbances, and substance abuse issues.

APPLICATION OF THE BODY MOVEMENT AND EXAGGERATION TECHNIQUE

Now apply the body movement and exaggeration technique to a current client or student you are working with or revisit the brief case studies presented at the beginning of this book. How can you use the body movement and exaggeration technique to address concerns and create movement in the counseling session?

CHAPTER 13

Role Reversal

ORIGINS OF THE ROLE REVERSAL TECHNIQUE

Role reversal is a technique derived from psychodrama and Gestalt theory. Gestalt therapists view existence as interconnected and use a holistic counseling approach. Role reversal is typically used when a professional counselor believes that client behavior is the reversal of some underlying feeling (Harman, 1974), and thus the client is behaving in a disconnected manner. By reversing roles, the professional counselor helps the client understand the polar issues at play and to integrate these polar opposites into a holistic perspective.

HOW TO IMPLEMENT THE ROLE REVERSAL TECHNIQUE

Professional counselors can use role reversal with clients who are experiencing a conflict, or a split, within themselves. The counselor takes an active role when using this technique, identifying the different roles that the client is undergoing in the paradoxical situation (Hackney & Cormier, 2017). Then the client is asked to take on the role that is causing the anxiety and to connect with those parts that have been denied (Corey, 2016). The counselor assists the client in a paradoxical examination of his views, attitudes, or beliefs. By playing the other role and examining both sides of the conflict, clients may heighten their awareness of the situation, deepen their emotional connections, and work out the underlying issues.

VARIATIONS OF THE ROLE REVERSAL TECHNIQUE

In one variation of the role reversal technique, clients were asked to play another person who was involved in the situation. By taking on someone else's role, clients have the opportunity to view themselves and the situation from a different perspective and gain further awareness (Doyle, 1998).

EXAMPLE OF THE ROLE REVERSAL TECHNIQUE

The following is a variation of the role reversal technique where the counselor asks the client to play the part of another person, considering the position of another, rather than role-playing a different aspect of self. However, some might say that even though Krista is technically viewing her daughter's position, in some ways she is role-playing an internal struggle because she views her daughter as representative of her child within and has transferred her hatred for herself onto her daughter. Thus, an adolescent experiencing interpersonal conflict with a parent or teacher could reverse roles and play the other person, attempting to connect with the emotions and motives apparent in that role.

Krista is a 34-year-old female who has had years of therapy with various providers throughout her childhood, adolescence, and adulthood. Severely abused sexually, physically, and emotionally as a child, she tried for years to be the perfect daughter. As a young teen, however, she stopped trying to be perfect and instead began to rebel. She recalls being filled with hatred for herself and for others and began using alcohol and drugs, stealing and vandalizing, running away repeatedly, and engaging in sexually deviant behavior. She spent much of her adolescence in various mental health hospitals, and upon each release she would return to the same behaviors and chaotic lifestyle. She eventually had two children and later married, and she continues to have episodes every few years during which she runs away from her husband and children and returns to this former lifestyle. Currently, she is employed and has been free of drugs for two years. She shows no physical indications of her former life and presents as a very attractive, well-groomed, stylish, and well-spoken young lady. Her chief complaint on entering counseling six weeks ago primarily centered on relational concerns with her mother, husband, and children. She also complains of an explosive temper and bouts of depression. She states that she doesn't understand what is wrong with her and feels she is pushing her husband away and emotionally damaging her daughter. Up to this point, much time has been spent developing a trusting relationship, gaining insight and knowledge into her previous and current diagnoses, evaluating her medication, and discussing various therapeutic techniques aimed at improving emotional regulation and reactivity, from mindfulness to identification and rebuttal of illogical beliefs.

Krista (K): I feel so hopeless again. I mean, I knew I wouldn't be instantly cured . . . but I was amazed at how quickly I was beginning to improve. I mean, I went six entire days without any major chaos . . . Six days! . . . I don't know that that's ever happened! I wasn't letting stuff at work, or the kids, or Josh get to me or anything. I was so proud of myself.

Counselor (C): And hopeful?

K: Definitely hopeful. Hopeful that maybe I could start feeling normal for the first time in my life. I'm so tired of feeling this way.

C: This way . . .

K: Like a crazy, evil monster. I got so angry yesterday at Kaley. I just get so damn angry . . . (Krista balls up both fists and grits her teeth.) . . . I could just pinch her head off. I'm still mad. *So* mad. I don't know why she gets to me the way she does, but boy does she. She knows *exactly* how to push my buttons, and she does it on purpose. Just to spite me. Why would she *want* me to get that mad with her? Surely she doesn't *enjoy* that! God . . . but she knows exactly what she's doing . . . little *brat*.

C: (Tentatively) You feel like her behavior is on purpose.

K: I know it is. Hell, you would have to be *stupid* to continue to act the way she does, *knowing* I'm going to go off on you.

C: Can you put yourself in Kaley's shoes for just a minute? I just want you to put yourself in her shoes for a moment . . . and respond to the statement you just made. If you were Kaley, how would you respond to "Your behavior is on purpose, Kaley . . . that or you must be stupid to act the way you do." How do you respond . . . as Kaley?

K: (Without hesitation) Maybe I do. Maybe I am. Maybe I do it on purpose. And maybe I *am* stupid. Maybe I *hate* you. Maybe *you're* stupid. If you're going to act like a lunatic, I'm not going to stop you. I'm sick and tired of trying to tiptoe around your precious feelings. We all are. I've learned to not give a *shit* about your stupid little feelings. It does . . . *no* . . . good! I tried for years to be what you wanted. Nothing was ever enough. I am *tired* of wasting my energy on you. I get nothing back! You are this vacuum . . . this black hole . . . you suck the life right out of me! I gave up on you. I gave up! (Pause) On you! (Pause; affect changes from anger to sarcasm) And now? . . . Well, I might as well be entertained by the lunatic.

Typically role reversal produces identification and empathy for the position of the other person.

Krista is both angry and projecting her own feelings about herself at age 14 years and transferring her feelings about her own mother at that age onto her daughter now. But there was another side to Krista at that age, and based on prior information that she has given the counselor about her daughter and their interactions, this verbalization is not entirely representative of her daughter either. Krista is presented with this and asked to bring to therapy next week a diary entry written from the perspective of her daughter. Writing will often tap into material difficult to reach through verbal expression.

C: Were you able to complete the diary entry we talked about last week?

K: I was, but it was really difficult.

C: Difficult how?

K: Upsetting, I guess.

C: Uh-huh. Okay, upsetting then.

K: Upsetting and difficult because it made me realize how she must feel. Kaley is a really good kid . . . . Here, just read it. (Hands a folded paper to the counselor and the counselor reads it aloud)

C: "Dear Diary, tonight my mom and I argued . . . again. I don't understand why she gets so angry at me. She doesn't do that to my brother. It's like she hates me sometimes. I can see it in her eyes and hear it in her voice. I'm not even sure why. And she goes crazy. I'm scared of her sometimes. I don't know what she's going to do next. I never know what to expect with her. Sometimes things that were okay yesterday aren't okay today. It's like the rules change with her, and I just never know what is safe and what isn't. It makes me feel like giving up. And it really hurts. I swear I do my best to be a good daughter. I'm not perfect. But I do try. I know I can be sassy sometimes. But isn't that normal for my age? Aren't I a pretty good kid? My teachers like me. They tell me they're glad to have me in their class. But I don't think my mom is glad to have me as

her daughter. And I think I'm starting to get angry. I can feel myself sometimes talking back to her in my head. I can feel myself getting tired of trying. I can feel myself giving up on being a good daughter. It's not getting me anywhere. And it hurts too bad to keep trying only to feel like you're hated anyway." (The counselor looks up, and Krista is crying.) What's upsetting you most now?

K: That I'm killing her. I'm emotionally killing her. I'm making her hate me. And she *is* such a great kid.

C: So last week you felt her behavior was purposeful and bratty and you were so angry at her, but today . . .

K: I understand her. And I hurt for her. I don't want to *hurt* her. I hurt *for* her. I've been so afraid that she had already crossed that line . . . the one I crossed at that age. And I hate myself for the things I did. And I think when I looked at her, I saw me at 14 and I hated what I saw. But I don't think she has yet . . . crossed that line. She's not me. She's not at all like I was at that age. She is still so good . . . she still has so much good in her. There's still a chance for her.

The empathy that role reversal is so useful at creating has now been achieved, and Krista is beginning to see her daughter separate from herself and with compassion rather than hatred.

USEFULNESS AND EVALUATION OF THE ROLE REVERSAL TECHNIQUE

No empirical studies exploring effectiveness of the role reversal technique were located in the extant literature. When implementing this technique, professional counselors initially may experience resistance from clients because the client is being asked to take on what may be an uncomfortable role. For this technique to be effective under this circumstance, the counselor needs to provide extra encouragement in a safe environment to help the client participate with comfort (Hackney & Cormier, 2017).

APPLICATION OF THE ROLE REVERSAL TECHNIQUE

Now apply the role reversal technique to a current client or student you are working with or revisit the brief case studies presented at the beginning of this book. How can you use the role reversal technique to address concerns and create movement in the counseling session?

Techniques Based on Mindfulness Approaches

Mindfulness involves a way of seeing, feeling, knowing, and loving that is present focused and facilitates greater centeredness of focus and awareness (Kabat-Zinn, 2006). It involves focused attention on the here and now and with nonjudgmental attitudes using the building blocks of intention, attention, and attitude. Mindfulness requires people to be open to and accepting of their present experience in order to develop tolerance for difficult feelings expressed within oneself and by others. The approach is very helpful for clients, and professional counselors can also benefit from the link between mindfulness and empathy (Schure, Christopher, & Christopher, 2008).

Historically embedded within the cognitive-behavioral tradition (Segal, Williams, & Teasdale, 2002), mindfulness techniques can also be found in dialectical behavior therapy (DBT; Linehan, 1993) and acceptance and commitment therapy (ACT; Hayes, Strosahl, & Wilson, 2003). Several commonly used techniques are based on the mindfulness approach and are particularly effective in reducing stress. The first three of the four techniques covered in this section are each based on Wolpe's (1990) principle of reciprocal inhibition, which basically means that you can't do two opposite things at the same time. As applied to counseling, a client cannot feel stressed and relaxed at the same time; think positive, reaffirming messages to oneself at the same time one is thinking negative, nasty thoughts; visualize positive, empowering scenes at the

same time one is visualizing disempowering, negative images; breathe quickly and slowly at the same time; or have a muscle that is both relaxed and tense at the same time. Thus, by using counseling techniques that engage in the positive dimension of these continua, the client effectively blocks out the negative dimension and the resulting stressful ramifications. These techniques are often used in concert to maximize effectiveness. For example, clients can be taught the techniques of self-talk, visual or guided imagery, deep breathing, and the progressive muscle relaxation technique (PMRT) in sequence and can be encouraged to use them simultaneously as homework in order to reduce stress by blocking out negative self-talk, negative visualizations, shallow breathing, and muscle tension. Self-talk is covered in Section 6 (cognitive-behavioral approach), and visual imagery, deep breathing, and PMRT are covered in Chapters 14, 15, and 16, respectively.

Visual or guided imagery can help clients block out intrusive visualizations by substituting a relaxing or empowering visualization or image. Guided imagery also allows a counselor to *covertly* (i.e., through the use of visual imagery) expose clients to empowering or relaxing images, ordinarily by having a client close her eyes and imagine a scene or series of actions the counselor suggests. Guided imagery is used very frequently in therapeutic approaches to relaxation, such as when a client imagines taking a walk along a stream through the woods and imagines the sights and sounds one might encounter, all suggested by the counselor or a relaxation recording. Guided imagery can also be used for covert modeling or role playing, in which the client imagines performing a certain skill or behavior before trying it out in the real world (see Chapter 32 on modeling).

Deep breathing and PMRT are both physiologically based mindfulness interventions that are very effective in reducing stress and anxiety after the stressor has occurred. Deep, slow, diaphragm-based breathing slows down one's metabolism and induces a relaxation response. PMRT provides a systematic process of tensing and relaxing muscle groups in order to achieve a deeper state of muscular relaxation. These three techniques (i.e., visual imagery, deep breathing, and PMRT) can also be taught to clients preparing for systematic desensitization (see Chapter 30), a very effective counseling technique for addressing simple phobias.

Finally, Chapter 17 introduces mindfulness meditation. Mindfulness involves formal and informal meditation practice. Formal meditation practice involves the more familiar meditation while sitting or lying down. Formal practice also includes mindfulness movement, such as hatha yoga or walking meditation. Informal meditation (everyday mindfulness) focuses attention and awareness into any facet of daily life. Although historically infused into spirituality and religion, mindfulness is secular and universal in its clinical application and has numerous social and psychological benefits.

MULTICULTURAL IMPLICATIONS OF THE TECHNIQUES BASED ON MINDFULNESS APPROACHES

The multicultural considerations for counselors using the mindfulness-based approaches are in many ways similar to the multicultural considerations for cognitive-behavioral approaches(see Section 6). Like humanistic/phenomenological, psychodynamic, and cognitive-behavioral approaches to counseling, mindfulness emphasizes rapport and therapeutic alliance, but it deemphasizes the sharing of intense emotions, intimate life details, and past life events. The mindfulness approach is a present-focused, nonthreatening process that many clients find empowering, and it may appeal to clients from a wide array of cultural backgrounds, particularly those whose cultures *may* discourage the sharing of family-related issues (e.g., Latino culture) or exploration or exhibition of intense emotions (e.g., Asian culture). The approach also transfers meaningfully across numerous cultural contexts, including gender, racial, ethnic, socioeconomic, disability, and sexual orientation contexts (Hays & Erford, 2018).

The mindfulness approach allows collaboration and behavioral change while still stressing the importance of the therapeutic relationship and does not question cultural values or practices. These approaches allow clients to decide whether to adhere to, give up, or modify the perceived rules, giving clients more freedom and flexibility in controlling levels of stress.

The mindfulness approach is directive, and the professional counselor is often perceived to be an expert by the client. Some clients from some cultures (e.g., Middle Eastern, Hispanic, Asian) may be very comfortable with the expert perception, whereas others (e.g., some males) may be less comfortable (Hays & Erford, 2018). Also, professional counselors should make efforts to avoid facilitating a dependency relationship with clients because clients should not look at the counselor as an expert with the answers. Clients from diverse racial, religious, and ethnic backgrounds often appreciate the straightforward, physiologically and cognitively based mindfulness approach because it focuses on the client's present thoughts, events, and behavior rather than on a person's nature, sociocultural background, or cultural beliefs. Other clients may feel uncomfortable with a mindfulness approach because it focuses on present-moment events rather than on self-awareness or insight derived from past experiences.

Many mindfulness-based approaches are based on Eastern religions and therefore appear as second nature to practitioners of Buddhism. In contrast, because it is linked to a Buddhist religious tradition, some practitioners of other faiths (e.g., Christianity, Islam) may view the procedures with great suspicion. Indeed, in the United States, citizens of some entire states or individual school districts have sought to restrict the practice of visual imagery, in particular because it was viewed as having a potential use as mind control in school settings, as if teaching students to control their minds, states of relaxation, affect, and stressors is a bad thing.

CHAPTER 14

Visual/Guided Imagery

ORIGINS OF THE VISUAL IMAGERY TECHNIQUE

The origins of visual imagery techniques began with Freud's dream interpretations in the late 1890s and were heavily influenced by Jung's so-called active imagination (Koziey & Andersen, 1990). Hypnagogic visions under deep relaxation were noted by Frank in 1913 and later in 1922 by Kretschmer, who named them *bildstreifendenken*, which means "thinking in the form of a movie" (Schoettle, 1980, p. 220). In the 1920s, Robert Desoille developed the guided daydream method as a therapeutic technique. He required the client to actively daydream, while in a state of muscular relaxation, about themes introduced by the psychotherapist. More modern influences for the technique are Leuner's guided affective imagery in the 1950s and Swartly's initiated symbol projection in 1965.

Today, visual imagery is used in many counseling approaches, including cognitive-behavioral, transpersonal, Gestalt, psychodynamic, and Ericksonian (Arbuthnott, Arbuthnott, & Rossiter, 2001; Seligman & Reichenberg, 2013). For example, behavioral therapists use imagery in the treatment of phobias and in relaxation and stress management training (Arbuthnott et al., 2001). Cognitive therapists employ imagery to access a client's key beliefs and urge reinterpretations of experiences. Psychodynamic therapists use imagery to help clients process difficult memories or thoughts. Gestalt therapists draw on imagery to help clients work through internal conflicts or alleviate anxiety. Solution-focused counselors use imagery to implement the miracle question (Murdock, 2013; also see Chapter 4).

There are several types of visual imagery. *Mental imagery* is the process through which a person focuses on a vivid mental picture of an experience. Mental imagery can help assess the relationship between the client's experiences and presenting symptoms and help determine how those experiences became intensified in the client's mind. *Positive imagery* is the visualization of any pleasant scene, real or imagined. Positive imagery can reduce tension, inhibit anxiety, or help a person cope with pain. *Goal-rehearsal imagery*, or *coping imagery*, requires the client to self-visualize successfully coping with each step of a process.

HOW TO IMPLEMENT THE VISUAL IMAGERY TECHNIQUE

Before beginning guided imagery, make sure that the room is quiet and the client is comfortable. Music may be used to create a soothing mood, but be aware that for some people music is a distraction. Help the client relax by suggesting closing the eyes and taking long, slow, deep breaths. Once the client is relaxed, start the guided imagery experience. Speak in a soft, soothing voice. It is preferable to script a story ahead to ensure that the words create the desired mood and direction. Guided imagery scripts do not need to be long, and it may take only a minute or two to lead a client through the experience, although some experiences may last more than 10 minutes. Keep the exercises simple at first. Arbuthnott et al. (2001) provided the following example of how multi-sensory guided imagery might be used in a counseling session:

Imagine that you are walking across a field of fresh green grass on a warm spring day. You feel the softness of the grass beneath your feet, the warmth of the air on your skin, and hear the sound of birds singing in the distance. You are moving toward a large tree that is near a creek. When you reach the tree, you sit down with your back supported by the trunk. Listening to the soft sound of the running water in the creek, you notice that you are filled with a sense of well-being. (p. 123)

Always allow the client to imagine something familiar and nonthreatening before moving on to scripts that pose serious dilemmas or require the client to confront specific issues. Bring closure to the guided imagery experience by posing a final question, telling the client to let her mind go blank again, or by informing the client that the experience is ending and she should open her eyes on the count of three. Discuss the guided imagery experience afterward. Ask the client how she felt about the activity and what she did or did not like about it.

VARIATIONS OF THE VISUAL IMAGERY TECHNIQUE

Guided imagery is a major subtype of visual imagery. Guided imagery can be used to help clients put emotional or interpersonal issues into words, to help clients generate goals for change, to help clients rehearse new behaviors, or to help clients exert control over their emotions or stress levels (Arbuthnott et al., 2001). In guided imagery, a person is led through a visualization process directed by stimulus words or sounds. Clients are encouraged to relax, imagine themselves in a situation, and then discuss and process the activity to gain insight. Counselors use three types of images in guided imagery (Vernon & Clemente, 2004). *Spontaneous images* arise without conscious direction of content. *Directed images* involve the counselor suggesting a specific image on which the client should concentrate. *Guided images* combine the other two types by giving the client a starting point and allowing the client to fill in the blanks. Guided imagery can be realistic or rely on fantasy or metaphors (Arbuthnott et al., 2001). The

timing, duration, and intensity of guided imagery should be modified to meet the needs of each individual (Seligman & Reichenberg, 2013). Imagery is most powerful when it appeals to the person's dominant senses (i.e., visual, auditory, tactile, olfactory) and when it is practiced between sessions.

EXAMPLES OF THE VISUAL IMAGERY TECHNIQUE

EXAMPLE 1: The use of visual imagery in a reciprocal inhibition procedure

Nick is a 35-year-old male referred for symptoms of depression and anxiety. In the course of treatment, he was introduced to the visualization insertion/blocking technique based on reciprocal inhibition.

Counselor (C):   . . . Because you know when you close your eyes and you can still see things and you can play things, movies, inside your mind's eye, things that may have happened in the past or things that you might like to happen in the future. A lot of people call it fantasizing or daydreaming.

Nick (N):   Yeah.

C: But we actually call it visualization and visual imagery, and it's really important because, again taking you back to the term *reciprocal inhibition*, it's actually impossible to run the negative nasty movies, the things you're worried about, while you're thinking about a calming and relaxing place that you might like to take yourself. One of the other assignments that I gave you before this session was to think about one or two calming and relaxing places you might like to take yourself whenever you're stressed out. What did you decide on?

N: Hawaii. Definitely Hawaii.

C: Oh, Hawaii. That's a good one.

N: The beach there was the calmest, most peaceful place I have ever been.

C: Great. What was so calm and relaxing?

N: I think it's just the environment, so beautiful.

C: Let's close our eyes, and you describe it to me so I can picture it in my head.

N: Um . . . well I picture myself on the sand with the blue ocean right there, and the palm trees, and the sky, the warm weather.

C: Yeah . . . How did it make you feel when you were there? Were you lying on the beach or walking around?

N: I was lying on the beach, and it was really calm and relaxing.

C: It sounds beautiful. Do you have pictures, videos, and things like that?

N: Yeah.

C: Some people are really good at visualizing it. It's almost like you close your eyes and you're there. And sometimes when you've not been there for quite some time, it starts to fade from memory and becomes more difficult to recall. And one of the things you can do is to look at the pictures or video of the beach with the surf and the waves and the sounds. And so whenever it doesn't seem as vivid, it doesn't seem like I'm right there when I close my eyes, I can actually look at it on the TV and hear the sounds and it kind of brings that back . . . What I want you to do right now is close your eyes and take yourself to Hawaii, on the beach. I want you to imagine that you're actually there, and I want you to imagine the peacefulness and the calm. (Pause for a minute or so as Nick closes his eyes and relaxes into his visual scene) And come on back to me whenever you're ready. There . . . feeling more relaxed? How did that feel?

N: Outstanding.

C: Sorry I had to bring you back. We still have some more work to do. Now I want you to close your eyes and visualize some of the unpleasant scenes that we were discussing earlier—your boss, ex-wife, that particularly nasty colleague. And when I tell you to, I want you to change the scene in your mind to Hawaii and relax, even do some deep breathing and some positive self-talk.

N: Got it. (Pause for a minute to let Nick visualize the stress-producing visualizations he presented with at counseling)

C: Now, Nick, I want you to take yourself to Hawaii.

N: With pleasure!

C: That's the idea . . . When you think and visualize sad and stressful things, you become sad and stressed. When you think about and visualize relaxing things, you become relaxed. (Pause for about a minute as Nick relaxes into his Hawaii scene) Okay. It's time to open your eyes and come back to me. You can go back there anytime you want, as you already know. (Introduction of the scaling technique) Now, on that scale of 1 to 10—with 10 being total relaxation, "This is just so fantastic," and 1 being "Eeek! I'm completely stressed out"—where are you whenever you're in Hawaii in your mind?

N: A 10. Definitely a 10!

C: A 10. Great, that sure beats the 2 that you were at when we were discussing those challenging people in your life.

N: You got that right!

EXAMPLE 2: Guided visual imagery

Numerous recordings of visual imagery exercises are available. Following is one of several excellent tracks available on *Stressbuster Relaxation Exercises* produced by Erford (2001) and available for purchase from the American Counseling Association (click on the link to Publications at www.counseling.org).

TROPICAL HIDEAWAY

Today we are going to take a trip to a deserted tropical beach. Before we go, we are going to do a deep breathing activity to prepare us for our relaxing journey.

Get into a comfortable position and close your eyes. Now put one hand on your stomach. Breathe in so that you can feel your hand go up as it rests on your stomach. Imagine that your stomach has a beach ball inside. As you breathe in, fill the beach ball with air. As you exhale, let the air out of the beach ball.

Let's try it. Take a slow deep breath in through your nose.

(Pause)

Now breathe out slowly.

(Pause)

Again, take a slow deep breath in through your nose.

(Pause)

And breathe out slowly.

(Pause)

One more time, breathe in slowly and fill the beach ball with air.

(Pause)

And breathe out slowly. Let the air out of the beach ball. Continue to take long, deep, slow breaths as you journey to your tropical hideaway.

(Pause)

Take a moment to listen to your breathing. See how calm and relaxed it is. You are now ready to take your trip. Imagine that you are on a tropical island; you have left your traveling party in search of a relaxing hideaway.

(Pause)

You see a trail that leads into the jungle. Feeling adventurous, you enter the trail. In front of you, you see many lush green plants and several hanging vines. You also see brightly colored tropical flowers. You hear the chatter of tropical birds and other small animals. You smell the sweet fragrant flowers and plant life. You follow the trail while enjoying the beautiful scenery. You eventually come to a clearing. In front of you, you see a white sandy beach surrounding a crystal-clear turquoise-colored lagoon. You notice that the beach is completely deserted. You can hardly believe that nobody is visiting this glorious place. You decide to walk toward the water. You feel the warmth of the sun on your body. You look up in the sky and see that it is completely clear. As you are walking, you hear the lapping of the waves against the sand. The closer you get to the water, the softer the sand becomes beneath your feet. Notice the feel of the warm, grainy sand on your feet.

(Pause)

Finally, you have reached the lagoon. You see the gentle ebb and flow of the water. You stand for a moment and watch the water lap gentle little waves against the beautiful white sand.

(Pause)

You feel your worries and concerns wash away with every ebb and flow of the crystal-clear water.

(Pause)

You decide to enjoy the cool, soothing, crystal-clear water. You submerge your feet in water. The tiny waves break gently against your lower legs. You stand alone in the lagoon, acclimating to the temperature. The water is cool yet refreshing. You decide to walk out a little farther from the shore. You feel the refreshing water on your knees.

(Pause)

On your thighs.

(Pause)

On your buttocks.

(Pause)

And on your stomach.

(Pause)

You stand for a moment submerged to your waist in the cool, crystal-clear water. You feel as if you could just float away. Your entire body feels relaxed and refreshed. After enjoying the tranquil calm of the lagoon, you walk back toward the white, sandy beach.

(Pause)

Once you reach the beach, you feel the warmth of the sand beneath your feet. You decide to get your beach blanket out of your backpack and put it down on the warm sand. You lie down on the blanket and look at the peaceful blue sky with puffy white clouds. You feel the sun warming your wet body. You close your eyes and listen to the lapping of the water. Take a moment and enjoy this peaceful, relaxing sensation.

(Pause)

After lying there a while, you decide it is time to get back to your traveling party. Get up from your blanket. Enjoy the beautiful view of the water and the white, sandy beach. Gather up your belongings and head back toward the tropical jungle feeling relaxed, peaceful, and calm. Walk through the jungle, enjoying the sound of the birds and the fragrant odor of the tropical flowers. Continue on the trail, thinking about your wonderful trip and how relaxed it has made you feel. Carry this positive

experience with you the entire day, knowing that you can return to your tropical hideaway whenever you desire.

To learn the effects of the guided visualization on the client or to add additional meaning to the experience, the professional counselor should ask several follow-up questions before ending or transitioning to another topic or activity. Possible follow-up queries include:

- What did you like about this activity?
- What did you not like about this activity?

USEFULNESS AND EVALUATION OF THE VISUAL IMAGERY TECHNIQUE

Visual imagery can be used in many developmental and therapeutic situations. Imagery can reduce anxiety, facilitate relaxation, promote a sense of control, improve problem solving and decision making, alleviate pain, and help people develop new perspectives on their lives (Seligman & Reichenberg, 2013). Imagery also can produce behavioral changes and enhance one's self-concept (Vernon & Clemente, 2004). Guided imagery has been shown to treat nonsuicidal self-injury (Kress, Adamson, DeMarco, Paylo, & Zoldan, 2013), stress, post-traumatic stress disorder, panic attacks, bulimia nervosa, phobias, depression, and chronic pain (Arbuthnott et al., 2001). Visual and guided imagery are used primarily to enhance relaxation (Laselle & Russell, 1993), but they are also helpful in addressing self-management (Penzien & Holroyd, 1994), pain management (Chaves, 1994; Cupal & Brewer, 2001; Gonsalkorale, 1996; Ross & Berger, 1996), and asthma (Peck, Bray, & Kehle, 2003). Guided imagery is also useful in treating enuresis and psychosomatic disorders (Myrick & Myrick, 1993) and leads to improved self-efficacy in pain management in some Hispanic clients (Menzies & Kim, 2008) and increases in lung function and decreases in anxiety levels in students with asthma and concomitant anxiety disorder (Kapoor, Bray, & Kehle, 2010).

Toth et al. (2007) conducted a small-scale, randomized, controlled trial and found that guided imagery delivered via recording reduced anxiety in hospitalized medical patients, leading to the possible efficacy of widespread application for people exposed to short- and long-term elevated stress levels. Jallo, Bourguignon, Taylor, and Utz (2008) conducted a 12-week study to determine whether a relaxation-guided imagery (R-GI) intervention would enhance stress management in African American women during the second trimester of pregnancy. They found that participants improved their breathing, level of relaxation, response to stress, and sleep cycle, and reduced levels of anxiety and anger. Wynd (2005) found that guided imagery had immediate and long-term usefulness in smoking cessation, leading to a 26% abstinence rate after 2 years compared to 12% in the placebo control group. Jewell and Elliff (2013) studied the effectiveness of a five-session group work program for juvenile detainees called Relaxation Skills Violence Prevention (RSVP), which integrated visual imagery and other relaxation skills (e.g., deep breathing, progressive muscle relaxation training [PMRT]). Participants experienced significantly increased anger and personal control compared to the control group.

Guided imagery can also allow clients to uncover and deal with highly complex emotions from experiences such as sexual abuse (Pearson, 1994). Imagery has shown minimal usefulness for clients with psychotic disorders and addictions (Schoettle, 1980). It is important to note that visual imagery may not be effective with young children who have difficulty separating fantasy from reality, who have trouble keeping their eyes closed and their body relaxed, or who repeat TV or movie plots rather than use their own imaginations.

In general, mindfulness approaches, including visual imagery, have been used to add psychological adjustment to serious physical illnesses (e.g., cancer; Smith, Richardson, Hoffman, & Pilkington, 2005), as well as to cope with work-related stressors (Shapiro, Astin, Bishop, & Cordova, 2005). Schure et al. (2008) found the mindfulness-based approaches effective in the training of professional counselors, particularly for empathy development and advanced listening skills.

APPLICATION OF THE VISUAL/GUIDED IMAGERY TECHNIQUE

Now apply the visual/guided imagery technique to a current client or student you are working with or revisit the brief case studies presented at the beginning of this book. How can you use the visual/guided imagery technique to address concerns and create movement in the counseling session?

CHAPTER 15

Deep Breathing

ORIGINS OF THE DEEP BREATHING TECHNIQUE

Breathing exercises, although relatively new techniques in Western culture, have been highly regarded by many other cultures for a long time and are commonly used mindfulness techniques. The early roots of deep breathing can be traced back to the Hindu yoga traditions. Hindu philosophers' belief in yoga centers on the concept of pranayama. *Prana* means "life energy" as well as "breath," and by being able to control one's breathing, it is thought that a person is able to control life energy. An ancient metaphor used to describe breath is the string that controls the kite: The kite represents the mind, and the string represents breath. To calm the body, many professional counselors now recommend using breathing techniques. By learning to breathe more deeply and efficiently, clients can learn to manage their stress (Kottler & Chen, 2011).

HOW TO IMPLEMENT THE DEEP BREATHING TECHNIQUE

Implementation varies widely, but some basic guidelines to follow when implementing the breathing technique include the following:

1. Breathe through the nose on the inhale, and exhale either through the nose or through pursed lips (almost like blowing a gentle kiss).
2. Between the deep breaths, take one or two normal breaths to avoid dizziness. When any lightheadedness passes, use consecutive, long, deep, slow breaths.
3. Practice the exercises initially while lying on your back, then sit or stand during the exercise after learning the basic techniques.
4. You may yawn frequently so that the body can establish equilibrium and begin to relax. This is common and is a sign that you are successfully relaxing.
5. You should note what your breathing is like before starting the exercises and compare it to progress made during the exercises.

It is also important to know that a person's exhale should take about twice as long as the inhale. For example, if a person inhaled for 3 seconds, the same breath should be exhaled over approximately 6 seconds. Also, common nasal congestion can make breathing through the nose uncomfortable or ineffective. In these cases, breathing through the mouth is acceptable. But clients should be urged to do so very slowly. It is the depth and rate of breathing that induce relaxation.

A person at rest is typically using only one third of his or her lung capacity. A professional counselor can use sessions with clients to teach how to breathe more effectively. Before learning the deep breathing technique, it is important for the person to know how to do diaphragmatic or abdominal breathing. To begin, clients should lie on their backs and notice how they are breathing. They can use their hands to get an understanding of how they are breathing. By putting one hand on the stomach and one hand on the chest, clients can feel how they are breathing. If the hand on the stomach rises, the client is breathing from the abdomen. If the hand on the chest rises, the client is breathing from the chest. The professional counselor can instruct clients to shift from chest to abdominal breathing to help them become more aware of the difference (Davis, Robbins-Eshelman, & McKay, 2009).

Once clients are able to breathe from the abdomen, the professional counselor can teach the clients the deep breathing technique. Davis et al. (2009, p. 27) provide the following procedures for implementing the deep breathing technique:

1. Lie down on a blanket, rug, mat, or pad on the floor. Bend your knees and move your feet hip-width (about 8 to 12 inches) apart, with your toes turned slightly outward. Make sure that your spine is straight.
2. Scan your body for tension.
3. Place one hand on your abdomen and one hand on your chest.
4. Inhale slowly and deeply through your nose into your abdomen to push up your hand as much as feels comfortable. Your chest should move only a little and only with your abdomen.
5. When you feel at ease with step 4, smile slightly and inhale through your nose and exhale through your mouth, making a quiet, relaxing whooshing sound like the wind as you blow out gently. Your mouth, tongue, and jaw will be relaxed. Take long, slow deep breaths that raise and lower your abdomen. Focus on the sound and feeling of breathing as you become more and more relaxed.
6. Continue deep breathing for about 5 or 10 minutes at a time, once or twice a day, for a couple of weeks. Then, if you like, extend this period to 20 minutes.
7. At the end of each deep breathing session, take a little time to scan your body once more for tension. Compare the tension you feel at the conclusion of the exercise with the tension you experienced when you began.
8. When you become at ease with breathing into your abdomen, practice it any time during the day when you feel like it and you are sitting down or standing still. Concentrate on your abdomen moving up and down, the air moving in and out of your lungs, and the feeling of relaxation that deep breathing gives you.
9. When you have learned to relax yourself using deep breathing, practice it whenever you feel yourself getting tense.

VARIATIONS OF THE DEEP BREATHING TECHNIQUE

The deep breathing technique comes in over two dozen variations, and the ones thought to be most useful to professional counselors are highlighted below. When a person is in a situation that causes feelings of anxiety, a variation of the deep breathing technique, called breathing down, can be used. In this exercise, the person sits in a comfortable position and places both hands over the bellybutton, with the right hand on top. The client imagines that there is a pouch at the point where the hands meet the stomach. As the person takes in a breath, he imagines the pouch is filling with air. He continues the breathing exercise to fill the pouch to the top. When the pouch is full, the person holds his breath, keeping the air in the pouch, and repeats "My body is calm." As the person exhales, emptying the pouch, he says, "My body is quiet." After repeating this exercise four times in a row, 10 times a day for a couple of weeks, the client will be better able to relax.

Two other variations of this technique have been around for decades. Vernon and Clemente (2004) instructed clients to toss their concerns away as they exhale. As they inhale, they are instructed to imagine a calmness filling their bodies. Similar to this variation is another one called "waiting in line, peacefully breathe." Faelton and Diamond (1990) suggested that people waiting in traffic jams or similar situations can use deep breathing to help their impatience dissipate. While waiting, it is important for the person to remind himself that being impatient makes the time pass slower.

Another variation of the deep breathing technique can be used with a group. A professional counselor can teach deep breathing to any of his or her groups whose members can benefit from this technique. After every member knows the technique, it can be used to open a session. The rolling breath is another variation of the deep breathing technique. It involves working with a partner to complete the exercise. In this variation, one person lies on the floor; the partner puts one hand on the person's stomach and one hand on the person's chest. The person inhales in two steps, first filling the abdomen and then the chest, watching his partner's hands move rhythmically. The person exhales the air in his chest and abdomen at the same time. After the first person has practiced this exercise and attained a rolling effect for several minutes, the partners switch places (Sam Houston State University Counseling Center, 2018).

The three-breath release is yet another variation of this technique. This alternative should be used at least once a day. The client needs to close her eyes if she is able to do so. When the client exhales, she needs to loosen her whole body and go limp. The client needs to make sure that while she is doing this exercise, she has something to balance on so she does not fall. This exercise should be done three times (Schafer, 1999).

"Controlling pain with imagery breath" is another variation described by Faelton and Diamond (1990). In this variation, the person does diaphragmatic breathing with his eyes closed. When inhaling, the person imagines the breath filling the painful spot with calmness. On the exhale, the person imagines the pain leaving his body. After 10 minutes, the person opens his eyes and stretches his body.

EXAMPLE OF THE DEEP BREATHING TECHNIQUE

The following transcript is just one of numerous renditions of a deep breathing exercise.

Counselor (C):   Okay, Sam. Lie down on your mat and close your eyes. Bend your knees a bit and keep your feet apart . . . great. Now I want you to place one hand on your abdomen and one hand on your chest . . . . Inhale slowly and deeply through your nose into your abdomen. You will notice that your hand over your abdomen will rise with your abdomen. The hand on your chest should move only a little. Now exhale very slowly through your mouth.

Just purse your lips slightly and allow the air to escape slowly . . . slowly, barely enough to make a candle flame flicker. Good. Continue to take long, slow deep breaths that raise and lower your abdomen. Focus on the sound and feeling of your breathing . . . (Pause) . . . Become more and more relaxed.

Sam continues to breathe with periodic encouragement and comments from the counselor for 5 to 10 minutes. The counselor then assigns homework: deep breathing for 5 to 10 minutes, three times per day, every day, until the next appointment.

USEFULNESS AND EVALUATION OF THE DEEP BREATHING TECHNIQUE

Slowing your breathing rate helps to reduce stress and promotes a mindfulness focus (Fontaine, 2014; Kabat-Zinn, 2006; Luskin & Pelletier, 2005). Breathing techniques are used for a variety of reasons. Most commonly, a professional counselor suggests this technique to a person who is working on controlling anxiety or managing stress. This technique is also used to reduce "generalized anxiety disorders, panic attacks and agoraphobia, depression, irritability, muscle tension, headaches, fatigue . . . breath-holding, hyperventilation, shallow breathing, and cold hands and feet" (Davis et al., 2009, p. 25).

A version of this technique is incorporated into a popular method of childbirth: Lamaze. The theory behind the Lamaze breathing techniques is that if the deep breathing exercises are performed, a part of the cortex will not respond to the pain. Nuernberger (2007) described how breathing techniques can be used when people have difficulty sleeping. Not only does this technique allow a person to fall asleep, but also the sleep will be more restful. The deep breathing exercise should be completed in the following way: "8 breaths lying on your back, 16 breaths lying on your right side, and 32 breaths lying on your left side" (p. 197). Most people fall asleep before they finish this exercise.

Kabat-Zinn (2006) described how deep breathing techniques can be used to help manage pain. During the time when a person is performing a deep breathing technique, he should attempt to go into the part of the body causing the pain. By being aware of the pain and his breathing, the client can penetrate the affected area and reduce stress.

Deep breathing exercises also can be used to help smokers quit. Some people smoke to relax, and when smoking, they take the time to inhale and exhale slowly. This habit has some of the same relaxing effects as the deep breathing exercises. By learning how to relax by breathing deeply without the cigarette, a person may be more successful in quitting smoking (Faelton & Diamond, 1990).

Deep breathing techniques also can be used to help manage one's anger. Anger is a normal response, yet it can cause problems if it is not handled well. One cool-down strategy recommended by Arenofsky (2001) is a deep breathing exercise. People can be taught to use deep breathing exercises before attempting to resolve their conflicts so that the chance of a peaceful outcome increases. Jewell & Elliff (2013) found that the five session Relaxation Skills Violence Prevention (RSVP) program, which combined deep breathing with PMRT and guided visual imagery, led to significant improvements in anger management and self-control in a sample of juvenile detainees compared to participants in the control group.

Likewise, mindfulness-based interventions are effective for reducing depressive, anxiety, stress, and sleep symptoms. In a magnetic resonance imagery study, Paul, Stanton, Greeson, Smoski, and Wang (2013) found deep breathing effective in reducing automatic emotional responding and reactivity. Lerma et al. (2017) integrated deep breathing into a five-week cognitive behavioral intervention treatment regimen, leading to lower levels of depression and anxiety and a higher quality of life assessment compared to the control condition. In a randomized control trial, Perciavalle et al. (2017) found that deep breathing was effective in improving mood and stress levels on self-report and objective physiological measures in just ten 90-minute sessions in healthy young university students. The effects were equivalent for men and women. In addition, clients with major depression receiving CBT with breathing relaxation experiences improved sleep quality at termination and follow-up (Chien, Chung, Yeh, &

Lee, 2015). Finally, in a double-blind, randomized, controlled trial (RCT), Borge et al. (2015) randomized participants into guided deep breathing, music listening, and sitting-still groups and found the deep breathing treatment group experienced better outcomes on most dependent variables compared to the other conditions at termination and follow-up. So the outcome literature supports the use of deep breathing for symptom relief of a wide range of internalizing disorders and problems.

A survey conducted by Laselle and Russell (1993) indicated that professional counselors were not commonly incorporating breathing techniques in their work with students, but it is a technique that could be valuable to many young people. By teaching students relaxation techniques, including deep breathing, professional counselors could help to reduce the number of behavior problems and conflicts in school. Noggle, Steiner, Minami, and Khalsa (2012) demonstrated that a breathing-enhanced yoga procedure resulted in reduced negative affect and increased positive affect and mood in comparison with the control condition in teenagers.

Brown and Uehara (1999) described how deep breathing techniques can be used in workplace settings where stress exists. Many times, stress is a factor when an employee chooses to leave a workplace or a profession. Stress also contributes to higher rates of absenteeism among staff members. Brown and Uehara recommend that, after becoming aware of stress, employees become involved in physiological training. In this process, employees learn coping strategies, including deep breathing techniques that are part of an effective stress management plan.

Van Dixhorn (1988) performed a randomized trial of relaxation therapy during which the main techniques taught were breathing awareness and diaphragmatic breathing. When compared to exercise alone, relaxation therapy was more effective in reducing the risk of abnormalities that suggest myocardial ischemia, a heart condition. At the two-year follow-up study, participants who learned the relaxation technique did not experience as many cardiac problems as the other participants. Cooley et al. (2009) looked at the difference in effect for naturopathic treatment for anxiety (e.g., dietary counseling, deep breathing relaxation techniques, a standard multivitamin, and the herbal medicine ashwagandha) and psychotherapy (with the same deep breathing techniques and placebo). Both groups of participants showed improvement in anxiety, with the naturopathic treatment group showing greater benefits. This study showed versatility of deep breathing in combination with many kinds of therapy.

Deep breathing exercises are commonly used by professional counselors with their clients for a variety of purposes. Perhaps one of the reasons this technique is popular is because it is quick and easy to perform. A person can engage in this exercise almost anywhere because it is not noticeable to others while it is performed. The deep breathing technique is a valuable relaxation exercise that is simple enough for nearly any person to learn.

APPLICATION OF THE DEEP BREATHING TECHNIQUE

Now apply the deep breathing technique to a current client or student you are working with or revisit the brief case studies presented at the beginning of this book. How can you use the deep breathing technique to address concerns and create movement in the counseling session?

CHAPTER 16

Progressive Muscle Relaxation Training (PMRT)

ORIGINS OF THE PMRT TECHNIQUE

Edmund Jacobson developed the technique of progressive relaxation years after noticing how anxious his father, a calm and quiet man, became after living through a house fire. Jacobson performed many studies examining human skeletal muscles and, in particular, what made the muscles tense and what helped them to relax. Through some of his studies, Jacobson showed that mental activity takes place in the neuromusculature as well as in the brain. By measuring the activity taking place in the neuromusculature when a person was tense and when a person was calm, Jacobson used data to help create the progressive relaxation training (Jacobson, 1977). A person learns to relax striated muscles through this process. Muscles are relaxed when a person does not have to use any energy.

The belief that underlies the technique of progressive muscle relaxation training (PMRT) is that a muscle cannot be both relaxed and tensed at the same time—a fact based on the principle of reciprocal inhibition. By learning to identify the ways muscles feel when they are tensed and when they are relaxed, a person can learn to relax, thereby reducing stress (Kottler & Chen, 2011).

HOW TO IMPLEMENT THE PMRT TECHNIQUE

When training a client in PMRT, the professional counselor should make sure that the space is free from any distractions. The client needs to find a place, such as a couch or a mat on the floor, to lie comfortably with her eyes closed. Progressive relaxation sessions typically last about 15 to 30 minutes and are performed in a dimly lit area. More often than not, six or seven sessions of progressive relaxation are enough to have a positive effect on a client's stress levels (Jacobson, 1977). Clients need to make sure to wear loose-fitting clothing and should take off their shoes before the session starts. Beginning with the toes and proceeding up the body, clients tighten each muscle group, and after noting the feeling, they quickly relax the given muscle group. It is important to repeat the muscle contraction exercises many times so that the client becomes aware of the difference that exists between a tense and a relaxed muscle. The professional counselor teaches the client to relax all of the different muscle groups in the body.

Although Jacobson initially suggested 30 muscle groups (implemented over 40 individual sessions!) most professional counselors currently use some or all of the following muscle groups implemented in a single session: right foot, right lower leg, right thigh, left foot, left lower leg, left thigh, buttocks, abdomen, right hand, right arm, left hand, left arm, lower back, shoulders, neck, lower face, upper face (see Table 16.1).

Ordinarily, the client is instructed to take in a deep breath, hold the breath for 5 seconds while tensing a muscle group, then release the tension in the muscle while slowly exhaling. The pairing of the tension release and exhale leads to deeper relaxation and a potential classically conditioned association.

Once the client knows how to relax each muscle group, the professional counselor can lead the client in a full session of PMRT, going through each of the groups. After practicing this technique, clients should be able to keep their muscle groups relaxed at the same time. At the end of

TABLE 16.1 Instructions for Tensing and Relaxing Major Muscle Groups

- Right arm—Take a deep breath and hold it for about 5 seconds as you make a fist, curl your wrist, flex your forearm, and flex your bicep. Then relax these muscles and release the tension as you exhale.
- Left arm—Take a deep breath and hold it for about 5 seconds as you make a fist, curl your wrist, flex your forearm, and flex your bicep. Then relax these muscles and release the tension as you exhale.
- Right leg—Take a deep breath and hold it for about 5 seconds as you curl your toes under, lift the ball of your foot to flex your shin, and flex your thigh muscle. Then relax these muscles and release the tension as you exhale.
- Left leg—Take a deep breath and hold it for about 5 seconds as you curl your toes under, lift the ball of your foot to flex your shin, and flex your thigh muscle. Then relax these muscles and release the tension as you exhale.
- Abdomen—Take a deep breath and hold it for about 5 seconds as you pull in your stomach and bend your waist to lean your shoulders forward about 6 inches. Then relax these muscles and release the tension as you exhale.
- Lower back and shoulders—Take a deep breath and hold it for about 5 seconds as you arch your back and push your elbows back while keeping your forearms parallel with the ground, effectively pushing together your shoulder blades. Then relax these muscles and release the tension as you exhale.
- Neck—Take a deep breath and hold it for about 5 seconds as you turn your head to the right and look out over your right shoulder. Then relax these muscles and release the tension as you exhale. Next, take a deep breath and hold it for about 5 seconds as you turn your head to the left and look out over your left shoulder. Then relax these muscles and release the tension as you exhale. Take a deep breath and hold it for about 5 seconds as you lean your head to the right and try to touch your right ear to your right shoulder. Then relax these muscles and release the tension as you exhale. Next, take a deep breath and hold it for about 5 seconds as you lean your head to the left and try to touch your left ear to your left shoulder. Then relax these muscles and release the tension as you exhale.
- Lower face (jaw, lips, and tongue)—Take a deep breath and hold it for about 5 seconds as you clench your teeth, press your lips together, and push your tongue up to the roof of your mouth. Then relax these muscles and release the tension as you exhale.
- Upper face (forehead, eyes, and nose)—Take a deep breath and hold it for about 5 seconds as you close your eyes tightly, wrinkle your nose, and knit your brows in a frown. Then relax these muscles and release the tension as you exhale.

each session, the client lies in silence for several minutes to allow progressive relaxation to have the greatest impact.

VARIATIONS OF THE PMRT TECHNIQUE

According to Jacobson (1987), there are three different types of progressive relaxation: general, relative, and specific. Clients relax every muscle group in their bodies when they are practicing general relaxation. Relative relaxation occurs when a person is doing something but relaxes as much as possible. For example, while sitting at her desk at work, a person could practice relative relaxation; she is not able to relax completely, but she relaxes as much as she can. A person is practicing specific relaxation when she relaxes and tenses only certain muscle groups. Lazarus called the general relaxation procedure total relaxation and the relative relaxation procedure differential relaxation. Carroll, Bates, and Johnson (2003) used PMRT in small-group work following a deep breathing exercise. They suggested using relative relaxation after completing the breathing exercise. The professional counselor should have the clients sit in chairs and relax the muscles that they do not need to use.

Another variation of progressive relaxation is audio-recorded training. In this alternative, the professional counselor records a session of PMRT with the client and then gives the client a copy of the recording to listen to at home. This recording takes the place of the in-session training, and the client practices the technique repeatedly in the comfort of her own home. There is some debate over this version because the professional counselor is not with the client throughout the learning process and cannot correct any mistakes made by the client. Using PMRT recordings as homework assignments may make treatment progress faster, however, for many clients.

EXAMPLE OF THE PMRT TECHNIQUE

In this session, Sam is learning how to use PMRT to enhance relaxation.

Counselor (C): I want you to get in a comfortable position for this activity. Sit up in your chair with your back supported. Take a few long, deep, slow breaths, and begin to feel yourself relax as your breathing slows . . . (Pause for a minute or two as Sam does his deep breathing) Now, Sam, you are going to learn a relaxation technique called progressive muscle relaxation training. *Progressive* means "step-by-step," so you are going to learn a step-by-step process to help you to relax the major muscle groups in your body. Begin by taking a couple of long, deep, slow breaths, just like we practiced over the past week.

Sam (S): (Closes his eyes and breathes deeply and slowly for about six breathing cycles)

C: PMRT is based on the fact that the same muscle groups cannot be tense and relaxed at the same time. So by relaxing the muscle groups one at a time, we can achieve total body relaxation. The basic process is to take in a deep breath, hold it for about 5 to 7 seconds while you tense the specific group of muscles, and then release the tension in the muscles as you exhale. The relaxation of the exhale is coupled with the relaxing of the muscle tension so that, after you practice this long enough, you may be able to just exhale and feel the tension leave your muscles.

S: That would be great! And save some time.

C: Right. So it is important that we become very good at this procedure and practice hard so that in the future, you're right, you can save a lot of time. By the way, this whole procedure works something like a physics concept known as resting potential. You see, you can estimate the tension in your muscle on a scale of 1 to 10 or 1 to 100, just like we have done with other concepts. If the resting potential—the present state of tension in your muscle—is, say, a 7, then when you tense the muscle group, the tension will rise to, say, a 9 or 10. Then when you release the tension, the muscle will relax to, say, a 5 or 6 . . . more relaxed than it was before we started.

S: Oh, I see. So by tensing and relaxing a muscle, you can actually get it to relax deeper.

C: Right. Now let's start with the first muscle group. That's your right arm. But first take in a couple more long, deep, slow breaths. (Pause for three breathing cycles) Okay, take a deep breath . . . and hold it for about 5 seconds as you take your right arm and make a fist, curl your wrist, flex your forearm, and flex your bicep. But keep your shoulder and the rest of your body relaxed. Just tense your right arm. Then, after about 5 seconds, relax these muscles and release the tension as you slowly exhale. Also, concentrate on the feeling of relaxation in your arm as you release the tension. Great. Do you understand the process now? Deep breath in, hold for 5 to 7 seconds as you tense the muscle group, then relax the muscles as you exhale . . . Now take a breath in and exhale before we go on to the next muscle group . . .

S: Got it—sounds pretty simple.

Because Sam caught on quickly, the counselor now proceeds through the remaining muscle groups.

C: Okay. Let's try the left arm. Take a deep breath . . . and hold it for about 5 seconds as you make a fist, curl your wrist, flex your forearm, and flex your bicep. Then relax these muscles and release the tension as you exhale . . .

Now your right leg. Take a deep breath . . . and hold it for about 5 seconds as you curl your toes under, lift the ball of your foot to flex your shin, and flex your thigh muscle. Then relax these muscles and release the tension as you exhale . . .

Left leg. Take a deep breath . . . and hold it for about 5 seconds as you curl your toes under, lift the ball of your foot to flex your shin, and flex your thigh muscle. Then relax these muscles and release the tension as you exhale . . .

Your abdomen. Take a deep breath . . . and hold it for about 5 seconds as you pull in your stomach and bend your waist to lean your shoulders forward about 6 inches. Then relax these muscles and release the tension as you exhale . . .

Your lower back and shoulders. Take a deep breath . . . and hold it for about 5 seconds as you arch your back and push your elbows back while keeping your forearms parallel with the ground, effectively pushing your shoulder blades together. Then relax these muscles and release the tension as you exhale . . .

The neck is a little more complex because it includes several sets of complementary muscles. Take a deep breath . . . and hold it for about 5 seconds as you turn your head to the right and look out over your right shoulder. Then relax these muscles and release the tension as you exhale. Next, take a deep breath . . . and hold it for about 5 seconds as you turn your head to the left and look out over your left shoulder. Then relax these muscles and release the tension as you exhale. Take a deep breath . . . and hold it for about 5 seconds as you lean your head to the right and try to touch your right ear to your right shoulder. Then relax these muscles and release the tension as you exhale. Next, take a deep breath . . . and hold it for about 5 seconds as you lean your head to the left and try to touch your left ear to your left shoulder. Then relax these muscles and release the tension as you exhale . . .

Now let's do your lower face—that is, your jaw, lips, and tongue. Take a deep breath . . . and hold it for about 5 seconds as you clench your teeth, press your lips together, and push your tongue up to the roof of your mouth. Then relax these muscles and release the tension as you exhale . . .

Finally, your upper face, which includes your forehead, eyes, and nose. Take a deep breath . . . and hold it for about 5 seconds as you close your eyes tightly, wrinkle your nose, and knit your brows in a frown. Then relax these muscles and release the tension as you exhale . . .

Okay. We have relaxed all of the major muscle groups in your body. Scan your whole body again and search for any muscles that are still tense. Tense and relax them as we did before.

S: (Tenses and relaxes the muscles in his lower back and shoulders one more time).

C: Now take a few more long, deep, slow breaths to end the exercise and concentrate on the feeling of relaxation in your muscles, allowing them to become even more relaxed as you continue to breathe.

S: (Completes another three or so breathing cycles)

C: Okay. Open your eyes and guess what your homework is.

S: Three times a day, every day, until I see you next time . . .

USEFULNESS AND EVALUATION OF THE PMRT TECHNIQUE

PMRT is effective in addressing a wide array of physical and psychological complaints. PMRT is a technique often used on its own, and it is also combined with techniques such as systematic desensitization, assertion training, self-management programs, biofeedback-induced relaxation, hypnosis, meditation, and autogenic training (Corey, 2016). Progressive relaxation is also used to alleviate an array of clinical problems, including anxiety, stress, high blood pressure and other cardiovascular problems, migraine headaches, asthma, and insomnia. When people experience stress due to the pressures they feel from work or their lifestyles, PMRT can often be beneficial. PMRT also has been used effectively as a method of reducing anxiety in gifted children (Roome & Romney, 1985), as well as facilitating coping in the workplace, and to treat chronic low back pain (Carlson & Hoyle, 1993). Bornmann, Mitelman, and Beer (2007) implemented a 13.5-hour PMRT program into a group intervention with inpatient school-age clients, resulting in significantly less aggression and angry explosions in comparison with the treatment-as-usual condition. They concluded that aggression and crisis situations might be preventable if relaxation and other anger management techniques were implemented on a larger scale.

The outcome literature on PMRT shows robust effects in the treatment of internalizing disorders and symptoms. Klainin-Yobas, Oo, Yew, and Lau (2015) reported on the effectiveness of PMRT, music, and yoga in treatment of depression. Michalopoulou, Tzamalouka, Chrousos, and Darviri (2015) randomly exposed Greek women who had experienced intimate partner violence to an 8-week PMRT training and standard shelter services and reported that the treatment group self-reported a significant decrease in perceived stress ($d = .45$) but not depression or other ways of coping. Sundram, Dahlui, and Chinna (2016) found an effect size of $d = 0.6$ in stress reduction when PMRT was compared to a control receiving an educational pamphlet in a worksite health promotion program. PMRT has even been used to enhance academic performance. For example, Hubbard and Blyler (2016) found that PMRT reduced state anxiety in a clinical trial of graduate students, thereby improving academic performance.

PMRT has also been used with medical patients to help alleviate physical symptoms of stress, especially for pregnancy, migraines, and cancer treatment. Muller and Hammill (2015) conducted a systematic review of the literature and found strong evidence that PMRT is effective in reducing anxiety and stress during pregnancy. Kropp et al. (2017) found that PMRT was

an effective treatment for migraines. Liao et al. (2017) found that PMRT combined with music therapy reduced anxiety and depression in cancer patients when compared to a no-treatment control condition. And Pelekasis, Matsouka, and Koumarianou (2016) conducted a systematic review of clinical trials and determined that PMRT reduced anxiety and side effects of discomfort associated with chemotherapy, except for vomiting. However, they caution that they could locate only five studies and that the quality of those studies was quite low.

Comparative studies are of interest when discerning treatment efficacy. Stevens, Hynan, Allen, Beaun, and McCart (2007) conducted a meta-analysis of 26 studies of PMRT, biofeedback, and so-called complex psychotherapies and concluded that the more complex therapies provided a small but significant improvement over PMRT and biofeedback. Of course, more complex psychotherapies generally require higher levels of training or expertise, which is generally not the case with PMRT. With new technological innovations come new possibilities for service delivery. Eonta et al. (2011) used a client's smartphone to personalize a PMRT exercise to aid in the treatment of agoraphobia and generalized anxiety disorder, allowing the client to engage in a relaxation exercise while out in the community. Such interventions are likely to increase in popularity as mobile digital technologies continue to improve.

Kiselica and Baker (1992) provided cautions for professional counselors who intend to use progressive relaxation. They warn counselors that, for some clients, the relaxation procedures can actually induce anxiety. To help clients who have anxiety about relaxing, professional counselors should inform their clients that they may feel some uncommon sensations during the procedure. Professional counselors can also talk to their clients about how progressive relaxation can increase, rather than decrease, their control over themselves. For some anxious clients, keeping the lights on may ease their concerns. Other clients may recall vivid memories that can be either disturbing or unpleasant. In either case, the counselor needs to help the client process the memory. When completing the progressive muscle relaxation training procedure, some clients may fall asleep. To help prevent this, a counselor can tell the client to stay awake, can make the room brighter, or can change the client's position. The professional counselor also can develop a signal for the client to use to let the counselor know that she is relaxed but awake.

APPLICATION OF THE PMRT TECHNIQUE

Now apply the PMRT technique to a current client or student you are working with or revisit the brief case studies presented at the beginning of this book. How can you use the PMRT technique to address concerns and create movement in the counseling session?

CHAPTER 17

Mindfulness Meditation

ORIGINS OF THE MINDFULNESS MEDITATION TECHNIQUE

By nature, humans are self-aware and attentive. But people vary in these characteristics, and how they cultivate self-awareness and attention. Mindfulness involves purposeful and nonjudgmental attention to the present moment (Kabat-Zinn, 2016) and self-regulation of thoughts, feelings, sensations, sights, and sounds in the here and now. Mindfulness is an attitude of openness, acceptance, and curiosity in both internal and external experience (Kabat-Zinn, 2016; Keng, Smoski, & Robins, 2011).

After an earlier history embedded in spirituality and contemplative religions (e.g., Buddhism, Taoism, Hinduism; Keng et al., 2011), mindfulness practices have generalized into more universal and secular applications and are associated with numerous psychological and social benefits. Zen Buddhism was introduced into Western cultures in the 1950s and 1960s, and "mindfulness meditation" was applied to Western medical health by Dr. Jon Kabat-Zinn, who founded the Stress Reduction Clinic at the University of Massachusetts Medical School in 1979. Kabat-Zinn (2016) developed mindfulness-based stress reduction (MBSR) to promote physical and psychological healing through the interaction of mind and body and by getting people to become active participants in their own mental and physical health care.

Today, mindfulness is accomplished through both formal and informal meditation practices. *Formal meditation* practice involves meditation while sitting or lying down, such as through mindfulness movement (e.g., hatha yoga, walking meditation). *Informal meditation* (or "everyday meditation") transfers awareness and attention to everyday life. MBSR has given rise to other mindfulness-oriented approaches, including mindfulness-based cognitive therapy (MBCT), dialectical behavior therapy (DBT), and acceptance and commitment therapy (ACT).

HOW TO IMPLEMENT THE MINDFULNESS MEDITATION TECHNIQUE

Maintaining a personal practice of mindfulness meditation will help counselors develop competence in mindfulness meditation and likely will result in a stronger therapeutic counselor–client alliance. By design, mindfulness meditation helps counselors develop the essential counselor characteristics of empathy, congruence, compassion, nonjudgment, and authenticity (Campbell & Christopher, 2012). Schure, Christopher, and Christopher (2008) proposed that mindfulness meditation enhances counselor attentiveness, responsiveness, stress management, and tolerance for negative emotions.

Some clients may have a preconceived notion that meditation is mystical or religious (Kabat-Zinn, 2016). Therefore, before implementing mindfulness meditation activities, the counselor should first identify and address any client objections to the approach, focusing on the self-awareness and attentiveness to existence in the here and now. The needs of the client are preeminent, and mindfulness meditation, which is initially directive, quickly becomes client directed and modified to focus on client breath, body, sounds, and thoughts. It also can be individualized to client schedules. Truly, quality is much more important than quantity. Mindfulness meditation can be implemented in individual, group, or classroom settings; what is critical is that the space is quiet, uncluttered, distraction free, and comfortable, allowing participants to sit or lie down. The following step-by-step instructions suggested by Kabat-Zinn (2016) are meant as a general guide that can be readily adapted to individual needs.

- **Step 1: Invite the client to find a comfortable position.** Typical positions include being seated upright in a chair, cross-legged on a mat, or lying on one's back on the floor or couch. The *mudra*, or hand positioning, is associated with different types of energy, and clients are encouraged to experiment and gain comfort with different *mudras* (e.g., clasp hands, palms open, palms facing up or down). What is essential is that the hands be placed in a comfortable position (e.g., lap, thighs, over the heart) throughout the entire meditation period. Clients may keep their eyes open, closed, or half open. For beginners, closed-eye meditation is suggested to eliminate distractions. As one becomes more experienced, open-eye meditation is suggested because it more closely mirrors outside world awareness and living. During eyes-open training, clients should focus on a spot on the wall or floor a few feet away.

- **Step 2: Mentally prepare the client for meditation.** Meditation is not about achieving an "altered state" but about leaving one's normal state of being and becoming internally and externally aware. As such, clients must learn to trust the experience, rather than become concerned about "doing it the right way."

- **Step 3: Commence active meditation by** *inviting the bell* **to sound three times.** Counselors gently chime the bell three times, then use a calm and soothing voice to tell the client to clear the mind, relax, and breathe normally. Clients should breathe through the nose,

while centering attention on the breath, which anchors them to the present moment. Clients are reminded that they are alive in the present moment, which is the only moment that matters. As each breath enters and leaves the body, clients enter a state of relaxed awareness and focus on each unfolding moment.

- **Step 4: Guided exercises.** Counselors verbally guide the client through a visualization exercise focused on attention, thoughts, feelings, sensations, sounds, and movement. The focus and depth of the exercises are individualized according to the session duration, experience, and client needs. Clients should be reminded periodically to focus on the breath and to stay in the here and now. Counselors may suggest that clients focus on awareness and sensations of various body parts or feelings, and they can suggest tensing and relaxing various muscle groups that are often tense or painful, as in the progressive muscle relaxation technique (PMRT). Negative cognitions, self-talk, or emotions can also become the focus of meditation, with the goal of expanding the field of awareness to thoughts and emotions by directing the client to view pleasant or unpleasant thoughts without judgment. Clients then release the thoughts and emotions and return to the present moment and breathing awareness.

- **Step 5: Reinforcing a commitment to mindfulness and encouraging self-appreciation.** Mindfulness awareness requires a lot of practice. Practice allows clients to understand how personal narratives distort experiences, as well as how we interpret our awareness of self and others. Mindfulness meditation helps establish intrapersonal and interpersonal boundaries and serves as a reminder to carry mindfulness throughout one's day and life. Clients are also encouraged to express self-gratitude and self-praise for engaging in mindfulness meditation. The session is ended by *inviting the bell* by ringing the bell three times.

VARIATIONS OF THE MINDFULNESS MEDITATION TECHNIQUE

Formal mindfulness meditation enhances focus, compassion, and awareness of thoughts, feelings, and sensations. *Informal mindfulness meditation* allows clients to refocus, relax, and come into the here and now throughout the day, such as while driving, eating, showering, and studying. Meditation strategies can be adapted for any age group. Kabat-Zinn (2016) suggested several formal, structured variations including the following:

- *Mountain meditation and lake meditation* are imagery-based formal methods, respectively, of sitting and lying-down meditation. Through visualization, clients are empowered to embody the properties and virtues of the mountain and lake. Mountains imply the strength and stability of rock, despite changing weather patterns (e.g., emotions, challenges). Lakes represent the peacefulness of water, while acknowledging short-term disturbances to the surface (e.g., reactions, impulses).
- *Loving kindness meditation* helps develop interpersonal and intrapersonal positive emotions and compassion, leading to enhanced life satisfaction and reduced depressive symptoms. This is accomplished by meditating on phrases that evoke caring and positive regard, then displaying unconditional and unselfish kindness to others and oneself. Importantly, the caring is first directed inward, reasoning that one is able to love others only after self-respect is accomplished. The nurturing phrases are then directed outward, toward loved ones, neutral relationships, difficult relationships, and community.
- *Walking meditation* is mindfulness in motion. Whether slow or fast, the walking must be deliberate and focused on the here and now. Distractions, memories, and worries may enter awareness, but the client returns focus to the breathing and bodily sensations experienced in the present.

Mindfulness meditation also can be modified for children and adolescents. Of course, part of the modification is to ensure the developmental appropriateness of time guidelines (e.g., matching the number of minutes with age, like 7 minutes for 7-year-olds), and then increasing the amount of time as appropriate.

EXAMPLES OF THE MINDFULNESS MEDITATION TECHNIQUE

EXAMPLE 1: Rituals

Starting with a ritual provides motivation and brings one back to the present moment fully concentrated on the experiences of the session. Rituals also can be done at the close of a session as a wrap-up.

Invite the bell three times to begin the meditation.

Bring attention to your posture. Sit upright and tall, with your backbone erect but not stiff. Relax your shoulders. Open your breathing.

Gently close your eyes for a few moments; focus on the present moment. Take a few breaths. Inhale and exhale fully and slowly.

Survey your body and mind to determine how you feel right now. There is no need to change anything. There is no right or wrong way to think, feel, or be right now. Just note what is present. Relax and let go of judgments, strivings, and expectations.

Take a few breaths . . . breathing in and out. Connect the present moment with each breath and open your eyes whenever you feel comfortable.

Invite the bell three times to end the meditation.

EXAMPLE 2: Mindful eating

The Raisin Exercise is a very common mindfulness exercise often applied at the first session of every mindfulness-based program. The aim of this exercise is to become aware of automatic reactions to everyday rituals and to understand the beginner's mind attitude of mindfulness, which means experiencing something as if it is the first time. This helps us to "come into our senses."

Invite the bell three times to begin the meditation.

Mindful eating is about being aware in the present moment while eating. It focuses on the process of eating while noticing how each sense encounters the food.

The aim here is to consciously pay full attention to a raisin. While doing this exercise, if your mind starts to wander just notice the thoughts and bring your attention back to the raisin.

- First, take a raisin and hold it between your finger and thumb. Become curious about the raisin as if you have never seen one before, as if you had dropped in from another universe at this moment.
- Bring your full attention to the raisin. Feel the texture and weight of it in your hand.
- Explore this raisin with your senses.
- *Touching:* Hold it between your fingers and feel it in your palm and next to your face. Note the various sensations. Note its degree of softness or hardness.
- *Seeing:* Take time to really focus on the raisin. Gaze at it with care and full attention, examining the highlights where the light shines, the darker hollows, the folds and ridges, and any unique features. Note the color, color variations, shape, size, and texture. Hold the raisin up to the light and note any changes.
- *Smelling:* Smell the raisin. Note the strength and type of the smell. Hold the raisin beneath your nose. With each inhalation, take in any smell that may arise. Slowly breathe in several times and focus on the different smells. Does smelling the raisin trigger anything else in your body?
- *Listening:* Bring the raisin close to your ears and listen for any sounds as you move it between your fingers. Listen for other sounds or people, but keep your focus on the raisin.
- *Tasting:* Bring the raisin to your mouth. Gently move it around in your mouth. Notice the texture and sensations in your mouth. Notice whether you can taste anything without biting into it. Note any changes happening in your mouth in anticipation. Gently begin the first bite. Note the sensation of taste. Is it one kind

of taste or more than one that you are experiencing? Without swallowing yet, notice the bare sensations of taste and texture in your mouth and how these sensations may change over time, moment by moment. Chew as many times as you can before swallowing. Stay in the moment. (Pause for 15 to 30 seconds.) Now swallow the raisin and note the sensations related to swallowing.

Invite the bell three times to end the meditation.

Processing Questions

- Compared to how you usually eat, how was this raisin experience?
- Rate your satisfaction with eating the raisin.
- How would eating be different if you ate this way most of the time?
- How could this experience modify your attitude toward eating?

EXAMPLE 3: Body and breath

Our body is always in the present moment. Becoming aware of our body and connecting to it rather than thinking about it makes us get in touch with "the now." Differences between muscle relaxation exercises and becoming aware of our body and body scan is not only the focus on our body and relaxing it but also experiencing whatever arises in our body and accepting all the bodily sensations in a kind and compassionate manner without judging and trying to change or fix the experiences.

Invite the bell three times to begin the meditation.

Bring attention to your posture. Sit upright and tall, with your spine erect but not stiff. Relax your shoulders and open your chest to your breathing. Rest your hands comfortably on your lap or knees. You may keep your eyes closed or open.

Mentally check your body from head to toe and consciously relax any tension. Notice how your body feels in this moment. Take a moment to notice any sounds in the distance and the temperature of the room.

Gently bring your attention to the breathing process. As you breathe in, notice that you are breathing in. And as you breathe out, notice that you are breathing out. Keep your attention and awareness on the breath. As you breathe, be aware of the rise and fall of your chest and abdomen. Attend to every detail of the inhalation and the exhalation. You do not need to manipulate your breathing. There is no right or wrong way to do this. Keep focusing on your breath in silence. Take note of your whole body and the sensations you are feeling.

As you keep your attention on the breathing process, your mind may wander. When you notice your mind has wandered, silently acknowledge the wandering mind and gently bring your attention back to the breathing process without judgment. Each time, let go of what came before and allow your attention to the breath to be a new and fresh experience.

Gently open your eyes, and take note of how your body, mind, and heart feel.

Invite the bell three times to end the meditation.

EXAMPLE 4: Using metaphors in mindfulness

Compassion and kindly living: The intention of this exercise is to experience compassion for yourself through phrases of well-being and becoming aware of the feeling of peace after these phrases.

Invite the bell three times to begin the meditation.

Picture yourself as you are now. Smile at your own image, and give your body the message of joy and ease. Bring tenderness and love to this image. Bring your attention toward yourself. Repeat these phrases of well-being, saying one every 15 seconds or so:

- May I be free of anger, resentment, hatred.
- May I be filled with compassion and kindness.
- May I be safe and protected from pain and suffering.
- May I be peaceful.
- May I live with ease and be free.
- May I be safe.
- May I be free of fear.
- May I be healthy.

Now bring your attention back to your breath and allow your heart to stay open to the love and kindness you have generated. Allow this kindness to stay with you for the rest of the day. Open your eyes.

Invite the bell three times to end the meditation.

USEFULNESS AND EVALUATION OF THE MINDFULNESS MEDITATION TECHNIQUE

Mindfulness-based approaches are used in counseling to address a variety of psychological symptoms for individuals or groups and have been effectively applied across a range of populations. The literature reports many recent randomized controlled trials (RCTs) of mindfulness meditation on a wide range of physical and emotional conditions. A meta-analysis of 47 mindfulness meditation clinical trials conducted by Goyal et al. (2014) concluded that meditation interventions resulted in small to medium reductions in symptoms of anxiety ($d = .38$), depression ($d = .22$), and pain ($d = .33$), but they were no more effective than other active treatments such as exercise, medication, or CBT. Goyal et al. also found nonsignificant effects on positive mood, attention, substance use, eating habits, sleep, and weight.

An 8-week MBSR training program that incorporated formal and informal mindfulness meditation was associated with reduced depression, anger, anxiety, rumination, general distress, post-traumatic avoidance symptoms, and cognitive disorganization (Anderson, Lau, Segal, & Bishop, 2007). Long- and short-term mindfulness meditation practices were associated with increases in psychologic al well-being, including greater self-compassion and sense of well-being (Carmody, Baer, Lykins, & Olendzki, 2009).

Because Kabat-Zinn originally applied MBSR in a medical clinic, many studies point to the physical and mental health benefits of MBSR. For example, mindfulness meditation may improve occupational functi oning and reduce use of healthcare services in adults with generalized anxiety disorder (Hoge et al., 2017). Also, Guardino et al. (2014) conducted an RCT and determined that mindfulness meditation reduced stress during pregnancy. For pain control, mindfulness meditation helps alleviate fibromyalgia in women (Cash et al., 2015) and chronic pain in children (Waelde et al., 2017).

Mindfulness meditation is also helpful in addressing sleep problems. Slomski (2015) found that meditation promoted better sleep in older adults. An RCT conducted by Black, O'Reilly, Olmstead, Breen, and Irwin (2015) found that mindfulness meditation improved sleep quality in individuals with sleep disturbance. Finally, a meta-analysis of six RCTs conducted by Gong et al. (2016) determined that mindfulness meditation significantly improved sleep quality and total wake time, but had no effect on "sleep onset latency, total sleep time, wake after sleep onset, sleep efficiency total wake time" (p. 1).

Finally, MBSR also has wide application in school settings. School-age youth receiving MBSR showed increased resilience to stress (Zenner, Herrnleben-Kurz, & Walach, 2014). In addition, Sidhu (2014) found mindfulness meditation promising for increasing the attention span of children with ADHD.

APPLICATION OF THE MINDFULNESS MEDITATION TECHNIQUE

Now apply the mindfulness meditation technique to a current client or student you are working with or revisit the brief case studies presented at the beginning of this book. How can you use the mindfulness meditation technique to address concerns and create movement in the counseling session?

Techniques Based on Humanistic-Phenomenological Approaches

Humanistic or phenomenological approaches are very relationship oriented, with a focus clearly on current and future functioning as opposed to past events and problems. This approach also stems from the realization that all people possess the freedom and responsibility to grow and develop. Indeed, humans have an innate capacity for self-growth and self-actualization (Rogers, 1995). But at the core of the humanistic approach is the client–counselor relationship and therapeutic alliance. Counselors must be willing to fully enter the subjective world of the client in order to focus on presenting issues from the perspective of the client.

Carl Rogers (1995) is the best-known proponent of humanistic counseling; he is most noted for developing the nondirective, person-centered counseling approach. Person-centered counseling is nondirective and useful for facilitating personal growth, adjustment, socialization, and autonomy. People strive to integrate their internal and external experiences, but unhealthy social or psychological influences can hinder self-actualization and lead to conflicts, especially when basic needs, such as the need for social approval, are lacking.

Rogers (1995) identified three essential counselor characteristics—empathy, genuineness, unconditional positive regard—needed to create a nonthreatening, anxiety-free relationship that will allow clients to resolve conflicts and reach deeper levels of self-understanding. Like mindfulness-based approaches, humanistic-phenomenological approaches focus on the here and now and are free of judgmental attitudes. Critics of humanistic-existential approaches indicate that insights do not usually lead to solutions. Successful actions lead to solutions. Still, humans frequently want to understand their internal world, including thoughts, feelings, and mood states, and humanistic techniques help facilitate this self-understanding and search for internally designed (i.e., intrinsic) motivations.

The four techniques covered in this section include self-disclosure, confrontation, motivational interviewing (MI), and strength bombardment. Self-disclosure, or, in this case, counselor disclosure, has been controversially applied to counseling since Freud's era, and the research on its application is admittedly sparse. Still, when skillfully applied, counselor disclosure can improve the therapeutic alliance and help create client insight. In a way, this makes perfect sense: If we believe that clients can benefit from the experiences of others, why can't previous experiences of the counselor provide that benefit? Confrontation is also an inevitable part of counseling and, when skillfully applied, helps move clients toward effective life changes. Thankfully, gone are the times when counselors used confrontation to force clients toward movement. Today, counselors are much more likely to use indirect confrontational styles or empathic confrontation (Ivey, Ivey, & Zalaquett, 2018) to encourage and facilitate client change.

Motivational interviewing is a process developed by Miller and Rollnick (2013) to help motivate clients to pursue agreed-upon changes. Miller and Rollnick identified four general principles of MI: expressing empathy, developing discrepancies, rolling with resistance, and supporting self-efficacy. Clients are helped to develop discrepancies through four person-centered techniques recalled using the acronym OARS: open-ended questions, affirmations, reflecting skills, and summaries. Originally developed for use with clients with addictions, motivational interviewing has been generalized for use with wide-ranging client issues for which motivation to change is a stumbling block. Finally, strength bombardment (when used with groups) and self-affirmation (when used with individuals) are used to underscore client strengths and positive attributes, serve as a wellspring of resilience and resources when clients encounter trials and challenges, or simply summarize and reaffirm client gifts, positive attributes, and characteristics. Strength bombardment is commonly used as a culminating activity during group-work termination.

MULTICULTURAL IMPLICATIONS OF HUMANISTIC-PHENOMENOLOGICAL APPROACHES

Person-centered counseling and other humanistic-phenomenological approaches have had a significant impact on diverse cultural groups around the world, but these approaches are not without critics. Multicultural limitations of the humanistic approach include lack of structure, difficulty translating core conditions to practice, and focus on internal rather than external evaluation (Corey, 2016). On the positive side, the humanistic approach discourages diagnoses and focuses on the client's personal frame of reference.

The counselor's role is to help the client gain insights and recognize what the client knows already

works. Humanistic approaches directly relate to feelings and issues presented by clients from disenfranchised or historically oppressed groups who may feel discouraged or alienated, and these approaches are therefore respectful of individual clients, their worldviews, and various cultural heritages. The more emotive aspects of the humanistic approach may be particularly appealing to women. Conversely, interactions that are highly intense and require self-disclosure of feelings and personal and/or family information may not be appropriate for individuals of Arab or Asian descent because individuals from these cultures may not feel comfortable expressing strong emotions. Thus, counselors using this approach must take additional care to gauge a client's comfort level by starting with commonly used techniques (Hays & Erford, 2018).

Humanistic approaches are not brief approaches and often require many months of counseling. The speed of these approaches may be problematic for some individuals, especially those who may be unable to afford the time and money required for a long-term therapeutic approach. In addition, these approaches often do not pursue concrete outcomes, making some clients uncomfortable investing the time required for changes to occur.

Humanistic approaches emphasize rapport, therapeutic alliance, and the sharing of intense emotions and intimate life details, involve present-focused, nonthreatening processes that many clients find empowering, and may appeal to clients from a wide array of cultural backgrounds. On the other hand, some cultures may discourage the sharing of family-related issues (e.g., Latino culture) or exploration or exhibition of intense emotional displays (e.g., Asian culture). The humanistic approach transfers meaningfully across numerous cultural contexts, including gender, racial, ethnic, socioeconomic, disability, and sexual orientation contexts, although clients from some cultures (e.g., Middle Eastern, Hispanic, Asian) may be uncomfortable with the nondirective approach (Hays & Erford, 2018).

CHAPTER 18

Self-Disclosure

ORIGINS OF THE SELF-DISCLOSURE TECHNIQUE

Many theoretical approaches to counseling have defined a position, or made recommendations, on counselor self-disclosure to the client. Some, like humanistic approaches, view counselor disclosure as a positive occurrence that shows the warm, real, human side of counselors and helps to build a therapeutic alliance (Williams, 2009); others, like psychodynamic approaches, view counselor disclosure as a potential contaminant that disempowers the client. Regardless, intentional or unintentional disclosure is part of the counseling process, many types of disclosure and goals of disclosure exist, and disclosures may or may not be noticed by clients. Thus, professional counselors are wise to become knowledgeable about self-disclosure to ensure proper usage—or strategic avoidance. Counselor disclosure has been embraced most prominently by the humanistic approach to counseling and has been included in this section.

HOW TO IMPLEMENT THE SELF-DISCLOSURE TECHNIQUE

As it pertains to informed consent, self-disclosure is an essential element of ethical counseling (Barnett, 2011). Counselors have an ethical responsibility to inform clients and students about the counselor's education, experience, background, approach, and other factors that could lead a client to determine that the counselor can appropriately address client goals. Objects that professional counselors keep in their offices may reveal a personal side to the counselor, as does informing clients of life situations that

may influence the seamless provision of services (e.g., death in the family, birth of a child, vacations). These instances of self-disclosure are intentional and unavoidable.

The professional counselor's appearance and cultural factors also disclose many details about the counselor, some serving to enhance or detract from the therapeutic alliance. Counselor race, age, gender, cultural dress, physical ability/disability, speech or language capabilities, and even whether or not one wears a wedding ring convey information and values about the counselor (Barnett, 2011). Cultural and appearance characteristics often lead clients to form assumptions, impressions, and even stereotypes about a counselor. These assumptions may be correct and provide valuable input about the potential of the counseling relationship to the client, or they may be incorrect and thwart counseling progress unnecessarily.

There are two primary ways to implement self-disclosure intentionally. The first method involves sharing a personal experience with the client with the goal of demonstrating genuineness and authenticity, with the ultimate goal of improving the therapeutic alliance (Rogers, 1995). In these circumstances, the counselor may have experienced an event or internal struggle similar to what a client expressed and hopes to develop and strengthen the bond with the client by expressing that similarity, thus validating the client's struggles.

A second method of intentional self-disclosure involves sharing genuine and authentic feelings that the professional counselor has in the session, such as feelings of pride, sorrow, or transference. This type of disclosure may help clients view their experiences more subjectively and may counteract negative client self-perceptions or interpretations (Aron, 2001). As such, the counselor would share and compare his understanding and point of view with the client's, helping both parties gain valuable insights into the counseling process and topic.

When using either method, it is vital that a solid therapeutic alliance already be in place and that the goal of the disclosure is to help the client; the potential for advertent and inadvertent abuse could exist if the disclosure is not used properly and with the right intentions. Open and honest consultation with other trusted professionals can help counselors decide appropriate and effective use of self-disclosure.

Accidental (inadvertent, unintentional) self-disclosure is an additional type of counselor disclosure of which professional counselors should be aware. Counselors are trained to be accepting and nonjudgmental, but clients sometimes say the darnedest things, and even seasoned counselors sometimes wince or gasp! After all, we are products of our own values, beliefs, and backgrounds, which is to say that counselors are humans too, and we all make mistakes. Barnett (2011) discussed how unintentional reactions and disclosures can harm or even cause ruptures in the therapeutic alliance. Expressions of counselor disapproval, shock, or surprise as well as other reactions can violate the neutrality of the counselor that clients often depend on as a pillar of a safe and trusting environment. It happens to all of us from time to time, and it is vital for counselors to immediately assess the impact of an accidental self-disclosure while in session with the client and repair any damage to the relationship that the accidental disclosure may have created.

VARIATIONS OF THE SELF-DISCLOSURE TECHNIQUE

Self-disclosure is a dynamic and versatile technique when skillfully applied, and different approaches have differing perspectives on its appropriate applications. For example, humanists may view self-disclosure as a way to equalize client–counselor power dynamics (Williams, 1997), existentialists may view it as a way to model for or coach

the client (Yalom, 2009), and feminists may see it as a way to help the client choose an appropriate counselor and understand or augment the power relationship between client and counselor (Simi & Mahalik, 1997). Contemporary psychodynamic practitioners view self-disclosure as unavoidable and are exploring how best to integrate it into an expanded approach (Farber, 2006), and contemporary cognitive-behavioral counselors use self-disclosure to normalize client experiences and fight negative thought patterns (Ziv-Beiman, 2013). Regardless, research supports the skillful application of self-disclosure when the therapeutic alliance is already strong in order to create insight, bonding, and healing (Farber, 2003, 2006).

EXAMPLES OF THE SELF-DISCLOSURE TECHNIQUE

Following are three brief examples of the use of self-disclosure in counseling sessions.

EXAMPLE 1: The case of Kim

Kim was referred to counseling by her physician for anxiety. Kim's father has long abused alcohol, and the perpetual stress of her home life has begun to affect her mental health. During their third session together, the counselor uses self-disclosure to normalize the client's feelings about a tough situation.

Kim (K):   I can't even believe what happened this weekend. I feel stupid for even having this story to tell.

Counselor (C):   This is a safe place to share what you're going through. I'm not judging you.

K: Okay . . . So on Friday, my mom and dad got in an argument. She was yelling at him for drinking again, not like it helps. So he leaves, and we wait for him to come home for like an hour. Then my mom is like "Forget him. Let's go to the movies." So I'm thinking cool, me and Mom can still have a normal life even with Dad drinking like crazy. This is a good thing, right? So we get some dinner and go to the movies together, and when we get home my dad is passed out in the driveway. Naked!

He was naked in the driveway! I mean, this is crazy, right? We were gone for like four hours. How long was he there? How did this happen? I've never seen anyone else's dad passed out naked in their driveway! Just me! Is this really happening to me?

C: Wow . . . So I'm not sure if you are angry or confused. Tell me more about this.

K: I don't know if I'm confused, but I'm definitely . . . baffled. I mean, this can't be real. When we saw him, all I could do was rub my eyes and hope that what I was seeing would go away. Like, this can't be real. It just can't. I must be crazy.

C: But you did see him. This is real.

K: No, it can't be. I must be crazy.

C: You saw it. Your mom saw it. You're here telling me now. You are not crazy. It did happen.

K: I must have the most messed-up life ever. I have got to be crazy.

C: One of the stresses of substance abuse is the potential for anything to happen.

K: I just don't believe it.

C: I believe it.

K: I don't see how. This is literally the stuff of movies and Internet memes. This stuff doesn't happen in real life.

C: I believe it does, Kim. I grew up with a mother who drank too much, and although she was never naked in the driveway, she did some pretty unbelievable stuff. I was often confused, like you said: baffled, angry, embarrassed. But you can't let it make you doubt your sanity. They are the ones doing these crazy things because they are under the effects of alcohol. You are not crazy. You saw alcohol abuse, and that can make people do crazy things.

In this disclosure, the counselor explained how she felt as the client did by citing an example from her personal life. She did not go into detail and kept the focus on the client. The client now understands that the counselor has had similar experiences and truly understands how she feels.

EXAMPLE 2: The case of Sam

Sam, a middle-age adult, is in counseling for anger problems. He is receiving court-ordered counseling after his arrest for disorderly conduct following a fight at a local convenience store. Sam is single and lives with his younger brother, Scott. During their sixth session together, the counselor uses self-disclosure to help Sam uncover how he really feels about his progress in counseling.

Counselor (C):   Sam, last time we talked, I asked you to think about what makes you happy. Were you able to think about this?

Sam (S):   Yeah, I thought about it. I like going to work. It makes me feel useful, and I make money. That makes me happy. I also like it when my truck is clean. I'm always happy after I wash my truck.

C: So accomplishing things makes you happy. You like to work and have something to show for it.

S: Yes, I like to get the rewards for my hard work.

C: Well, you have done a lot of hard work here. What will your reward be?

S: I don't know. I don't have to come back . . .

C: There are no other rewards for your hard work here?

S: No. I only came here because the judge said I had to!

C: Over the past six weeks, we have talked a lot about how you have gotten yourself in trouble when you got angry. You weren't proud of any of those stories. But listening to you now, talking about the rewards you get from your accomplishments, you are happy. Can you not see the reward you are getting from this accomplishment?

S: No, I can't.

C: This makes me feel very sad and afraid for you, Sam.

S: Well, I feel that way too.

C: What are you sad about, Sam?

S: I'm not really sad. But I am afraid.

C: What are you afraid of, Sam?

S: I'm afraid of turning back into the old me.

In this example, the counselor shared his feelings about Sam's attitude toward his progress in counseling. This helped Sam to see that he has similar feelings as the counselor.

EXAMPLE 3: The case of Marsha

This last example shows how a counselor may accidentally self-disclose personal feelings and/or values to clients, as well as how to identify and rectify this occurrence to prevent a rupture or tear in the therapeutic relationship. Marsha is a recent college graduate who has just started a high-pressure job on Wall Street. She moved alone to New York City and has not had time to make new friends. She is seeking counseling for depression. In their second session together, the counselor accidentally reacts in a way that lets Marsha know that the counselor does not approve of her choices. It is then up to the counselor to address this situation and ensure that it does not affect the therapeutic alliance.

Marsha (M):   Well I managed to meet some co-workers for drinks after work on Thursday. I thought it was weird to go out on a weeknight, but I went anyway.

Counselor (C):   And did you enjoy yourself?

M: I mean, I guess so. They were drinking so much. I kept up with them because I wanted them to like me, but before I knew it I was really drunk.

C: So what did you do? Order something to eat?

M: No. I went to the bathroom and made myself throw up. Then I had a glass of water.

At this point, the counselor unintentionally reacts with a look of shock to Marsha's statement about drinking too much to be liked and making herself throw up. Marsha finishes her story with very little detail and has nothing else she wants to tell the counselor. The counselor realizes what has occurred and addresses the issue head-on with Marsha.

C: Marsha, something has happened between us that made you decide you do not wish to share with me anymore. This issue must be addressed so that we can continue to work together effectively. Perhaps it was the surprise and concern I felt and likely displayed when you told me that you made yourself throw up at the bar, after drinking more than you thought you should have. I want to share with you why I feel this way. This type of behavior concerns me because many women who engage in this type of behavior cause harm to themselves. I would like to talk more about why you acted as you did so that I can understand your reasoning. I am not judging you. I only want to ensure that you are safe and will continue to be safe in other future situations.

One hopes that Marsha now understands why the counselor reacted the way she did and will now feel more comfortable discussing this experience. Although a potential rupture has occurred, the counseling relationship is not broken by this misstep; indeed, there is great potential for growth in the alliance between Marsha and her counselor.

USEFULNESS AND EVALUATION OF THE SELF-DISCLOSURE TECHNIQUE

Self-disclosure has enjoyed a roller-coaster ride of controversy in counseling history, and various paradigms view its use differently. Although outcome research is mixed, it is clear that the appropriateness of self-disclosure is situation dependent, and when, how much, and how self-disclosure occurs have much to do with your counseling style and the topics under discussion. Indeed, client perceptions of the therapeutic alliance have a differential impact (Myers & Hayes, 2006): Clients in positive alliances perceived the counselor disclosures to be more expert, whereas clients in negative alliances perceived the counselor disclosures as less expert. Indeed, Audet and Everall (2010) found the effects of disclosure on clients to be quite complex and identified three primary themes in their research: (1) It helps to form an initial connection between client and counselor, (2) it indicates the counselor is authentic and genuine, and (3) it serves to engage clients in the therapeutic alliance. However, Audet and Everall urged further study due to their small sample size and potential individual differences. Ziv-Beiman, Keinan, Livneh, Malone, and Shahar (2017) differentiated between immediate self-disclosure (i.e., expressing feelings toward the relationship or person in session) and nonimmediate self-disclosure (i.e., expressing information related to the therapist's life outside the treatment) and found that the former created a more favorable client perception of the relationship and therapeutic alliance.

Several studies explored the effects of counselor self-disclosure with diverse clients. Kronner (2013) found, in general, that counselors and gay clients rated higher levels of therapeutic connectedness when counselor self-disclosure was increased. East Asian American clients working with European American counselors rated disclosures, in general, as more helpful when they related to strategy as opposed to facts, approval, or counselor feelings (Kim et al., 2003). Finally, although more research is certainly needed, from a brain and neuroscience perspective, Quillman (2012) indicated counselor disclosure has great potential for helping clients connect in deeper, more meaningful ways with both their counselors and themselves.

APPLICATION OF THE SELF-DISCLOSURE TECHNIQUE

Now apply the self-disclosure technique to a current client or student you are working with or revisit the brief case studies presented at the beginning of this book. How can you use the self-disclosure technique to address concerns and create movement in the counseling session?

CHAPTER 19

Confrontation

ORIGINS OF THE CONFRONTATION TECHNIQUE

The confrontation technique was originally used most prominently in Gestalt therapy, but it has emerged in numerous other approaches and is comfortably ensconced in humanistic-existential and microskills approaches (Ivey, Ivey, & Zalaquett, 2018). Perls used a highly confrontational approach in Gestalt therapy (see Section 3) while trying to help clients recognize avoidance behaviors. Corey (2016) reported that many clients (and counselors) perceived the approach to be overly harsh and insensitive. In the modern era, the confrontation technique has evolved to a more kind and compassionate usage and is now conveyed with greater empathy in a relational context.

HOW TO IMPLEMENT THE CONFRONTATION TECHNIQUE

Empathic confrontation (Ivey et al., 2018), also known as the challenge technique, can be implemented to help clients analyze their narratives for discrepancies and contradictions between words and deeds. Theoretically, these contradictions create dissonance and motivate clients to resolve the discrepancies and become "unstuck." Effective application of confrontation and empathic confrontation help clients change their behavior, become congruent, and live a healthier, more fully functioning lifestyle (Corey, 2016; Ivey et al., 2018; MacCluskie, 2010; Young, 2013).

Some Initial Considerations

When skillfully applied, confrontation can lead to effective client outcomes (Bratter, Esparat, Kaufman, & Sinsheimer, 2008; Corey, 2016; Ivey et al., 2018; MacCluskie, 2010). But unskillful application, in the wrong context, or without an appropriate therapeutic alliance, can result in tears or ruptures in the counseling relationship. Many novice counselors are hesitant to use confrontation, viewing it as harsh and potentially damaging to the therapeutic alliance. However, movement in counseling is often accomplished by leading clients to understand how their behaviors and choices are affecting them, and skillful, empathic, and compassionate application of confrontation is one way to help clients understand the consequences of their behaviors and actions. Key to promoting client understanding is active listening and helping clients to express their attitudes and behaviors, interpersonal and intrapersonal conflicts, and irrational beliefs and defense mechanisms that keep them stuck where they are. Once discussed openly, empathic confrontation can be used to create forward momentum and get the client unstuck.

Underlying the effective implementation of confrontation is a strong therapeutic alliance. Client–counselor trust and respect must be strong for confrontation to be received at all, let alone successfully. Thus, relationship building via person-centered strategies and approaches is a key prerequisite to confrontation. Mutual trust, respect, understanding, and genuine caring are accomplished through unconditional positive regard. It is the strength of this foundational relationship that creates the client motivation to work with the professional counselor, especially when confrontations occur about discrepancies between what the client says and how the client behaves (Corey, 2016; MacCluskie, 2010).

Timing is a second critical component of successful confrontation. Factors around timing ordinarily include the stage of the counseling process in which the confrontation is implemented, client readiness, client behavioral risk factors, and client emotional stability. Inappropriately gauging the timing could damage the therapeutic alliance (MacCluskie, 2010). Furthermore, confrontation should not be antagonistic or harsh; instead, counselor training in the use of confrontation must reflect caring and support of the client, focusing on positive, not negative, client characteristics in order to help clients recognize their discrepancies in thought and action and become motivated to address these discrepancies.

Thus, a strong relationship that reflects genuine understanding and care is more likely to result in empathic confrontations that motivate clients to self-examine discrepancies among thoughts, feelings, and behaviors and to address those discrepancies in ways that will promote client progress. The focus on client strengths and positives, coupled with active counselor support, increases the likelihood of successful outcomes and therapeutic movement. With this as prerequisite context, we are now ready to analyze the steps of the confrontation technique.

How to Implement the Confrontation Technique

A four-step process is ordinarily used to implement a confrontation technique: (1) listen for discrepancies, (2) summarize and clarify, (3) confront empathically, and (4) observe and evaluate. During each of these steps, professional counselors should continue to use other person-centered or counseling microskills to understand client thoughts, feelings, and behaviors, including active listening, paraphrasing, reflection of feelings, and summarizing (Ivey et al., 2018; Young, 2017).

Step 1: The counselor actively listens to the client for discrepancies, ambivalence, and mixed messages (Young, 2017). Ivey et al. (2018) identified six types of discrepancies counselors should be listening for, including discrepancies between a client's (1) verbal and nonverbal messages, (2) beliefs and experiences, (3) values and behavior, (4) talk and behavior, (5) experiences and plans, and (6) verbal messages.

Step 2: The counselor helps to summarize and clarify client discrepancies, then uses additional observation and listening skills to help the client resolve internal or external conflicts caused by these discrepancies. It is often helpful to bring these internal and external conflicts to the surface and to discuss them openly, including how the conflicts are helping to keep the client stuck, what needs are being met by perpetuating the discrepancy, and what needs are not being met because of the discrepancy. In other words, the professional counselor strives to identify the conflicts, identify client needs, and help the client work through discrepancies in a supportive, empathic way.

Step 3: The counselor confronts the client empathically (Ivey et al., 2018). This is done in a manner acceptable to the client. Knowing the manner that may or may not be acceptable to the client takes a great deal of insight, skill, and experience. Ordinarily, a confrontation can be best integrated into a session using positively focused questioning and reflection of feelings. The contradiction should be challenged in a way that gently finesses the issue. For example, "On one hand, you said _____, whereas on the other hand, you said _____" or "You say that you _____, but you actually did _____ (behavior)." This helps clients to recognize where the discrepancy lies—using positive, supportive language—and leads the client to consider the natural and logical consequences of meeting or not meeting the challenge to change.

Step 4: The counselor observes and evaluates the effectiveness of the confrontation. Two scales of confrontation evaluation have been suggested: the client change scale (CCS; Ivey et al., 2018) and the client adjustment scale (CAS; Young, 2017). CCS uses a five-level scale to determine effectiveness of the confrontation and where the client is in the change process: (1) client denied the discrepancy, (2) client examined only a portion of the discrepancy, (3) client accepted the confrontation but no change resulted, (4) client is ready to try new solutions to the discrepancy, and (5) client accepted the discrepancy and is generating and applying new behaviors to address the discrepancy. Although some clients follow a linear progression through this process, others do not, depending on the type or depth of conflict experienced. The CAS (Young, 2017) is a three-level assessment: (1) client denied the discrepancy, (2) client accepted only part of the discrepancy/confrontation, and (3) client fully accepted the confrontation and acts on the discrepancy. When clients reach the final levels of these processes, they are ready to get unstuck, change behaviors, and experience a more positive view of themselves.

In cases where the confrontation is not accepted by the client, the counselor should revert to additional listening, questioning, and clarifying, and perhaps use less direct language in framing the next challenge (Ivey et al., 2018; MacCluskie, 2010; Young, 2017). It is essential to keep the therapeutic alliance at a high level throughout this process and to assess whether tears or ruptures have occurred.

VARIATIONS OF THE CONFRONTATION TECHNIQUE

As with many other counseling techniques, the effective implementation of confrontation must be done with cultural sensitivity. Clients from cultures that value more direct and open confrontation (e.g., some European Americans, some males) often respond to confrontation in counseling more positively because it resembles real-life interactions that the clients encounter in the media and everyday life (Ivey et al., 2018; MacCluskie, 2010). Clients from other cultural backgrounds often prefer a more subtle and polite, less directive approach to confrontation (e.g., some Asian Americans, some females). Client gender is a particularly important consideration given the variations in how some men and women view the roles of power and structure in society. Again, understanding a client's worldview and cultural intersectionality, and building a strong client–counselor bond are critical to effective implementation of the confrontation technique.

A variation on this technique is self-confrontation, wherein clients confront themselves after direct observations of their behaviors and statements (usually through video recordings) and which leads to self-identification of feelings, defenses, and behaviors (Popadiuk, Young, & Valach, 2008; Young, 2017). In a study of self-confrontation with suicidal clients, Popadiuk et al. (2008) used video-recorded focus groups and video-recorded self-confrontation sessions to allow clients to see their contradictions in talk, feelings, and behaviors. Clients found self-confrontation to be a powerful mechanism for gaining immediate feedback and to work on both cognitions and feelings. Clinicians believed the video recordings allowed clients to see things and develop insights in ways not possible in a standard counseling session.

In a family counseling adaptation, Gold and Hartnett (2004) used strength-focused confrontations to allow the family to challenge more powerful members of a family hierarchy and thereby to focus on the identified client's strengths as opposed to failures or problems. This leads the entire family to consider a more balanced approach to understanding family context and environment, as well as helping to reframe potential family problems and solutions.

Counselors' different theoretical approaches can also lead to differing implementation strategies of confrontation (Strong & Zeman, 2010). For example, counselors using an Adlerian approach ordinarily confront a client's private logic and behavior, whereas counselors using a rational-emotive behavior therapy (REBT) approach use disputation procedures aimed at challenging irrational client thoughts and beliefs. Some clients may find the use of humor or exaggeration by the professional counselor to be less harsh or "mean" and more fun, which helps put client behaviors or discrepancies in a more positive light and allows clients to own the discrepancies (Young, 2017).

EXAMPLE OF THE CONFRONTATION TECHNIQUE

The professional counselor and Sandra are entering their fourth session and have developed a very strong therapeutic alliance. Sandra is a 41-year-old female who is seeking counseling after her twin sons went off to college. Sandra has been a stay-at-home mom since her sons were born, but now that the boys are in college, her husband would like Sandra to get a part-time job to keep her busy and help with the added expenses of college. Sandra doesn't see why she should get a job, yet she has also shared that she often feels lonely and down when her husband is at work. When asked how she feels about her sons leaving home, Sandra says that she is happy. She is proud that the boys got into good colleges and that they seem to be adjusting well. The counselor believes Sandra may not be dealing with the feelings of sadness and loss that accompany a transition, such as children leaving the home.

Counselor (C):   Sandra, last time we talked, you shared with me your daily routine since your sons have left for college. You said that you enjoy having less laundry to take care of, but that you often feel lonely while your husband is at work. Would you like to continue to discuss this?

Sandra (S):   Yes I would. I've had simply the worst week. I think I may be coming down with something. I haven't had any energy at all. I've had to take a nap almost every day. I don't understand. I've always been a fireball! Running around to football practice, swimming, and tutoring. It's a good thing my sons aren't here—I wouldn't be any good to them!

C: So feeling this way—tired and sometimes lonely and sad—is new to you?

S: Yes. I've never felt this way before. It's a drag!

C: How do you think you should be feeling, Sandra?

S: I should be pretty carefree right now. My boys are out on their own. I have way less to do at home.

C: Sandra, how often do you think about your boys?

S: Oh, every day, of course.

C: And you miss them.

S: Of course! But this is a part of life. They grow up. I'm so happy for them. I'm so proud of them. (Sandra has pulled her arms around herself and has begun to stroke her arm with her hand, seeming to try to comfort herself.)

C: (Initiating an empathic confrontation and pointing out the discrepancy) Sandra, I hear you say you are a proud mother and happy that your boys are off in college, but you also say that you are grateful to be relieved of some of the housework that goes along with caring for a big family. And you don't seem happy right now talking about your boys growing up.

S: Of course I'm happy. Everyone wants their children to grow up and be successful. Going off to college is the first step. I couldn't be anything but happy.

C: You are happy for your children. But how do you feel for yourself?

S: I feel proud. (Sandra sits up and puffs her chest out proudly as she says this, but then she sinks back into the seat and pulls her arms around herself again.)

C: What about the changes that this transition has caused in your day-to-day life? What about your husband's expectation that you will get a part-time job now that you don't have children to care for? How do you feel about that?

S: Well, I'm overwhelmed by the idea of going back to work. I really don't know where to begin with that. And I don't have a lot to do around the house anymore, but I still don't feel like I should be doing something else.

C: So you're overwhelmed with some of the changes in your life right now.

S: And I guess I'm underwhelmed by what I have to do around the house. I hardly ever have to go to the store anymore now that I'm not feeding two teenage boys!

C: So you have less to do in your role as a mother than you did before?

S: Yes, I guess that's right. Wow, that is true. That's kind of sad, isn't it?

C: You have dedicated yourself to being a mother to your sons for their whole lives, and now they're off at college and you can't do as much for them.

S: I guess they don't need me as much anymore. And I don't need to be home in case of any little emergency . . . you know . . . forgotten homework or rides home from practice.

C: Not feeling as needed as you used to, even for a good reason like your boys going away to college, can still make you feel lonely and sad.

S: I'm proud of my boys, but I do miss seeing them and doing things for them. I often wonder if they're getting enough to eat and if they have clean clothes. These are things I never had to worry about before. Now I feel like it's not my place to worry because they've left me. I'm here, and they're not. They went off and now they have to take care of themselves.

Sandra has now begun to link her feelings of loneliness and sadness to her sons going off to college. Sandra probably never thought about how she would lose some of her identity as a mother through this transition, and so she wasn't prepared for her life to change as it has. Now the professional counselor can help Sandra begin to deal with these emotions of loss, grief, and sadness to adjust to the changes in her life.

USEFULNESS AND EVALUATION OF THE CONFRONTATION TECHNIQUE

Outcome research indicates that use of the confrontation technique is most appropriate and effective when helping clients get unstuck, as well as to motivate them to pursue a fuller life rather than accepting or settling for the way things are. The counselor–client relationship must be strong prior to attempting this technique, however, and counselors must be well aware of each client's worldview. The confrontation technique has been implemented successfully with clients in danger of harming themselves (i.e., they are suicidal; Polcin, Galloway, Bond, Korcha, & Greenfield, 2010; Popadiuk et al., 2008) and clients with addictions, including nicotine (Kotz, Huibers, West, Wesseling, & van Schayck, 2009). For example, Polcin et al. (2010) found the confrontation technique most effective for participants with severe alcohol, drug, psychiatric, and interrelated problems upon follow-up at 6 and 12 months. Also, Popadiuk et al. (2008) found self-confrontation most successful with suicidal clients because video recordings were used to teach clients about their suicidal triggers and how to confront their perceived discrepancies immediately.

The confrontation technique is not appropriate for all clients, and professional counselors must recognize this early in the relationship. For example, in a study of smoking cessation in public housing residents, Boardman, Catley, Grobe, Little, and Ahluwalia (2006) verified that inappropriate confrontation strategies can tear or rupture the therapeutic alliance, and they are significantly related to poor outcomes. On the other hand, appropriate use of confrontation resulted in enhanced client ability to experience emotions in the here and now in at least one study (Town, Hardy, McCullough, & Stride, 2012). In general, clients who are self-centered or narcissistic resist confrontations (Shechtman & Yanov, 2001).

Confrontation is most useful with clients who are stuck and unable to move closer to achieving their counseling goals. Building an effective, empathic relationship with the client is essential to effective implementation of the confrontation technique (Corey, 2016; Ivey et al., 2018; Young, 2017) and culturally appropriate variations are needed when working with clients from diverse backgrounds and characteristics (Cheung & Nguyen, 2012; Ivey et al., 2018; MacCluskie, 2010; Popadiuk et al., 2008; Strong & Zeman, 2010; Young, 2017).

APPLICATION OF THE CONFRONTATION TECHNIQUE

Now apply the confrontation technique to a current client or student you are working with or revisit the brief case studies presented at the beginning of this book. How can you use the confrontation technique to address concerns and create movement in the counseling session?

CHAPTER 20

Motivational Interviewing

ORIGINS OF THE MOTIVATIONAL INTERVIEWING TECHNIQUE

Counseling is about change, and the case was made immediately in this text that professional counselors use different approaches, strategies, and techniques to help clients change to accomplish counseling goals and objectives. But what is a professional counselor to do when a client doesn't appear to want to change? I have often encountered clients presenting with substance use disorders, disruptive behavior problems, and a host of other difficulties who did not appear motivated to change. I often liken the treatment of such clients to precounseling, or counseling aimed at helping to motivate clients to get to the point where they are actually ready for counseling.

Miller and Rollnick (2013) systematized this process by developing motivational interviewing (MI), which helps clients develop the intrinsic motivation to change and accomplish counseling goals. MI was conceived in 1983 when William Miller developed a short-term intervention for chronic alcohol users (Naar-King & Suarez, 2011) because he noticed that the more confrontational styles prevalent during that time period increased client resistance (Lewis, 2014). Then in 1992, Miller and Rollnick wrote *Motivational Interviewing: Preparing People to Change Addictive Behavior*. Originally designed to address resistance in clients with substance use disorders, MI has been generalized for use with other health and mental health behaviors (Naar-King & Suarez, 2011).

The development of MI was influenced primarily by the work of two individuals: Carl Rogers and James Prochaska. Miller and Rollnick (2013) adapted Rogers's client-centered core areas of empathy, warmth, genuineness, and unconditional positive regard, reasoning that a strong therapeutic alliance was vital to working through (or with) client resistance and helping clients change. However, Miller and Rollnick purposely deviated from Rogers's nondirective style, believing that a more straightforward approach in dealing with client ambivalence and resistance would help develop intrinsic motivation and self-efficacy, and thereby propel clients toward change. Prochaska's five-stage transtheoretical model of change (Lewis, 2014) also influences the MI approach: (1) *precontemplation*, the client sees no need for change; (2) *contemplation*, the client is ambivalent but willing to weigh the positives and negatives; (3) *determination*, the client recognizes that change is needed but is not committed to a path for change; (4) *action*, the client is committed to change and actively pursues agreed-upon counseling goals; and (5) *maintenance*, the client integrates the changes into a new way of living.

Miller and Rollnick (2013) identified three key components of MI: collaboration, evocation, and autonomy. *Collaboration* involves the professional counselor and client co-exploring client motivations in a supportive manner. *Evocation* involves the professional counselor drawing out a client's motivation. *Autonomy* places responsibility for change squarely on the client, which respects a client's free will. MI is less a theory or technique than an approach, a process, or a "way of being" with the client—in classic Rogerian style. Naar-King and Suarez (2011) called it "a gentle, respectful method for communicating with others about their difficulties with change and the possibilities to engage in different, healthier behaviors that are in accord with their own goals and values to maximize human potential" (p. 5).

HOW TO IMPLEMENT THE MOTIVATIONAL INTERVIEWING TECHNIQUE

MI can be used as a comprehensive method or as a way to jump-start a client's motivation before switching to another counseling approach (Lewis, 2014). Tahan and Sminkey (2012) also proposed that counselors using MI must have substantial emotional intelligence and an awareness of emotions, reactions, strengths, and areas of challenge both within oneself and others. Being emotionally tuned in helps the professional counselor monitor client communications and motivations and allows the counselor to know when to push against or ride with client resistance.

Miller and Rollnick (2013) identified four general principles of MI: expressing empathy, developing discrepancies, rolling with resistance, and supporting self-efficacy. *Expressing empathy* involves displaying Rogers's core conditions and developing a strong therapeutic alliance. Professional counselors must display unconditional client acceptance and use reflective and active listening skills to ensure that clients feel understood and to ensure that the clients understand the significance of their own thoughts, feelings, and behaviors (Tahan & Sminkey, 2012). It is also important that the counselor highlight and accept clients' ambivalent feelings about change (Miller & Rollnick, 2013). *Developing discrepancies* entails the professional counselor skillfully helping clients to verbalize thoughts, feelings, and conflicts so that the counselor can point out the discrepancies between how clients are living and the way the clients would like to live.

Miller and Rollnick (2013) suggested a set of skills that are helpful in developing client discrepancies using the acronym OARS: open-ended questions, affirmations, reflecting skills, and summaries. *Open-ended questions* (O) cannot be answered with a simple yes or no and therefore encourage clients to divulge more information and clarify responses. Asking clients to describe typical days also can help professional counselors discern patterns in client thoughts, feelings, and behaviors (Naar-King & Suarez, 2011). *Affirmations* convey value for what the client is saying (Lewis, 2014) and help clients to recognize inner strengths and resources. Affirmations should reflect honestly specific client behaviors or attributes and are aimed at increasing client self-efficacy. When providing affirmations, it is important for the professional counselor to avoid using the word *I* so that the client does not feel evaluated. Use of *reflecting skills* conveys empathy, reveals underlying feelings and meanings of client statements, allows clients to know they are understood, and allows counselors to track the conversation, highlighting important information the client may not realize is important at the time. However, Naar-King and Suarez (2011) also pointed out that more complex, double-sided reflections can reveal clients' mixed feelings about change, thus aiding in developing discrepancies. Finally, *summaries* are used to review and connect what the client has said in order to facilitate forward movement (Young, 2013). Lewis (2014) suggested that summaries should include client feelings and attitudes about change—called change talk—a necessary step prior to goal setting. Although summaries are often offered at the end of a session, MI proposes that several summaries should be offered at various junctures or transition points during a typical MI session.

The third principle, *rolling with resistance*, proposes that instead of fighting against a client's resistance to change, the professional counselor should acknowledge that resistance is an important and commonly experienced part of the change process (Watson, 2011). After all, if resistance did not occur, change would be easy and would have happened already! Using reflecting skills, counselors provide feedback, reframe questions from varying perspectives, and even recall earlier client statements about motivation to change. Here, it is important to help clients explore the pros and cons of change (Lewis, 2014), and counselors can even add a twist by acknowledging the client's resistance while adding an additional thought or reframing something that the client may not have previously considered, thus leading the client in a possible new direction. When rolling with resistance, it is essential to keep the client responsible for the problem and any resistance to addressing the problem (Miller & Rollnick, 2013).

The fourth principle is *supporting self-efficacy* (Miller & Rollnick, 2013), which reinforces client beliefs in promoting change to improve one's life. Lewis (2014) suggested that self-efficacy can be bolstered by having the client share stories about how the client overcame past obstacles and achieved success. Clients should be encouraged to use change talk; Watson (2011) indicated that use of change talk indicates increasing levels of self-efficacy and subsequent commitment to change. Indeed, increased use of change talk is an important indicator that clients are ready to set goals and pursue a plan of action (Naar-King & Suarez, 2011).

Finally, Tahan and Sminkey (2012) proposed several suggestions for professional counselors who want to help clients make the desire for change permanent. In addition to making clients aware of their need to change, counselors should provide space in the relationship for clients to accept the need to change, provide strategies to the client on how to change, and provide constructive feedback as positive behavioral changes are observed.

VARIATIONS OF THE MOTIVATIONAL INTERVIEWING TECHNIQUE

MI was originally used in addictions counseling, but subsequent adaptations have transformed MI so that it is now effective in couples counseling, health care, and the criminal justice system. Adaptations of MI have been particularly useful in group work and in counseling with adolescents and young adults who lack the intrinsic motivation to change. Young (2013) suggested that MI modifications can be quite valuable in the early stages of group work when the concepts of autonomy (recognition and respect of all group members), collaboration (working hand in hand, commitment to individual member and group goals), and evocation (conversation that evokes change talk and new thoughts and behaviors) are introduced. Group workers can also introduce OARS skills to support members as they develop the motivation to construct and achieve goals.

MI has become very popular in counseling with adolescents and young adults who need to develop the motivation to change, especially around issues such as substance use, smoking, risky sexual behaviors, eating disorders, and disruptive behavior (Naar-King & Suarez, 2011). Setting short- and long-term goals may be a new construct for young adolescents, and they may struggle to see the logic behind goal setting. Autonomy is an important developmental consideration for all adolescents and young adults, who often use resistance. Rolling with resistance is a strength of MI and makes it a good match for this young population.

EXAMPLE OF THE MOTIVATIONAL INTERVIEWING TECHNIQUE

Shawn is a 15-year-old white male who is under court order for counseling after a drug charge. Shawn is resistant to counseling because he does not want to be there. He believes that others around him are overreacting and trying to control him and that they are responsible for his trouble. He insists that if people would leave him alone and let him be more independent, then they would see that everything would turn out fine.

Counselor (C): Shawn, last time we talked about your drug habits, you shared with me that you enjoy smoking pot and that it isn't dangerous to you. You also shared with me that your mother is furious when she finds you with drugs and that she believes this habit to be a major cause for concern. Would you like to continue talking about this?

Shawn (S): I guess so because my mom found some pot in my room again and is now threatening to call my parole officer. She is so stupid! She says she doesn't want me to get in trouble, but then she's going to call and get me in trouble. It doesn't make sense, and I wish she would just leave me alone!

C: So you're angry at your mom because she might call your parole officer.

S: I'm angry at her for not minding her own business.

C: So if she stayed out of your business, what would happen?

S: Nothing. Absolutely nothing. I wouldn't get caught, and I wouldn't get in trouble.

Sum

C: So if your mother would ignore your drug habit, then you would be able to smoke pot with no repercussions?

S: Well, maybe . . . no, that's right. No problems at all.

C: What do you mean by "maybe"?

S: Well, I applied for this job with this painting company, and I guess if they made me take a drug test, then I might not get the job.

C: Do you want the job?

S: Yes.

C: Even if you have to quit smoking pot?

S: Well, I wouldn't have to quit, I would just have to stop for a while.

C: When would you have to stop?

S: I don't know.

C: Well, why not stop now and get your mom off your back and get ready for this job?

S: No. I don't need to stop now. I don't care what my mom thinks, and they'll tell me when they want me to take a drug test for the job.

C: What will continuing to smoke pot do for you?

S: Well, I like smoking pot. It's not a big deal, and I like it.

C: So you would be happy?

S: Yes, I would be happy.

C: What else?

S: What do you mean "what else"? I would be happy. Isn't that enough?

C: What else would smoking pot do for you?

S: Well, nothing.

C: If you stopped smoking pot what would happen?

S: My stupid mom would be happy.

C: You would make your mom happy. What about the painting job?

S: I would be ready for it whenever.

C: And you want the job, so that would also make you happy, right?

S: Sure.

C: So, if you stopped smoking pot, your mom would get off your back and you would be ready to work for the painting company. These are two things that you want.

S: Yes.

C: So how can you get these things and still smoke pot?

S: If my mom would leave me alone and not get me in trouble.

C: What can *you* do, Shawn?

S: I could stop smoking pot. But I don't want to.

At this point, Shawn is thinking about why it may be good to make some changes. The counselor has used Shawn's resistance to drop his drug habit to juxtapose Shawn's different goals. He may begin to see how smoking pot interferes with things he cares about in his life, even if one of them isn't making his mother happy. This is motivation for change, as is evident in Shawn's last statement of "I could stop smoking pot." Even though he states that he doesn't want to, he has now realized that it is an option for him. MI often involves a lengthy process, and this transcript provides just a small snippet of the overall process.

USEFULNESS AND EVALUATION OF THE MOTIVATIONAL INTERVIEWING TECHNIQUE

Miller and Rollnick's (2013) book has been translated into at least eight languages and is used in countries around the globe (Lewis, 2014). More than 200 clinical trials have tested the efficacy of MI (Fisher & Harrison, 2013), and the Substance Abuse and Mental Health Services Administration's (SAMHSA's) National Registry of Evidence-based Programs (https://www.samhsa.gov/nrepp) reports that MI received an overall rating of 3.9 on a 4.0 scale. It is best applied to situations in which specific behavior changes are desired and measurable (e.g., wearing a condom during sex, eating a nutritious diet, limiting alcohol intake; Koken, Outlaw, & Green-Jones, 2011; Lewis, 2014). MI has demonstrated effectiveness in reducing adolescent risky behavior (Koken et al., 2011) and in improving academic achievement and attendance (Kaplan, Engle, Austin, & Wagner, 2011), including a 10% reduction in the high school dropout rate. VanBuskirk and Wetherell (2014) conducted a meta-analysis of MI randomized control trials (RCTs) and concluded that one or more MI sessions would be effective in enhancing a client's readiness to obtain goals related to healthy behaviors.

Medical professionals have employed MI with some success. The American Medical Association endorsed the use of MI for low-intensity interventions promoting health-related outcomes (e.g., weight loss), so Hardcastle, Taylor, Bailey, Harley, and Haggar (2013) explored use of five face-to-face MI interviews during a six-month low-intensity intervention with patients with cardiovascular disease and found substantial improvement at post-treatment for blood pressure, weight, and body mass index, although these improvements were not maintained at one-year follow-up. In a second study, MI used with participants with cardiovascular disease led to lower levels of blood pressure, body weight, and cholesterol when compared to participants in a treatment-as-usual condition (Groeneveld, Proper, van der Beek, & van Mechelen, 2010). In a randomized controlled trial, Fleming et al. (2010) used MI, which was implemented through two 15-minute counseling visits and two follow-up phone calls by physicians, to significantly reduce 28-day drinking totals among a large sample of college students and to reduce scores on the Rutgers Alcohol Problem Index. No differences were noted in the frequency of heavy drinking, healthcare utilization, injuries, drunk driving, depression, and tobacco use.

Of course, MI has been used most commonly with substance use clients, and the outcome research supports continued application of MI to prevent dropout and improve treatment adherence in substance use and other conditions. In a clinical trial of adolescents with anxiety and mood disorders, Dean, Britt, Bell, Stanley, and Collings (2016) reported that participants randomly assigned to an MI condition attended significantly more group therapy sessions and demonstrated greater treatment readiness and initiation than did participants in an active control condition. Westra, Constantino, and Antony (2016) found a trend in treatment retention

($p = .09$), finding that 23% more clients dropped out of CBT treatment alone, compared to motivational interviewing enhanced CBT. A meta-analysis by Lundahl et al. (2013) explored the effectiveness of MI in medical settings, reviewing 48 RCTs ($n = 9618$), and concluding that MI showed promise related to "HIV viral load, dental outcomes, death rate, body weight, alcohol and tobacco use, sedentary behavior, self-monitoring, confidence in change, and approach to treatment" (p. 157). In sum, MI is a robust intervention to address motivational and adherence problems related to a wide range of behavioral issues.

Some researchers have also experienced success with MI implemented over the telephone. Bombardier et al. (2013) used a telephone-based MI physical activity treatment with patients with multiple sclerosis and major depressive disorder, and found the intervention resulted in significantly lower depression outcomes when compared with a waitlist control. Also, Seal et al. (2012) used telephone-administered MI with veterans with mental health problems to increase the likelihood that the veterans will pursue mental health treatment to address their specific concerns. Jiang, Wu, and Gao (2017) conducted a qualitative systematic review of 25 articles on the effectiveness of motivational interviewing in preventing and treating substance abuse when delivered through modes other than individual face-to-face counseling. They found that MI delivered via telephone was an effective intervention mode for preventing and treating substance abuse, whereas inconclusive results were obtained for short message system (SMS), Internet MI, and MI delivered through a group format.

The use of change talk is a strength of MI, and when OARS is implemented to encourage change talk, clients experience higher levels of behavior change (Morgenstern et al., 2012). Significant others can influence client change talk. In a study aimed at reducing alcohol use (Apadoca, Magill, Longabaugh, Jackson, & Monti, 2013), participants whose significant others engaged in supportive talk were more likely to make positive change statements themselves and actually accomplish higher degrees of behavioral change. D'Amico et al. (2015) explored interventions aimed at change talk versus sustain talk. Change talk, an important element of MI, was associated with decreased alcohol use and heavy drinking at three-month follow-up, whereas sustain talk was associated with a decrease in change motivation, as well as increased expectancies of alcohol and marijuana use.

So how MI is implemented and supplemented either can have positive results or can lead to no differences. For example, Sussman, Sun, Rohrbach, and Spruijt-Metz (2011) found no difference between a 12-session high school classroom guidance program aimed at reducing both substance use and risky sexual behavior and the same 12-session program supplemented with three 20-minute MI sessions, two sessions of which were conducted by telephone.

APPLICATION OF THE MOTIVATIONAL INTERVIEWING TECHNIQUE

Now apply the motivational interviewing technique to a current client or student you are working with or revisit the brief case studies presented at the beginning of this book. How can you use the motivational interviewing technique to address concerns and create movement in the counseling session?

CHAPTER 21

Strength Bombardment

ORIGINS OF THE STRENGTH BOMBARDMENT TECHNIQUE

The strength bombardment technique stems from the humanistic-existential and, to a lesser extent, cognitive-behavioral paradigms. The premise underlying use of the strength bombardment technique is that mood, self-perception, and self-image can improve when clients receive strength-based communications from others and internalize these communications into their own internal dialogue. Rather than focusing on past experiences (psychoanalytic) or behaviors (behaviorism), strength bombardment molds client perceptions and feelings in the present. After these strength-based positive perceptions and feelings are internalized, they can be called on as a source of resilience when the client experiences future troubling or traumatic events.

HOW TO IMPLEMENT THE STRENGTH BOMBARDMENT TECHNIQUE

Strength bombardment can be used in both individual and small-group counseling situations. Whether used in the individual or group context, it is essential that a strong therapeutic alliance be formed from the outset that is based on mutual respect and genuineness so that, when the strength bombardment technique is used, it is perceived as a genuine extension of the relationship and is genuinely appreciated. Otherwise, clients may negate the attempts at self-affirmation and discount their feelings, thoughts, and actions.

Steele (1988) referred to strength bombardment, when used in individual counseling, as a self-affirmation technique. Self-affirmation can be used in combination with the exception technique discussed in Chapter 2. To implement strength bombardment (self-affirmation) with an individual client, ask the client to recall times and situations when the client encountered similar challenges or troubles but she successfully, or at least partially successfully, handled the situations. Then focus on and help the client identify and compile a listing of the strengths and success characteristics demonstrated during those events.

Some clients may struggle to recall past successful events or to identify strengths displayed in the process, so the professional counselor may need to use effective interviewing skills to bring that information and those experiences to light. For example, the counselor may remind the client "Even though that situation was hard and challenging, you made it through. What did you do to make it through?" or "How did you feel when you prevailed? What did you say to yourself?" Sometimes clients downplay the successes or are overly critical if things didn't work out perfectly. It is important to counter the negative perceptions and focus on the feelings of accomplishment and success, no matter how small, that stemmed from the actions, thoughts, and feelings of the client.

Strength bombardment has been used as a small-group intervention to help clients hear their strengths from other group members, which thus allows them to internalize the affirmations and improve their self-images. The subsequent focus is then on how clients can use the strengths to resolve future situations and dilemmas they may encounter. In this way, it is used as a classic strengths-based approach to counseling, and the resulting strength bombardment content serves as a well of resiliency to cope with future trials. When implemented in small-group work, the strength bombardment technique ordinarily focuses on one group member at a time and is framed by a statement such as "Let's do a quick round, and everyone tell Shambar one thing you have noticed about him that you believe is a positive characteristic or skill" or "Let's help Sally identify some of her character traits or strengths that she could use to solve problems like the one she is facing." The strength bombardment technique is also frequently used during the termination stage of group work, often as a culminating activity, when the group leader instructs each member to do something like the following: "Identify one thing about [the target member] that you really like or appreciate." The leader then facilitates a quick round focusing on each group member so that every member has the opportunity to hear what others think about them, as well as to tell each member one thing he or she likes or appreciates. Of course, it is essential to be sure that the comments shared reflect positive characteristics. It is also important to note that the strength bombardment prompt should be tailored to the individual needs of the group.

Whether the strength bombardment technique is implemented with an individual client or small group of clients, it is important for the professional counselor to check with each target client to understand how the content is being received and integrated, as well as to reframe the information as positive and productive whenever possible. Sometimes the professional counselor will need to restate, elaborate on, or clarify information shared by group members for maximum effect. This check-in also allows the client to give evaluative feedback on the effectiveness of the intervention and gives other group members feedback on how helpful their input has been. One hopes all will realize that a strengths-based approach is helpful for the target client and the contributors, leaving everyone feeling empowered, validated, and positive.

VARIATIONS OF THE STRENGTH BOMBARDMENT TECHNIQUE

A helpful variation of the strength bombardment technique is to write down all of the strengths identified and assign a daily self-talk homework activity in which the client reviews the content and incorporates the identified strengths into the client's self-talk. Clients can also be assigned homework whereby each client is to keep a list of strengths noticed throughout the week. This can be done whether the strength bombardment activity originally occurred in an individual or group context.

With an individual client, strength bombardment or self-affirmation can be used as an inoculation or relapse prevention procedure, much like the flagging the minefield technique described in Chapter 5. In this way, clients can be protected from future threats to their self-esteem. The professional counselor engages the client in a detailed discussion about her problem-resolution strengths, interests, and values, constructing a protective layer against future situations that may threaten the client's self-concept. Follow-up conversations can involve reminding the client of the strong identity features previously acknowledged and how they can prevent the client from experiencing the ill effects of current or future struggles by remembering the successful handling of the previous events. Showing resiliency and self-affirmation in the face of current struggles not only helps to resolve the challenges more effectively but also reaffirms the strengths and resiliency facets (Lannin, Guyll, Vogel, & Madon, 2013).

Numerous creative adaptations can be implemented in group work. For example, the professional counselor can give each group member an index card and instruct all members to place their name at the top. Then the card is rotated around the circle of chairs as each group member adds to the list of strengths, admired qualities, and so forth. When the cards make their way back to the person whose name is at the top, everyone can share a few of the list entries and how they feel about the affirmations and the activity. The list on the index card can become a stimulus for expanding the list even further and can be revisited during challenging times to help the clients remember their strengths and positive qualities.

EXAMPLES OF THE STRENGTH BOMBARDMENT TECHNIQUE

EXAMPLE 1: The Case of Sara

The following is an example of a variation on strength bombardment in an individual counseling session, also referred to as self-affirmation. Sara is a 27-year-old new mother who is struggling with postpartum depression. She has been in and out of counseling for depression for many years. In preparing for the changes that would come with having a child, Sara's counselor had Sara write a letter to herself outlining past successes and detailing her many strengths. Her baby is now 3 months old, and Sara has returned for help. The counselor asks Sara to begin the session by reading the letter she wrote months ago.

Sara (S):   Dear Sara. Hi, it's me, Sara, and I'm here to remind you that things aren't so bad. You have a tendency to beat yourself up, and you really shouldn't do that. You are a resilient and strong woman. You are also very brave. You have been through a lot of tough situations and, although it was hard at the time, at this moment you are able to look back at them and be proud of yourself. There is nothing you have been through that hasn't made you stronger. Remember when your best friend died in that car accident? You thought you would never have fun again, but just last Friday you went out and had fun with your friends. Yes, it was sad that she wasn't there, but you didn't let that stop you because she wouldn't want you to do that. And you don't want to do that either. Chances are, if you're reading this, you are at the base of yet another mountain that you have to climb. Remember that nothing is stopping you from climbing that mountain and doing a damn good job at it too! Things that look tough are often the most rewarding, so go get your reward! You deserve it. Most important, remember that I love you, and I am proud of whatever it is that you do. Love, Sara

Counselor (C):   Wow. What incredibly powerful words you wrote to yourself. Do you remember how you felt when you wrote that?

S: Yeah, I . . . I felt great. I felt like a strong person because, at the time, things were going great. And when things go great I have no problem feeling great. But with a new baby, things hardly ever go "great."

C: Having a baby can be hard work and unpredictable, but is it really not "great"?

S: I mean, look at me! I don't get any sleep, my house is a wreck, and I feel like I can't get anything done anymore . . .

C: How is your baby?

S: He's a good baby. He only cries when he's hungry or needs to be changed, and then he's very content.

C: So when he cries you are able to give him what he needs, and then he is happy?

S: Yes.

C: It sounds to me like you are a very attentive mother.

S: Oh, yes . . . I always have him near me, or at least the monitor when he is sleeping.

C: So you are a good mother.

S: I guess so . . .

C: Say it aloud: I am a good mother.

S: I am a good mother.

C: I am doing a good job climbing that mountain of motherhood.

S: (Laughing) I am doing a good job climbing that mountain of motherhood!

C: Do you think you were honest in your letter to yourself?

S: Yes. All of those things are true, even if I forget sometimes.

C: Do you believe them now, hearing them later?

S: Yes, I believe them because I wrote them and it all makes sense. I guess I just forgot and was afraid that things weren't going well.

C: In your letter you reminded yourself that things aren't always easy.

S: But I'll still get through it, and it will be rewarding, and having my son is definitely rewarding.

Sara is now empowered because she gave herself a tool to fight off her negative thinking. It is easier for Sara to get back her positive self-concept because she created it in the first place. This technique has reinforced truths that Sara already believed, and more practice at this technique will only make this easier for her.

EXAMPLE 2: Strength bombardment in a group session

In this next example, the professional counselor uses strength bombardment as a culminating activity in a small-group intervention with adults. The group members are terminating from a group focused on overcoming stress and depression.

Counselor (C):   As we end our final group session, I would like you to participate in a strength bombardment or affirmation activity meant to highlight some of the strengths and characteristics you will be taking from the group after we finish. Sylvia, if it is okay with you, because you are sitting next to me, I would like to start with you.

Sylvia (S):   Sure!

C: We will go around the circle, and each of you will tell Sylvia one thing you appreciate about her. This could be something you see as a personal strength or characteristic that you admire about her. As always, anyone can take a pass. Javier, would you like to start?

Javier (J):   Hmm. Okay. That's an easy one. Whenever someone was feeling particularly low, Sylvia always had something kind and supportive to say. Whether it was directed at me or not, I always felt better after she said it.

C: Thank you, Javier! That was a very kind thing for you to say. I will write each of these down so we will each have a list of what was said. Ebony?

Ebony (E):   Her smile. I always felt happier just by seeing that thousand-watt smile!

S: (Beaming with all 1,000 watts) Thank you, Ebony!

Michael (M):   My turn. We talked about empathy and emotions a lot, and there were a lot of times I could tell that Sylvia really felt the anguish I was feeling, like she really cared about me,

about all of us. It made it easier to come to group and share really personal stuff knowing that she and everybody else really cared about me, my emotions . . . hell, all of us and our emotions. Thanks for caring so much about us.

The process continued until everyone had an opportunity to make a comment, then the counselor moved to the next member of the group, Javier, and the process repeated.

The counselor needs to decide whether to participate or simply facilitate. Also, this example used a systematic process of going around the circle, and a random process works just as well, allowing group members to chime in when each feels it is time. In this more random process, the professional counselor must ensure that no one is left out.

USEFULNESS AND EVALUATION OF THE STRENGTH BOMBARDMENT TECHNIQUE

Very little outcome research has been published on the topic of strength bombardment, although some recent research on self-affirmation indicates that it is effective in improving mood and self-confidence. Also, many studies embedded self-affirmation into a larger treatment package, so it is difficult to parse out the exclusive effects of the affirmation and strength focus.

Armitage (2012) explored the effects of self-affirmation activities on perceptions of body shape and weight in a sample of adolescent girls. Armitage found that participation in self-affirmation activities led to greater body satisfaction and a lower level of threat from the actual self-rating process when the results were compared to girls in the control group. In a study of Latino and Latina students, Sherman et al. (2013) found that self-affirmation exercises helped inoculate participants from stereotyping and identity threats, leading those students to attain higher levels of academic achievement than did control participants not exposed to the affirmation activities. Scott, Brown, Phair, Westland, and Schüz (2013) demonstrated that self-affirmations led to reduced alcohol consumption.

In an older study, Healy (1974) explored the use of strength bombardment in the group setting, using exercises in career counseling as a means to grow efficacy and self-esteem for group members. Strength bombardment is also useful within groups for elementary-age and special needs children. Finally, it is possible that other mediums of expression (e.g., drawings, stickers, beads, stamps, clay models, toys, and emerging technologies) could be useful in allowing clients to develop self-affirmations or provide affirmations to other group members.

APPLICATION OF THE STRENGTH BOMBARDMENT TECHNIQUE

Now apply the strength bombardment technique to a current client or student you are working with or revisit the brief case studies presented at the beginning of this book. How can you use the strength bombardment technique to address concerns and create movement in the counseling session?

Techniques Based on Cognitive-Behavioral Approaches

ognitive therapy emerged in reaction to behavioral approaches that minimized or even denied the importance of thoughts in promoting changes within counseling (see Section 9 and Section 10). Over the past several decades, the passions that created both the behavioral and cognitive approaches to counseling have abated, and more and more counselors have recognized that, although thoughts alone and behaviors alone can lead to helpful changes, the synergistic integration of these two approaches may be even more effective. Thus, the integrated practice of cognitive-behavioral approaches to counseling emerged. Pioneers such as Albert Ellis, William Glasser, Donald Meichenbaum, and others developed theories of counseling based on cognitive-behavioral approaches. An additional force behind the emergence of cognitive-behavioral approaches was the prominence of managed-care programs, which promoted cognitive-behavioral therapy (CBT) as a time- and cost-effective treatment. In Section 6, nine cognitive-behavioral techniques will be presented.

Self-talk empowers clients to monitor their internal dialogue, which most people are able to do by the time they are 8 years old, and to alter that dialogue in order to think positive and affirming self-messages (which I refer to as a positive spin cycle) while simultaneously blocking self-defeating and negative self-messages (which I refer to as a negative spin cycle).

Reframing requires a counselor to take a client-perceived problem situation and adapt (reframe) it in a more positive or productive manner. For example, the behavior of a defiant adolescent could be reframed as a need to develop independent or autonomous decision-making practices. As such, the problem is viewed not as maladaptive or pathological but as developmental or even prosocial (e.g., she is telling you she is trying to become an adult). Reframing is often considered an Adlerian technique, but it is covered here because of its strong cognitive component. (How's that for a reframe?!)

Thought stopping is particularly effective in ending repetitive thought cycles, which sometimes even reach the point of obsession. The technique physically breaks a cognitive spin cycle and substitutes positive self-talk and statements. Cognitive restructuring helps clients systematically analyze, process, and resolve cognitively based issues by replacing negative thoughts and interpretations with more positive thoughts and interpretations.

Rational-emotive behavior therapy (REBT) is also included in this section. Albert Ellis would probably turn in his grave if he knew his REBT was being referred to as a technique; however, it is more like a process that can be taught and implemented using a step-by-step procedure that helps clients alter distorted thinking. Thus, I have featured the ABCDEF model of REBT and the rational-emotive imagery technique as key elements of the REBT approach to counseling.

Research has shown that a number of cognitive-behavioral techniques are particularly effective in reducing stress and addressing simple phobias. Systematic desensitization, also based on reciprocal inhibition, incorporates the subjective units of distress scale (SUDS), which is a modified scaling technique, and a fear hierarchy into a procedure that allows clients to experience a fear-producing event during a relaxed state. Doing so breaks the classically conditioned phobic cycle.

The final technique covered in this section is stress inoculation training. Stress inoculation training, originally developed by Donald Meichenbaum, helps clients systematically process and resolve cognitively based stressors.

MULTICULTURAL IMPLICATIONS OF THE TECHNIQUES BASED ON COGNITIVE-BEHAVIORAL APPROACHES

Like humanistic-phenomenological or psychodynamic approaches to counseling, cognitive-behavioral approaches to counseling emphasize the importance of rapport and the therapeutic alliance. But unlike these other approaches, the cognitive-behavioral approach does not require clients to reveal intimate details of their lives or past events or to focus on intense emotions. Cognitive-behavioral approaches deal with the present and use a logical and clear process in a nonthreatening manner that many clients find empowering; it especially appeals to clients who are systematic thinkers. As a result, cognitive-behavioral approaches ordinarily appeal to clients from a wide array of cultural backgrounds, particularly those whose cultures may discourage the sharing of family-related issues (e.g., Latino culture) or exploration or exhibition of intense emotional displays (e.g., Asian culture).

The approach also lends itself to the use of numerous techniques that transfer meaningfully across numerous cultural contexts, including gender, racial, ethnic, socioeconomic, disability, and sexual orientation contexts (Beck & Weishaar, 2013). Cognitive-behavioral approaches were particularly

helpful in exploring negative expectations and creating more positive expectations among clients of African descent. Clients from lower socioeconomic strata often find that cognitive approaches help them discover that they can control the events and perceptions of events in their environment, thus empowering them to develop positive expectations and positive steps to change their lives.

Cognitive-behavioral counselors often use a time-limited approach that requires clients to think clearly and logically, and many clients find the approach to be superficial or unable to meet their emotional needs or needs for self-awareness. Of course, like other approaches, some techniques based on cognitive-behavioral approaches require more training and sophistication. Counselors using a cognitive-behavioral approach with clients are, at their core, nonjudgmental, nonthreatening, and accepting of clients from diverse backgrounds and worldviews because they do not view clients or client problems and behaviors as bad or inferior; they view client issues as stemming from distorted thoughts that can be analyzed and modified to adjust to a complex and fluid sociocultural environment.

Cognitive-behavioral approaches allow clients and counselors to modify beliefs, cognitions, and actions collaboratively while still stressing the importance of the therapeutic relationship. An approach like REBT does not question cultural values or practices; instead, it challenges the inflexible application of the shoulds and musts that stem from a client's views of cultural rules. These approaches allow clients to decide whether to adhere to, give up, or modify the perceived rules, giving clients more freedom and flexibility related to their own thoughts, feelings, and behaviors.

Professional counselors must be careful not to challenge client beliefs before understanding the cultural context within which those beliefs developed because many clients are hesitant or resistant to questioning their own basic cultural values. For example, some Arab American clients adhere to very strict customs and beliefs related to religion, family, and child rearing. Disputing or even questioning motives or behaviors related to these customs could create additional dilemmas for these clients.

The cognitive-behavioral approach is quite directive, and the counselor is frequently perceived to be an expert by the client. Some clients from some cultures (e.g., Middle Eastern, Hispanic, Asian) may be very comfortable with this expert perception of the counselor, whereas others (e.g., some males) may be less comfortable (Hays & Erford, 2018). It is essential that counselors not facilitate a dependency relationship with clients, which is a possibility when clients perceive the counselor as an expert with all of the answers. Ordinarily, clients from diverse racial, religious, and ethnic backgrounds appreciate the straightforward, even no-nonsense, cognitive-behavioral approach because it focuses on the client's thinking and subsequent behavior rather than on a person's nature, sociocultural background, or cultural beliefs.

CHAPTER 22

Self-Talk

ORIGINS OF THE SELF-TALK TECHNIQUE

Seligman and Reichenberg (2013) described self-talk as a positive pep talk that a person gives to oneself each day. When using self-talk, a person repeatedly states a helpful, supportive phrase when faced with a troubling issue. Self-talk is a technique that stems from rational-emotive behavior therapy (REBT) and other cognitive-behavioral approaches to counseling (see Chapter 26). REBT holds that "people make irrational demands on themselves" that lead to psychological disturbances (Ellis, 1993, p. 200). People's conversations with themselves are based on their beliefs about themselves. Self-talk is self-fulfilling, and it is important for people to learn ways to challenge irrational beliefs. Self-talk is a technique that can be used to dispute these irrational beliefs and develop healthier thoughts, which will lead to more positive self-talk. It is a way for people to deal with the negative messages that they send to themselves.

A person may use two types of self-talk: positive and negative (Egan, 2013). A person's self-talk can be influenced by what other people (e.g., parents, teachers, peers) say about the person. Positive self-talk, as described above, is the type that professional counselors want to teach their clients to use. When people use positive self-talk, they are much more likely to remain motivated to reach their goals. Negative self-talk is often self-defeating and prevents clients from improving and succeeding because it is dominated by pessimism and anxiety. Borton, Markowitz, and Dieterich (2005) conducted a study to examine the most common types of thoughts associated with negative self-talk. The top three concerns the researchers found included interpersonal concerns, physical appearance, and personality characteristics. Schafer (1999) identified at least 16 different types of negative self-talk: negativizing (i.e., focusing on the negative aspects), awfulizing (i.e., perceiving situations as awful), catastrophizing (i.e., perceiving situations to be catastrophes), overgeneralizing, minimizing, blaming, perfectionism, musterbation (i.e., perceiving that one "must" do something), personalizing, judging human worth, control fallacy (i.e., perception that everything is within one's control), polarized thinking (i.e., an all-or-none mentality), being right, fallacy of fairness (i.e., the belief that life should be fair), shoulding (i.e., perceiving that one "should" do something), and magnifying. By using self-talk to change their absolutist ways of thinking, clients can gain more control over situations. A person's negative self-talk is not always unhealthy because it sometimes helps a person recognize a risky situation; a balance between positive and negative self-talk is important.

HOW TO IMPLEMENT THE SELF-TALK TECHNIQUE

Before teaching a client how to use the self-talk technique, it is helpful if the professional counselor first works with the client to develop a positive attitude about self-talk and the client. To do this, the professional counselor and client should evaluate the client's self-thoughts to figure out which thoughts are helpful to the client's well-being. Later in the process of teaching the client to use self-talk, the professional counselor can have the client focus on these thoughts.

A popular four-step method to reduce negative self-talk is called the countering method (Young, 2017). In the first step, the goal is to detect and discuss negative self-talk. To enhance effectiveness, it is necessary for the professional counselor to know in which type(s) of negative self-talk the client engages, how often negative self-talk occurs, and the types of situations that bring about negative self-talk. Young suggested having clients carry an index card to record any self-criticisms made. This index card will provide the professional counselor with valuable information and may also assist the client to understand the feelings that the self-criticisms produce.

After one full week of self-monitoring, the professional counselor and client are ready to begin step two of the countering method. In this second step, the goal is to examine what purpose is served by the client's negative self-talk. Three or four common themes typically emerge when the professional counselor and client review the index card. It is important for the professional counselor to help the client understand the basis of the beliefs. Most of the time, clients will not easily let go of their beliefs because of habit and self-protection (Young, 2017). To explore the function of the negative self-talk, the professional counselor can ask the client questions such as, "What does this negative thought help me do or feel?" (p. 157). Not only will investigating this area help the client and professional counselor understand the basis for negative self-talk, but the client also may realize that there is something else he would like to work on during the counseling sessions.

Once the client is aware of the reason he uses negative self-talk, the professional counselor can help the client develop counters: self-statements that are incompatible with the thought (Young, 2017). The most effective counters dispute the irrational belief and are consistent with the client's values. They are also in the same mode as the statement that is being challenged: images are countered with images, and thoughts are countered with thoughts. Words like *I* and *me* can be used as personalized counters. Counters also should be worded positively and in the present tense, and they should be realistic, easily memorized, and repeated often. If a professional counselor has a client who

"musterbates" (e.g., simply *must* have everything he wants), an effective counter could be "I never must have what I want, I only prefer it" (Ellis, 1997a, p. 97).

The goal of the last step of the countering method is for the client to review the counters after practicing them. The amount of time that clients need to practice their counters varies, but they frequently will need more than one week. The subjective units of distress scale (SUDS; see Chapter 29) can be used to evaluate the effectiveness of a counter. First, the client identifies the negative self-statement and rates the discomfort on the 100-point SUDS scale. Then the client identifies one of the counters and again rates the new level of discomfort on the SUDS scale. The effectiveness of the counter can be measured by subtracting the second rating from the first rating. If there is a reduction in the feelings of discomfort, the counter can be considered effective. Of course, the greater the drop of the second rating, the more effective the counter. Counters that are evaluated as ineffective need to be revised, practiced, and evaluated again until an effective counter is found (Young, 2017).

VARIATIONS OF THE SELF-TALK TECHNIQUE

A variation of the self-talk technique is the P and Q method. In this method, when negative self-talk begins, clients pause (P), breathe deeply, and question (Q) themselves to figure out what is upsetting about the situation. One of the questions should address an alternative way of interpreting what happened so that the client can deal with his feelings appropriately (Schafer, 1999).

Instant replay is another variation of self-talk. When a client notices that he is responding to something in an unwanted way, he needs to "catch the negative self-talk, challenge it, and change it" (Schafer, 1999, p. 373). To challenge his negative self-talk, the client can evaluate whether it is factual or distorted, moderate or extreme, and helpful or harmful. Southam-Gerow and Kendall (2000) suggested that when working with children and attempting to identify their self-talk, the professional counselor can ask the children to imagine thoughts as thought bubbles. The children can picture these thought bubbles running through their heads, just like in a comic strip. This alternative helps make the concept of self-talk more understandable for young children.

EXAMPLE OF THE SELF-TALK TECHNIQUE

Nicole is a 17-year-old high school senior with a test phobia. The following transcript is the initial segment in a series over several chapters throughout the book covering self-talk and culminating in the implementation of systematic desensitization. This transcript provides some preliminary information regarding Nicole's symptoms and how they affect her, then ends with the implementation of a scaling technique. During her treatment, Nicole was also taught the techniques of visual imagery and progressive muscle relaxation. Nicole was initially referred for psychoeducational evaluation to rule out learning disorders and attention problems. During the evaluation, it became clear that a test phobia was the primary concern.

Counselor (C):   About a month or two ago, we talked about how you sometimes have some fears or anxieties that are related to testing, tests and taking tests, and things like that. Tell me about this so I can understand more about what happens to you in these situations.

Nicole (N):   Um . . . I get really nervous before I take an exam or SATs and it affects the way I perform on my tests because I'm so nervous.

C: When you say it affects your performance on the tests, what do you mean?

N: I bomb them 'cause I'm worrying.

C: And what kind of thoughts go through your mind whenever you're worrying and thinking that you're not going to do well?

N: "Oh, my God! What if I don't do good?" Um . . . what's going to happen if I do bad, the outcome, things like that.

C: Do you say things to yourself? Do you carry on a conversation in your mind?

N: I tell myself to calm down.

C: You tell yourself to calm down. Do you tell yourself other things, things that make you more anxious and nervous sometimes?

N: I'll tell myself, like, you gotta do good or else you're in big trouble.

C: Or else get in big trouble. What is big trouble?

N: Big trouble means like I won't get into a good college, I'll fail, stuff like that.

C: And whenever you say those things to yourself, how do you feel?

N: Bad. Nervous. Like a failure.

C: Do you feel those things in your body, too?

N: My stomach, neck.

C: Anyplace else?

N: No.

C: So butterflies in the stomach and a pain in the neck?

N: Yes.

C: One of the assignments that I gave you before you came to session today was to write down a couple of things that you might be able to say to yourself when you are anxious and upset. We call that cognitive self-talk. It's whenever you think inside your own mind and say things to yourself. Because either you can think negative, nasty, hurtful things and spin yourself up into a frenzy where you get the butterflies in your stomach and start to feel the tension in your neck, or you can think positive and affirming types of things.

N: Right.

C: And if you're thinking the positive and affirming types of things, then it's impossible to think about . . .

N: The bad stuff.

C: The bad stuff, right, and we call that reciprocal inhibition. That basically means that you can't do two opposite things at the same time. So if you're thinking the positive and uplifting thoughts, then it's impossible to think the negative and hurtful types of things.

N: Okay.

C: So one of the things that I'd like you to do is share with me a couple of things that you could be saying to yourself instead of "I better do good or I'm going to get into big trouble or not get into a good college." These types of thoughts can really get the anxiety and worry flowing. So what kinds of things could you say? (At this moment, Nicole reaches into her pocket and pulls out a slip of paper with the self-talk phrases written on it.) Ah, you have them written down.

N: I wrote them down for homework.

C: I can tell that you're very serious about these problems, and I really appreciate your efforts so far. What is on the paper?

N: Um . . . I tell myself stuff like "Don't worry because in the end everything's going to be all right, so it's no use stressing over it."

C: (Writes this down.) Don't worry, no use stressing over it. Anything else?

N: I tell myself to take a deep breath and relax.

C: Good, deep breath and relax. Have you ever taken a deep breath?

N: A couple of times. If I'm really losing it, I will.

C: How does that feel?

N: It's okay, it works . . .

C: Okay. Lean back in your chair and close your eyes. And say out loud the things that you used to say. Things like "I gotta do good on this test," "I gotta get into a good college," and so forth, and I want you to feel the tension inside your body . . . (Pause for about 15 seconds) Now I want you to say these calming and relaxing things to yourself. I want you to say "Don't worry because everything's going to be all right, don't stress over it, take a deep breath and relax." (Pause for a half minute) How was that?

N: Pretty good. I stopped feeling so nervous and felt more positive, like I could really do it without being scared. I wonder if it'll work in class . . .

C: Good. So what you're finding is that whenever you are thinking these bad, nasty things,

about how life's gonna end if you don't get a good score on those SATs or something like that, then you're feeling really anxious and stressed out. Way up there on the scale. But whenever you think these calming and relaxing thoughts—and I could see you actually taking a deep breath when you were saying that to yourself—then you start to relax and feel better.

N: Uh-huh.

C: Great. That was called cognitive self-talk and that's based on that principle of reciprocal inhibition, which again means you can't think nasty things and calming and relaxing things at the same time, so you block all that nasty stuff that comes into your mind. All those hurtful and stressful things that you say to yourself, you block it with all these calming and relaxing phrases, and that's one very helpful way to keep you from feeling stressed out. It's also a very helpful way for you to calm yourself back down so that you can focus and get the work done that you need to get done. For your homework I want you to practice positive self-talk five times a day for at least 1 minute each time, every day until I see you next week. Spread them out during the day so that you do one or two practices each morning, afternoon, and evening.

USEFULNESS AND EVALUATION OF THE SELF-TALK TECHNIQUE

Self-talk is a technique that is commonly used to deal with issues of perfectionism, worry, self-esteem, and anger management (Corey, 2016). This technique also can be used with clients who need to develop motivation. For example, if a client wanted to motivate himself to exercise, he could list positive statements about exercising on index cards and pick several of them to recite each day. This helps to change the person's statements from negative to positive, and in turn the person develops a better attitude about exercising (Schafer, 1999). Professional counselors can teach this technique to clients who need help managing stress. Because negative self-talk can result in stress, it makes sense that positive self-talk can result in less stress. By altering the effect that the stressful situation has on the client, stress can be reduced (Corey, Corey, & Corey, 2018). Positive self-talk is used to help children focus on the positive rather than the negative and to reinforce their coping skills. The goal is to have the child identify the negative thoughts or self-talk and to recognize that the situation is usually not as terrible or disastrous as it seems. This strategy is not intended to diminish the child's feelings or to be an oversimplified, think-positive approach—it is intended as a way of helping a child who is having unrealistic negative thoughts to identify this negative pattern and develop a more realistic and adaptive outlook (Pearlman, D'Angelo Schwalbe, & Cloltre, 2010).

Weikle (1993) suggested using self-talk with clients who have an internal locus of control and value health. This technique has also been shown to work with coaches and athletes when it comes to coaching behavior and athletes' self-talk. The self-talk of an athlete affects cognitive, motivational, behavioral, and affective mechanisms, and therefore sports performance (Hardy, Oliver, & Tod, 2008). Coaches' esteem support was related to positive self-talk in athletes (Zourbanos, Theodorakis, & Hatzigeorgiadis, 2006), and according to Zourbanos, Hatzigeorgiadis, and Theodorakis (2007), the positive and negative statements made by coaches were related to positive and negative self-talk, respectively, in athletes.

Smith (2002) described using self-talk as part of a cognitive-behavioral intervention that teachers can use with students who have behavioral deficits.

Vernon and Clemente (2004) described using self-talk with high school students who had hostile reactions when confronted by an authority figure. When students find themselves in situations where they want to react with hostility, they can repeat "I'm okay. I don't agree with the way X is treating me, but that's his (her) problem. I'm okay." By focusing on their "okay-ness," the students feel less victimized and more in control of the situation and typically react with less hostility.

Many studies provide support for the efficacy of self-talk in addressing issues of control (Thompson, Sobolew-Shubin, Galbraith, Schwankovsky, & Cruzen, 1993), self-regulating academic behavior (Wolters, 1999), and anxiety (Prins & Hanewald, 1999; Treadwell & Kendall, 1996). Grainger (1991) cautioned that it is important for a person not to dismiss all negative thinking. Instead, professional counselors need to help their clients distinguish between negative thinking that leads to negative self-talk and negative thinking that helps keep them safe. Negative thinking is necessary, especially when a person is in a high-risk situation. This type of thinking sometimes helps a person realize that he must create a plan to be able to live and/or work effectively.

APPLICATION OF THE SELF-TALK TECHNIQUE

Now apply the self-talk technique to a current client or student you are working with or revisit the brief case studies presented at the beginning of this book. How can you use the self-talk technique to address concerns and create movement in the counseling session?

CHAPTER 23

Reframing

ORIGINS OF THE REFRAMING TECHNIQUE

Reframing takes a problematic situation and presents it in a new way that allows the client to adopt a more positive, constructive perspective. Reframing changes the conceptual or emotional viewpoint of a situation and changes its meaning by placing it in another contextual framework that also fits the same facts of the original situation. The goal of reframing is to help the client see the situation from another vantage point, making it seem less problematic and more normal, and thus more open to solution. Reframing and metaphors create hope and motivation by amplifying strengths (Scheel, Davis, & Henderson, 2013).

When reframing, the professional counselor offers a new point of view to the client in the hope that the client will see the situation differently and thus act more suitably. This alternative point of view must fit the situation as well as or even better than the client's original point of view in order to be convincing to the client. If successful, reframing may result in the client seeing a previously unsolvable problem as solvable or seeing it as no longer a problem at all (Hackney & Cormier, 2017). Other times, reframing may allow the client to take a fresh approach to the presenting problem. At any rate, reframing is effective only when the alternative meaning is seen as totally credible.

Historically, reframing is a type of paradoxical strategy used in cognitive-behavioral, Adlerian, strategic family, and structural family therapies. The reframing technique actually evolved from Adlerian theory, but it is addressed here because of its cognitive dimension. In family systems and solution-focused therapies, reframing emphasizes the redefining of experiences and problems in the context of social and cultural systems (Becvar & Becvar, 2012).

In addition, reframing is one of the six influencing skills included in Ivey, Ivey, and Zalaquett's (2018) counseling microskills approach. At its base, reframing operates on the premise that behavioral and emotional problems are caused not by events but by how the events are viewed. Problems arise when events are perceived as blocking a client's goals or as interfering with client values, beliefs, or purposes. The reframing technique also involves the assumption that people have all the resources they need to make a desired change. Reframing accepts the client's worldview and works within this framework to create a solution. Reframing is especially useful when the situation involves redefining offensive motives or behaviors as problematic but well intended (Hackney & Cormier, 2017).

Because problematic behavior patterns often become ingrained, reframing works to reinterpret these behavior patterns. The assumption behind the reframing technique is that, by altering perspectives on a behavior pattern, new behaviors will develop that accommodate this interpretation. Reframing can also move the client from blaming others to taking more responsibility for personal behavior (Young, 2017) and can be used with both intrapersonal and interpersonal issues.

HOW TO IMPLEMENT THE REFRAMING TECHNIQUE

Reframing can be implemented using three simple steps. First, the professional counselor must use a nonjudgmental listening cycle to gain a complete understanding of the client's problem (Young, 2017). This is an essential starting point because reframing must be based on firm knowledge of the client and the client's worldview so that the client can relate to the new frame of reference (i.e., the reframe). Second, once the professional counselor understands the problem, the professional counselor may then build a bridge from the client's point of view to a new way of looking at the problem. At this point it is important to include some aspect of the client's perspective while also suggesting the new one. Finally, the professional counselor must reinforce the bridge until a shift in perspective develops. One way of emphasizing the new perspective is to give the client homework that forces her to see the problem in the new way.

VARIATIONS OF THE REFRAMING TECHNIQUE

There are several varieties of reframing techniques. Reframing is also referred to as relabeling, denominalizing, and positive connotation (Eckstein, 1997). *Relabeling* is a specific type of reframing that consists of replacing a negative adjective with one that is more positive in connotation. For instance, if a woman describes her husband as "hovering or enmeshed," this label could be replaced with the description "caring." *Denominalizing* is the process of removing a diagnostic label and replacing it with a specific behavior that can be controlled. For example, a girl with anorexia may be seen as one who refuses to eat. *Positive connotation* simply describes the symptomatic behavior as being positively motivated. For instance, the statement "My mother never lets me do anything" can be reframed as "My mother loves me enough to set limits" (Vernon & Clemente, 2004).

EXAMPLE OF THE REFRAMING TECHNIQUE

Lori is a 34-year-old female who is experiencing depressed mood, helplessness, and despair. She reports that, prior to her current circumstances taking shape, she has never had any major episodes with depression and typically felt quite happy and in control of her life. She feels her current state of mind is in direct relation to her current situation.

Counselor (C): Well, from what I can tell, you seem like an insightful person. And you say this depressed mood you are feeling is related to your current situation. I'll certainly take your word for that. So tell me more about this current situation of yours.

Lori (L): Okay. Let's see. Up until about 6 months ago, life was good. I have a master's in accounting and am a CPA. Or *was* I should say.

C: You are no longer?

L: Well, technically I am. But it doesn't feel like it since I no longer work as one.

C: I see. Go on.

L: Okay, so anyway, life was good. I completed my master's before meeting my husband. I always knew I wanted to be an accountant, and I went straight through school and took a lot of pride in my abilities as a student and later as an accountant. I went straight to work after graduation, landed an awesome job at a large medical corporation where I eventually worked my way up to a partial supervisory position. By that time, I had met Terry, that's my husband, and then we married 3 years ago. I became pregnant fairly soon after we married and now have beautiful twin boys. We hired someone to care for the children in our home, and I returned to work after maternity leave. Life continued to be good.

C: Okay. It sounds like life has been agreeable for you. You got your education out of the way and had time to focus on your career before meeting your husband. You had children, you hired a nanny, and you got to continue your career, which sounds very important to you.

L: Very. It's something I'm really good at. I feel valuable and appreciated. We all want to feel that, right? And it's not that I don't get that from my family . . . it's just different, you know? It's like, how valuable can you feel changing dirty diapers? Not that I don't adore my children. They're great . . . really! But they don't say things like "Wow, Lori, amazing work on the Bradford account! How about a pay raise?"

C: No, I don't suppose they do.

L: So, it's not that I'm pouting for ungrateful 1-year-olds. That's really not it. It's more that I really valued my career and the sense of worth that it gave me. I worked hard to get where I was. Even sacrificed being with my children to return to it . . . which was really hard . . . especially when they cried for me or were sick . . . . Anyway, everything was still working out. I had it all . . . what every woman wants . . . and then . . . bam!

C: Bam?

L: Yeah, bam! All of a sudden, it's all gone . . . taken from me! I can't believe how much I'm talking. I guess I'm just so relieved to be talking about this to someone without an agenda.

C: I'm very glad to hear that. Talking about it, being able to say out loud what it is you feel, can bring great relief. (Pause) So, it's gone . . . your career, I assume?

L: Yep. All of that hard work just gone. Thanks to my husband. See, he's really close to his parents. And ever since the twins were born, they've been nagging at him and pulling at him and complaining that we lived too far away for them to see their grandchildren grow up. Becoming a father really changed his perspective on things too, and he began to really question my drive to have a career and instead wanted me to focus more on being a parent. It's really not fair that women feel like they have to choose between the two or kill themselves doing both. Well, anyway, out of the blue, supposedly, he received a job offer back home that was just too good to be true . . . almost double the salary . . . which is important to him. He said it must be fate because he wasn't even in the market for a new job. I don't know if I believe him or not. But that's what he said, and he said it was too great an offer to turn down. Looking back, I

should have seen it coming. But at the time, I was completely blindsided. To make matters worse, he told his parents about the offer, and they just took it to mean it was a done deal. They were so excited and talking as if we were already there and one big happy family again. Then I started to feel guilty, like maybe my place should be at home with the kids. And then he felt obligated to his parents and didn't want to break his mother's heart. It was this huge mess, and we ended up here before I could even absorb it all. He put our house on the market, he started his new position, I left my old one, and now the kids and I are at our new home.

C: So that's how everything unfolded to result in your current situation.

L: That's how it unfolded.

C: Can you tell me what exactly about the way things are now that is most troubling to you . . . that has your mood so depressed?

L: I feel like I'm talking too much. Am I talking too much?

C: Not at all. I want to get a very clear idea of what is important to you and what is troubling to you.

Recall that it is extremely important to get the full picture and to understand the client's perspective and worldview in order to present an accurate reframe that will be acceptable to the client.

L: Okay, good. What is it about the way things are now. . . . (Pauses for some time to really pinpoint what is most troubling) Um, I guess . . . (Begins to slow her speech down) . . . that it feels so out of my control? . . . That it feels like a huge mistake? . . . That there's nothing I can do about it? . . . That he was so selfish? . . . And that I feel I have no meaning . . . no purpose . . . (Begins to cry) . . . that all that hard work was wasted, and I'll never have that kind of career again.

C: Uh-huh. Yes, I think I see now. What gave you the most meaning is now gone, through no fault of your own, and now you feel meaningless.

L: Completely.

C: I can see how sad this must make you feel.

L: I'm totally depressed.

C: I can also sense some anger.

L: Yeah, I haven't wanted to admit that, but it's definitely there.

C: That's not surprising, you know. Anger and depression sometimes go hand in hand. Sometimes when we feel we can't do anything to change what we're angry about, we just give up and become depressed.

L: Makes sense. I would say that applies to me. Definitely applies.

There are many ways to arrive at the information needed to offer a reframe to a client. The following exemplifies one such method, but it is certainly not the only one.

C: Okay, Lori, what I'd like to do for just a moment is brainstorm. I want us to work together to come up with a few possible options or exceptions to the current perspective we have on this situation.

L: Okay . . . I think.

C: Okay. Let's play devil's advocate for just a moment. I'm going to make a statement based on what you've told me here today, and I want you to make a statement in return that argues against it. Make sense?

L: Sure.

C: Okay. I'll start with "I have *no* control over my daily life."

L: Ah . . . hmm . . . and I just say something back that goes against that?

C: Yes, but make it true to you.

L: Okay. In some areas of my life, I have more freedom than I've ever had. I can schedule my day any way I like. I can stay up late. I don't have a boss telling me what to do. Like that?

C: Exactly like that. Okay, another one. "*Nothing* in my life gives me meaning."

L: (Talking to self) Nothing in my life gives me meaning . . . argue that . . . well . . . I get meaning from being a mom, and a sister, and a friend. And I have a few hobbies that I'm really good at . . . they give me a sense of pride, I guess.

C: Okay. "There are *no* benefits to being home with my children."

L: Oh, that's not true at all. They will never be 1-year-olds again. I never realized how much I was missing out on before. They'll never be exactly as they are right now.

C: Good. We've got just two more. "I will *never* have a career again."

L: Well, it seems silly to say it like that. Of course I will have a career again, eventually. It just seems impossible in this town to have the kind I want. But I don't suppose I have to stay here forever. So *eventually* I'll have a career again.

C: All right. Last one. "My husband is *completely* self-serving."

L: Oh dear. That's a hard one to argue. I mean, maybe he's not completely self-serving in everything he does, but in this situation, that's certainly hard to argue against. (Pauses and thinks for several moments) I can't come up with anything.

C: Okay, I think I can help with this one. Sometimes when we understand someone's position or motives, when we feel compassion or empathy for them and their choices, we find it impossible to be angry at them—that is, if you don't *want* to be angry anymore.

L: I don't want to be angry anymore. I don't want to be angry or depressed.

C: Okay then, what I mean is that understanding can negate anger. Assume, for instance, when someone cuts me off in traffic, that I immediately conjure up a reason or two why that person may be having the worst day of her life. I say to myself "I bet she just got laid off from her job" or "I bet she just got dumped by her boyfriend." Something like that.

L: Okay. That's funny. I guess then it's hard to be mad at them for cutting you off.

C: Exactly. So, let's do that for your husband. Now you said earlier that this new job opportunity of his came with a large pay increase. Is that right?

L: Yes.

C: Could we possibly conjure up that he was worried about finances prior to that job offer?

L: Oh, we don't have to conjure. He has always worried about finances. And then when we had twins, he panicked. He was always afraid there wouldn't be enough to provide for all of us.

The counselor is about to offer a relabeling of the husband, from "selfish" to "provider." Recall that relabeling is a type of reframe, often used within a larger reframe. Also recall that it is especially helpful to redefine offensive motives as problematic but well intended.

C: Would it be possible, then, to think of your husband as being motivated by the need to be a *provider* for his family rather than having a purely selfish motive?

L: Yes, it would be possible for me to consider that.

C: (Standing up and walking to the window and opening the blinds) What do you see outside my window?

L: (Somewhat puzzled) A dumpster! No wonder you keep the blinds closed!

C: Great view here on the backside of the building, isn't it? What else do you see?

L: I see a few small flowers. Oh, I see that beautiful dogwood tree behind the dumpster.

C: Yes, they grow wild here. Isn't it a sight?

L: Yeah, too bad that big green piece of metal is in front of it!

C: Yes, I don't suppose we can move that, can we?

L: Doubt it.

C: Probably can't change much of anything about what's already out there. (Pauses to let Lori think and returns to chair) From the view we have here, that dumpster is in front of that dogwood. See that building on the other side there?

L: Yes.

C: Suppose my office was in that building. Suppose we went over to that office and looked out that window instead of this one.

L: Okay.

C: The scenery wouldn't have changed, would it?

L: No. The dumpster would still be there.

C: That's right. But do you suppose it might look different from that angle?

L: Well, yes . . . it would . . . because from that window, the dogwood would be in front of the dumpster. You could still see the dumpster, of course, but just barely because the dogwood would be the most obvious.

C: I believe you are exactly right. And I agree with you completely. Suppose that view out there is your life as you've described it early in this session. And suppose that I cannot for one minute change the situation that is your life. I cannot remove that dumpster. But I can lead you to that other window, with the different view. And even though that dumpster would still be there, it wouldn't be the focus of the view. Do you think that would be helpful for you at all?

L: I think that sounds like a fine idea.

C: Well, you've provided plenty of good material. So here goes . . . When you arrived today, you were most troubled by your current situation. You felt both anger and sadness because you viewed your situation as out of your control, your life as meaningless, your career as over, and your husband as selfish. Now, I cannot change the *realities* of your situation, but I can offer you a new frame within which to view it. From this newly framed window, that very same scenery takes on new meaning. As it turns out, you have much control within your current situation. In fact, in some ways, you have more freedom than you've ever had. You have no boss to answer to. You set your daily schedule. You make many independent choices every day. Your life has meaning. You are a mother, and a sister, and a friend. You have hobbies that you are very skilled at and that you take pride in. These things give your life meaning and purpose. . . . Your salaried career is on hold for the moment, and that is temporary. That does not mean that you will never have a career again. It only means that it will be just a while longer. And in the meantime, you get to soak up every little morsel of joy those 1-year-olds have to offer. You don't have to miss one moment of their lives, which will never be as it is now. . . . Finally, it turns out that your husband may be more motivated by his need to provide for the financial welfare of his family than by purely selfish needs, and it is difficult to stay angry at that kind of motivation.

Pauses a few moments to let Lori take all this in.

L: My gosh! If I could keep telling myself that, and really focusing on that part of the picture, I believe I could feel so much better and maybe even actually *enjoy* my current situation.

Notice that the facts of the situation never changed. But with the counselor's help in arguing Lori's points, a credible and alternative meaning was given.

USEFULNESS AND EVALUATION OF THE REFRAMING TECHNIQUE

Reframing can be used in many different situations. It is especially valuable when redefining the problem situation changes the view of the problem so that it is more understandable, acceptable, or solvable. Individuals can use reframing to construct new meanings from previously distressing behaviors or moods caused by irrational thoughts (Wicks & Buck, 2011). Robbins, Alexander, and Turner (2000) showed that reframing was effective in altering client attitudes toward counseling.

Reframing is effectively used in family counseling approaches. Frain et al. (2007) used reframing in their work with families of clients in need of disability rehabilitation services. They helped to alter the family's view of disability as a challenge and opportunity rather than as a career-ending disability. Davidson and Horvath (1997) indicated that reframing was beneficial in couples counseling when addressing dyadic adjustment and marital conflict.

Reframing can be used in family therapy to reduce the blame among family members by attributing negative consequences to situational causes rather than individual family members (Eckstein, 1997). For example, a child's curfew may be seen as a concern for safety rather than a lack of trust. Positive reframing of a negative behavior has been shown to intervene in the scapegoating process within a family as well as to refocus from the problematic aspects of the behavior to the positive functioning of the action (Jessee, Jurkovic, Wilkie, & Chiglinsky, 1982). Reframing can also be applied with those who are addicted to substances or those who are enablers or codependent. LaClave and Brack (1989) presented several case examples in which positive reframing was used to deal successfully with client resistance.

Research on the reframing technique is limited and dated, but some studies have shown that positive reframing is effective in reducing negative emotions and mild to moderate depression (Swoboda et al., 1990). Kraft et al. (1985) evaluated the use of positive reframing against a control group for participants reporting negative emotions. Positive reframing produced greater improvement on outcome measures of depression and mood. Swoboda et al. (1990), compared the effectiveness of positive reframing, paradoxical restraining directives, and a pseudotherapy control for the treatment of depression. Statements such as "being alone and feeling down shows a great tolerance for solitude and basic self-satisfaction" and "feeling badly about yourself rather than taking grievances out on others shows a willingness to sacrifice for the good of others" (p. 256) were used with the positive reframing group. The participants in this reframing group showed the greatest improvement on several outcome measures, suggesting that reframing is a powerful technique for overcoming depression.

APPLICATION OF THE REFRAMING TECHNIQUE

Now apply the reframing technique to a current client or student you are working with or revisit the brief case studies presented at the beginning of this book. How can you use the reframing technique to address concerns and create movement in the counseling session?

CHAPTER 24

Thought Stopping

ORIGINS OF THE THOUGHT STOPPING TECHNIQUE

Thought stopping refers to a group of procedures used to increase a person's ability to block a response sequence cognitively (Bakker, 2009). It was first used in 1875 to treat a man who was preoccupied with thoughts of nude women (Wolpe, 1991). However, many give credit to Alexander Bain for introducing thought stopping in his 1928 book *Thought Control in Everyday Life* (Davis, Robbins-Eshelman, & McKay, 2009). Thought stopping entered the behavior therapy domain after it was suggested by James G. Taylor and adapted by Joseph Wolpe for the treatment of obsessive and phobic thoughts (Davis et al., 2009; Wolpe, 1991). Today, thought stopping procedures are commonly used with sex offenders (Worling, 2012). Thought stopping trains the client to exclude, at the earliest moment possible, every undesirable thought (Wolpe, 1991), usually by invoking the command "Stop" to interrupt unwanted thoughts (Davis et al., 2009).

Thought stopping is successful for several reasons (Davis et al., 2009). First, the command "Stop" serves as a punishment, thus decreasing the likelihood that the thought will recur. Also, the imperative "Stop" acts as a distractor and is incompatible with the unwanted thought. Finally, the command "Stop" can be followed by thought substitutions to help ensure that the unwanted thoughts will not return. For instance, self-accepting statements may be substituted for undesired negative thoughts about the self, a process based on the principle of reciprocal inhibition.

HOW TO IMPLEMENT THE THOUGHT STOPPING TECHNIQUE

Thought stopping involves four steps. First, the client and professional counselor must decide together which thoughts are going to be targeted in the thought stopping procedure (Wolpe, 1991). Second, the client closes his or her eyes and imagines a situation in which the target thought is likely to occur (Davis et al., 2009). Third, the target thought is interrupted by the command "Stop." The last step in thought stopping is to substitute a more positive thought for the unwanted thought. This step begins with the client's overt use of a thought substitution and then progresses to covert (imagery-based) thought substitution. A typical thought stopping session requires 15 to 20 minutes for client self-monitoring. The goal is to have the intrusive thoughts occur less frequently and bring their removal under the control of the client.

Thought interruption, the third step specified above, follows a four-stage process, shifting control from the professional counselor to the client. First, the professional counselor interrupts the client's overt target thoughts until the client signals that the thoughts have subsided. As the client relays his thoughts aloud, the counselor yells "Stop" anytime the client mentions the target thought. Second, the counselor attempts to stop the client's covert thoughts. When the client signals with a silent gesture that he is experiencing the target thought, the therapist yells "Stop!" Eventually, by yelling "Stop" aloud whenever he experiences the target thoughts, the client learns to interrupt his silent thoughts overtly. Finally, the client interrupts his silent thoughts covertly. In his head, the client commands himself to stop whenever he experiences the target thought.

VARIATIONS OF THE THOUGHT STOPPING TECHNIQUE

For some clients, the command "Stop" is not sufficient to suppress unwanted thoughts. In these cases, stronger methods of interruption may be used. Clients may keep a rubber band around their wrist and snap the rubber band when unwanted thoughts occur (Davis et al., 2009). They may also pinch themselves or press their fingernails into their palms in order to stop negative thoughts. In addition, using the "Stop" command while pressing a loud buzzer when unwanted thoughts occur may disrupt the negative thoughts successfully (Wolpe, 1991). Some clients find it helpful to do something physical to break the thought cycle, such as stand up and sit down, turn around several times, or simply cross their legs. Similar to the rubber band and pinching, the physical activity breaks the cognitive "spin cycle."

EXAMPLE OF THE THOUGHT STOPPING TECHNIQUE

Nong is a 17-year-old with anxious-perfectionistic characteristics. She thinks constantly about maintaining high levels of school performance in order to meet future goals of attending a top-tier college. In the process, she creates a great deal of stress in her life. She has sought counseling to help her to stop what she perceives to be constant, perhaps obsessional, thoughts.

Counselor (C):   Okay. What kinds of things specifically do you say to yourself and think about all the time?

Nong (N):   I think that I have to do well in school, or my grades will go down. I have to do well so I can, like, accomplish my goals, you know, do well and succeed.

C: What'll happen if you don't?

N: Oh (nervous laughter), I'll feel bad about myself and, like, my self-confidence will go down . . . I won't feel, like, smart or anything.

C: Is that something you think about a lot?

N: Yeah, like, all the time. I think about it *all* the time. (Pauses and begins to think)

C: You are worried about doing well in school and being smart.

N: What? Yeah, I guess I am.

C: What do you tell yourself specifically? I mean, to hear you tell it now, you're making it sound like an intellectual activity. "Oh, I just want to feel confident about myself." But what do you really say to yourself?

N: I'm dumb or I feel dumb, or I'm going to fail a test, or not get into a good college—stuff like that . . . sometimes, you know, I'm really down there.

C: What does that feel like, when you're really down there?

N: Bad, yeah, horrible.

C: On a scale of 1 to 10? (Introduces scaling procedure)

N: Like a 1 or a 2—pretty bad.

C: And how often does that happen, when you think things like that to yourself?

N: Well, it usually happens if I'm really overloaded, which seems like all the time lately.

C: Okay . . . So how often has that happened in the last week or two, would you say?

N: Um, all the time, especially at the end of, like, a semester, or you know when teachers are cramming in all the . . .

C: It's crunch time?

N: Yeah, end of the quarter, that's when it usually happens.

C: Would you like to learn something that can help with that?

N: Yep. That's why I'm here.

C: Right. Well, saying "I'm dumb" or "I feel stupid" or things like that are kind of self-disrespectful and even destructive. Saying these to yourself, you can understand why you might not feel good about yourself.

N: Right.

C: Because those are kind of nasty, negative things to think about yourself. What I'm going to show you is a technique called thought stopping.

N: Okay.

C: And this will work not just when you're saying things like "I'm dumb" or "I'm stupid" but also when you're saying anything that's kind of nasty and self-destructive, whenever you tend to think about it over and over and over again. We call it obsessive thinking, when you're thinking about something over and over and you just can't get it out of your head. We talked last time about how that happens a lot at bedtime, when you're thinking about some things and you can't get to sleep. You keep thinking and thinking and thinking and just keep going and going and going. So thought stopping is a way of getting you to break the cycle of that obsessive thinking in order to think about something more positive. To start, I want you to think out loud, so I can hear you, the things you say to yourself. Go ahead and say it out loud.

N: I'm stupid, and I feel dumb.

C: Oh, come on, say it like you really mean it.

N: I'm stupid. And I feel dumb!

C: There you go, that's the way you say it in your own mind, right? You don't really go "Oh well, gosh, gee, shucks, Dr. E., I feel stupid." You say "Ugh, that was such a dumb thing to do, that was so stupid, I feel like an idiot!" Those are the types of things that you say, right?

N: Absolutely! That's exactly the way I say it!

C: Okay, now whenever you start to say those things to yourself, I want you to shout out loud "Stop it!" Okay? Try it again out loud.

N: Okay. I'm such a stupid idiot for bombing that test. How dumb could I be? . . . Stop it!

C: Great. Now, doing something physical like saying "Stop it" actually physically interrupts your negative thought cycle. You actually need to do something physical that will break that thought pattern and allow you to switch your thoughts to something that's a more positive

thing to say to yourself, which is your self-talk message, which is what?

N: Everything's going to be okay.

C: Everything's going to be okay. Don't worry, everything's going to be okay. And then you can also use some visual imagery if you want, take yourself to some relaxing, calming place. So, again, you want to break that cycle by saying "Stop it" out loud. You can scream it if you want, then insert your positive self-talk phrase, repeating "Everything is going to be okay" over and over, taking a deep breath, and going to a calming visual image, okay?

N: Okay.

C: Let's try it one more time.

N: I am stupid, I am dumb, I'm an idiot. Stop it! (Pauses for insertion of positive self-talk, breathing, and imagery)

C: Okay, how did that feel?

N: Relaxing.

C: On a scale of 1 to 10?

N: A 6—pretty relaxing, actually.

C: Excellent. All right, now whenever you're out in public, at school, shopping, at the gas station, and you start to think these things about yourself, immediately out in the middle of all these people, you're going to shout. . . .

N: (Starts to laugh) Oh, my, would that ever be embarrassing! You'd have to change my diagnosis pretty quick, huh?

C: Oh, yeah. So when you are out in public, we want to modify this technique somewhat. So, I have brought for you your very own rubber band for your wrist. (Counselor puts the rubber band on Nong's wrist) Ta-da!

N: Wow. Thank you. I'll treasure it always.

C: To be sure. Now instead of shouting out loud "Stop it," instead you will say "Stop it" to yourself inside your head, while at the same time reaching down to your rubber band and snapping yourself on your wrist. (Nong snaps the rubber band against her wrist.) You feel that? How's that feel?

N:　Stings a little, but not too bad.

C:　Yeah, it's a little sting, some physical action to break your negative cognitive spin cycle. I want you to snap it once or, if you don't stop, do it twice while saying "Stop it" inside your mind, and then I want you to switch to a more positive thought, take your deep breath, and even begin a calming visualization if you like. Let's try it one more time—to yourself this time. Think the nasty, negative thoughts, snap the band as you say "Stop it" to yourself, then take your deep breath, take yourself to your calming and relaxing spot, and change your thoughts to something that's more positive, something more productive.

Nong engages in the thought stopping technique by herself.

C:　How was that?

N:　Great. I've got it.

C:　Okay, so wear this rubber band all the time until I see you again, and use it when the obsessive thoughts begin.

N:　Yeah.

The professional counselor and Nong then explore other times when thought stopping may be appropriate to help her generalize use of the technique.

C:　(In conclusion) If you're starting to think these negative things, you just can't get your mind off them, you know that you're just dragging yourself down. And you're just making your life more difficult and more miserable by telling yourself negative and nasty things. Go ahead and yell to yourself "Stop it," snap your rubber band at the same time, then substitute your positive self-talk, breathe deeply, and take yourself to a more calming spot—just relax. Collect your thoughts, and then in a short time you're feeling calmer, and you can make a good decision.

USEFULNESS AND EVALUATION OF THE THOUGHT STOPPING TECHNIQUE

Although used with a variety of problems, thought stopping is most often used with episodic brooding, obsessions, and phobic thoughts, including sexual preoccupation, hypochondriasis, thoughts of failure, thoughts of sexual inadequacy, obsessive memories, and common fears (Davis et al., 2009). It is frequently used with sex offenders who experience intrusive thoughts and visualizations related to their offending behavior (Worling, 2012). Dawood and Jehan (2013) used thought stopping as a part of a CBT treatment that led to significant improvement in OCD with depression.

Dekker (2015) randomized 42 inpatients with depressive symptoms to treatment as usual (TAU) and a brief cognitive therapy treatment that featured thought stopping. Although both conditions led to improvements in quality of life, depression, and negativistic thinking at termination and three-month follow-up, the CT with thought stopping group experienced fewer cardiovascular emergency events and survival than did the TAU condition participants.

Thought stopping has been used to reduce negative self-thoughts. Fernández-Marcos and Calero-Elvira (2015) randomly assigned 60 participants to three conditions: thought stopping, cognitive defusion, and control group. They concluded that both treatment groups self-reported significantly decreased discomfort and thought stopping, which led to higher levels of self-perceived usefulness and ability to deal with intrusive thoughts. Thought stopping has also been used to reduce smoking and visual and auditory hallucinations (Horton & Johnson, 1977) and insomnia (Katofsky et al., 2012). Samaan (1975) reported a case study of a woman who experienced hallucinations, obsessions, and depressive spells. After 10 sessions of thought stopping, flooding, and reciprocal reinforcement treatment, the woman's disturbed behavior decreased from 22 hallucinations, 14 obsessions, and 8 depressive spells per week to an average of 1 or 2 of these events per week during the early part of treatment and eventually to an absence of any of these three disturbances. In addition, Peden, Rayens, Hall, and Beebe (2001) used thought stopping as part of a multicomponent cognitive-behavioral group intervention to treat college women with depression. They found that this intervention resulted in significantly lowered depressive symptoms, especially the symptom of negative thinking, and that these results lasted even through the 18-month follow-up.

Some researchers (Macrae, Bodenhausen, Milne, & Jetten, 1994; Wegner, Schneider, Carter, & White, 1987; Wenzlaff, Wegner, & Roper, 1988) reported that attempts to suppress negative, obsessional thoughts may actually lead to greater expression of these thoughts, whereas other researchers reached the opposite conclusion (Purdon & Clark, 2001; Roemer & Burkovec, 1994; Rutledge, 1998). Han et al. (2013) concluded that thought stopping may not be helpful in the treatment of generalized anxiety disorder. So, thought stopping is a technique that should be used planfully and thoughtfully. Bakker (2009) provided an excellent analysis of the effective use of thought stopping embedded within a cognitive-behavioral therapy (CBT) process, indicating that thought stopping is a specific and specialized form of thought suppression that is highly effective and enhances client coping. The technique has been criticized, however, because some proponents have advocated using mild shocks as the aversive stimulus; shocks should *not* be used.

APPLICATION OF THE THOUGHT STOPPING TECHNIQUE

Now apply the thought stopping technique to a current client or student you are working with or revisit the brief case studies presented at the beginning of this book. How can you use the thought stopping technique to address concerns and create movement in the counseling session?

CHAPTER 25

Cognitive Restructuring

ORIGINS OF THE COGNITIVE RESTRUCTURING TECHNIQUE

Cognitive restructuring is a technique that emerged from cognitive therapy and is usually credited to the work of Albert Ellis, Aaron Beck, and Don Meichenbaum. Sometimes the technique is called correcting cognitive distortions. Cognitive restructuring involves the application of learning principles to thought. The technique is designed to help attain a better emotional response by changing habitual appraisal habits so that they can become less biased. Cognitive restructuring strategy is based on two assumptions: (1) irrational thoughts and defective cognitions lead to self-defeating behaviors, and (2) these thoughts and self-statements can be changed through alterations of personal views and cognitions (James & Gilliland, 2003). Typically, professional counselors use cognitive restructuring with clients who need help replacing negative thoughts and interpretations with more positive thoughts and actions.

HOW TO IMPLEMENT THE COGNITIVE RESTRUCTURING TECHNIQUE

Doyle (1998) described a specific, seven-step procedure for professional counselors to follow when using cognitive restructuring with their clients:

1. Gather background information to discover how the client handled past and current problems.
2. Assist the client in becoming aware of her thought process. Discuss real-life examples that support the client's conclusions and discuss different interpretations of the evidence.
3. Examine the process of rational thinking, focusing on how the client's thoughts affect well-being. The professional counselor can exaggerate irrational thinking to make the point more visible for the client.
4. Provide assistance to the client to evaluate client beliefs about self and others' logical thought patterns.
5. Help the client learn to change internal beliefs and assumptions.
6. Go over the rational thought process again, this time drilling the client on the important aspects using real-life examples. Help the client form reasonable goals that the client will be able to attain.
7. "Combine thought stopping with simulations, homework, and relaxation until logical patterns become set." (p. 92).

Hofmann and Asmundson (2008) discussed how cognitive restructuring allows the professional counselor and client to collaboratively recognize irrational or maladaptive thoughts and to use specific strategies, such as logical disputation, Socratic questioning, and behavioral experiments, to challenge their reality. Meichenbaum (2003) described three goals of the cognitive restructuring technique that the professional counselor and client can meet while going through the seven steps described by Doyle (1998) above:

1. Clients need to become aware of their thoughts; this goal can be worked on during Doyle's (1998) second step. To do this, Meichenbaum (2003) recommended asking the client questions directly related to thoughts and feelings.

The professional counselor also can help the client use imagery reconstruction to access specific thoughts. This process involves the client imagining a situation in slow motion, so to speak, so that the client can describe thoughts and feelings surrounding the incident. It may be easier for the client if the professional counselor asks the client to give advice to a person who experiences stress from a similar situation as the client. Meichenbaum also recommended that clients record their thoughts by self-monitoring. Any time the client becomes troubled, the client should describe, in a journal, the incident and any thoughts and feelings experienced.

2. Clients need to alter their thought processes. During Doyle's (1998) fourth step, the professional counselor can help the client meet this goal and learn to change thinking patterns. Professional counselors can assist clients in becoming aware of the changes in thought process that need to be made by helping the clients to "evaluate their thoughts and beliefs, elicit predictions, explore alternatives, and question faulty logic" (Meichenbaum, 2003, p. 422). When evaluating the client's thoughts and beliefs, the professional counselor can ask questions that help the client define any self-given labels. By having the client make predictions, the professional counselor helps the client realize which thoughts are rational and which are self-defeating. For example, the professional counselor can ask "What do you picture happening or think will happen when X occurs? How can we find out? How do you know that will indeed happen?" (p. 423). The point in exploring alternatives is for the client to take a different perspective. If the client can generate an alternative that is rational instead of self-defeating, progress is being made. Throughout this step, the professional counselor should be sure to question the client's faulty logic including "dichotomous thinking, all or none thinking, overgeneralization, and personalization" (p. 424).

3. Clients need to experiment to explore and change their ideas about themselves and the world; this goal can be worked on during step 5 of Doyle's (1998) process. The professional counselor can start by having the client perform personal experiments in the therapeutic setting and move on to a real-life situation when the client is ready. A scheme diary can also aid in altering a client's beliefs (Meichenbaum, 2003). The following is an excerpt from Meichenbaum (p. 429) outlining how a client can set up a scheme diary:

> *Triggers:* (What set off my reactions?)
> *Emotions:* (What was I feeling?)
> *Thoughts:* (What was I thinking?)
> *Behaviors:* (What did I actually do?)
> *Life traps:* (Which of my "buttons" got pushed? What early life experiences might be related?)
> *Coping:* (Realistic concerns: In what ways were my reactions justified? What did I do to cause or worsen the situation? Is there anyone I can check this out with?)
> *Overreactions:* (In what ways did I exaggerate or misinterpret the situation?)
> *Problem-solve:* (In what ways could I cope better in the future or solve the problem?)
> *Learned:* (What have I learned from this situation that I can apply in the future?)

VARIATIONS OF THE COGNITIVE RESTRUCTURING TECHNIQUE

One variation of this technique requires the client to be aware of and journal thoughts and feelings before, during, and after having a stressful incident. The professional counselor reads the client's journal and analyzes it, paying special attention to any self-defeating thoughts and specific instances that seem to cause the client stress. Once these details are identified, the professional counselor helps the client replace the self-defeating thoughts with coping thoughts.

Doyle (1998) described another variation that clients can use to analyze themselves. The client can use a three-column method to learn more about self-thoughts. The client records the situations that cause anxiety in the first column. The client's thoughts about the situations are noted in the second column. In the third column, the client records the inaccuracies observed in the thought process.

Hackney and Cormier (2017) described how to use coping thoughts in cognitive restructuring. The professional counselor needs to work with the client to identify thoughts the client has that are self-defeating. After the client is aware of her negative thoughts, coping statements must be formed. A coping statement is a positive thought that is a rational response to a self-defeating statement. For example, instead of thinking "I am afraid of this airplane" (a self-defeating statement), a client can think "This airplane has just been inspected by a specialist in aviation safety" (a coping thought) (p. 195).

Southam-Gerow and Kendall (2000) posed another variation of cognitive restructuring that they use with children. When a professional counselor and client are in step 2, attempting to identify the client's self-talk, the professional counselor can ask the child to imagine thoughts as thought bubbles. The child can picture these thought bubbles running through the child's head, just like in a comic strip. This alternative helps make the concept of self-talk more understandable for young children.

EXAMPLE OF THE COGNITIVE RESTRUCTURING TECHNIQUE

Kay is a 48-year-old female who initially presented for counseling about relationship issues. After a few counseling sessions, it became apparent that Kay became angry with family members several times daily, often resulting in spending an entire day feeling hostile, upset, and irritable.

Counselor (C):   I see you have several sheets of paper here with you today.

Kay (K):   Yep. I did what we talked about last time.

C: You wrote down each situation that made you angry this week?

K: Yeah. And I even jotted down why it made me so mad. Want to see?

C: I'd rather you tell me about a few of them, if you don't mind.

K: Sure . . . okay . . . um . . . well . . . I'll just start with the first one. Um, so, as soon as I left here last week, my husband called me on the phone and asked where I was. Well, I had already told him I had a counseling appointment that afternoon, and so first I got mad that he had forgotten and that he was calling me asking where I was. Then he said he was calling to tell me to pick up the ingredients I needed to make dinner because he forgot to get them earlier like I had asked him to do. Well, that really made me mad because he should have already done it.

C: I'd like to get a better idea of what "mad" in this situation means exactly. As a result of this phone call, how mad would you say you were on a scale of 1 to 10, with 10 being just slightly irritated and 1 being . . .

K: Ready to smash windows?

C: Okay, 1 being ready to smash windows.

K: That's easy. I was a 1. By the time I got home, I could have smashed every window in that house and on every one of those stupid cars he works on.

C: Alright. I get the idea. And one more . . . thinking about your husband's behavior and comments during that phone call, on a scale of 1 to 10 again, with 10 being just a little thoughtless but probably not on purpose and a 1 being the worst thing a person could ever do to you . . .

K: I'd say a 1 again.

C: Okay, we'll come back to that a little later.

Next, the counselor uses a technique known as laddering, which is helpful in uncovering the core beliefs behind a person's feelings and behaviors.

C: Now, thinking about this one situation, and I know you went to a lot of trouble this week to write down others, and we will get to them after we talk this one through, but just thinking about the phone call right now, you said two things made you really mad about this call. One was that your husband didn't even remember you had told him you had a counseling session and was calling to ask where you were. Number two was that he asked you to pick up ingredients he was supposed to have gotten already. Is that right?

K: Exactly.

C: Your husband didn't remember you had a counseling session and called to ask where you were. What does this mean to you?

K: That he doesn't listen to what I tell him.

C: Okay, so your husband doesn't listen to what you tell him. What does this mean to you?

K: That he's not paying attention to me.

C: Alright, and your husband doesn't pay attention to you. What does that mean to you?

K: That he doesn't care about me! (Head down, thinks for a few moments, looks up) If he cared, he would pay attention. Right? Wouldn't he pay attention if he cared?

Kay has just discovered an underlying belief and is now questioning it herself.

C: Good, Kay. I know this is hard, but let's keep going. And now, if he doesn't care about you, what does that mean to you?

K: That no one cares about me. I am unlovable. (She speaks this very softly and then gets loud and angry again.) Who would care about me if my own husband doesn't?

C: That's right, Kay. You believe that when he doesn't pay attention to you, or doesn't remember what you say, then he must not care for you. And if he does not care for you, then you are unlovable and no one can care for you.

K: Yes! You get it! That's exactly right!

The counselor suspects there is a theme to Kay's anger and that "all roads will lead to the same destination," showing that her anger is predominantly tied to feeling unloved and uncared for.

C: Okay, let's go back to the phone call if you are ready. You said there was another part to that conversation that upset you. He asked you to pick up ingredients he was supposed to get

himself. You said that he should have already done it.

K: Yes, he should have already done it! I'm the one that has to cook the meal to begin with, and I had a really bad week—you remember, I told you about it last week. I was so fed up with everything and everyone and he knew that! The least he could have done was get the ingredients from the store when he had plenty of time and little else to do! He knew how tired I was, and yet he chose not to lift a finger to help me out! (Is angry again)

C: Okay, this is going to sound familiar, but we are going to do the same thing we've just done to help us get to the heart of the matter. You are saying that he knew you were tired and that you had a bad week, and yet he "chose" not to help you. What does this mean to you?

K: Oh, I see where this is going. Well, okay. He knew I was tired and already sick of everything, yet he didn't do what I asked him to do anyway. Well, that means I'm not a priority to him, doesn't it?

C: Okay, so you are not a priority to him. What does that mean?

K: I guess it means I'm not too important.

C: Uh-huh. And if you're not too important to him, what does that mean to you?

K: Hell, I guess it means what I already know . . . that I'm not important, period. I'm no damn good.

C: Alright, Kay. Do you notice any similarities between this statement and the one you said a few moments ago?

K: You mean when I said that no one cares about me?

C: Yes, that's what I mean.

There is silence for a few moments as Kay thinks this over. It is probably very difficult for her to acknowledge how her thoughts may be related to her anger at her husband because she much prefers to blame him.

K: And just now when I said that I'm not important . . . that I'm no good?

C: Yes, that's right.

K: Okay, I can see where those are similar. I'm unlovable . . . I'm no good. They're similar.

C: Kay, everybody has these sorts of beliefs, and we carry them around with us every day. Sometimes we don't even know what they are or that they're there because they've been a part of us for so long that we don't even notice they exist. But believe me, they control how we interpret things, how we feel and what we do, because they are so strong and we believe in them so much. I would bet, Kay, that these beliefs that we just uncovered, these beliefs that you have, are at the heart of much of what you have on that paper there in your hand. I would bet that if we repeated this same process with every situation on that list, we might find a very similar belief for most of them. What do you think, Kay?

K: (Looks at list, thinks over several of the situations, is quiet for one or two minutes) I can see that, yes. I just sort of did that questioning thing in my head, and I can see that that is where it is going . . . to the same sort of thing, yes. But the way he acts sometimes is not fair to me. And I don't want to excuse all of the crappy things he does. I'm not taking responsibility for his behavior!

C: No, Kay, you're not. Not at all. We won't take responsibility for his behavior, and we can't necessarily change his behavior. But what we can do instead is focus on how it makes you feel, on your reaction and your angry feelings . . . those feelings that make you feel so awful about yourself.

K: Okay. We can do that.

C: I want to tackle this in two ways. First, I want us to think of alternative reasons for your husband's behavior. Then, I want us to rethink how others' behavior defines you. Okay?

K: Okay. Well, I can think of a few other reasons for his behavior.

C: Good. Good.

K: Well, when I told him about my counseling session, he was underneath the hood of a car

and probably really had to pay attention to what he was doing and maybe I just picked a bad time to tell him.

C: Good. What else?

K: (Thinks for a moment) Well, he did sound worried when he called. Like, when he couldn't find me, he got worried or something. Probably not though. He was probably just worried about what he was going to eat for supper. I don't know, maybe.

C: It's possible, then, that he was so preoccupied with his work that he didn't really absorb your appointment time, and then it is also possible that he was worried about you when he couldn't find you.

K: Yes, it's possible.

C: Good. So remember earlier when I asked you to rate his behavior during that phone call on a scale of 1 to 10, with 10 being just a little thoughtless but probably not on purpose and a 1 being the worst thing a person could ever do to you?

K: Yep.

C: And you said a 1, absolutely a 1.

K: I did.

C: Now, just taking those possibilities that we just discussed into account, now how would you rate his behavior on that same 1 to 10 scale?

K: Um. Yeah. Well, that would have to be much higher, like maybe 8 or 7.

C: And is it entirely possible that these are more accurate reasons for his behavior?

K: Very possible now that I think about it rationally. Yes.

C: So given that this is possible, and you now rate his behavior an 8 or a 7, but your reaction was a "smashing windows" 1, what do you make of that?

K: It seems a little extreme. I have to admit that a lot of my reactions are that way. Sometimes I feel bad afterward, but then I just get mad again and don't even have time to correct it or apologize for it. It's, like, as soon as I think maybe I overreacted, one of them makes me mad again.

C: Yes, it's easier for that to happen when every time a person forgets what you said, or forgets to do what you asked them to do, you interpret it to mean that you are no good and unlovable.

K: Makes a lot of sense. What am I going to do about it?

C: Good question. We've made so much progress already. You've worked very hard today. And I want you to know that these beliefs, they didn't develop overnight. They've been taking shape for well over 40 years now, and they are going to take some time to change.

K: Not 40 more years, I hope!

C: No. Not 40 more years. But it will take some time and a lot of hard work, like what we've been doing here today.

K: I can do that.

C: Well, then let's move on to the second way I want to tackle this. Remember I said I first wanted us to think of alternative reasons for your husband's behavior, and we did that just now. Then, I said I wanted us to rethink how others' behavior defines you. Remember?

K: I remember. Let's do that.

C: Okay. Then at the risk of you getting angry again, let's assume for just a moment that it is possible after all that your husband does not care about you, that you are not important to him. You said earlier that means you are unlovable and no good. But does it really? Does it really have to mean that, Kay?

K: Well, it's pretty bad when your own husband doesn't care. It must mean something.

C: Yes, it does. It does mean something. To me, it means your husband doesn't care. But does it have to mean anything else? Do his thoughts and feelings about you have to define you?

K: You mean, does it have to mean that nobody thinks I'm important or good or lovable?

C: Exactly! Does it have to mean that?

K: No. I guess it doesn't. It just means that he doesn't.

C: And would that be terrible?

K: It would hurt.

C: Yes, it would hurt very much, but . . .

K: But it wouldn't be the most terrible thing ever. And it wouldn't mean that everybody feels the way he feels.

C: That's right, Kay! See? You're getting there. Doesn't that feel different?

K: It feels weird to say that.

C: It's very new for you to think this way, yes. But assume you were thinking this way during the phone conversation. A moment ago, we changed your perception and rating of his behavior. Now let's assume that you had had this perception during the phone call. Do you think your reaction would have been a "smashing windows" 1?

K: Not even close. I might have actually felt a little sad instead of angry. You know sad might be a nice change from being so damn mad all the time.

USEFULNESS AND EVALUATION OF THE COGNITIVE RESTRUCTURING TECHNIQUE

Johnco, Wuthrich, and Rapee (2012) found that cognitive flexibility in adults was an important predictor of whether an adult will be able to acquire and master cognitive restructuring coping strategies. Although cognitive restructuring could be practiced with groups, clients tend to open up more if it is used on a one-on-one basis (Madu & Adadu, 2011). Cognitive restructuring is commonly used with individuals who are polarized thinkers, display fear and anxiety in certain situations, and overreact to typical life issues using extreme measures. Velting, Setzer, and Albano (2004) suggested using cognitive restructuring with adolescents and children who have anxiety disorders. By identifying thoughts that lead to anxious feelings, children can learn to challenge their own self-defeating thoughts with coping thoughts.

Cognitive restructuring has been used in recent years to treat post-traumatic stress disorder (PTSD) in adolescents (Rosenberg, Jankowski, Fortuna, Rosenberg, & Mueser, 2011) and adults (Bryant et al., 2008), although the additive effect of cognitive restructuring did not improve upon gains made using the more traditional prolonged exposure approaches used to treat PTSD (Foa et al., 2005). Cognitive restructuring has also been shown to be effective in reducing feelings of contamination in adult survivors of childhood sexual abuse when coupled with imagery activities (Jung & Steil, 2012). Cognitive restructuring has also been used successfully with clients with depression (Evans, Velsor, & Schumacher, 2002), panic disorder (Beamish, Granello, & Belcastro, 2002; Beck, Berchick, Clark, Solkol, & Wright, 1992; Overholser, 2000), self-esteem issues (Horan, 1996), stress (Hains & Szyjakowski, 1990), negative self-referential thoughts

(Deacon, Fawzy, Lickel, & Wolitzky-Taylor, 2011), anxiety (Courtney, 2015; Shurick et al., 2012), social phobia, obsessive compulsive disorder, panic disorder, phobia, and substance abuse (Saltzberg & Dattilio, 1996). In a study attempting to reduce test anxiety during high-stakes tests, cognitive restructuring was equal in effectiveness to more traditional treatment using systematic desensitization (Baspinar Can, Dereboy, & Eskin, 2012).

APPLICATION OF THE COGNITIVE RESTRUCTURING TECHNIQUE

Now apply the cognitive restructuring technique to a current client or student you are working with or revisit the brief case studies presented at the beginning of this book. How can you use the cognitive restructuring technique to address concerns and create movement in the counseling session?

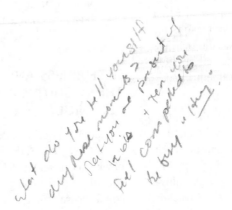

CHAPTER 26

Rational-Emotive Behavior Therapy (REBT): The ABCDEF Model and Rational-Emotive Imagery

ORIGINS OF THE ABCDEF MODEL AND THE RATIONAL-EMOTIVE IMAGERY TECHNIQUE

Rational-emotive behavior therapy (REBT) was created by Albert Ellis in the 1950s after he determined that Rogerian therapy and psychoanalysis were ineffective methods of treatment because they failed to focus on a client's current thoughts and beliefs. REBT has undergone several transformations, from rational therapy to rational-emotive therapy, to its current name, REBT, in an attempt to encompass thinking, feeling, and behaving. When Ellis changed the name to REBT, he recognized that emotions, behaviors, and thoughts are not separable (Seligman & Reichenberg, 2013).

In REBT, emotions are important; however, a person's cognitions are the source of psychological issues. The professional counselor needs to help the client understand that feelings are not caused by events, other people, or the past but, rather, by the thoughts the person has developed surrounding the situation. The basic idea of the theory is that by changing one's irrational beliefs into more flexible and rational ones, a more adaptive change in behavioral and emotional consequences can occur

(Davies, 2006). One major goal of REBT is to help clients strive for unconditional self-acceptance (USA), unconditional other-acceptance (UOA), and unconditional life-acceptance (ULA) (Dryden & David, 2008).

HOW TO IMPLEMENT THE ABCDEF MODEL AND THE RATIONAL-EMOTIVE IMAGERY TECHNIQUE

What follows is a somewhat simplified or deconstructed version of REBT. In REBT, the professional counselor takes a directive approach in helping the client, and treatment is brief (Seligman & Reichenberg, 2013). The professional counselor needs to remain somewhat detached from the client in order to have an objective view of the client's irrational beliefs. In this approach, the therapeutic alliance is desirable but not a necessary aspect of treatment. REBT has three goals: (1) to help clients gain insight into their self-talk, (2) to help clients assess their thoughts, feelings, and behaviors, and (3) to train clients in the principles of REBT so that they will function more effectively in the future without the aid of a professional counselor (Ellis & Wilde, 2002).

A core concept of Ellis's REBT is the ABCDE model. (Corey, Corey, and Corey [2018] expanded on the ABCDE model by adding F. F stands for the new feeling that a client has if disputing was effective.) The activating event (A) is the situation that triggers a client's beliefs; it can be an event that happened or is inferred, is external or internal, or it may refer to the past, present, or future (Dryden & Branch, 2008). It is important for the professional counselor to understand what actually happened during the event as well as the client's perceptions of what happened. The professional counselor needs to help the client give the right amount of details about A; some clients will want to give more details than necessary and others will be too vague. If the client describes many A's, the professional counselor needs to help the client choose one to begin working.

According to REBT, there are two types of beliefs (B), rational and irrational (Hackney & Cormier, 2017). A person's beliefs affect both thoughts and actions. Rational beliefs are realistic and can be supported by evidence. They are flexible and logical, and they help the client reach goals. Irrational beliefs are not realistic and are often based on "absolutistic musts" (Ellis, 1999). They are rigid and illogical, and they do not help the client reach goals. To identify a client's irrational belief system, a professional counselor needs to examine the client's shoulds and musts, awfulizings, can't-stand-its, feelings of worthlessness, and overgeneralizations (Ellis, 2015). Usually, a client's irrational beliefs will be related to self-denigration or a blaming/condemning of others' intolerance of frustration. Typically, irrational beliefs fall under one of the following 11 statements (Hackney & Cormier, 2017):

1. I believe I must be loved or approved of by virtually everyone with whom I come in contact.
2. I believe I should be perfectly competent, adequate, and achieving to be considered worthwhile.
3. Some people are bad, wicked, and villainous, and therefore should be blamed and punished.
4. It is a terrible catastrophe when things are not as I would want them to be.
5. Unhappiness is caused by circumstances that are out of my control.
6. Dangerous or fearsome things are sources of great concern and their possibility for harm should be a constant concern for me.
7. It is easier to avoid certain difficulties and responsibilities than it is to face them.
8. I should be dependent to some extent on other persons and should have some person on whom I can rely to take care of me.
9. Past experiences and events are what determine my present behavior; the influence of the past cannot ever be erased.
10. I should be quite upset over other people's problems and disturbances.
11. There is always a right or perfect solution to every problem, and it must be found or the results will be catastrophic. (p. 82)

The consequence (C) should be assessed after A but before B. C is the client's emotional or behavioral response to beliefs the client holds about the activating event. This is usually what sparks the client to initially seek counseling. Negative emotions such as concern, sadness, remorse, and sorrow are healthy responses, whereas anxiety, depression, guilt, and hurt are unhealthy responses (Dryden & Branch, 2008).

After A, B, and C are identified and assessed, the professional counselor facilitates a dispute (D) of the client's irrational belief "by asking questions that encourage the person to question the empirical, logical, and pragmatic status of" the irrational belief (Dryden, 1995, p. 34). There are three steps to D: debating, discriminating, and defining (James & Gilliland, 2003). The professional counselor debates the client's belief system surrounding A, helps the client discriminate between rational and irrational reactions, and helps the client define statements in a more rational way. When debating, the professional counselor can use some of the following questions: "Is that good logic?" "If a friend held that idea, would you accept it?" "Why does it have to be so?" "Where's the evidence?" (Hackney & Cormier, 2017), as well as "What would happen if . . . ?" "Why must . . . ?" or "Can you be happy even if you don't get what you want?"

D can be achieved through cognitive, emotive, and behavioral techniques. Professional counselors can choose to use logical disputes in which they attack the accuracy of the client's argument, empirical disputes in which they center on the truth of the client's irrational beliefs, or functional disputes in which they focus on changing the belief to reduce the amount of discomfort experienced at C. Rational self-analysis can also be used for disputing. In rational self-analysis, the client examines A, B, C, and D, and describes an alternative reaction.

After disputing, the professional counselor and client evaluate the effects (E) of D. If D is successful, the client will alter feelings and actions because he has altered his beliefs. When A occurs, the client will be able to make more rational conclusions.

Dryden (1995) outlined a fairly specific 13-step process for implementing REBT:

1. Ask the client what brought him to counseling.
2. Agree on a target problem to discuss and goals for counseling.
3. Assess the activating event (A). It is important to determine the action that triggered an irrational belief. (An alternative is to have step 4 precede step 3.)
4. Assess the consequence (C) of the issue that resulted in seeking counseling. The consequence may be behavioral, emotional, or cognitive.
5. Identify and assess a client's secondary emotional problems, if any.
6. Teach the client that beliefs behind A were directly related to C.
7. Assess B, distinguishing between absolutist (traditional) thinking and more rational thoughts.
8. Make the connection between the irrational B and C.
9. Help the client dispute (D) the irrational belief and facilitate a deeper understanding of the irrational B.
10. Help the client deepen his confidence in the new rational belief.
11. Assign homework allowing the client to put into practice what has been learned.
12. Check the client's progress on the homework during the next session.
13. Help the client work through any difficulties with the issue or homework and generalize use of the process to other issues.

I observed Albert Ellis in action, both in person and on video, on numerous occasions consistently using the following seven-step process with clients.

1. *Accessing the client's self-talk:* The client is encouraged to talk about a presenting issue in order to assess the A and C. Particular attention is given to what self-messages the client is thinking, making these messages explicit.
2. *Determining the client's underlying belief:* From the explicit self-talk messages, the client's B is determined. If this belief is irrational, consensus is gained to alter the belief and thus reach a more desirable feeling and consequence.
3. *Agreeing on a more rational belief:* Together, the client and professional counselor can reach agreement on a more rational and appropriate belief to obtain the more desirable feeling and consequence.
4. *Performing rational-emotive imagery (REI):* Refer to the REI section that follows for a discussion of these procedures. REI is practiced in the session at least once to be sure the client understands how to implement the technique properly.
5. *Assigning homework:* The client is required to practice REI using the presenting issue three to five times every day until the next session in order to develop the more rational belief.
6. *Positive consequence:* The client self-rewards for complying with the homework each day.
7. *Negative consequence:* The client self-punishes for not complying with the homework each day.

Ordinarily, processing a client issue using REBT procedures requires 20 to 50 minutes.

Rational-Emotive Imagery

Often subsumed within the REBT process, the technique of rational-emotive imagery (REI) was developed by Maultsby in 1984 and involves intense mental practice to establish patterns of emotional adaptation. With the help of the professional counselor, the client visualizes himself thinking, feeling, and behaving just as he would like to be able to do in everyday life. The primary goal of REI is for the client to change emotions from unhealthy to healthy with the help of the professional counselor (Seligman & Reichenberg, 2013).

Before implementing this technique, it is important for the professional counselor to help the client perform a rational self-analysis to ensure that the client understands the irrational beliefs surrounding the distressing situation (Maultsby, 1990). It is also necessary for the professional counselor to understand the ABCDEFs of REBT. Once the client has identified his irrational beliefs, the professional counselor and client can begin the following seven-step process (Seligman & Reichenberg, 2013):

1. *Visualize an unpleasant activating event:* The professional counselor should tell the client to imagine the details of the event vividly.
2. *Experience the unhealthy negative emotions:* The client needs to get in touch with the emotions that surface during the activating event and then spend several minutes facing the emotions. Imagining these inappropriate emotions is called negative imagery. It is important for the client to picture himself in the situation vividly.
3. *Changing the emotions:* Once the client has experienced the unhealthy emotions, he needs to spend time changing them into appropriate responses by visualizing himself responding with healthy emotions to the activating event. When the client imagines the healthy response, it is called positive imagery.
4. *Examine the process:* In this step, the professional counselor needs to help the client understand how changing his belief system (B) affected the activating event (A) and the resulting emotional consequence (C). It is essential that the client understand how his self-talk changed from the old belief to bring about the more rational, new belief.
5. *Repetition and practice:* The client needs to repeat steps 1 to 3 for at least 10 minutes every

day until he no longer experiences unhealthy emotions in response to the activating event.
6. *Reinforcing the goal:* After several weeks, the client should be able to experience healthy, appropriate emotions while experiencing little, if any, of the previously experienced inappropriate emotions when he encounters the activating event.
7. *Generalization of skills:* Once the client has learned this technique, he can use it for other activating events that also trigger inappropriate emotional responses.

VARIATIONS OF THE ABCDEF MODEL AND THE RATIONAL-EMOTIVE IMAGERY TECHNIQUE

General REBT is used with clients who have a wide range of concerns, and elegant REBT is used with clients who seek deeper, more meaningful philosophical changes (Seligman & Reichenberg, 2013). When using elegant REBT, the professional counselor frequently engages the client in rational, positive coping statements. The client writes down irrational beliefs, disputes, and effective rational beliefs. The professional counselor can record the client reciting the effective rational beliefs so that the client can view the recording at home and so work from the sessions will be reinforced.

EXAMPLE OF THE ABCDEF MODEL AND THE RATIONAL-EMOTIVE IMAGERY TECHNIQUE

Barb is an adult female teacher and mother of two teenagers who has struggled with perfectionism since childhood. The following case exemplifies the use of REBT and rational-emotive imagery (REI). Barb initially presented with panic disorder, and that condition was successfully treated first. Her struggle with perfectionism is being addressed as a secondary issue during the fourth session. The activating event (A) (perfectionism-related occurrences) has already been identified, and Barb has given several examples of how the events affect her (C). The counselor starts by accessing Barb's self-talk (step 1).

Counselor (C):   How do you know that the perfectionism is there? What kinds of things do you notice about your life and actions?

Barb (B):   Well, first of all, I don't handle it very well when things don't go according to my plan. If everything isn't just right, I get very upset and I get very . . . I'm very much . . . um . . . very much afraid that . . . um . . . if everything isn't just right, that nothing's going to be right, and if it's not just right, that it's my fault that it's not just right. I get very stressed.

C: And the stress comes. What effect does it have on your life, and the general way that you live your life?

The counselor is helping Barb explore the C.

B: Um . . . I can be neurotic sometimes about planning things and making things just right, and you know my expectations have gotten very high. I think I've gotten better over time. When I was younger it used to be really bad, if I couldn't accomplish something immediately, then I assumed that I couldn't do it and it was probably my fault that I couldn't do it, and I wasn't even going to try any more. Some things I probably could have done, and now it's just, you know I've gotten better, but it's made me afraid to try things because if I don't accomplish them successfully, I'm afraid what other people will think, that there's something wrong.

C: All right. That's interesting because I hear you say that your perfectionism keeps you from trying new things because you may get kind of frustrated and take your hands off things. Other people sometimes decide that they will get even more controlling, sort of "I'm gonna master this no matter what."

B: I'm more of the former. If I don't think I can do it, I avoid it, more afraid to fail—or at least of others seeing that I fail.

C: And you avoid it. Okay, so that's where we're at today. We want to deal with this issue of perfectionism, and I'd like to use this process with a big, fancy name called rational-emotive

behavior therapy, which has about all the components of someone's psychological being wrapped up in there somewhere: the rational thinking self, the emotive feeling self, and, of course, the behaving, or acting, self. We're going to try to do something to counteract your thoughts of perfectionism and the accompanying feelings and actions. So I hear you say a number of things about the perfectionism. One thing that I heard you say is that everything has to be just right, and whenever everything has to be just right, you're saying these things to yourself, some kind of conversation going on inside your brain. And I heard some of that self-talk conversation in the first minute or two, "If everything isn't just right, nothing is going to be right, and it's all my fault," and that makes you behave in a stressed out, worried, and perfectionistic manner.

B: Right.

Counselor begins step 2: Determining the client's underlying belief (B).

C: So what I want you to focus on now is, what do you think the values and beliefs are that underlie those thoughts going on in your brain?

B: Oh . . . um . . . well, that if it's worth doing, if something's worth doing, it's worth doing right! Um . . . so I feel like, I feel like I've got to do everything I do well. Because if I'm doing something, then I have to do it well. That failure isn't really something that you're allowed to do, you know. I can't really mess up.

C: I'm even hearing that it's more than just if I'm going to do something, then I have to do it well. It's almost as if I *must* do it well, I *should* do it well, and if I *don't* do it well, then . . . (Pause)

B: I fail . . . then something's wrong with me!

C: I have failed, I have failed (Writes this down), something is wrong with me. Now we're getting somewhere. Something is wrong with you, and what is wrong with you? Because I know you've been thinking about this for a long time.

B: Um . . . oh . . . I'm not perfect, and I'm not a good person, and people will think that I'm not a good person, and, you know, people will judge me to be inferior. You know, I will be inferior to them, inferior to co-workers, or inferior to friends.

C: So what kind of emotional reaction do you get, when you think "Oh, I am not perfect, I am inferior to all of my friends and neighbors and colleagues?"

B: Oh, it's like this big welling up, like your heart fills up and you're crushed and you know, you get overwhelmed sometimes with it, like you don't know what to do next and you don't know how to fix it, and, oh, my gosh, I've gotta do, I've gotta do something to fix it. So with me it's always been, well, I just won't do it at all because if I can't do it well, I'll just make up some reason that I'm not doing it anymore, instead of just soldiering on and trying to just do the best I can at something. I'm not doing it right, so I shouldn't be doing it at all.

C: Okay, so you get this visceral reaction; you can feel it inside your body and get all tensed up. I can see from your hands that you get kind of edgy and fidgety about this.

B: Definitely.

C: Okay, good.

B: Good?

C: I mean it's good that you're able to describe all those things because that's what we're trying to do something about here, so that really helps me understand.

Introduce scaling procedure—see Chapter 1.

C: Now on a scale of 1 to 10, with 10 being calm, cool, relaxed, no problems at all, and 1 being on the edge of that panic attack, emotionally upset, and the stomach turning and all that. Whenever you're saying these things to yourself, like "I'm not perfect" or "I'm inferior to all my colleagues, friends, and neighbors," where are you on that scale?

B: Oh, I'm probably 1 or 2.

C: So you're way down there—1 or 2—on the verge of something really negative happening.

B: Uh-huh.

C: Okay, so I'm not perfect, I'm inferior to all these other folks. What's so horrible about realizing that you're not perfect that would lead everybody else to think that you're inferior or no good, or is that just what you're saying to yourself?

B: Well, I'm saying that to myself, you know, it's like this little thing that goes on in your head. Like, if they knew that I wasn't perfect, if they knew I couldn't do this well, they wouldn't like me, or hire me, or live near me, or be my friend. They wouldn't talk to me or sit by me at sporting events or whatever. If people think I'm not perfect, they're not gonna like me. If I'm not perfect, they're not going to accept me.

C: Okay. That's a pretty powerful belief. Now, what's the emotional consequence of these thoughts? If you could label these feelings, what do they lead you to? "Okay, I have to be perfect, I have to be superior, I have to be as good as everyone else or even better than everyone else. And if I'm not, then it's awful and horrible"?

B: Yeah.

C: But where does it lead in the way of your emotional reaction? I mean, if you could label it, what would you call it?

B: Um, it depends. Sometimes it makes me put on this front of . . . appearance . . . it makes me . . . I don't know . . . seem superficial.

C: Right, now that's how you *cope* with the emotional reaction. I'm hearing you say something more like you get extraordinarily anxious, worried, and . . .

B: Hurt, like emotionally hurt, like someone has done something to me. You've already accepted the judgment, you don't know, I don't know if anyone is really making it, but a little voice in the back of my head is telling me "Yes, they are, and they're judging you, and they're judging you negatively."

C: Everyone's looking at you and judging you. Okay, so we get worried and hurt and this real anxiety, this kind of visceral anxiousness happening every time. You think, "I'm not perfect, and it's horrible and awful, and if I can only be perfect, my life would be so much better."

B: Uh-huh.

C: Has your life ever been perfect?

B: Oh, no.

C: No. Has anyone's life ever been perfect?

B: No. (Starts laughing)

C: Okay, so you're aware of this on the cognitive level. You're thinking, "Okay, I know that this is kind of irrational, that this is not the way I should be thinking, but I just can't help it. You know, I just have this way of thinking, and it leads me to this almost panic reaction, this worry and this anxiety." Is this rational?

B: No way.

The counselor begins step 3: Agreeing on a more rational belief and emotional consequence.

C: Rather than intense anxiety, worrying, or panic when you are not perfect, what would be a more rational response to these situations?

B: I dunno. Maybe . . . maybe others would just be disappointed, or just suck it up and go on. I dunno.

C: Okay, disappointed. (Writes this down). And so what we need to do now is do something about it. So you're about a 1 or a 2 on the scale when these types of things happen, and you're saying them to yourself. You're kind of realizing, "Hey, I'm bringing a lot of these things on myself. In fact, probably just about all of it, I'm bringing it on myself." And now what we need to do is get you a little bit closer to what a normal reaction might be. You see, it's normal to make mistakes sometimes. You kind of feel "Wow, you know, I should have done better, because I'm a bright, articulate, capable woman, and I should be able to get things done in a fairly efficient manner. Not necessarily perfectly but fairly efficiently." We want to get you back closer to more of a normal reaction. So what I want to do with you right now is a technique called rational-emotive imagery.

Begin step 4—REI.

So I want you to close your eyes, and I want you to imagine that something is happening, and you are basically failing at it, that it's not going well. And you're saying to yourself things like "I can't believe this. I'm not perfect. What would the neighbors think? What would my colleagues think? They're going to think that I'm inferior." And I really want you to feel it inside your stomach and inside your body that you're up there at 1 or 2 on the scale and that this is just a horrible, awful thing that happened to you. Can you feel that?

B: (Laughs, smiles, and shakes her head in an obvious "yes" gesture) Oh, yeah. . . .

C: Yeah, that's pretty easy to do. I want you to sit there with that feeling for a bit and just really feel all that churning going on inside you. (Pause for about a minute) And now I want you to change that emotion or that feeling from this horrible, awful 1 or 2. I want you to just be, instead of anxious and churning, and really worried and upset, I want you to be somewhat disappointed in yourself. Just slightly disappointed. Not *really* disappointed, way out there at the end of the scale. I just want you to be somewhat disappointed. That, yeah, you probably could've, if you had had more time, put a little bit more effort into it, maybe things would have gone better. But, hey, everything is going to be all right. Just be slightly disappointed that you didn't do everything perfectly. And then give me a little sign that you're able to do that. You might even want to do some of your deep breathing to calm yourself down. So go ahead and bring yourself up to just slightly disappointed. Disappointed . . . but not worried and upset and angry about everything. (Pauses for a minute until Barb gives a nod) Are you there?

B: Yeah.

REI helps transition to the (D) disputation phase by creating a new internal dialogue.

C: Okay. Now, what did you do to get from the 1 or 2? You can open your eyes now and look again. What did you do to get from the 1 or the 2 up to just slightly disappointed? What kinds of things did you say to yourself? What kinds of things went on in your brain?

B: Um . . . I don't have to be perfect.

C: Okay.

B: I'm not perfect. Nobody's perfect. The other person's not perfect. Um . . . nobody's . . . uh . . . you know, the worst consequences, we've talked about this. Nobody's going to . . . uh . . . take you out back and shoot you or bludgeon you to death. Nobody's going to fire you or tell you to get lost. They'll give you a chance to explain yourself. Even if not, well, you know, don't worry about it, 'cause the worst consequence is not gonna be as bad as all that.

C: Okay. Has it ever been as bad as you thought it was going to be?

B: Maybe once in my entire life.

C: Yeah. Okay. So maybe once in a great while it might be a very negative, nasty consequence. But what you're saying is that it's hardly ever that way. It is very rarely the worst consequence. And so a lot of that worrying is just basically having an effect on you and on your body and on your mind, but it's not really having an effect on your life. As far as other people can see.

B: Yeah.

C: Just making you a nervous wreck and everything.

B: (Laughs out loud)

The counselor is ready to move to step 5: assigning homework, but completes step 6: positive consequence and step 7: negative consequence before making the homework assignment.

C: Okay, good. What I want you to do now is to tell me something that you really like to do. Something that you find rewarding or kind of fun and something you would do just to kind of reward yourself.

B: Shopping.

C: Go shopping, all right.

B: Or read for pleasure.

C: All right, go shopping, read for pleasure. I'm certain that your husband would prefer if you read for pleasure.

B: Yeah, definitely.

C: Okay, now tell me something that you don't like to do, something that you'd rather avoid.

B: Ironing!

C: Okay. For your homework, I want you to practice your rational-emotive imagery five times a day, every day, until I see you next week. Spread them out, a couple in the morning, afternoon, and evening. When you practice your rational-emotive imagery five times during the day, I want you to reward yourself with 30 minutes of pleasure reading and, if you do not practice five times, I want you to do 30 minutes of ironing. Start with the clothes that need to be ironed in your house, then pull clothes out of your closet and iron them again, even call your relatives and neighbors to ask if they have any ironing for you to do.

B: (Laughing at the humor in the situation) Gee. Should I do what I'm supposed to do and get something I like, or not do it and iron all night? Hmm, which should I choose?

C: Reward or punish yourself this way each day until I see you next week.

The counselor goes to (E) evaluation and (F) feelings by exploring with Barb how the process worked for her today.

USEFULNESS AND EVALUATION OF THE ABCDEF MODEL AND THE RATIONAL-EMOTIVE IMAGERY TECHNIQUE

Professional counselors can use REBT with clients who have a variety of different presenting problems, including high levels of stress (Abrams & Ellis, 1994), relationship problems, and coping with disabilities (Ellis, 1997b). Yankura and Dryden (1997) described using REBT with "children and adolescents, culturally diverse clients, clients with disabilities, families, and ongoing therapy groups" (p. 1) and provided models for professional counselors to use when working with these populations. REBT is useful when working with women, couples, and adults (Seligman & Reichenberg, 2013). REBT can be applied to individual, couples, family, and group therapy (Ellis & Dryden, 2007). It can be used with clinical issues, such as addictive behaviors, anxiety, borderline personality disorder, depression, morbid jealousy, obsessive-compulsive disorder, and post-traumatic stress disorder (Ellis, 2001), and it is applicable to emotional education (Ellis, 1971), encounter groups (Ellis, 1969), executive leadership, and marathons and other intensive group-work experiences (Ellis & Dryden, 2007).

REBT is praised as being effective and leading to quick decreases in symptoms and major changes in a client's philosophy (Seligman & Reichenberg, 2013). The implementation of REBT with children and adults has been successful for problems such as anxiety, depression, low frustration tolerance, perfectionism, obsessive-compulsive disorders, post-traumatic stress disorders (Ellis, 2003), self-esteem, test-anxiety, emotional disturbance (Banks, 2006), learning disabilities, and academic performance (Ellis & Wilde, 2002; Hajzler & Bernard, 1991). It has been effective in reducing disruptive behaviors of children and adolescents (Gonzalez et al., 2004), anxiety, and feelings of regret (Weinrach et al., 2001).

It is an effective way to "help people to think more rationally, to feel less anxious, depressed, and enraged when they fail and get rejected" (Ellis, Shaughnessy, & Mahan, 2002, p. 356). For example, Iftene, Predescu, Stefan, and David (2015) conducted an RCT of 88 Romanian youth with depression and found no difference among the three treatment conditions: group REBT/CBT, pharmacotherapy, and a combination of pharmacotherapy. And Turner, Slater, and Barker (2014) reported that a single REBT educational workshop reduced irrational thoughts in elite youth soccer athletes, although no long-term follow-up was conducted. It can also increase treatment adherence. For example, Surilena et al. (2014) concluded that eight weeks of REBT for women with HIV/AIDS improved general mental health factors, which led to increased treatment adherence. REBT is also an effective technique to use with clients from different cultural backgrounds (Lega & Ellis, 2001) and people experiencing emotional problems after bereavement (Boelen, Kip, Voorsluijs, & van den Bout, 2004).

REBT is effective, but it also has its limitations. It is criticized for overlooking the client's past and having a too-fast pace (Seligman & Reichenberg, 2013). In addition, the efficacy of REBT is limited when working with clients who have severe personality disorders (Ellis et al., 2002) and impulse control disorders (e.g., alcohol abuse, burglary, pedophilia, voyeurism) unless the client is truly motivated to change.

APPLICATION OF THE ABCDEF MODEL AND REI TECHNIQUE

Now apply the ABCDEF model and REI technique to a current client or student you are working with or revisit the brief case studies presented at the beginning of this book. How can you use the ABCDEF model and REI technique to address concerns and create movement in the counseling session?

CHAPTER 27

Systematic Desensitization

ORIGINS OF THE SYSTEMATIC DESENSITIZATION TECHNIQUE

In the late 1950s, Joseph Wolpe (1958) developed systematic desensitization, one of the most common techniques used to treat anxiety and phobias. This technique, originally considered to be strictly behavioral, is now considered to include cognitive components as well, thus creating the rationale for including it in this section on techniques based on cognitive-behavioral approaches. Systematic desensitization is a procedure in which clients repeatedly recall, imagine, or experience anxiety-provoking events and then use relaxation techniques to suppress the anxiety caused by the event.

The basis for systematic desensitization stems from classical conditioning, counterconditioning, and, in particular, a concept reviewed earlier called reciprocal inhibition (Seligman & Reichenberg, 2013)—that is, two competing responses cannot occur simultaneously. It is not possible to be fearful and calm at the same time. The key is strengthening the desirable response (calm) to block out the undesirable response (fear). In the case of systematic desensitization, the relaxation technique learned and used by the client decreases the likelihood that the event will trigger an anxious response in the client. Anxiety and relaxation are incompatible responses, so the client, with gradual exposure to the feared event and relaxation training, becomes less sensitive to the event (Young, 2017). Examples of phobias for which systematic desensitization can be used include fear of an animal or insect (e.g., dog, bee, spider), heights, or closed spaces (e.g., elevator, closet).

Systematic desensitization can be conducted either covertly, through visualization in the professional counselor's office (e.g., visually imagine the feared insect or animal, or standing at a great height), or in vivo, translated as real-life exposure to the fear-producing stimulus (e.g., actually exposing the client to bees or standing at great heights). I advocate for use of covert imagery because it gives the professional counselor greater control over the environment and counseling process. Both are equally effective.

HOW TO IMPLEMENT THE SYSTEMATIC DESENSITIZATION TECHNIQUE

The process of systematic desensitization has three general components. First, the client is taught relaxation techniques (e.g., deep breathing, progressive muscle relaxation technique [PMRT]) in which she needs to become proficient. Second, an anxiety hierarchy scale is created. The third component is presenting the anxiety-provoking stimuli during relaxation (Young, 2017). Before the client and counselor get to the point that they are ready to begin the actual desensitization process, the first two components must be accomplished to a satisfactory level.

After the counseling relationship is formed between the client and the counselor, the first step in systematic desensitization is to discover the behavior on which to focus the intervention. To do this, the professional counselor needs to gather a complete history of the client. By extensively questioning the client, the counselor can analyze the client's problem and connect it with other events occurring in the client's life (Young, 2017). In addition to learning general information about the client, the counselor also learns which situations and circumstances bring out the client's anxiety, which will help with the second step of the process.

In step 2, the professional counselor works with the client to discover any factors that are linked to the client's anxiety. It is important for the client to give accounts filled with details of the anxiety-provoking situations. For systematic desensitization to be most effective, the counselor needs to know all of the situations that cause the client distress. This information is learned via discussion, although the *Fear Survey Schedule*, *Willoughby Questionnaire*, or *Bernsenter Self-Sufficiency Inventory* are also methods the counselor may use to discover the client's fears (Young, 2017).

Next, the professional counselor assists the client in constructing an anxiety hierarchy. It is important that the hierarchies are realistic and concrete (Young, 2017). The *Willoughby Questionnaire* provides some of the raw data needed. The professional counselor should also assign the client, as homework, the task of creating a list of stimuli related to the fear. If needed, the counselor should help the client come up with at least 10 items; typically, the list should not have more than 15. The counselor then reviews the list and groups together items related to a specific fear. The client views the divided list and ranks the themed items using the subjective units of distress scale (SUDS; see the example later in this chapter about Nicole). The hierarchy is then constructed by placing the situations that cause the most anxiety at the bottom of the list and those situations that cause the least anxiety at the top of the list, in order (see Table 27.1 in the example).

Once the hierarchy is created, the client is ready to learn relaxation techniques. Although Wolpe (1958) suggests hypnosis, the technique most commonly taught to clients is PMRT (see Chapter 16). Clients learn to relax all of the different muscle groups in their bodies. For systematic desensitization to be most effective, the client needs to be able to relax completely. To become proficient in relaxation techniques, the client should practice them for homework.

The professional counselor next needs to create a plan to present the scenarios from the hierarchy to the client (Young, 2017). Typically, there is a slow progression from covert to more overt scenes and from lower intensity to higher intensity or more realistic situations. The professional counselor and client need to agree on a signal that the client will give to the counselor if she becomes distressed; a slight raise of the hand or twitch of a finger usually works just fine.

When the client and counselor are ready to begin the desensitization process, the client needs to reach the state of deep relaxation learned earlier. The client's eyes should be closed. The counselor begins by introducing a neutral scene not found on the client's hierarchy. If the client can imagine this scene without experiencing anxiety, the counselor asks the client to imagine the situation at the bottom of the hierarchy (Corey, 2016). After a few seconds to a half minute, the counselor asks the client to imagine the situation that is next on the gradual progression of the hierarchy. If the client feels any anxiety during this process, the client is to use the agreed-upon signal to let the counselor know. When the client experiences anxiety, she is to stop imagining the scene and return to a state of deep relaxation. Once the client is relaxed, the professional counselor can continue presenting scenes from the hierarchy. Usually, accomplishing five to six steps on the hierarchy is enough for a single session. The content of the second session is determined by how far along the client progressed through the hierarchy during the first session. Scenes to which the client had no adverse reaction are taken out of the hierarchy. If the client had significant anxiety to the weakest situation, it must be replaced with a weaker one. If a stimulus that is too strong is presented, harm may be done; a counselor should always err on the side of presenting a stimulus that is weak because no harm comes of it. Following sessions should be conducted in a similar way. Wolpe (1991) indicated that treatment typically takes 10 to 25 sessions of systematic desensitization, although a hierarchy of 15 items related to a mild to moderately severe fear can often be accomplished in 4 to 6 sessions. When a client can imagine the situation at the top of the hierarchy while remaining in a relaxed state, treatment is complete.

The last step is for the counselor and client to develop a follow-up plan. This plan should involve having the client practice the technique at home once the sessions have ended. The counselor should also schedule follow-up visits with the client because reinforcement may be necessary to ensure the success of the treatment.

Subjective Units of Distress Scale

To measure shifts in levels of client anxiety, Joseph Wolpe created the subjective units of distress scale (SUDS). SUDS is a more specific example of the general procedure known as scaling, which was presented in Chapter 1. The SUDS was originally designed for use with clients during systematic desensitization procedures (Kaplan & Smith, 1995). The SUDS is used so that the professional counselor can assess and understand which situations cause the most anxiety for the client. To introduce the SUDS to the client, Wolpe (1991) suggested posing the following scenario:

> Think of the worst anxiety you can imagine and assign to it the number 100. Then think of being absolutely calm—that is, no anxiety at all—and call this number 0. Now you have a scale of anxiety. At every moment of your waking life, you must be somewhere between 0 and 100. How do you rate yourself at this moment? (p. 91)

Usually the 0 to 100 scale is used because of the flexibility of range it provides. However, a scale of 0 to 10 can also be used, making the SUDS similar to the scaling technique discussed previously. The client's self-report on the SUDS establishes a baseline in terms of the client's anxiety level (Wolpe, 1991). When a client is experiencing anxiety about several different things, the professional counselor can have the client use the SUDS to figure out which situation is the most anxiety provoking. With this knowledge, the professional counselor can help focus the session on just one situation (Shapiro, 2001).

Wolpe (1991) described how the SUDS can be used to create an anxiety hierarchy that is "a thematically related list of anxiety-evoking stimuli, ranked according to the amount of anxiety they evoke" (p. 160). The subject of the hierarchy can be internal to the client, but most commonly it is something external. To create the hierarchy, the professional counselor and client make a list consisting of the scope of the client's thoughts about the anxiety-provoking stimuli. Then the client rates each of the items using the SUDS. Finally, the professional counselor creates the hierarchy by arranging the statements from the least anxiety provoking to the most anxiety provoking according to the magnitude of the SUDS score (Thorpe & Olson, 1997). This provides the framework for the professional counselor to implement systematic desensitization with the client.

VARIATIONS OF THE SYSTEMATIC DESENSITIZATION TECHNIQUE

Corey (2016) described a common variation of systematic desensitization: in vivo desensitization. Although the procedure described above calls for the client to imagine the scenarios herself, in her mind, in vivo desensitization includes exposing the clients to the real feared situation. When appropriate, the client can self-manage in vivo desensitization. If necessary, the counselor can go with the client to face the anxiety-provoking situation. Supporters of this alternative say that the results of treatment are more effective because the client is better able to generalize the learning experience.

Young (2017) suggested another variation of systematic desensitization with a focus on anxiety reduction rather than fear reduction. Instead of subdividing the client's list and having several hierarchies to work through with the client, only one hierarchy is constructed. The treatment plan consists of only six sessions; relaxation is still taught, and a hierarchy is still constructed. Each situation from the list is written on a separate index card. The session begins with the client becoming relaxed and imagining a neutral scene. Then the counselor begins by reading the description on the lowest anxiety-provoking situation card. If the client is able to stay relaxed, the counselor can go on to the next situation card. On each card, the counselor records the ranking number, the original SUDS score, a description of the anxiety-provoking situation, the trial number, how long the client was able to stay relaxed, and the SUDS level associated with each trial number. Young recommends introducing in vivo desensitization to the client when appropriate.

Another variation, self-administered systematic desensitization, is described by Richmond (2017). It contains the same three components as the original version of systematic desensitization. The client first needs to become familiar with a relaxation technique and then needs to create an anxiety hierarchy, including detailed descriptions of the situations. Richmond suggests having 10 to 15 situations, each written on a separate card, and using the SUDS to rate each situation. After sorting the cards, the person should order them from lowest to highest anxiety provoking. The next day, the person can start matching items from the hierarchy with relaxing situations. Each session should last 30 minutes, and the client should attempt to work on three situations per session. A deep state of relaxation should be attained at the end of each session for several minutes.

Clients should be prohibited from trying systematic desensitization on their own between sessions. However, it is a good practice for the professional counselor to assign homework between sessions, including practicing and strengthening client skills in deep breathing, PMRT, visual imagery, and self-talk.

EXAMPLE OF THE SYSTEMATIC DESENSITIZATION TECHNIQUE

Systematic desensitization is composed of three facets: (1) teaching relaxation, (2) constructing an anxiety hierarchy and scaling it using the SUDS, and (3) systematically applying the relaxation to the hierarchy to accomplish desensitization. Earlier in this session, Nicole was taught the techniques of positive self-talk, visualization, deep breathing, and PMRT—what I call The Big Four. She is now ready to begin the process known as systematic desensitization to treat her test phobia. Nicole's treatment was conducted using an imagery implementation strategy in the counseling office (*covert desensitization*) rather than in real life (in vivo). The imagery-based method gives the counselor more control over the anxiety-producing stimulus (it is easier to handle panic reactions related to fear of enclosed spaces

when the client is sitting in a chair in your office imagining she is in an elevator than when she is actually in the elevator) and is generally as effective as in vivo desensitization. The following transcript demonstrates creation of an anxiety hierarchy, implementation of the SUDS, and development of the imagery-based systematic desensitization procedure.

Counselor (C):   All right, so we've learned about positive self-talk and visual imagery. We've done some deep breathing and some progressive muscle relaxation. We are now ready to deal with your presenting concern, a test phobia, using what is called systematic desensitization. That's a big fancy term, but it basically means that we are going to help you get used to a testing situation step by step and replace your anxiety with relaxation. We are going to do this by accomplishing two more things. We're going to construct what's called an anxiety hierarchy with some things that have to do with testing that aren't very anxiety producing at all, and then we will proceed all the way up to the things about a testing situation that make you incredibly anxious, like where you're actually sitting there taking your SAT test, and shaking and "it's the end of the world" and you're getting up to that 9 or that 10 on the panic scale, frightening and anxiety-producing things.

Nicole (N):   (Laughing) Okay.

C: And then we're also going to use the relaxation training, which you've already learned how to do. So these two parts, fear hierarchy and relaxation, will be used in the third part, systematic desensitization, okay?

N: Let's do it.

C: Let's talk for a few minutes about the fear hierarchy. We want to get somewhere between 10 and 15 steps on this hierarchy. What are some anxiety-producing things that you've experienced in the way of testing, from minor stuff to the times that you've been the most frightened or fearful?

N: Just involving tests?

C: Yes, the test anxiety.

N: You mean, like, when I, when I get stressed out the most?

C: Okay, sure. Something that would be real close to a 9 or a 10 on that scale.

N: Probably when I'm stuck, something really bad. Like I'm actually in the test, I'm taking it, and there's a question or a part that I don't understand whatsoever. It's probably the worst, I think.

C: Okay, so you're in the test and you're stuck on a question you don't understand? (Counselor writes down this and subsequent contributions.)

N: Yeah.

C: Okay, well, what else? What other kinds of things do you run into?

N: I'm watching, and I see all kinds of people are done, and I see everyone else is done and I'm still frantically working. That's pretty bad.

C: So they . . .

N: They have their pencils down or are sitting there.

C: What else?

N: If I'm running out of time, that's a big one, and I'm not anywhere near finished, or I still have a lot left to do in a short period of time.

C: Okay. What else?

N: In the beginning, I guess, or if I see that the test is a lot . . . like a lot of pages or a lot of questions . . . I may panic because I may feel like I'm never going to finish it all.

C: Okay. You've got some things at that high end of the scale, we need some things kind of in the middle, maybe even things down at the bottom that aren't really so anxiety producing but are still things that kind of get you a little bit churned up. What's some, what might some of those things be?

N: Well, maybe when the teacher announces that we are going to have a test soon. In the middle somewhere would probably be more the fact that I know that the test is coming up soon and I need to prepare more.

C: You need to prepare more?

N: Yeah.

C: That would be even more stressful than the teacher announcing the test?

N: Yes.

C: (Constructing a test phobia hierarchy is fairly predictable, so the counselor helps to fill in some low- and medium-range responses.) And then we could probably even say things like, well, you know, some on the morning of the test?

N: Yes.

C: Okay, and the night before the test?

N: (Nods head yes)

C: Maybe even the day before if you're in class?

N: (Nods head yes)

C: And how much time do they usually give you from the time they say, that the teacher says, oh, there's going to be a test? Is it usually like a week ahead or a couple of days?

N: A week, sometimes a couple of days.

C: A couple of days?

N: A week. Usually they'll give us a week.

C: Okay, I'm writing like two days ahead, three days, four days ahead.

N: Okay.

C: Anything else that you can think of?

N: That's pretty much everything that I can think of.

C: There's probably a lot that happens between when you wake on the morning of the test and when the test occurs, as you are getting closer and closer to when the test starts.

N: I guess when I wake up and I'm going through the information again. Reviewing it all.

C: So you're reviewing on the morning of?

N: Uh-huh.

C: What else? How about on your way to school?

N: Yeah, it does. Really nervous.

C: How about when you arrive?

N: Yes, when I get there. Basically all the way up until the test.

C: So, is there anything that happens from the time that you arrive at school to the time that you actually . . . that the teacher passes out the test?

N: I'm more anxious and more nervous. When it's getting closer and closer and time is getting less and less before the test.

C: Okay. And that would kind of be the waiting time?

N: Yeah.

C: And then there's the waiting time in between it, and then there's the time that the teacher actually passes the tests out, okay, and then you see that there's a lot of pages or questions on the test. You're running out of time and you have a lot left to do, you see other people already have their pencils down and so forth, and then you're stuck on a question that you don't understand.

N: Yeah.

C: Okay? So by my count, we've got 2, 4, 6, 8, 10, 12, 14, 16. Okay, we can add or scratch a few because we're coming up on the close of our session right now. The next thing we're going to do is what's called the subjective units of distress scale, or SUDS, where you actually get to rank each of these on a scale of 1 to 100.

N: Okay.

C: On how much anxiety you feel whenever these things happen. Some of them might be close to 90 or 100, and some of them might be down close to, you know, a 10 or a 15 or a 20.

N: Right.

C: And so what will happen, we will have all these ranked in order of how much anxiety they produce in you and we will go ahead and do the systematic desensitization. I will have you close your eyes, and we'll imagine each one of these things is happening. We'll start at a really low one, and you will relax yourself while you are imagining these things. While imagining these scenes, you will be relaxing using your deep breathing. And you'll have your progressive muscle relaxation training— positive self-talk—and you'll be able to switch your image to the beach to calm yourself down if you need to, okay?

N: Okay.

C: As we kind of move our way up this hierarchy—and we'll probably get through four or five of them in each of the next few sessions—from now on our sessions will be a lot quicker because we'll only do four or five of these things, and then we'll stop, and then do four or five the next time, and so on, until we get to the top of the scale without having you feel like you're really upset and anxious about things.

Begin session 2.

C: All right, Nicole, another week until school starts, huh?

N: Yep.

C: Whoa . . . you think they are going to give you any tests this year?

N: Yes, a lot.

C: All right, you think so? A lot of tests. You're expecting a ton of tests.

N: Yep.

Counselor reviews activities from the previous session and checks to make sure all homework assignments were completed before continuing with systematic desensitization. Nicole's anxiety hierarchy prepared during this session is illustrated in Table 27.1.

C: Since last session, I took the anxiety hierarchy listing and put the events in what seems to me a reasonable starting order, and I have them listed on my paper here. So the first thing that we want to do today is to apply the subjective units of distress scale, SUDS, to this fear hierarchy list. And what that does is helps us to rate each of these events that you imagine would happen or do happen in real life. You need to rate each one so we can put them

TABLE 27.1 Nicole's Anxiety Hierarchy

Subjective Units of Distress Scale (SUDS)	Event
015	The teacher is announcing there will be a test in a week.
025	It is 4 days before the test will be administered.
032	It is 3 days before the test will be administered.
040	It is 2 days before the test will be administered.
055	The test is coming up, and you need to prepare.
068	It is the day before the test.
078	It is the night before the test.
084	It is the morning of the test.
086	You are on your way to school on the morning of the test.
087	You arrive at school on the morning of the test.
089	The teacher passes out the test and is ready to begin.
091	You see a lot of pages and questions on the test.
094	You get stuck on a question.
096	Other people are finishing and have their pencils down on their desks.
097	You are running out of time but still have a lot to do.

in order from lowest, or the least stress producing events, up to the highest, or the most stress-producing ones to do with test anxiety. When we are finished with the list, we will be able to start at the bottom of that list and work our way up to the highest events, using our relaxation, visual imagery, self-talk, and deep breathing, so that you'll be able to relax while you're imagining the nasty stuff happening. What will eventually happen then is you'll become desensitized to the nasty stuff because you're relaxed while you're thinking about it, imagining it. And then, when you go into real life, you'll be relaxed because you've taken care of this in the office here. All right?

N: Okay.

C: So the first thing we need to do is the subjective units of distress scale. Have you ever seen an alarm clock with an LCD—a liquid crystal display—readout? It's the numbers that show up, the background is dark, and red or some other colored numbers flash up? I want you to imagine an LCD panel with three spots for digits on it, where three numbers can come up, and the numbers can go anywhere from 000 to 100. So 000 means you're not stressed out at all, you're totally relaxed, this doesn't bother you at all, and 100 is whenever you are ready to have a panic attack and everything because you're just so upset and stressed out. Okay?

N: Okay.

C: So what we want to do is, on that scale from 0 to 100, we want you to read each one of these little comments that we have, each one of these activities or events that'll happen, so we can put them in order. I'm just going to read some of them. Close your eyes. I'm going to say one of them, and I want you to go ahead and imagine it happening in your mind. That's why I want you to close your eyes. I want you to visually imagine that this is happening to you, and I want you to put that little LCD panel up in the top right-hand corner of your mind's eye.

N: Okay.

C: Does that make sense?

N: Sure, that makes sense.

C: Nicole, I want you to imagine yourself in the classroom and in whatever subject you like to imagine yourself being in. I want you to imagine that the teacher is announcing that there will be a test a week from now on the subject. On that scale from 0 to 100, with 0 being absolutely stress free and 100 being totally stressed out, where would you be on that scale?

N: 015.

C: 015. So that's pretty close to stress free, right?

N: Yeah.

C: Now I want you to imagine that you're now four days away, four days from the test being administered. Where are you on that scale?

N: 025.

C: 025? Okay, so we're getting a little bit higher there.

N: Yep.

C: How about three days away?

N: 040.

C: A test is coming up, and you need to prepare.

N: 055.

C: Okay, how about two days away?

N: 050.

C: Okay. How about a day before the test?

N: It's going up more. About 068.

C: 068. So, really, that last day before the test, that day before the test is where you start really getting stressed out.

N: Yes.

C: Okay. How about the night before the test? You are at 068 on the day, knowing it's the next day?

N: 078.

C: 078. Okay, how about the morning of the test?

N: 087. Oh, no, actually 084.

C: 084. Okay. And you're reviewing. You just woke up, and you're reviewing for that test in the morning.

N: 086.

C: Okay, and now you're on your way to school.

N: Probably about the same. 086. It really doesn't usually change.

C: How about right when you arrive at school?

N: Probably like 087.

C: Okay, just a little tiny bit higher.

N: Yeah.

C: The teacher passes out the test, and you're waiting to begin.

N: That's bad. 089.

C: 089. Okay, you're stuck on a question, you're taking the test, and you're stuck on a question that you don't understand.

N: That's pretty high because I usually panic at that point so that would probably be 094. Yeah.

C: Okay. Now other people have their pencils down.

N: Oh, gosh. So high. 096.

C: And you're running out of time, and you have a lot left to do.

N: That's probably the highest, I think. That would probably be like 097.

C: 097?

N: Yeah.

C: Okay, so you're really close to 100.

N: Yeah.

C: What would 100 be, by the way? Is there something that would put you at 100?

N: I don't think I'd ever really get to 100, but I'd probably get really close. I'm sure I'd lose it.

C: We'd be carrying you out of the room or something?

N: Yeah.

C: All right. So you've got some down here, the teacher announces that the test will be a week away, that was about a 015, and as the test gets closer you're starting to feel more stress until the morning of the test. And on your way to school, you arrive at school, you're getting real close to 070, and then as the teacher is passing it out, you're right at 089. And you see there are a lot of pages, you get stuck on a question that you do not understand. Other people seem to be finishing, and you're running out of time and you have a lot of questions left.

N: Yeah, that's the worst.

C: Was there anything as you were kind of running your way through that list, is there anything that you want to add at this point? Anything that you think is something particularly problematic for you that we've forgotten?

N: I think that pretty much covers everything. I think that's everything I need.

C: All right, and because you gave two of them the same rating, anxiety on the way to school and reviewing on the morning of the test, I'm just going to delete one, and that will leave us 15 steps on the anxiety hierarchy. Is there anything else that I need to know about before we begin?

N: Nope.

The professional counselor now begins the actual systematic desensitization procedure.

C: Okay, well, let's go ahead then, and we'll start at the bottom of the list, and we'll work through about three or four or maybe five today and see how you do.

N: Okay.

C: Now I want you to just kind of get comfortable, even use some deep breathing and progressive muscle relaxation training to work out any kinks you might have in your body. I want you to take a couple of deep breaths. Okay?

N: You want me to start now?

C: Yep. Take a couple of deep breaths, close your eyes. You might even want to take yourself to the beach right now or use some positive self-talk to reach a deep state of relaxation. (Pause for a couple of minutes or so)

C: Okay. Now for this next step, we're going to take a nice, calming, deep, slow breath, and

then I'm going to have you imagine what's on the list here, what we were just talking about. I'm going to start at the lowest one, and I want you to imagine that scene in your mind's eye. And then, I want you to, while you're imagining it, keep taking deep slow breaths. If you become very anxious or stressed, I want you to block out the testing image and replace it with your beach scene. Okay?

N: Okay.

C: Also, I want you to give me a little sign that you are relaxed and ready to move on to the next step. When you have visualized the scene in your mind and have regained a state of calm and relaxation, just twitch your finger to let me know you are ready to move on.

N: Like this? (Lifts her finger as a signal)

C: Exactly . . . great. Let's start with the first one. I want you to imagine, visually imagine, that your teacher has announced that there will be a test about a week from now. So picture that and keep breathing and relaxing, and then give me another little finger sign when you're ready to go on, when you are able to imagine the scene while remaining calm and relaxed. (Pause) Okay, now open your eyes for a second and come back to me. How do you feel right now on that scale from 0 to 100?

N: Probably about a 003, maybe. I'm really relaxed right now.

C: Originally that one was a 015. And now it is a 003, pretty calm and relaxed? Not really stressed out at all?

N: No.

C: Okay, go ahead and close your eyes and take another couple of deep breaths, and give me a finger sign and we'll go on to the next one, and we'll probably go through the next three or four. (Pause until finger twitch) Okay, now I want you to imagine that it's now four days away from the test . . . four days. Imagine it, keep breathing, and keep relaxing. (Pause until finger twitch) All right. Now I want you to imagine that there are three days until the test. (Pause until finger twitch) Good. Now I want you to imagine there are only two days until the test is going to be administered. Try to stay calm with good breathing. (Pause until finger twitch) Good. Now I want you to imagine that the test is coming up very soon and you need to prepare for the test. Imagine yourself needing to prepare. (Pause until finger twitch) Okay, Nicole, now come back to me slowly and, when you are ready, open your eyes. (Pause and wait) Where on that scale of 1 to 100 are you now?

N: (Nicole yawns and stretches) 010.

C: 010?

N: Or maybe a 008.

C: That's good, that's great, that's fantastic. . . . You are doing a great job. You made it a third of the way up your hierarchy, okay, so you're already at the 055 point and you're understanding now what I mean. You're going to get up there. Here you were imagining something that was about a 055, and you're now able to visualize that scene and keep yourself all the way back down to about a 008 or 010 on your scale. This is basically what we are going to do over the next three to five sessions. We're going to do a few more next time and try to keep you calm and relaxed while imagining those things, so that whenever you take tests in real life, the stress won't be so bad. You'll be able to be calm and relaxed and use your deep breathing when you're in real-life situations and be able to control your thoughts and the pictures in your mind so that you'll be able to cope with all those stresses, all right?

N: All right.

C: Now—and this is very important—do *not* try to do this on your own outside our sessions. Got it? It is only for inside our sessions when I am here to make sure you are doing it correctly and safely.

N: No problem.

During session 3, Nicole backed up and began with step 4 on her anxiety hierarchy, then completed steps 5 through 10 without incident. During session 4, Nicole backed up and began with step 9 on her anxiety hierarchy, then completed steps 10 through 14 without incident. At this point the treatment was

nearly completed. Had she experienced any adverse reaction during these steps, I would have used reciprocal inhibition to block the stressful visualization, along with deep breathing, self-talk, and PMRT to return her to a relaxed state, ending the session for the day. As fate would have it, Nicole missed a session between sessions 4 and 5 and had several tests in school during the week before the final session. Then we began session 5.

C: Missed you last week. Bring me up to date on what is happening in school.

N: Well, I had a couple of tests.

C: Really? How did they go? Any tough ones?

N: Oh, yeah. Precalc and chem were tough. But the weird thing was I didn't panic or feel sick or anything. I just took deep breaths when things got hard and kept the nasty stuff out of my mind.

At this point, the treatment was obviously having the desired effect. The counselor finished the session by beginning with step 13 and proceeding through step 15, completing the hierarchy, then used the flagging the minefield technique (see Chapter 5). Nicole finished her senior year with no adverse testing reactions, raised her SAT score by 150 points (math and reading combined score), and got into her first-choice university and desired major.

USEFULNESS AND EVALUATION OF THE SYSTEMATIC DESENSITIZATION TECHNIQUE

Systematic desensitization is commonly used to treat specific phobias, and in some cases using in vivo desensitization can be achieved in a single session (Ost, 1989; Zinbarg, Barlow, Brown, & Hertz, 1992). A specific phobia occurs when a person's anxiety is related to a specific situation, such as test taking or standing at a great height. For example, Triscari, Faraci, D'Angelo, Urso, and Catalisano (2011) determined that cognitive-behavioral therapy (CBT) combined with systematic desensitization was effective in the treatment of fear of flying. The use of systematic desensitization is most appropriate when the client possesses the necessary coping skills but avoids situations because of her high level of anxiety.

Egbochukuand and Obodo (2005) and Austin and Partridge (1995) suggested use of systematic desensitization with students to alleviate stressful responses, like test anxiety. Both cognitive restructuring and systematic desensitization were equally effective in the treatment of high-stakes test anxiety (Baspinar Can, Dereboy, & Eskin, 2012). Crawford (1998) described using systematic desensitization with preservice teachers who had reading anxiety.

Most professional counselors are in agreement that systematic desensitization is successful in treating phobias; however, there is disagreement over whether imagining (covert) or in vivo exposure is more effective (Zinbarg et al., 1992). Graziano, DeGiovanni, and Garcia (1979) conducted a review of the literature focused on behavioral treatments of children's phobias and found that systematic desensitization, whether applied individually or in groups, whether actually experienced overtly or covertly applied, is more effective in reducing certain phobias and anxiety related to situations than are other types of treatments. Such findings make the discussion of superior effectiveness between imagery-based and in vivo approaches moot. Indeed, it may well be that covert and in vivo approaches complement each other and cater to client preferences. For example, Pagoto, Kozak, Spates, and Spring (2006) reported that an older woman who refused in vivo desensitization did well with the imagery-based systematic desensitization.

Several recent studies have applied systematic desensitization to medical and dental treatment environments. Sajadi, Goudarzi, Khosravi, Farahani, and Mohammadbeig (2017) reported that systematic desensitization was effective in decreasing anxiety in a sample of nurses compared to a control group. Heaton, Leroux, Ruff, and Coldwell (2013) studied the use of Computer Assisted Relaxation Learning (CARL), a self-paced systematic desensitization-based computerized treatment for dental injection fear and found that twice as many treatment group participants (35%) as control participants reading an educational pamphlet (17%) opted for the injection.

Some supporters claim that this technique works because of reciprocal inhibition (Wolpe, 1991). Others claim that systematic desensitization is successful because the clients learn through repeated exposure that the stimulus will not harm them (Young, 2017). Another explanation is that clients gain insight during the time it takes to complete the desensitization process. Meichenbaum (as cited in Young, 2017) suggested that actual cognitive changes occur during the process, and clients change their expectations about the anxiety-provoking situations. Yet another explanation of the efficacy of this technique is that the client learns a new, more effective coping skill (relaxation) to help deal with anxiety.

Systematic desensitization is not always the appropriate technique to use with a client experiencing anxiety. For this technique to be effective, the client must become proficient with progressive muscle relaxation or another relaxation technique. If the client cannot learn to relax, another technique should be chosen. Also, some clients cannot imagine the situations vividly enough, which generally causes systematic desensitization to be ineffective (Young, 2017). If a client continues to experience high levels of anxiety even after numerous exposures to the items on the hierarchy, Richmond (2017) suggested that the professional counselor consider several things. First, the ranking that the client gave the item may be too low. Second, the item may be described in so much detail that it contains aspects of scenes farther along in the hierarchy. The professional counselor should also be sure that the client is not focusing too long on a scene without giving the professional counselor the distress signal.

APPLICATION OF THE SYSTEMATIC DESENSITIZATION TECHNIQUE

Now apply the systematic desensitization technique to a current client or student you are working with or revisit the brief case studies presented at the beginning of this book. How can you use the systematic desensitization technique to address concerns and create movement in the counseling session?

CHAPTER 28

Stress Inoculation Training

ORIGINS OF THE STRESS INOCULATION TRAINING TECHNIQUE

Stress inoculation training (SIT), a technique developed by Donald Meichenbaum, is based on the idea that helping clients cope with mild stressors will allow them to develop a tolerance for more severe forms of distress. Meichenbaum believed that clients could increase their ability to cope by modifying their beliefs about their own performance in stressful situations. SIT seeks to enhance the client's set of coping skills and to encourage the client to use the coping skills already possessed (Meichenbaum, 2003). SIT combines elements of Socratic and didactic teaching, client self-monitoring, cognitive restructuring, problem solving, relaxation training, behavior rehearsal, and environmental change. However, SIT is not a formula treatment that can be applied blindly to all distressed clients; instead, SIT is composed of general principles and clinical procedures that must be tailored to fit the individual client.

SIT was introduced by Meichenbaum in the early 1970s. The first clients were individuals who experienced multiple fears, who had difficulty controlling their anger, and who had problems coping with physical pain (Meichenbaum, 2003). Meichenbaum stressed cognitive behavior modification, which concentrated on changing the client's self-talk. SIT involves a cognitive component that focuses on helping clients modify their self-instructions in order to cope more effectively with the problems they encounter. SIT assists clients in conceptualizing and reframing stress, allowing them to rescript their lives or develop a new narrative about their ability to cope.

SIT is based on a transactional view of stress, which states that stress occurs whenever the perceived demands of a situation outweigh the perceived ability of the system to meet the demands (Meichenbaum, 2003). Stress is therefore defined as a relationship between the person and the environment in which the person sees the current demands as exceeding his coping resources. SIT seeks to boost the client's coping skills and increase the client's confidence in his coping abilities, thus enabling him to deal more effectively with life stressors.

SIT has several goals. First, clients learn to see their stress as a normal, adaptive reaction (Meichenbaum, 2003). Clients also discover the course of their disorder, the transactional nature of stress, and their own role in maintaining their stress level. In addition, clients learn to manage stress by changing their conceptualization of it and by understanding the difference between changeable and unchangeable aspects of stressful situations. Finally, clients work on breaking down large stressors into specific short-term, intermediate, and long-term coping goals.

HOW TO IMPLEMENT THE STRESS INOCULATION TRAINING TECHNIQUE

SIT can be conducted with individuals, couples, small groups, or large groups (Meichenbaum, 2003). Typically SIT consists of 8 to 15 sessions, plus booster or follow-up sessions scheduled over 3 to 12 months. SIT involves three phases: (1) conceptualization, (2) skill acquisition and rehearsal, and (3) application and follow-through.

The first phase of SIT, the conceptualization phase, teaches the client the nature of stress as well as the client's role in creating stress. The client and professional counselor work together to identify the presenting problem (Meichenbaum, 2003). Once global stressors have been identified, the professional counselor can help the client break down these stressors into specific stressful situations and evaluate the client's present coping efforts. The client then develops short-term, intermediate, and long-term behaviorally specific goals with the understanding that some aspects of stress are changeable and some are unchangeable. The client also self-monitors the internal dialogue, feelings, and behaviors that occur during stressful situations. The professional counselor can then use the client's self-reports to help develop a new conceptualization of the distress.

During the second phase, the skill acquisition and rehearsal phase, clients learn a variety of behavioral and cognitive coping techniques to use in stressful situations (Corey, 2016). These coping skills may include collecting information about the stressful situation; planning for resources and escape routes; cognitive restructuring of negative self-statements; task-oriented self-instruction; problem solving; and behavioral techniques such as relaxation, assertiveness, or self-rewarding for coping (Meichenbaum & Deffenbacher, 1988). Other important coping skills are social skills, time management, developing support systems, and reevaluating priorities (Corey, 2016). Once the client has been taught a number of coping strategies, skills can be reinforced through behavioral and imagery rehearsal, coping modeling, and self-instruction training (Meichenbaum, 2003). The professional counselor should also discuss with the client possible barriers and obstacles to using the coping techniques.

The third phase, the application and follow-through phase, allows for transfer of skills from the therapeutic setting to the real world (Corey, 2016). In this stage, skills are rehearsed in role plays, simulations, imagery, and graduated in vivo practice. As skills are mastered, they are integrated into the external world through graded homework assignments. Another important aspect of this last phase is relapse prevention (Meichenbaum, 2003). To prevent relapses, the client and professional counselor work together to identify high-risk situations,

anticipate stressful reactions, and rehearse coping responses. Also, SIT frequently includes follow-up or booster sessions and may involve significant others in the training to assist the client.

VARIATION OF THE STRESS INOCULATION TRAINING TECHNIQUE

Only one variation of the SIT technique has been reported. A five-step process to help children learn to deal with stress has been developed by Dr. Archibald Hart (Shapiro, 1994). Hart suggested that children be gradually exposed to problems. Children should be told age-appropriate information about family problems and not be overprotected. Parents should resist the urge to rescue children; rather, they should allow children to solve their own problems. Parents should also teach their children to use healthy self-talk, to say encouraging, rational things to themselves. Children should be allowed adequate time for recovery after a stressful period and should be taught to give themselves this time. Last, children need to learn to filter stressors in order to determine what events are worthy of a stressful reaction.

EXAMPLE OF THE STRESS INOCULATION TRAINING TECHNIQUE

Sarah is a 21-year-old college student seeking counseling due to feeling overwhelmed and unable to cope with the ramifications of a previous rape. Approximately 10 months ago, at the end of the spring semester, Sarah was raped at an off-campus party. At the insistence of her mother, she immediately entered into counseling with a professional counselor located in her hometown and withdrew from summer classes as well as fall courses. After four months of counseling, she terminated counseling because she felt she had made significant improvements in her emotional state and reenrolled for spring semester courses. On her return to campus, she has had much difficulty coping with the past trauma. The following excerpt is from the second session with a professional counselor practicing in the city where the university is located.

Sarah (S):   I just feel I should be over it by now. It is so frustrating to me that it is still affecting my life this way. I had no idea it would be this difficult to come back. I feel like maybe I should go back home again.

Counselor (C):   You felt safe there.

S: Exactly. And I don't feel safe at all here. There are all these reminders, and I'm so afraid I will run into him at any moment.

C: I can see where that would be very difficult for you.

S: It's so unfair. And there is nobody that would even begin to understand. I don't even keep in touch with any of the friends I had last year. They probably think I'm some moron for leaving so quickly and running home to my mom.

C: Or they might think you are brave for coming back.

S: Maybe. I don't know.

C: You did make the choice to come back. You felt strong enough.

S: I did. But then it felt a lot different when I got here. Now I feel like I am going to fall apart at any moment. I feel just like I did almost a year ago when it happened. I really don't think I can deal with this. I mean, what if I see him? What if everyone knows about it and thinks I deserved it? What if they are all siding with him and still think he is just this incredibly great guy? And I can't even begin to think about the court dates coming up. I wish I had never told my mom. She made me press charges, and it was just awful. And I think all of that is about to come up, and I am going to have to face him again. I can't do it. I just want to go home and forget it ever happened.

C: You know, I would love to tell you that all of these things you worry about are nothing to worry about at all. But instead, I have to say that everything you've mentioned . . . well, they are possibilities. You may run into him on campus or when you're out. There may be some people who don't understand what that is like, and they may judge you inaccurately.

There may be people who still think he is a wonderful person. And court hearings will eventually take place, and you will see him. These are all possibilities, if not certainties. And they are all situations that you can cope with.

S: I just don't see how.

C: Well, first what I'd like to do is determine what things we can change and what things we cannot change.

S: What do you mean? I can't change any of it. It is all out of my hands. That's the worst part.

C: Well, some things, like if you run into him, we cannot change. But we can change how that affects you and how you respond to it when it happens. He raped you—that we cannot change either. But you've already seen how much control you were able to have over how that affected you. You coped with that terrible tragedy, and you will cope with these problems as well. They are problems to be solved.

The professional counselor is working to build a relationship and therapeutic alliance. The counselor is also looking for problems in thinking, such as avoidance, rumination, and catastrophizing. The professional counselor attempts to reframe threats that feel overwhelming into problems to be solved, problems that are neither overwhelming nor debilitating. The professional counselor wants to begin laying the groundwork for the client to see that she always has control—if not direct control—to change the facts of the situation, then emotional control to direct her response to the facts.

The following excerpt is from the fourth session.

The professional counselor wants to create small stressors and successes prior to the court date in order to prepare Sarah for it. The court date will surely be a large stressor requiring much resiliency.

C: So, I'm curious, what might it be like for you to run into him, into Tray, I mean?

S: Hmm. (Begins to fidget with the bottom of her T-shirt) Do I have to think about that?

C: Seems to me you probably already think about it. I would guess you think about it often.

S: True enough. I imagine it in my mind.

C: Tell me about what you imagine it to be like.

S: Well, for some reason I always think it's going to be right outside the library when it happens. Like I'd be walking in and he'd be walking out or something like that. I can see him coming long before I get to where he is. And I panic. I stop in my tracks and just stare. I start to shake, and I want to scream really loud for someone to help me. I want someone to jump in between me and him to protect me . . . to guard me. But no one does. And I can't scream. My voice seems to be completely gone. And then I start to feel sick . . . really sick . . . like I'm going to throw up.

C: Then what?

S: Then I start to focus on my stomach and the image goes away.

C: Wow, Sarah. (Takes a deep breath) That sounds like a pretty terrible feeling you are imagining.

S: It scares me to death.

C: Remember how I said before about how all these things that upset you are problems to be solved, and that at least one aspect of each of them is within your control?

S: Yes, I remember. And I like that. It's comforting . . . even though I don't understand how just yet.

C: Okay. Well, taking this situation for an example, the eventual encounter with Tray, what can we control about this problem?

S: Well, I remember you said if we can't change the facts of a situation, we can control how we react to the facts or how they affect us.

C: That's right. And do you suppose that this image you've created for yourself, the one where you freeze and your voice is gone and you want to scream but you can't, and then you feel sick enough to throw up, is this image making it more likely for you to actually respond this way to your eventual encounter, or less likely?

S: I would say thinking about that scenario over and over, playing it through my mind, that probably makes me more likely to actually react that way.

C: That's what I would say too. But let me ask you . . . is that how you want to react? If you could decide right now how that situation might play out, is that what you would choose?

S: No! No, not at all. That's how I'm afraid it will play out.

C: And you thinking it may in fact be making it more likely.

S: Yes.

C: So, tell me, how you would want it to happen, just *if* you could choose? *If* you could control it?

S: Well, I would definitely want to appear strong and unfazed.

C: And how would strong and unfazed look exactly on a typical campus sidewalk outside the library?

S: Well, let's see . . . I would stand up straight, and I would look straight ahead with my head held high. And I would not have an expression on my face.

C: Can you show me? Can you stand up and go to the door and walk across the office just like you've described?

S: That's silly.

C: But this situation, that will eventually happen, is not silly. We have to get prepared.

S: (Sarah nods her head in agreement and changes demeanor from embarrassed to serious. She stands up and walks across the office in the strong and unfazed manner she described.) I want to do it again.

C: Of course. (Sarah walks back across the office and back to the door with her head held even higher.) That was very good, Sarah. Now I'd like you to do it a couple more times, and I want you to repeat out loud "I am strong. I am in control." (Sarah rehearses this several times, walking strong, looking unfazed, and repeating her statements out loud.) Great, Sarah! You certainly look strong and unfazed to me.

S: I do?

C: You do. But this is just in my office. Do you think you can practice this week?

S: What do you mean?

C: Five times a day, I want you to pick some random guy on campus who is walking your way, and pretend that he is Tray. Would that be too frightening for you?

The professional counselor is careful to assess the degree of emotional risk with this exercise because he wants to create positive and strengthening experiences for practice, experiences that will arouse Sarah's defenses but not overwhelm her so that she has a negative outcome.

S: No, I can do that. Because I would know it wasn't really him.

C: Very well. So five times a day, I want you to choose some random guy and, as he is walking toward you, I want you to say to yourself "Okay, this is it. I have to be strong and unfazed." And I want you to immediately assume the posture and stance you've just displayed in here and walk past him with your head held high and your face expressionless. Got it?

S: I'm going to enjoy this.

Sarah is already making the shift from viewing this potential occurrence as scaring her to death to enjoyable.

The following is an excerpt from the fifth session.

C: So, you feel fairly certain that the comment was directed toward you?

S: Yeah, it seemed pretty obvious. I didn't know how to react or what to say, so I just left and went home.

C: What about your friends who were there with you?

S: I told them I didn't feel well, and I just left some cash to pay for my meal.

C: I see. So it ruined your whole evening. And next time, you would want to address comments like these?

S: Yes, because otherwise I'll just feel helpless again. But I wouldn't know what to say.

C: All right. What do you say I pretend to be you for a moment, and you pretend to be one of the guys in the restaurant?

S: Okay.

C: Okay. So were you standing up or sitting down? What was going on when this was said?

S: I had just ordered my food and had to use the restroom. I was walking out of the restroom when I passed their table and heard it.

C: Okay. So go right ahead and say what it is you heard them say to you.

S: Okay. "Oh, look, there's Tray's girlfriend." And then another said, "Hey, isn't she the one that . . ."

C: And I might respond with "Yes, as a matter of fact I am. And I would prefer that you not refer to me as his girlfriend." How's that?

S: That would have been good. It was strong and unashamed and unemotional.

C: What do you say we role-play a few other possible remarks and situations you might encounter?

The following is an excerpt from the sixth session.

C: So this is something that you really want to do?

S: I really do. I feel like as long as I avoid it, it has power over me. And I've been a lot of things this past year—mostly fearful and anxious. But now I think I'm actually ready to grieve like we talked about last time. I lost something back there. Something I may never have again. And I need to grieve that. I owe myself that. And with the one-year mark coming up, I think this would be an excellent way for me to stop avoiding the place, to grieve what happened, and to move past another hurdle as a way to commemorate the one-year anniversary. I'm ready. It's time. I know it's a huge step, but I feel more confident. I mean, I know it won't be easy at all. But I'm ready for this next step.

C: Okay. You've decided to do this, so I want to help equip you with everything necessary to ensure a healthy outcome. You've already spoken to your mom?

S: Yes, and she's fine with coming up to support me. She definitely wants to be there for me if I need her.

C: Okay. So what we'll do is learn and practice muscle relaxation and deep breathing today. And if we feel comfortable with it after today, you'll take these tools we've practiced home with you and practice no less than three times a day. Then, at the end of the week, if you are ready, you will revisit the place that this happened . . . the place where Tray raped you. And Mom will be there waiting to offer support.

S: Yes.

C: Okay, sit comfortably in your chair and close your eyes. And feel the weight of your body in the chair . . . and now you are very aware of how the chair feels on your back . . . and the back of your legs . . . and you want to squeeze your toes together . . . as tight as you can . . . and hold them like that for a moment . . . and release . . . and you want to now tense the arches of both your feet . . . and hold them very tightly now . . . hold them just like that . . . and now release and feel all that energy leaving your body . . . and squeeze your calf muscles . . . and really focus on your calves and your lower legs and how tense it feels now as you squeeze it . . . and now let all of that go . . .

The professional counselor continues to help Sarah tense and relax each part of her body (i.e., upper thighs, buttocks, stomach, lower back, chest, upper back, fingers, hands, arms, shoulders, neck, and face).

S: I can't believe how good that feels.

C: And imagine you can do that and feel that good three times a day now. Here (hands a compact disc to Sarah), I have it all on CD for you to listen to and do each time. You will find that, by the end of the week, you've become so good at it that your body has learned to relax much sooner and more easily. That's why it's so important to practice plenty before the moment comes when you really need it.

USEFULNESS AND EVALUATION OF THE STRESS INOCULATION TRAINING TECHNIQUE

SIT can be used for both remediation and prevention. It has been applied to a variety of issues, such as speech anxiety, test anxiety, phobias, anger, assertion training, social incompetence, depression, and social withdrawal in children (Corey, 2016). For more than two decades, SIT has remained the dominant model for worksite stress management training (Flaxman & Bond, 2010). This training has also been used with medical patients, athletes, teachers, military personnel, police officers, and persons coping with life transitions (Meichenbaum, 2003).

Numerous studies show the effectiveness of SIT. Sheely and Horan (2004) studied stress among law students and discovered that students receiving SIT exhibited a decline in stress and irrational beliefs, which endured throughout a follow-up period. In addition, Schuler, Gilner, Austrin, and Davenport (1982) examined the effectiveness of SIT with and without the education phase as a treatment for public speaking anxiety. Those receiving full SIT, including the education phase, reduced anxiety significantly more than those who experienced only the rehearsal and application phases of the training. Those receiving full SIT reported higher levels of confidence as a speaker and lower levels of communication apprehension. No studies were located that indicated any adverse effects of SIT.

SIT has also been used to treat anxiety, depression, and sleep disorders. Jokar and Rahmati (2015) reported that SIT relieved symptoms of anxiety and sleep disorder. And Kashani, Kashani, Moghimian, and Shakour (2015) randomly assigned 40 cancer patients to treatment as usual (TAU) and to TAU plus an eight-week (90 minutes per week) SIT program, finding that the SIT group experienced lower levels of stress, anxiety, and depression.

A good deal of outcome research has been conducted on the use of SIT in treating post-traumatic stress disorder (PTSD). In one clinical trial, SIT was slightly less effective in treating PTSD in sexual assault victims than prolonged exposure alone at post-treatment and six-month follow-up (Foa et al., 1999). Vickerman and Margolin (2009) reviewed 32 articles chronicling treatment of PTSD in sexual assault victims and indicated SIT showed some efficacy, although not as much as prolonged exposure and cognitive processing therapy. On the other hand, in a meta-analysis of eight clinical trials, Kehle-Forbes et al. (2013) reported that, although neither approach was effective in the treatment of PTSD in terms of statistical significance, prolonged exposure plus SIT was more effective than prolonged exposure alone. In a review of empirically supported treatments for PTSD in adults, Ponniah and Hollon (2009) determined SIT to be a "possibly efficacious" treatment, whereas in a meta-analysis of PTSD treatment clinical trials, Lee et al. (2016) found that the initial effects of SIT were large but decreased over time.

Two studies explored the effectiveness of SIT with war-related populations. Houram et al. (2011) used SIT to treat trauma exposure and combat-related stressors in deployed military personnel. Hensel-Dittmann et al. (2011) used SIT and found no significant reduction in PTSD symptoms (effect size [ES] = .12) for victims traumatized by war and torture.

One outcome study used SIT to reduce stress in hypertensive patients. In a small randomized clinical trial of hypertensive patients conducted by Ansari, Molavi, and Neshatdoost (2010), SIT had a better outcome on general health than the control condition.

Several studies exploring the educational adaptations of SIT have been conducted. Szabo and Marian (2012) conducted a large-group guidance intervention and demonstrated that a classroom-wide SIT intervention was more effective than a classroom stress education program in helping students reduce perceived stress and response to stress. Cook-Vienot and Taylor (2012) found that both eye movement desensitization and reprocessing (EMDR) and a combination treatment of biofeedback and SIT were effective in treating test anxiety in 30 college students.

APPLICATION OF THE STRESS INOCULATION TRAINING TECHNIQUE

Now apply the SIT technique to a current client or student you are working with or revisit the brief case studies presented at the beginning of this book. How can you use the SIT technique to address concerns and create movement in the counseling session?

Techniques for Use Within and Between Sessions

Section 4 made an excellent case that counselors are well advised to focus on the core conditions of effective helping. However, establishing an effective therapeutic alliance is only part of achieving effective outcomes. In a classic study that frames our view of treatment outcomes even to this day, Lambert (1991) concluded that 30% of therapeutic outcome is because of these core conditions and strength of therapeutic alliance, 15% is due to the specific technique or approach used (e.g., CBT, Adlerian, SFBC), 15% is due to client expectations (e.g., is this going to work, am I ready for change), and, importantly, 40% is due to factors outside of the counseling setting. It is this latter percentage that forms the core of this fifth section of the book: How do we help people between the time that they leave session until the time that they return for the next session?

This is an essential question of effectiveness that is often not even considered by counselors—unfortunately. Often counselors and clients think counseling only occurs in the counselor's office. Incorrect! Much of counseling is aimed at getting clients and students to think, feel, and behave differently *in the real world!* Clients need to transfer and generalize what they learn in counseling sessions to life outside the office.

Of course, life outside of the counseling session can cut both ways: good and bad stuff can happen to the clients. When the client hits the sidewalk or parking lot after a counseling session, they can encounter a wide range of experiences that can either improve or degrade their quality of life. I think about the depressed young woman who left me in my office wondering what the next week would present that would worsen her condition only to find during the next session that she was "over the moon happy" because she went out to socialize with some friends (a homework assignment from counseling) and met the "love of her life"! So happy, depressive symptoms . . . bye, bye! I did not plan for that to happen. She did not plan for that to happen. It just happened, and her depression scale outcome scores diminished quickly. Success!

A colleague tells of a young man whose partner threatened to leave him because of their financial woes. The week of the counseling session, the client had just made a big career change (a previous goal of counseling) that resulted in much higher pay, and he was ecstatically looking forward to a higher standard of living for his family and a better marital relationship. When he left the office, the client was 100% optimism, 0% depression. When he got home, all of the furniture was gone, and a message was written on the mirror, "F— you! You will always be a loser!" My colleague found all of this out that evening during a visit to the hospital after the client attempted to kill himself.

The point is that life happens to clients in between sessions, and you and the client cannot predict or control all these events. Despite this reality, the purpose of this section is to help counselors get some control over this other 40% of treatment outcome by structuring activities outside of the session time and keeping clients and students focused on pursuing the goals of counseling between sessions. Over the next three chapters, we will cover three techniques that help accomplish this goal: assigning homework, bibliotherapy, and journaling. In fairness, the latter two techniques can be implemented inside the counseling session as well as in between sessions, and each means exactly as it sounds. Homework involves the counselor assigning some out-of-session work to be accomplished and discussed during a subsequent session. This could involve practicing deep breathing or self-talk skills, going out with friends or co-workers to socialize, or self-monitoring and recording the frequency of some behavior the client is hoping to change.

Bibliotherapy involves using media to explore themes and ideas related to the counseling goals. This could mean reading a book on eating disorders, depression, or ADHD, or watching a movie about obsessions or trauma. Bibliotherapy is a technique claimed by several theoretical approaches and is a literacy-based approach to counseling in which the counselor and/or client reads a story or passage and engages in discussion about the story's content, meaning, and implications for the client.

Journaling (or a technological equivalent like blogging) also allows clients to self-monitor, express thoughts and feelings, and preserve timely insights into problems and solutions. Journaling also has the benefit of being conducted outside counseling sessions, so it extends the counseling experience and keeps the client focused on counseling goals, processes, and outcomes between counseling sessions. For example, a client or student may write for 5 to 10 minutes each night about how they reacted in an interpersonal situation that day and implemented some of the strategies covered in counseling sessions. As such, they are asked to record how they are transferring and generalizing the skills from session to the real world.

Assigning homework, bibliotherapy, and journaling are ways to structure client time within and between sessions. They are also excellent methods for keeping clients and students focused on goals of counseling every day and capture some of that 40% of counseling outcome that occurs outside of the counselor's office!

MULTICULTURAL IMPLICATIONS OF THE TECHNIQUES USED TO STRUCTURE EXPERIENCES OUTSIDE OF THE COUNSELING SESSION

Humanistic-phenomenological, psychodynamic, and cognitive-behavioral (CBT) approaches to counseling all emphasize the importance of rapport and the therapeutic alliance. Approaches like journaling and bibliotherapy deal with the present and use a logical and clear process in a nonthreatening manner that many clients find empowering; it especially appeals to clients who are systematic thinkers. As a result, these approaches ordinarily appeal to clients from a wide array of cultural backgrounds, particularly those whose cultures may discourage the sharing of family-related issues (e.g., Latino culture) or exploration or exhibition of intense emotional displays (e.g., Asian culture).

Techniques such as bibliotherapy and journaling may be particularly accepted by cultures with storytelling traditions (Hays & Erford, 2018). For example, Native American cultures have a very strong oral storytelling tradition, and *cuento* therapy was designed for use with Latinos and Latinas. This approach uses historical and cultural stories to underscore important lessons to help ground clients in an understanding of, and to help them to adapt to, life situations.

These out-of-session approaches are nonjudgmental, nonthreatening, and accepting of clients from diverse backgrounds and worldviews because they do not view clients or client problems and behaviors as bad or inferior; rather, they view client issues as stemming from distorted thoughts that can be analyzed and modified to adjust to a complex and fluid sociocultural environment.

Professional counselors must be careful not to challenge client beliefs before understanding the cultural context within which those beliefs developed because many clients hesitate or resist questioning their own basic cultural values. For example, some Arab American clients adhere to very strict customs and beliefs related to religion, family, and child rearing. Disputing or even questioning motives or behaviors related to these customs could create additional dilemmas for these clients. Ordinarily, clients from diverse racial, religious, and ethnic backgrounds appreciate these straightforward interventions because they focus on the client's thinking and subsequent behavior rather than on a person's nature, sociocultural background, or cultural beliefs.

CHAPTER 29

Assigning Homework

ORIGINS OF THE ASSIGNING HOMEWORK TECHNIQUE

Homework is any activity collaboratively developed by a client and counselor that takes place outside of the counseling session to accomplish counseling goals (Neimeyer, Kazantzis, Kassler, Baker, & Fletcher, 2008). Homework assignments are a fundamental part of numerous approaches to counseling; thus, the origins of this technique are multifaceted and allow clients to accomplish behavioral, cognitive, social, emotional, or attitudinal changes between sessions (Corey, 2016).

Historically, the use of homework in counseling increased dramatically during the rise of the cognitive-behavioral (CBT) paradigm. Existential approaches, such as Gestalt therapy and logotherapy, also used homework and out of session "experiments" to create change. Adler encouraged clients to act "as if" (Watts, 2003), and Kelly's theory of personal constructivism helped people organize their experiences by asking clients to "try on" a new role as a psychologically different persona by experimenting with new thought and behavioral styles. As such, homework assignments often help clients stuck in a cycle of ineffective problem solving to incorporate new experiences and perspectives, thereby creating opportunities for change.

HOW TO IMPLEMENT THE ASSIGNING HOMEWORK TECHNIQUE

Scheel, Hanson, and Razzhavaikina (2004) suggested a self-explanatory six-phase process for developing homework interventions, stemming from their systematic review of 16 empirical studies of assigning homework to clients: "1: Client-Therapist formulation of homework . . . 2: Therapist delivers homework recommendation . . . 3: Receipt of homework by client . . . 4: Client out-of-session implementation of homework recommendation . . . 5: Next session, therapist asks client about homework experience . . . 6: Client reports about homework experience . . . " (p. 50). Assigning homework is helpful across numerous client types and problem conditions. For example, a client working on anger management may learn several helpful strategies in session; the professional counselor should then follow this skill development with a homework assignment to practice these several strategies on a daily basis at various times of the day and during times when the client's anger arises. Professional counselors who practice rational-emotive behavior therapy (REBT) may direct clients to keep a list of uncomfortable emotions and accompanying irrational thoughts and beliefs that occur throughout the day, and then to practice disputing those beliefs. Likewise, clients are frequently asked to practice rational-emotive imagery activities, deep breathing, self-talk, or visual imagery. When teaching students any of these techniques, I regularly ask them to "practice this skill three times a day every day until I see you again—and teach it to someone else." The three-times-a-day homework assignment is basically behavioral rehearsal and skill development to facilitate mastery and automaticity. Teaching the skill to someone else stems from my observation that the best way to know that you have truly learned something is to teach it to someone else. This also helps to perpetuate use of the skill: Imagine myriad school-age students teaching their parents how to take calm, slow, deep relaxed breaths; imagine anxious mothers teaching their anxious sons, daughters, and partners how to use visual imagery.

Perhaps most important, professional counselors need to adequately connect the homework assignment to counseling goals in order to enhance compliance and clinical outcomes—that is, clients need to understand why it is essential for them to complete the homework. Houlding, Schmidt, and Walker (2010) found that more than 75% of the 32 surveyed counselors used some common elements. They praised clients for homework completion, used noncompliance as a learning opportunity in session, adequately aligned counseling goals with an appropriate rationale for completing the homework, adapted homework assignments to the client's strengths and abilities, collaboratively developed homework assignments, spent time on follow-through, problem-solved through barriers to homework completion, and built upon past successes when designing homework assignments.

VARIATIONS OF THE ASSIGNING HOMEWORK TECHNIQUE

Assigning homework is frequently used and discussed in the context of CBT; however, the assigning homework technique can be easily adapted to other counseling approaches, such as Adlerian therapy, solution-focused brief counseling (Kazantzis, Deane, & Ronan, 2000), systemic and family approaches (Carr, 1997), and multi-family group therapy (Deane, Mercer, Talyarkhan, Lambert, & Pickard, 2012). For example, individuals or families are assigned homework to enact during the week to apply and master strategies and achieve goals outside of the counseling sessions. A client experiencing a brief solution-focused counseling approach may be assigned to enact an agreed-upon plan, write notes on implementation and how it worked, then return the following session to share what was done and evaluate how well it worked. From an Adlerian orientation, a professional counselor might ask the client to "act as if" (or first "reflect as if") he could interact with co-workers with confidence in the workplace (see Chapter 7).

EXAMPLES OF THE ASSIGNING HOMEWORK TECHNIQUE

EXAMPLE 1

Do you recall Sam and the deep breathing technique example in Chapter 15?

Sam continues to breathe with periodic encouragement and comments from the counselor for between 5 and 10 minutes. The counselor then assigns homework: deep breathing for 5 to 10 minutes, three times per day, every day, until the next appointment.

By the time Sam returns for his next session, all of that practice should lead to a high skill level and eventual mastery.

EXAMPLE 2

Later in this book in Chapter 33, David will try to control his anger in the session with the counselor by trying various relaxation and anger control techniques like deep breathing, walking away, counting to 10, and going to a corner of the room to sit down, close his eyes, and relax or meditate.

David's homework was to continue practicing his behavioral rehearsal, to try it in real life after he felt comfortable with the technique, and to immediately report the results to the counselor.

EXAMPLE 3

Do you remember Justin and the mutual storytelling technique from Chapter 9? At the end of the session, the following interchange occurred:

J: That was a great story—I like tigers!

C: Great. Now I want you to take this recording home with you and watch this story again every night until the next time I see you. Okay?

J: No problemo! Can my mom and little brother watch it too?

By reexperiencing the storytelling via the recording every evening, and hopefully discussing things with

*his mother and brother (Mom was asked to partici-
pate and reinforce), Justin has an increased chance
of internalizing and implementing some of the suggested strategies.*

USEFULNESS AND EVALUATION OF THE ASSIGNING HOMEWORK TECHNIQUE

All too often clients think of counseling as a one-hour-per-week experience. Homework assignments help clients accomplish counseling goals by extending what occurs in session to the real-world contexts and getting clients to think about their counseling every day of the week (Leucht & Tan, 1996). Observing and monitoring homework allows counselors and clients to understand how well session content is grasped and generalized to the real world (Kazantzis & Lampropoulos, 2002; Leucht & Tan, 1996), and how future treatment should be modified (Hay & Kinnier, 1998).

Homework assignments are flexible and applicable to a wide range of clinical conditions, including correctional rehabilitation (McDonald & Morgan, 2013), pediatric obsessive-compulsive disorder (Park et al., 2013), obsessive-compulsive disorder (Sukhodolsky, Gorman, Scahill, Findley, & McGuire, 2013), depression (Neimeyer et al., 2008), social phobia (Leung & Heimberg, 1996), generalized anxiety disorder (Newman & Fisher, 2010), personality disorders (Freeman & Rosenfield, 2002), schizophrenia (Deane et al., 2012), and agoraphobia (Edelman & Chambless, 1993).

A meta-analysis by Kazantzis et al. (2000) explored the relationship between homework assignments ($r = .36$) or homework compliance

($r = .22$) with clinical outcomes. Murdoch and Connor-Greene (2000) found that the use of e-mail to monitor, report, and provide feedback on homework assignments enhanced not only clinical outcomes but also the client–counselor relationship. Riley (2015) examined the effect of CBT-oriented homework engagement with a sample of 45 adults with problematic gambling who completed outcome measures and found that engaging in homework was strongly predictive of outcome at termination and one-month follow-up.

Using homework assignments may be particularly useful with clients with depression. Neimeyer et al.'s (2008) path analysis revealed that a client's openness to and completion of homework assignments predicts treatment outcomes for depression. Jungbluth and Shirk (2013) studied homework adherence and resistance in CBT approaches to treatment of 50 adolescents with depression. They found that counselors who spent more time and provided a stronger rationale for the importance of homework in session 1 predicted homework compliance at session 2. Troubleshooting and reaction elicitation in session 2 predicted compliance at session 3. Thus, these strategies bolster adherence in teens who are depressed and initially less engaged in treatment.

APPLICATION OF THE ASSIGNING HOMEWORK TECHNIQUES

Now apply the assigning homework technique to a current client or student you are working with or revisit the brief case studies presented at the beginning of this book. How can you use the assigning homework technique to address concerns and create movement in the counseling session?

CHAPTER 30

Bibliotherapy

ORIGINS OF THE BIBLIOTHERAPY TECHNIQUE

Bibliotherapy is a term coined by Samuel Crothers in 1916 to describe the use of books as part of the counseling process (Jackson, 2001). Although several theoretical counseling approaches integrate or use bibliotherapy, it is included here in the cognitive-behavioral section for convenience. The popularity of bibliotherapy was advanced during the 1930s by librarians and professional counselors who put together lists of books that aided in altering the readers' thoughts, feelings, or behaviors (Abdullah, 2002). Today, bibliotherapy is a technique that is frequently used by professional counselors whose clients need to modify their ways of thinking (Seligman & Reichenberg, 2013). Bibliotherapy aims to affect lives by helping the client find both pleasure in reading and release from mental distress (Brewster, 2008). One of the major propositions underlying this technique is that the client needs to be able to identify with one of the characters who is experiencing a problem similar to the client's issue. By reading a book and being able to identify with a character, clients can "learn vicariously how to solve their problems" and "release emotions, gain new directions in life, and explore new ways of interacting" (Abdullah, 2002, p. 2). Films, videos, and movies also can be used during bibliotherapy; the technique is not limited to books. Bibliotherapy has five goals (Vernon & Clemente, 2004):

> (1) teaching constructive and positive thinking, (2) encouraging free expression of problems, (3) assisting the client in analyzing his or her attitudes and behaviors. (4) fostering the search for alternative solutions to problems, (5) allowing the client to discover that his or her problem is similar to others' problems. (p. 93)

HOW TO IMPLEMENT THE BIBLIOTHERAPY TECHNIQUE

Four "stages" are involved in implementing bibliotherapy: identification, selection, presentation, and follow-up (Abdullah, 2002). In the first stage, it is necessary for the professional counselor to identify the client's needs. Next, the professional counselor needs to select books that will be appropriate for the client's situation. Books need to be written at a level that the client will be able to understand, and the characters in the story need to be believable (Jackson, 2001). The professional counselor should recommend only books that the counselor has read personally and that are in line with the client's values and goals (Young, 2017). In the presentation stage, the client reads the book, usually independently, outside session time, and during counseling sessions, she discusses important aspects of the book with the counselor. For younger children, the book is frequently read together within the counseling session. The professional counselor can request that the client underline key points in the book or keep a journal if it would help the client.

Jackson (2001) described how to help the client identify with a character in the story. The professional counselor needs to have the client retell the story, and the client can choose how she would like to do so (orally, artistically, etc.). During this process, it is important to have the client concentrate on the feelings experienced by the character in the story. The next step is to help the client point out transformations in the character's feelings, relationships, or behaviors. The professional counselor then assists the client in making comparisons between the client and the character from the story. One essential part of this stage is for the client to identify alternative solutions for the character's problems and to discuss the consequences of each.

In the final stage of bibliotherapy, follow-up, the professional counselor and the client discuss what the client has learned as well as what has been gained from identification with the character (Abdullah, 2002). The client can express her experience through discussion, role play, an artistic medium, or a variety of other creative ways (Jackson, 2001). Throughout the implementation of this technique, it is important that the professional counselor keep the reality of the client in mind.

VARIATIONS OF THE BIBLIOTHERAPY TECHNIQUE

According to Brewster (2008), there are three different types of bibliotherapy. *Self-help bibliotherapy* involves the prescription of nonfiction, advisory books about mental health conditions. *Creative bibliotherapy* involves the use of fiction, poetry, biographical writing, and creative writing to improve mental health and well-being. *Informal bibliotherapy* involves a focus on creative bibliotherapy techniques in an unstructured manner, including the use of reading groups, recommendations from library staff members, and displays in the library.

There are also many variations of bibliotherapy. *Traditional bibliotherapy*, as described above, tends to be reactive in nature—that is, the client has a problem and the professional counselor selects a book for the client to read that will help resolve the problem. *Interactive bibliotherapy* involves clients participating in ways that will allow them to reflect on their readings. The ways in which professional counselors have the clients participate vary, but they can include group discussion or journaling. *Clinical bibliotherapy* is used only by trained professional counselors to help clients who are experiencing severe emotional problems (Abdullah, 2002), and it may use journal writing, role playing, or drawing. *Cognitive bibliotherapy* is used to teach

cognitive-behavioral therapy to clients who suffer from depression, with the intention that depression levels will be reduced (Gregory, Canning, Lee, & Wise, 2004). Teachers typically use *developmental bibliotherapy* with their students during group guidance or literacy-based educational experiences, helping to promote normal health (Abdullah, 2002).

When using bibliotherapy with students, make sure to capture student interest at the beginning of the lesson. One idea is to have students make puppets to use as the characters in the story. The teacher should also engage the students in a follow-up discussion requiring higher-level thinking (Johnson, Wan, Templeton, Graham, & Sattler, 2000). Johnson et al. outlined a five-step process for implementing bibliotherapy in the classroom: (1) motivate students with introductory activities, (2) allow reading time, (3) allow incubation time, (4) engage in follow-up discussion time, and (5) end with closure and evaluation. Many books are now available in an audiobook format and can be listened to by the client at home or in the car. Also, videos, movies, and video clips can be helpful aids.

EXAMPLE OF THE BIBLIOTHERAPY TECHNIQUE

An excellent example of the use of bibliotherapy with children who have experienced the loss of a father stems from an in-session reading of the story *When My Dad Died* (or *When My Mom Died*) by J. M. Hammond (1981). The story does an excellent job of conveying the situational emotions, beliefs, and behaviors experienced by young children who experience the loss of a parent or guardian. But good bibliotherapy goes beyond the simple reading of stories. Following are some guided prompts that accompany *When My Dad Died*:

When my dad died, I felt _____.
Sometimes I worry about _____.
These are some things I remember about my dad: _____.
Some things I enjoy are _____.
Now I'm feeling _____.
Now that I've finished the book, here are some things that I learned: _____.

It is the follow-up discussion between client and counselor of the experienced story that makes this bibliotherapy. And the deeper the discussion, the more therapeutic.

USEFULNESS AND EVALUATION OF THE BIBLIOTHERAPY TECHNIQUE

Professional counselors choose to use bibliotherapy with their clients for different issues, including illness, death, self-destructive behaviors, family relationships, identity, violence and abuse, race and prejudice, sex and sexuality, and gender (Christenbury & Beale, 1996). Other populations who may benefit from this technique include students with math anxiety (Hebert & Furner, 1997), females with body-image issues (Corey, 2016), people with depression (Mahalik & Kivlighan, 1988), gay and lesbian youth (Vare & Norton, 2004), and children of divorce (Yauman, 1991). According to Couser (2008), bibliotherapy has advantages as a worksite mental health intervention by reducing or eliminating potential stigmatization. The material could be broadly distributed without pre-identifying employees at risk for mental health problems.

Bibliotherapy helps to reinforce rational thoughts, promote other viewpoints, and instill social interest, and it can be used at any point during the therapeutic process (Jackson, 2001). Books can allow clients to have insight into a part of themselves that they otherwise might not have recognized. Bibliotherapy is used to "stimulate discussion about problems, communicate new values and attitudes, and provide realistic solutions to problems" (Abdullah, 2002, p. 3). This technique can be used to promote therapeutic goals (Schumacher & Wantz, 1995) or can be assigned as homework (Young, 2017). Professional school counselors can use bibliotherapy in classroom guidance lessons, small-group sessions, and individual counseling (Gladding & Gladding, 1991).

Bibliotherapy has been used to address a wide range of issues, although many outcome studies focused on its use with depressed and anxious clientele. Jeffcoat and Hayes (2012) found that a bibliotherapy-based self-help program on acceptance and commitment therapy (ACT) reduced symptoms of depression and anxiety, and it improved general mental health functioning in a group of adult educators. Songprakun and McCann (2012) found that a manual-guided bibliotherapy procedure was effective in reducing symptoms of depression and psychological distress in a sample of depressed Thai adults. Finally, Moldovan, Cobeanu, and David (2013) found that cognitive bibliotherapy reduced depressive symptoms and cognitions at both termination and follow-up compared to placebo, delayed treatment, and no treatment groups. It was also determined that automatic thoughts significantly mediated the effect of bibliotherapy on depressive symptoms.

Much of the research on bibliotherapy points out the cost-effectiveness of the approach compared with traditional face-to-face counseling approaches. Kilfedder et al. (2010) conducted a randomized intent-to-treat comparison of face-to-face counseling, telephone-based counseling, and bibliotherapy to treat occupational stress and found all three approaches to be effective, and they found no significant differences among the three approaches at termination. Bibliotherapy can be delivered at only a fraction of the cost of more traditional, time-intensive approaches, so Kilfedder et al. recommended bibliotherapy as a first course of treatment. In a randomized depression prevention trial with adolescents, Stice, Rohde, Seely, and Gau (2008) compared group cognitive-behavioral therapy (CBT), supportive group therapy, and bibliotherapy to a waitlist condition. Although the group CBT condition led to improvement in depression, social adjustment, and substance use compared to all other conditions at termination and at three- and six-month follow-ups, bibliotherapy participants showed improved depressive symptoms compared to the control condition at six-month follow-up, making it a cost-effective prevention strategy. Similarly, Stice, Rohde, Gau, and Wade (2010) demonstrated the cost-effectiveness of a cognitive-behavioral bibliotherapy approach in reducing risk for depression, even though a group cognitive-behavioral intervention was more effective in the overall clinical trial.

Bibliotherapy can even be used in an online capacity to support hard-to-reach clientele who have serious mental disorders. For example, Moritz et al.

(2016) reported that online treatment supplemented with bibliotherapy may help meet the needs of people with schizophrenia.

Many practicing professional counselors use this technique because of their belief in its efficacy (Jackson, 2001). Studies showed that bibliotherapy was effective in reducing aggressive behavior among adolescents with behavior problems (Shechtman, 2000), reducing depression levels for people who have a high internal locus of control (Mahalik & Kivlighan, 1988), and promoting developmental growth in elementary school children (Borders & Paisley, 1992).

Reading and comprehending bibliotherapy materials are important activities, yet it is possible that the more active component of bibliotherapy treatment is the follow-up questioning and exchange that occurs after the readings. For example, in a randomized controlled trial of mildly depressed, very old adults, Joling et al. (2011) found no differences between the bibliotherapy group and a usual-care group. In this study, the researcher simply distributed the reading materials to the community-based citizens with no active discussion component. Nordin, Carlbring, Cuijpers, and Andersson (2010) found unassisted (no clinician contact) bibliotherapy superior to waitlist control at termination and follow-up. Likewise, in a randomized clinical trial Rapee, Abbott, and Lyneham (2006) found that parent-facilitated bibliotherapy (with no therapist contact) was effective in comparison with waitlist control, but it was significantly less effective than a standard group treatment for childhood anxiety. Again, perhaps clinician-facilitated procedures would have yielded more positive results. Furmark et al. (2009) directly compared self-help (no counselor assistance) bibliotherapy to an Internet-based bibliotherapy intervention with counselor-guided online group discussions and waitlist control in the treatment of social anxiety disorders. They found that both treatment conditions were superior to waitlist both at termination and at one-year follow-up. No statistically significant difference was noted between the two treatment conditions, but Furmark et al. reported that effect sizes were somewhat higher for the counselor-assisted treatment. Dixon, Mansell, Rawlinson, and Gibson (2011) conducted

two studies that independently tested the efficacy of a minimally guided bibliotherapy approach, which effectively improved the main phobia of interest, and an unguided approach, which effectively improved general psychological distress. Not surprisingly, minimally guided, self-help procedures are superior to no treatment at all. Abramowitz, Moore, Braddock, and Harrington (2009) reported reductions in anxiety and depression in participants with social phobia in a minimally guided bibliotherapy treatment (self-help workbook) compared to waitlist participants at termination and three-month follow-up.

Thus, although some evidence promotes the contrary result, the preponderance of evidence indicates that counselor-guided approaches yield better clinical outcomes than undirected, self-guided approaches to bibliotherapy. Of course, the subject matter for all bibliotherapy intervention is not the same, and clinical trials should report effect sizes for specific books and a standardized set of discussion questions so that replication and extension studies can be conducted, as well as so that counselors will know which topical reading matter will yield the most effective results. Also, the speed or pacing with which bibliotherapy is implemented also appears to make no difference. Carlbring et al. (2011) found that variations in the pacing of bibliographic readings made no difference in treatment outcomes for adult clients in a randomized controlled study with panic disorder. Both slower and quicker-paced conditions resulted in two-year follow-up single-group effect sizes of close to 1.00. Importantly, although bibliotherapy that is not supported by counselors in session yields small short-term effects, bibliotherapy without counselor support may yield longer term effects by increasing awareness and positive attitudes toward treatment (Ruwaard et al., 2013).

Riordan and Wilson (1989) reviewed the research surrounding bibliotherapy and found mixed results, especially in its efficacy in changing attitudes, views of self-concept, and behavior. Professional counselors also must be aware that clients may "project their own motives onto characters and thus reinforce their own perspectives and solutions" (Gladding & Gladding, 1991, p. 8).

Bibliotherapy may be ineffective when participants have the following limitations: "lack of social and emotional experiences, failure, flights into fantasy, and defensiveness" (Gladding & Gladding, 1991, p. 9). Clients may not be ready to change or they may not be willing to use this technique. Another limitation of bibliotherapy may be that material on a given subject may not be available (Abdullah, 2002).

APPLICATION OF THE BIBLIOTHERAPY TECHNIQUE

Now apply the bibliotherapy technique to a current client or student you are working with or revisit the brief case studies presented at the beginning of this book. How can you use the bibliotherapy technique to address concerns and create movement in the counseling session?

CHAPTER 31

Journaling

ORIGINS OF THE JOURNALING TECHNIQUE

Journal writing allows clients to express and externalize their thoughts, feelings, and needs—expressions that are ordinarily reserved for the internalized, private realm. People have been journaling in diaries for centuries through formal and informal means. What makes journaling a therapeutic technique is that these written expressions are brought into the counseling sessions and shared openly with the counselor, becoming grist for the counseling process. Journaling also helps keep clients focused on counseling objectives when they are not in counseling sessions.

Counselors using the journaling technique generally ask clients to make journal entries between sessions, sometimes daily, and to share those reflections during the next session. Often, the client can write about anything the client wants; at other times, the professional counselor may assign specific topical content to increase the focus on client goals (Young, 2017).

Kerner and Fitzpatrick (2007) described two main types of therapeutic writing: affective/emotional and cognitive/constructivist. Affective/emotional journaling allows clients to chronicle free-flowing ideas with the goal of emotional expression and release. This process often helps clients access, externalize, and regulate their emotions.

Cognitive/constructivist journaling is a more structured writing approach that focuses on client cognitions and meaning making, often with the goal of promoting insight and reframing (see Chapter 23). Not surprisingly, the affective/emotional journaling is more closely aligned with humanistic-phenomenological approaches, and cognitive/constructivist journaling is more closely aligned with cognitive-behavioral counseling approaches. Whichever approach the professional counselor uses, clients are encouraged to develop a more comprehensive understanding of personal thoughts, feelings, and behaviors (Young, 2017).

The theoretical origins for cognitive or thought journals emerged primarily from rational-emotive behavior therapy (REBT; see Chapter 26), which proposed that distorted, irrational thoughts and beliefs affected client feelings and behaviors, often leading to distress. Ellis's ABCDEF serves as a helpful model for client analysis of the irrational thoughts and beliefs (B) stemming from the activating events (A) and leading to the emotional consequences (C). Clients can gain practice at analyzing the dynamics behind these distressing beliefs, writing down the specifics of scenarios encountered, and eventually internalizing the process through active engagement (Dryden, David, & Ellis, 2010).

Carl Rogers, founder of person-centered theory, also found journaling to have a valuable role in the counseling process. As opposed to the more directive approach of cognitive-behavioral practitioners, Rogers believed clients needed very little direction in order to develop and integrate insights into an authentic self, thus increasing the likelihood of better problem-resolution skills when dealing with future issues and problems. Journaling could be used for the purposes of self-discovery, growth, and self-actualization by channeling feelings and emotions through creative expression and writing processes.

HOW TO IMPLEMENT THE JOURNALING TECHNIQUE

Implementation of the journaling technique can range from nondirective free-flow writing assignments to structured worksheets, but the critical element in any journaling exercise is to match the method with the needs of the client. Young (2017) suggested that the writing should occur daily, guidelines should be agreed to by both the counselor and client, and adjustments should be made as needed. Instructions can be as simple as "Write about anything you like for at least five minutes every day" to "Record the circumstances each time you think about drinking alcohol." The general steps for any journal writing assignment include (1) describe the purpose and content of the exercise, (2) engage in the journaling activity, (3) check client progress and engage the client in meaningful exchanges stemming from the journal content and process, and (4) encourage the client and modify the exercise as necessary (Lent, 2009; Young, 2017). It is important to clarify or determine ahead whether the journal entries will be shared with the counselor. As stated earlier, sharing and discussing the journal content with the professional counselor amplify the therapeutic gains and usually lead to heightened client insights and discussions around changing client thoughts, feelings, and behaviors.

VARIATIONS OF THE JOURNALING TECHNIQUE

Many variations of journaling are available, including self-expression through other media (e.g., paint, dance, and music; Corey, 2016). Kerner and Fitzpatrick (2007) grouped therapeutic writing into six categories: (1) programmed writing, (2) homework diaries, (3) journaling, (4) autobiography/memoir, (5) storytelling, and (6) poetry. Lent (2009) also explored the use of blogging as an adaptation of therapeutic journaling, although he issued a strong warning that use of the Internet often presents challenges to confidentiality. Other creative journaling approaches involve the use of fiction, poetry, biographical writing, and creative writing to improve mental health and well-being.

EXAMPLE OF THE JOURNALING TECHNIQUE

Kottler and Chen (2011) suggested a simple yet effective method to promote cognitive journaling. Basically, the client divides a page into three columns or sections, with the first section labeled "Situation," the second "Feelings," and the third "Accompanying Thoughts." Table 31.1 provides an example of this style of thought or cognitive journaling.

TABLE 31.1 Some Example Entries in a Thought Journal

Situation	Feelings	Accompanying Thoughts
I put on too much weight recently.	Inadequate, unattractive, overweight, undesirable, unlovable	People will find me unattractive if I don't maintain a slim figure.
My paper is not ready to be turned in on time for preview by the teacher.	Stupid, lazy, embarrassed, procrastinator	I am an inferior student, and I am going to fail these classes and be kicked out of the program.
My workload has increased significantly because my supervisor lacks effective management skills.	Irate, resentful, mega-stressed, overwhelmed, depressed, hopeless	Everyone counts on me. Success or failure reflects on me.

Young (2017) encourages clients to integrate journaling into their everyday life routine. The following example is a low-commitment, five-minute, nondirective, free-flowing entry:

> I was running late and trying to make up some time by speeding on the interstate highway. It was working too, until that moron cut me off! He did it on purpose, and all I could think was "Great! I am going to be late because of this jerk! I should teach him a LESSON!" Then I caught myself again, took five or six deep breaths, and used my self-talk. "Everything will be okay." "I need to be sure to leave the house a bit earlier from now on—a little better planning on my part will help me avoid this last-minute drama." "Mr. Jerk is probably running late too." "We all need to get through rush hour safe and sound." I could actually feel myself lightening up, the stress dissipating. Then I switched what I was listening to from an up-tempo song to something more laid back and relaxed, but not gooey—I hate gooey! I settled into my seat, relaxed my grip on the wheel, and made it to work in a much better mood than usual—and 30 seconds early!

USEFULNESS AND EVALUATION OF THE JOURNALING TECHNIQUE

Journaling is an inexpensive, effective therapeutic technique widely used to keep clients motivated and focused between counseling sessions. It also helps clients remember important events and examples that occur throughout the week, allowing the professional counselor access to critical events and information external to the counseling session. Journaling has cross-cultural applications across many different client populations and can be empowering for clients.

Journaling has resulted in various therapeutic outcomes, including decreases in somatic illness, increases in working memory, and promotion of positive growth (Kerner & Fitzpatrick, 2007). Utley and Garza (2011) found journaling to be effective in reducing traumatic symptoms. In a randomized controlled trial with clients diagnosed with post-traumatic stress disorder (PTSD), Smyth, Hockemeyer, and Tulloch (2008) investigated the use of journaling about the traumatic experience compared with placebo control-group participants who wrote about generic time management issues. Results indicated journaling-group participants experienced significant elevations in mood and cortisol reductions.

Journaling improves mood and alters belief or thought structures. McManus, Van Doorn, and Yiend (2012) found significant belief changes when using "thought records" in comparison with the waitlist control-group condition. Chan and Horneffer (2006) conducted a randomized trial comparing participants engaging in a 15-minute journaling activity, a 15-minute drawing activity, and a no-treatment condition, and they found the journaling activity resulted in a greater decrease in psychological symptoms and stress than either of the other two groups. Keeling and Bermudez (2006) used journaling and sculpting in a four-week counseling intervention and found the intervention "helped participants express emotions, increased their awareness of personal resources and agency, helped separate problems from self, decreased symptoms and problem behaviors, and fostered a sense of empowerment" (p. 405).

Journaling also has been used to good effect in treating addictions. Kleinpeter, Brocato, Fischer, and Ireland (2009) found that a specialty group approach focused on journaling was an effective adjunctive therapy to traditional drug court services. Journaling led to higher program retention and successful completion rates for drug court participants. Dwyer, Piquette, Buckle, and McCaslin (2013) found the reflective and intellectual processes in journaling to be an effective intervention with adult females in treatment for a gambling addiction. Journaling can even be used with parents of children and adolescents being treated. Ahmed (2017) reported that daily gratitude journaling by parents of young children led to large effect sizes in decreasing parenting stress and life satisfaction compared to weekly gratitude journaling and a control condition. Unfortunately, this was only a small sample pilot study, so no statistically significant results were noted. Thus, journaling is widely applicable across populations and an effective method for sustaining client and other stakeholder attention to therapeutic goals between sessions.

APPLICATION OF THE JOURNALING TECHNIQUE

Now apply the journaling technique to a current client or student you are working with or revisit the brief case studies presented at the beginning of this book. How can you use the journaling technique to address concerns and create movement in the counseling session?

Techniques Based on Social Learning Approaches

Albert Bandura's (2006) social learning theory proposes that much human learning occurs without the contingencies associated with reinforcement and punishment. Bandura broke away from traditional behavior therapy based on operant conditioning (see Section 9 and Section 10) because he viewed it as simplistic and lacking a cognitive component. Bandura noticed that human beings often did a lot of observation, preplanning, and thinking before engaging in behaviors, and behaviorism ignored all of these essential components. Bandura noticed that a reciprocal interaction among the person, behavior, and environment were at the core of most behaviors.

Bandura (2006) noticed that clients frequently learned to perform tasks and behaviors simply by watching others and imitating the observed behaviors. He referred to this process as vicarious learning, and he and subsequent counselors applying social learning theory to counseling developed a number of techniques helpful to clients, including modeling, behavioral rehearsal, and role playing. Modeling involves demonstrating a certain skill or sequence of skills to a client so that the client may imitate the modeled behavior. For example, a professional counselor may demonstrate the appropriate manner for a client to introduce herself to an adult or how to handle a conflict with a peer assertively.

After a client understands how to perform a given task or interpersonal interaction, behavioral rehearsal usually ensues. Behavioral rehearsal is the actual practicing of social behaviors with constructive feedback from the professional counselor or other counseling participants. Role play allows a free-flowing, dynamic interchange between client and counselor (or another counseling participant) to try new behaviors in mock situations with constructive feedback. A primary advantage of role play stems from the players' abilities to improvise and introduce real-life twists and turns that clients may encounter when implementing the newly learned skills outside the counselor's office. Techniques based on social learning theory can yield powerful learning opportunities.

MULTICULTURAL IMPLICATIONS OF THE TECHNIQUES BASED ON SOCIAL LEARNING APPROACHES

Techniques based on social learning have wide applications across cultures because they allow clients and counselors to consider the essential interchanges of a client's cultural and social dimensions. Social learning approaches allow clients to conceptualize social difficulties within a cultural context, establish specific goals, plan therapeutic conditions to maximize success, and use social interactions between the client and counselor or other individuals to accomplish these goals. Clients of some cultures (e.g., Latino, Arab American, Asian American men) may prefer action-oriented, instructional strategies stemming from concrete goals and objectives, and they also may prefer to avoid emotional expression and catharsis (Hays & Erford, 2018).

In particular, counselors should be knowledgeable about what is considered normal and abnormal behavior within a client's multicultural context and how the client defines and conceptualizes the presenting problems (Hays & Erford, 2018).

Behavioral approaches based on social learning accommodate these culturally based preferences by focusing on specific behaviors and allowing clients to solve problems through social interaction. A final advantage of social learning approaches when used in a multicultural context is that traditional behavioral approaches have been criticized for viewing the problem as one internal to an individual. Ethnically diverse individuals often appreciate the more neutral and inclusive social learning approach for appropriately focusing on social interactions and skill enhancement in the sociocultural context.

CHAPTER 32

Modeling

ORIGINS OF THE MODELING TECHNIQUE

Modeling is the process by which individuals learn from watching others. It is a component of the social learning theory developed by Albert Bandura (Bandura, 2006) and has become one of the most widely used, well-researched, and highly regarded psychologically based training interventions (Taylor, Russ-Eft, & Chan, 2005). Modeling also has been referred to as imitation, identification, observational learning, and vicarious learning. Early research on modeling was conducted by Miller and Dollard (2003), who found that, through reinforcement, participants could learn to imitate one model, learn not to imitate another model, learn to distinguish between these two models, and generalize this discrimination of whether or not to copy the behavior to other, similar persons.

There are three basic types of modeling. *Overt modeling* (or live modeling) occurs when one or more persons demonstrate the behavior to be learned (Hackney & Cormier, 2017). Live models can include the professional counselor, a teacher, or the client's peers. Sometimes it can be helpful for clients to observe more than one model in order to draw on the strengths and styles of different people. *Symbolic modeling* involves illustrating the target behavior through video or audio recordings. Symbolic modeling allows the professional counselor to have more control over the accuracy of the behavioral demonstration. Also, once an appropriate symbolic model is developed, it can be easily stored for repeated use. Self-as-a-model activities involve recording the client performing the target behavior. The client can then either observe the recording

directly or use positive self-imagery to recall performing the skill successfully. *Covert modeling* requires the client to imagine the target behavior being successfully completed, either by herself or by someone else.

Modeling can produce three different types of responses (Bandura, 2006). Clients may acquire new patterns of behavior by watching others, which is termed an *observation learning effect*. Modeling may strengthen or weaken the client's inhibition of already learned behaviors, referred to as *inhibitory effects* (when strengthened) or *disinhibitory effects* (when weakened). Modeled behaviors may serve as social cues to signal the client to perform a certain known response, which is called *response facilitation effects*.

For clients to learn a modeled behavior successfully, four interrelated subprocesses must exist. First, the client must be able to attend to the modeling demonstration (*attention*). Second, the client must be able to retain the observation of the modeled event (*retention*). Attention and retention phases are necessary to acquire the behavior. Third, the client needs to be motorically capable of reproducing the modeled behavior (*reproduction*). Last, the client must be motivated, either internally (i.e., intrinsic motivation) or through external reinforcement (i.e., extrinsic motivation), to perform the target behavior (*motivation*). Reproduction and motivation are required to perform the behavior. Bandura (2006) referred to the first two subprocesses as the acquisition phase and the second two processes as the performance phase. Bandura distinguished between acquisition and performance phases primarily to underscore the reality that just because a client has acquired a behavior does not mean the client will be motivated to perform the behavior!

Several other factors influence the success of observational learning. Research shows that modeling is more effective when the client perceives the model to be similar to herself (Hallenbeck & Kauffman, 1995). In addition, clients more readily imitate a model who seems to be acquiring the modeled skills rather than those who are already highly skilled at the behavior. The characteristics of the observer also play a role in how willing the client is to imitate modeled behavior. Gender, age, motivation, cognitive capacity, and prior social learning are all factors in the success of modeling. Successful social learning relies heavily on reinforcements. Reinforcement can be directly applied to the client's external behavior, whether or not the client performs the target behavior. Or clients can observe vicarious reinforcement, where the model is either rewarded or punished for performing the target behavior. In general, imitative behavior is increased by observed rewards and decreased by observed punishment.

HOW TO IMPLEMENT THE MODELING TECHNIQUE

Before modeling can begin, the client and professional counselor must select an alternative behavior that will be taught to replace the undesirable behavior. The professional counselor should also provide the client with a rationale for the use of modeling (Hackney & Cormier, 2017). The modeling scenario should minimize the stress that the client might experience and also should break down complex behaviors into small, simple steps. As the target behavior is performed, either the model or the professional counselor should describe the steps to carry out the modeled behavior. Once the target behavior has been demonstrated, the professional counselor should lead the client in a discussion of the behavior. During this discussion, the professional counselor can verbally reinforce the client.

The client should be allowed many opportunities to practice the target behavior after the modeling has occurred. Frequent, short sessions are more effective than longer sessions. The professional counselor can also assign homework for the client to practice the behavior when she is not in a session. Self-guided practice can help the client apply the modeled behavior to real-life situations. However, the professional counselor should be careful not to expect too much too soon; teaching new behaviors often creates resistance, especially if clients do not understand the reasoning behind the target behavior.

VARIATIONS OF THE MODELING TECHNIQUE

Cognitive modeling was developed to help clients avoid negative, self-defeating thoughts and behaviors by replacing them with positive statements (James & Gilliland, 2003). Cognitive modeling involves five steps. First, the professional counselor models the behavior as if the counselor were the client. Then the client performs the task while the professional counselor talks the client through each step. Third, the client performs the task again, this time instructing herself aloud. Fourth, the client performs the task a third time while whispering the instructions to herself. Finally, the client performs the task while instructing herself covertly (i.e., through imagery or subvocalization).

Skills training is a counseling intervention that is composed of many different techniques, including modeling (Hackney & Cormier, 2017). In skills training, the professional counselor and client determine the skills to be learned. Then the skills are arranged in order from least difficult to most difficult. The training proceeds by modeling the skills, having the client imitate the skills as modeled, providing feedback to the client, and repeating the sequence until the skills are mastered.

EXAMPLE OF THE MODELING TECHNIQUE

Two case examples of modeling are provided here, and each continues in the next chapter with an example on behavioral rehearsal. The first transcript demonstrating modeling involves teaching a 17-year-old female client, Nicole, a deep breathing technique. Chapter 33, on behavioral rehearsal, provides a complementary transcript immediately following this one in the session to demonstrate the practice phase that frequently occurs in a modeling procedure. Prior to the moment the transcript begins, Nicole and the counselor agreed that an effective way to help her relax was to help her calm her breathing from shallow, quick breathing (which led to stress and hyperventilation) to long, deep, slow breathing— that is, they selected an alternative behavior. Next, the counselor discussed the rationale for the use of modeling and behavioral rehearsal. Finally, the counselor began to explain the steps of the deep breathing technique and the reason why deep breathing works.

Counselor (C):   When you slow your breathing, you will slow down your whole central nervous system, just like Johnny did in the picture, making you calm and relaxed. Just inhale and exhale at a slow, yet comfortable pace . . . Don't hold your breath when you complete your inhale, but I want you to breathe in until you can't get any more air into your lungs. Then I want you to breathe right back out. I will model for you and then we can practice.

Nicole (N):   Okay.

C: Okay, I'm going to show you how to do it correctly. I'll show you when I'm finished inhaling and when I start to exhale. (Pause for inhale) . . . Okay, now I've got about as much air in me as I can, and now I'm going to purse my lips and exhale slowly. (Pause for exhale) . . . There, did you see how I did that? I can even exhale a bit longer if I need to. The interesting thing is your exhale usually is longer than your inhale.

N: Yeah, I noticed that.

C: Ordinarily, when I get to deeper levels of relaxation, I can get down to two breaths per minute, sometimes even about one and a half per minute. So I'm actually breathing in for about 10 or 15 seconds on my inhale.

N: Uh-huh.

C: And you don't hold it; you immediately start your exhale, and I can ordinarily exhale for about 15 to 25 seconds. So my whole breath might take, you know, 30 or 40 seconds from the time that I begin to inhale and then finish my exhale and then begin again. Now your lung capacity may not be as large, so try to slow down your breathing to a level that is comfortable for you.

The counselor leads a guided discussion of the steps again, verbally reinforces her as Nicole performs the practice steps, and answers any questions Nicole has.

C: Do you want me to show you again, or are you ready to try it?

N: I'm okay.

C: Alright. I want you to slow your breathing down, again to about eight or six or even four breaths per minute so you can take your body into that relaxing state . . . So let's go ahead, and I want you to concentrate again on breathing very slowly on your inhale and then very slowly again on your exhale . . .

Note: This transcript continues in the next chapter to demonstrate how modeling is often followed by behavioral rehearsal.

The second transcript demonstrating modeling involves teaching a 10-year-old male client, David, a social skill: self-control in the context of being teased or taunted. Chapter 33, on behavioral rehearsal, provides a complementary transcript immediately following this one in the session to demonstrate the practice phase that frequently occurs in a modeling procedure. Prior to the moment the transcript begins, David explained the emotional frustration he feels when being teased by other boys who are just trying to get him in trouble for fighting. David has been referred to the principal's office several times already this year for fighting, and his reputation as a hothead has led to more baiting by peers and punishment by teachers.

David (D):   I just go off, lose control. Y'know, like a volcano exploding, blowing up. I can't stop it. These two kids are so mean; they just do it on purpose to get me in trouble. But I have to defend myself, don't I? I can't just let them diss me, y'know?

Counselor (C):   You surely do deserve to be treated respectfully, David, but it sounds like you need a strategy to control your emotions and keep out of trouble. It doesn't seem fair that they bait you, but you are the one who gets into trouble.

D: Exactly. Not fair at all. So, you will fix all this with Mr. Edwards?

C: Not exactly. You see, David, when you fight with other kids, you are breaking school rules, and Mr. Edwards needs to bring on the consequences just like he would for anyone else who fights.

D: But *they* are the ones *starting* it!

C: Right, but they are not the ones punching. You are. So, you end up in trouble, not them.

D: Then what do I do? I don't know what to do if I can't defend myself from all of the teasing! What am I supposed to do?

C: Well, I suppose we can both agree that what you are currently doing is not working so well. You end up in trouble and the teasers seem to be teasing you more than ever.

D: You got *that* right. It's not fair.

The counselor uses a sports metaphor related to David's favorite football team.

C: What would happen if the Steelers ran the same play over and over again?

D: They wouldn't get very far. Everybody would know what to expect.

C: Exactly. Which is why they have so many different plays. It keeps the other team guessing what they are going to do. It gives them choices on how to reach the goal.

D: Right?

C: See any similarity to your strategy with the bullies?

D: Um, oh, you mean how I always react the same way . . . do the same stupid thing and get in trouble?

C: Exactly. Maybe we should mix up our plays. Maybe we should try a different approach. Different choices. We know that fighting back

is not a good option. But what are some other things you could do instead?

The counselor and David brainstorm for some choices and come up with a list: count to 10; take several deep breaths to relax; do some visual imagery to relax; do some muscle relaxation; walk away; talk to someone you trust about it; write your feelings in a journal; do some self-talk with positive, self-affirming statements.

D: Wow. Eight things to try instead of fighting. I didn't think I had this many choices.

The counselor now uses modeling to demonstrate the skill for David.

C: Let me demonstrate how this might work for you in the future. Let's pretend that those two boys are teasing you and saying mean things and trying to pick a fight with you. In that situation, here is what I would do. I will think out loud so you can hear me, but you would be doing this in your head at the time, of course. I can feel myself getting upset about the teasing, so I think about my list of choices, take a few deep breaths as I count to 10. (The counselor looks at David and takes a deep breath, which David mimics, and counts to ten on fingers, which David also mimics.) The teasing hasn't stopped, so I turn and walk away and look for a friend or teacher to talk to, or find a place to sit by myself to do a relaxation exercise. (Looks to David) Did that make sense?

D: Sort of. Can I practice it a few times?

C: Sure.

And so ends the modeling procedure. This transcript is continued in the next chapter on behavioral rehearsal.

USEFULNESS AND EVALUATION OF THE MODELING TECHNIQUE

Modeling can be used to teach clients many different skills. In general, live modeling seems to be more effective in teaching personal and social skills, whereas symbolic modeling is helpful with more cognitive problems. Video modeling and video self-modeling have been used successfully with individuals who have developmental disabilities and externalizing issues, such as disruptive or aggressive behavior (Green et al., 2013). Self-as-a-model procedures are effective with self-acceptance problems, interpersonal skill development, and teaching or counseling skill development. Positive results from video self-modeling have been recorded in children with autism spectrum disorder who exhibit problem behaviors (Buggey, 2005).

Modeling also can be used to help teens deal with peer pressure, to help family members learn new communication patterns, or in any other situation where the client does not have an appropriate alternative response (Hackney & Cormier, 2017). Modeling has been used to teach autistic children to speak; to teach coping skills to hospital patients, new behaviors to children who are socially disturbed, interpersonal skills to people who abuse drugs and alcohol, and survival skills to individuals with intellectual disabilities; and to treat phobias (Corey, 2016). Modeling has been applied in developing training programs for supervisory, communications, sales, and customer service skills, and it has been extended to a broader range of applications, including cross-cultural skills (Taylor et al., 2005).

Elias (1983) investigated the effects of viewing social problem–solving videos on the behavior of boys who were socially disturbed. Elias observed that during the five-week program, those children who participated in video discussions showed a decrease in social isolation and an increase in popularity. They also were noted to show an increase in self-control, an improved ability to delay gratification, a decrease

in emotional detachment, and an overall decrease in personality problems. These results suggested that symbolic modeling, as observed through problem-solving videos, is effective in improving children's social skills.

Flowers (1991) studied the effects of modeling on self-confidence, as measured by students' willingness to answer trivia questions. He found that low self-confidence students, who observed other previously low self-confidence students, increased in confidence and showed an increase in self-confidence when compared to a control group and a group that observed only high-confidence students. This study confirmed that modeling is most effective when clients perceive that models are similar to themselves. Hallenbeck and Kauffman (1995) reported that students with emotional or behavioral disorders often do not learn effectively from the modeling of well-adjusted peers because they do not perceive themselves as similar to these peers. These observations suggested that students who are emotionally or behaviorally disturbed would benefit more from modeling by others with similar disorders who have acquired some success at overcoming their tendency to behave poorly.

APPLICATION OF THE MODELING TECHNIQUE

Now apply the modeling technique to a current client or student you are working with or revisit the brief case studies presented at the beginning of this book. How can you use the modeling technique to address concerns and create movement in the counseling session?

CHAPTER 33

Behavioral Rehearsal

ORIGINS OF THE BEHAVIORAL REHEARSAL TECHNIQUE

Behavioral rehearsal is one of the many techniques stemming from behavior therapy, but it has been adapted for use by counselors using a social learning approach. This technique, first labeled behavioristic psychodrama, is a blend of "Salter's conditioned reflex therapy, Moreno's psychodrama technique, and Kelly's fixed role therapy" (Thorpe & Olson, 1997, p. 44). Professional counselors typically use behavioral rehearsal with clients who need to become completely aware of themselves. It is a form of role play in which the client is learning a new type of behavior to use in response to certain situations and people outside the counseling situation. Behavioral rehearsal includes several key components: modeling the behavior, receiving feedback from the counselor, and frequently practicing the desired behavior.

HOW TO IMPLEMENT THE BEHAVIORAL REHEARSAL TECHNIQUE

When implementing behavioral rehearsal, events that occur in daily life are role-played by the client and professional counselor in an attempt to decrease any anxieties the client may have when expressing himself. The client acts as himself, and the professional counselor plays the role of the person about whom the client has surrounding anxieties. The professional counselor instructs the client to communicate feelings about the anxiety-producing person or circumstance. The client needs to use a strong voice and repeat a feelings statement or appropriate behavior, while the professional counselor gives feedback

to the client. The client continues rehearsing until the professional counselor indicates the statement or behavior was communicated effectively (Wolpe, 1991). Naugle and Maher (2008) suggested that the professional counselor and client should attempt and master simple skills first, and only then move on to more complex skills. Naugle and Maher provided the following steps for the professional counselor to use in implementing the behavioral rehearsal technique: (1) practice the behavior to be modeled; (2) build the client's motivation through positive reinforcement strategies (see Section 8); (3) give the client plenty of focused, concrete feedback to help the client master the skill; and (4) use positive reinforcement strategies to shape and hone the skill behaviors (e.g., successive approximation).

For behavioral rehearsal to be effective, Bootzin (1975) suggested clients practice the following six rules: (1) express emotions verbally; (2) present feelings nonverbally using body language; (3) contradict others when one disagrees with them; (4) speak in the first person, using the word *I* regularly; (5) agree with the counselor's praise; and (6) "improvise, live for the moment" (p. 105).

VARIATIONS OF THE BEHAVIORAL REHEARSAL TECHNIQUE

Naugle and Maher (2008) claimed that in vivo rehearsal could make the treatment even more effective by helping the client engage in the desired behavior in a natural setting. They warned that the professional counselor must provide comments and feedback that are specific to the desired client behavior. Then, after initial successes, the behavioral tasks assigned by the professional counselor can become progressively more difficult and practiced outside the counseling session.

Seligman and Reichenberg (2013) suggested that professional counselors have clients practice behavioral rehearsal not only in counseling sessions but also in outside settings. Clients could practice the tasks with friends in their daily lives. Seligman and Reichenberg also suggested that professional counselors record clients engaging in the behavioral rehearsal or encourage clients to practice in front of the mirror, thus allowing the client to monitor himself and provide his own feedback.

Smokowski (2003) incorporated technology into behavioral rehearsal sessions with clients by video-recording them and using computer simulations. In this variation, Smokowski used the video camera in a group session. He suggested having the camera represent the person who is working on a desired behavior and having the group members role-play the situations or people involved in the behavioral rehearsal. At the point in the role play when a response is needed from the camera, the recording is stopped and the member responds. Because the beginning part of the rehearsal is recorded, the member can practice several different responses. Smokowski also suggested having a member play the role he is having trouble responding to. By playing the role of the antagonist, the member can work on building his own assertiveness.

EXAMPLE OF THE BEHAVIORAL REHEARSAL TECHNIQUE

Two transcripts follow; both are continuations of the transcripts from Chapter 32, which discusses modeling. Modeling is usually followed immediately by behavioral rehearsal and then often by role playing (see Chapter 34). The following transcript is an excerpt of instruction and behavioral rehearsal of a deep breathing procedure. This transcript picks up with Nicole at the point that the transcript for Chapter 32 left off.

Counselor (C):   All right. I want you to slow down your breathing again to about eight or six or even four breaths per minute so you can take your body into that relaxing state . . . I want you to concentrate again on breathing very slowly on your inhale and then very slowly again on your exhale . . . (Nicole inhales.) Great. You breathed through your nose, and your lungs are full. Now exhale. (Nicole exhales.) Your lips are pursed, and I can barely feel your exhale. Very good. Now inhale.

Nicole (N):   (Pauses to inhale and exhale) I feel a little lightheaded . . .

C: Okay, now you might feel a little bit lightheaded as you start to do that, as you slow down, as you slow down your breathing from the normal rate to a slower and relaxed rate. Sometimes you feel a little bit lightheaded, but usually by the time you take your fourth or fifth breath the lightheadedness subsides.

N: Okay. (Continues to breathe several more cycles) You were right. I'm not lightheaded anymore.

C: Keep going. Your mind told your body to adjust, and the relaxation response kicked in, slowing down your entire central nervous system. Do you feel any anxiety or anything?

N: (Continues to breathe) None at all. In fact, I am starting to feel (Yawns) a little sleepy.

C: That's your body relaxing. Sometimes you get so relaxed, you fall asleep. This is why a lot of people practice deep breathing and progressive muscle relaxation training before they go to sleep—it helps them fall asleep quicker and gives them a head start on deep, relaxing sleep.

N: I can understand why! (Nicole practices a half dozen more times with feedback from the counselor, then breathes deeply on her own for three minutes.)

C: Okay, so you're already at four breaths per minute. Was that comfortable for you to breathe that way?

N: Wow, I didn't even know that. Four? Really? Yeah, that was comfortable.

C: You're a pretty quick learner. You learned this deep breathing technique like you've been breathing all your life.

N: Well, I have. (Laughs)

C: All right, you know what I'm going to tell you to do next . . .

N: More homework?

C: Right, practice this deep breathing activity five times a day for at least 3 minutes each time—and preferably 5 to 10 minutes each time. I want you to take nice, long, deep, slow breaths in and out. For a couple of minutes, about 3 or more minutes . . . I want you to practice that first thing in the morning before you jump out of bed. I want you to practice this right after breakfast or so, before lunch, before dinner, and then again at bedtime.

This next transcript is a continuation of the modeling procedure (see Chapter 32) used with 10-year-old David, who is learning choices to implement for improving his self-control and avoiding physical fighting.

David (D):   Can we write down my choices so I can remember them better?

Counselor (C):   Sure. We can even add to the list as new ideas come along.

The counselor composes the list: count to 10; take several deep breaths to relax; do some visual imagery to relax; do some muscle relaxation; walk away; talk to someone you trust about it; write your feelings in a journal; do some self-talk with positive, self-affirming statements. David starts his behavioral rehearsal, after imagining the boys are baiting him, by taking an exaggerated deep breath.

David (D):   (Breathes deeply, turns, walks away from the imaginary boys, and approaches the counselor) Dr. Erford, can I talk with you about a teasing problem?

Counselor (C):   That was excellent, David. I could see that you took some deep breaths, you walked away, and it took you at least 10 seconds to make your way slowly over to me, so I assume you also counted to 10, and then you asked an adult you trust to talk about it. Well done.

D: Thanks! Can I try another one?

This time David takes some deep breaths, turns away, walks to the corner of the room, sits down, and closes his eyes. The counselor provides more specific, critical feedback, and they practice a dozen more times until David feels comfortable with the choices he is making. At this point, the counselor began role-playing various scenarios with David so he could refine and adapt his strategies to changing conditions. His homework was to continue practicing his behavioral rehearsal, to try it in real life once after he felt comfortable with the technique, and immediately report the results to the counselor.

USEFULNESS AND EVALUATION OF THE BEHAVIORAL REHEARSAL TECHNIQUE

Turner, Calhoun, and Adams (1992) indicated behavioral rehearsal has been used successfully with clients dealing with anger, frustration, anxiety, phobias, panic attacks, and depression. Professional counselors often use the behavioral rehearsal technique with clients experiencing difficulty interacting with others in specific, anticipated situations. This technique is used frequently to achieve catharsis, attitudinal change, or specific targeted behaviors (Hackney & Cormier, 2017).

Walsh (2002) found behavioral rehearsal useful when working with people who have social anxiety. The client first learns new ways of thinking or behaving and gets to practice these new responses in the counseling situation. Then the client practices the new behaviors in a naturalistic setting. By practicing first in a safe environment, clients are able to develop more confidence before having to act in the real-life setting. The hope is that the client will master these altered ways of thinking and behaving and eventually shed shy or inappropriate behavioral tendencies. Turner et al. (1992) found the behavioral rehearsal technique useful in working with heterosexual males who had anxiety surrounding dating, resulting in reduced anxiety, increased assertiveness, and an increased number of dates these men scheduled on follow-up. Behavioral rehearsal has also been used with people who have been told what not to do and do not know what to do. The counselor can help stop the incorrect behavior and have the client replace it with a correct, prosocial behavior. By using this technique, people understand that mistakes are okay and that we can all learn from and fix inappropriate behaviors (Alvord & Grados, 2005).

Although there is little empirical research focusing on the behavioral rehearsal technique, it is a method that is widely used among professional counselors for a variety of reasons. This technique is not dangerous for clients; it is not associated with any substantial risks. It is efficient in terms of both time and money, and it works with many populations, including those who are challenged cognitively, socially, and emotionally (Naugle & Maher, 2008). Implementation of this technique is fairly simple, and change can be seen quickly, sometimes even in several sessions. Still, Naugle and Maher cautioned professional counselors to be careful when using this technique with clients who (1) cannot take responsibility for their behaviors; (2) are scared of the consequences, whether or not they are real; (3) will not practice the rehearsal; (4) will not complete the out-of-session assignments; (5) have

daily crises; and/or (6) "experience severe psychomotor agitation or retardation" (p. 241).

In a study conducted by Kantor and Shomer (1997), the researchers studied the effects of a stress management program on the participants' lifestyles. Behavioral rehearsal was one of the coping resources taught to the participants. Although the program was effective in some of the areas evaluated, the difference in coping resources was not statistically significant. It appeared that the participants were not using the techniques taught to them consistently. The results of this study remind professional counselors of the necessity that clients repeat the behavioral rehearsal frequently and receive frequent and specific feedback.

APPLICATION OF THE BEHAVIORAL REHEARSAL TECHNIQUE

Now apply the behavioral rehearsal technique to a current client or student you are working with or revisit the brief case studies presented at the beginning of this book. How can you use the behavioral rehearsal technique to address concerns and create movement in the counseling session?

CHAPTER 34

Role Play

ORIGINS OF THE ROLE PLAY TECHNIQUE

Role play is a technique used by counselors of different theoretical orientations with clients who need to develop a deeper understanding of, or change within, themselves. Within a role play, clients can perform a decided-upon behavior in a safe, risk-free environment. Role play is a blend of conditioned reflex therapy, psychodrama technique, and fixed-role therapy (Hackney & Cormier, 2017). Hackney and Cormier described four aspects commonly found in role plays. In most role plays, a person reenacts herself, another person, a set of circumstances surrounding a situation, or her own reactions. The person then receives feedback from the professional counselor or from group members when the role play is instituted in a group-work context. Role plays occur in the present, not the past or the future; it is common to begin with scenes that are easier to reenact and to work progressively toward scenes that are more complex.

HOW TO IMPLEMENT THE ROLE PLAY TECHNIQUE

Before implementing this technique, it is helpful for professional counselors to understand the four elements and three phases found within role plays. The first element is called the *encounter*, which in this situation means being able to understand the perspective of another person. This is a necessary part of the role play because the client will sometimes switch roles and play the part of another individual involved in the situation. The next element, the *stage*, is space with simple props that can provide

a realistic experience (Young, 2017). The *soliloquy*, the third aspect, is another term that professional counselors must know; it is a speech in which the client expresses her private thoughts and associated feelings. Professional counselors can learn more about their clients, including their irrational beliefs, through the soliloquy. The last element, *doubling*, leads to increased awareness on the part of the client and occurs when the professional counselor or another group member stands behind the client while the client is acting out the scene. The counselor then expresses the client's unexpressed thoughts or feelings.

The three phases in a role play include warm-up, action, and sharing and analysis. There is a debate about splitting the third phase and thus having four phases. The goal of the warm-up phase is to encourage the client to become connected with the situation, including the related emotions that will be reenacted. The warm-up activity can be performed either mentally or physically. In the action phase, the professional counselor helps the client set the scene by going over the details of the situation. The professional counselor also has to guide the client from reality to the imagined situation and back to reality. In the sharing and analysis phase, the professional counselor and group members (if performed in a group setting) share what they experienced during the role play. The analysis often occurs in a follow-up session because the client is typically emotionally aroused at the end of the role play. In this session, the client has a chance to process information and receive feedback.

Young (2017) provides a seven-step process for professional counselors to follow when implementing the role play technique with a client:

1. ***Warm-up:*** The professional counselor explains the technique to the client, and the client provides a detailed description of the behavior, attitude, or performance she would like to change. The client should be encouraged to discuss any reluctance she may have about the role play technique.
2. ***Scene setting:*** The professional counselor assists the client in setting the stage. If necessary, furnishings can be rearranged.
3. ***Selecting roles:*** The client names and describes the significant people involved in the scene.
4. ***Enactment:*** The client acts out the target behavior, and if she has difficulty doing so, the professional counselor can model the behavior. The client should begin with the scenes that are the least difficult and gradually move on to those that are more difficult. During this step, the professional counselor can interrupt the client in order to show the client what she is doing that contributes to her disturbance.
5. ***Sharing and feedback:*** The counselor gives the client feedback that is specific, simple, observable, and understandable.
6. ***Reenactment:*** The client repeatedly practices the targeted behavior in and outside the counseling sessions until she and the professional counselor believe that the goal has been met.
7. ***Follow-up:*** The client informs the professional counselor of her practice results and progress.

VARIATIONS OF THE ROLE PLAY TECHNIQUE

Behavioral rehearsal is one of the most common variations of role playing. When the client performs the target behaviors, she is reinforced and rewarded, first by the professional counselor and second by the client's self-praise (Young, 2017). To learn more about this variation, read the chapter focused on behavioral rehearsal in this text (see Chapter 33).

An alternative five-step process for implementing the role play technique is (1) specify the behavior to be learned; (2) determine the context or environment of a particular event; (3) start with small scenes and then build to scenes with greater complexity; (4) in session, engage in role plays with minimum risk and work up to situations that involve higher risk; and (5) apply the role playing in real-life situations, again starting with situations of minimum risk and working up to situations with higher risk. Video-recording the role plays can be extremely helpful in analyzing a client's strengths and struggles in a given role.

Young (2017) described another variation of the role play: the mirror technique in group therapy. In this version, the member who is reenacting the scene takes a seat at the very moment when the critical behavior occurs. Another group member takes this member's place and, sometimes exaggeratedly, reenacts the behavior or response of the original performer. The original performer can watch and evaluate her response. A new response can be discussed, and the original performer can then practice it.

In a variation used commonly by Gestalt therapists, two chairs are used in place of other people who are involved in the scene. The chairs can symbolize a variety of different things, including the client and any other person with whom the client is experiencing an issue, two parts within the same person (e.g., logic and desire), conflicting emotions, and so on (Seligman & Reichenberg, 2013). The client sits in each chair and needs to speak the point of view that each chair holds. Feelings or thoughts that are truthful, but until that time unsaid, are often expressed.

Another variation of this technique is useful when working with children. If possible, the child can put on different costumes when switching roles. This may help the child understand that he is not just acting like himself (Vernon & Clemente, 2004).

Shepard (1992) described yet another variation of the role play technique he uses when training beginning counselors. Often, counselors-in-training are asked to role-play with each other to gain experience using the different techniques that they are learning. Shepard taught students to role-play using screenwriting techniques, and commonly the result was more realistic role plays. The first step for the class was to create a character. Class members needed to describe the general characteristics of the character, including name, age, ethnicity, profession, relationship status, and family. A back story, which includes personal history and key influences on a character's life, also has to be created. The character's dreams, fantasies, goals, crises, conscious and unconscious desires, and societal influences should all be considered. Another important piece of the back story is deciding what the character's family life was like when growing up. Professional and personal forces faced by the client should be decided upon, as should the event that motivated the character to seek counseling. The presenting problem needs to be realistic and have at least one of the following manifestations: affective, cognitive, somatic, or behavioral. After the example is created in class, the students create their own characters using this model. Throughout the semester, Shepard created plot turns (major events) in the lives of students' characters.

EXAMPLE OF THE ROLE PLAY TECHNIQUE

The counseling intervention in this example takes place in a group counseling setting for high school juniors and seniors who are working on improved emotional expression and social interactions with their peers and family members. Tina, the focus in this part of the session, is one such group member with a history of being passive in her relationships with others, often ignoring her own needs in order to maintain friendships, keep the peace, or curry a person's favor.

Counselor (C):   Okay, we've checked in with everyone but you, Tina. You seem to have something on your mind.

Tina (T):   Yeah, I guess I do. Um . . . I guess I could tell you all about it. I mean . . . if you want.

C: (Looks around group, sees heads nod in favor) We'd like that, Tina.

T: Well, this might seem super-shallow to some of you, but it's like a big deal to me, and it's completely stuck in my head, and I don't know what to do about it. (She looks around to check the facial expressions of the other

group members before proceeding.) Okay, so some of you are going to know who I'm talking about, and I just want to make sure that what we say in group stays in group.

C: I'm glad you brought that up. I think it's good to remind everyone of that from time to time and just make sure that we all agree to keep this information between us . . . not talking about it to others who aren't here, and not talking to each other about it outside here either, right? (Group members reassure Tina by nodding their heads again.)

Jerome (J1):   Don't worry, Tina, we got your back. We ain't saying nothing to nobody.

T: I know. I just had to make sure. Okay. Um . . . (Deep breath). So I heard that my best friend of, like, four years has been talking bad about me to some of our other friends. At first, I didn't think it was true, but then I noticed she was acting funny toward me, like ignoring me when I was talking, or cutting me off when I was saying something. I swear I think she even rolled her eyes at me yesterday. And then today, I felt like she was avoiding me 'cause I've hardly seen her and usually we meet up in the hallways between classes.

J1:   Man, I'm glad I'm not a girl. Guys don't play that mess. My heart goes out to you, Tina, 'cause you're a stronger person than I am for even caring.

Susanna (S):   I totally get it, Tina. Having your best friend mad at you, or whatever it is, is like the worst feeling in the world. It messes with your head and makes everything seem like drama.

T: Yeah, exactly.

C: So tell me, Tina, how has all of this affected you this week?

T: I've been super-paranoid and paying way too much attention to every little thing. I've thought and thought about what I might have done to make her mad at me or tired of me or whatever. I swear I can't think of anything. I've even tried extra hard to be way nice to her and go along with whatever she wanted to do even if I didn't feel like it, just so she would be, like, normal to me again. I just really want this all straightened out. More than anything, I just need to know if it's for real or just in my head.

Jessie (J2):   Why don't you just ask her?

Nate (N):   Yeah, just talk to her about it. Just come out and be like "Are you mad at me or tired of me or what is up with how you've been lately?"

C: Have you considered talking to her about it?

T: I want to. I know I need to and that is the only way for this to get resolved. But I don't do so well with that sort of thing.

C: You mean, you've tried this sort of thing in the past, and it's not gone well?

T: Yeah. It's like whatever I say just comes out wrong or I'm never prepared for what the other person is going to say and it just . . . I just . . . I'm not very good at it or something. (Pauses for a moment) But I do know I'm going to have to do it. I kept thinking it would all just miraculously disappear, but obviously it isn't, and I know I need to talk to her about it before I drive myself nuts. I'm just scared to . . . I don't know what I'd say.

C: Would you be willing to try it out here today?

T: What do you mean?

C: Well, this sort of issue, not being able to express yourself or confront uncomfortable situations, seems to be something you've dealt with before. I think role-playing the conversation you want to have, actually having you try it out here with us, could help. I'd bet the other group members could learn from it as well. What do you say?

T: Well, I'd feel silly, but I guess if it would help me . . .

C: All right then. Is there anything else we should know about the situation before we begin?

T: Um . . . like what?

C: Well, perhaps you could just reiterate what you want the goal of the conversation to be.

T: I just want to know if she's mad and why.

C: Okay. Anything else?

T: Yeah, I guess I would like to be able to tell her how I've been feeling all week.

C: Okay. So with those goals in mind, to find out her feelings, and to express your own feelings, let's think about when you might want this conversation to really take place and where.

T: Um . . . you mean, like, for real where and when?

C: Uh-huh.

T: Well, we have basketball practice tomorrow after school. Usually we hang out afterward, just us two. That would probably be the best time.

C: And you would be at the basketball gym?

T: Yeah, we'd be there shooting hoops.

C: Okay. Is there anything here in this room that we can move around or do differently to make it resemble where you'll be having this conversation tomorrow?

T: (Looks around; thinks for a moment) Nah, not really. I mean we'll be standing up, so I should probably do that, but nothing else really. I'll have a basketball in my hand, but I don't see one in here, so I can just stand up.

C: Okay. So we understand the problem you are having with your best friend and how much it is bothering you. We understand that you want and need to have an open and honest conversation with her but that it is difficult for you to do. We also heard you say that you want to know how she feels, and you want her to know how you feel as a result of the conversation. And we know when and where the conversation is to take place. Now, the last thing I need you to do before we begin is to select a group member to play the part of your best friend.

Up to this point, the professional counselor has guided the client through the warm-up phase, identification of a behavior in need of change, and scene selection and setting. As soon as roles are selected, enactment can begin.

T: (Looks around the group, grins a little) I pick Kenya.

C: Kenya? Okay, very well. (Looking toward Kenya) Would you be willing to play Tina's best friend?

Kenya (K):   Sure. I'll do it!

C: Thanks, Kenya. Do you have any questions for Tina before we begin?

K: Well, I was wondering if she could tell us a little more about what her best friend is like, so I'll know how to play my part better.

C: Good point, Kenya. Tina?

T: Well . . . um . . . It's hard to say how she normally is with everything going so different this week. Let's see . . . She's loud, very outgoing, fun, everybody loves to be around her, and she is definitely a leader. She always has cool ideas and usually makes the decisions for everyone else when it comes to social events and get-togethers and stuff. But she can also be very defensive . . . and weird reactions sometimes . . . and she disses others, I guess. Yeah, that's all. Is that enough?

K: I think so. That helps.

T: Oh, and don't go easy on me (speaking to Kenya) . . . I mean . . . make it a little bit hard for me so I'll be prepared if it really goes that way.

C: Okay. (Standing up and motioning for Tina and Kenya, as the best friend, to stand as well) I'm going to ask everyone to push their chairs back just a bit so we have some more room. (Pauses while chairs are moving) Thanks, guys. And, Tina, if you don't mind, I'm going to stand behind you and to your right, like this, and there may be times during the role play when I feel you're stuck or struggling to get to the crux of the matter . . . and what I'm going to do is something we call *doubling*, and all that means is that I may speak on your behalf, say what it is I believe is going unsaid . . . to help you out. Is that okay?

T: Sure, that'd be helpful.

C: Good. And when I do that, I may put my hand on your shoulder, if that's okay. (Tina nods, seemingly relieved to have the support.) And what I want you to do is either accept what I say as your own and repeat it aloud for yourself, or change it to better reflect how you feel and then state that aloud. Does that make sense?

T: I think I've got it, yes.

C: Okay. Now imagine tomorrow being much like today. You get through the day much the same as all week, assuming nothing has changed, and now basketball practice is coming to an end and everyone is leaving and the two of you stay behind to practice shooting.

Remember, the professional counselor is responsible for moving the client from reality into the imagined situation.

T: Yeah, okay.

C: And now it's just you and your best friend . . . what's her name?

T: Stacy.

C: Okay, so now it's just you and Stacy in the gym shooting. And you have this important conversation that you need to have with her . . . whenever you're ready.

T: Okay . . . this is hard . . . I can do this . . .

C: You can do this . . . we're supporting you.

T: Okay. Stacy, I want to talk to you about something.

Kenya as Stacy (S):   Yeah, okay, what's up? (Shooting baskets)

T: Well, it seems like lately, this week mostly, that you've been acting different.

S: What do you mean? (Still shooting her baskets)

T: Um . . . well . . . I mean you just haven't been yourself.

S: Sure I have. What are you talking about? (Taking somewhat of a defensive tone and still shooting)

T: I just feel like you've been treating me different, and I was wondering . . .

S: *What* are you talking about? (Obviously aggravated to be bothered with this)

T: (Turns to the counselor) I can't do this.

C: (Doubling with hand on Tina's shoulder) This is important to me. I'm talking about how *I* feel. And I feel like you've been ignoring me this week.

T: Yeah, this *is* important to me, and I feel like you've been ignoring me this week.

S: So, what if I have?

T: I was wondering if I did something wrong?

S: I don't know, maybe. Not really. I don't know. Why are you freaking out?

T: I don't know. I guess I shouldn't. (Looks down at floor, clearly feeling ashamed for bringing it up and ashamed of feeling the way she feels. Long pause.)

C: (Doubling) Because you've been my best friend for a long time, and it really hurts to think that might change. This week, feeling like you are mad at me, has been really hard.

T: I care about our friendship, and I don't want to lose it. It *has* been really hard this week, and I *have* been hurt by the way you've acted.

S: (With a change in demeanor, less flippant, and now taking Tina's concerns seriously) Okay, so let's talk. (Thinking) I don't want to hurt your feelings. Really, I don't. It's just that sometimes you are right under me, and you try too hard. You should know by now that we are the best of friends. You don't always have to try so hard. It's a little annoying at times. I guess I should have just talked to you about it instead of acting the way I did. I just didn't want to hurt your feelings. But now I see that I did anyway . . . and I'm sorry.

T: Really? I mean, so you still want to be my best friend? You just want me to give you some space sometimes?

S: Yeah.

T: I can do that. I can totally do that. As long as I know you're not mad at me or anything. (Tina looks relieved, and there is a long silence.)

C: Okay. Tina, do you feel done with this?

T: (Breathing a sigh of relief) Yeah . . . yeah . . . I feel done. I think I can do this tomorrow.

C: Good! All right, we can sit back down now, and I'd like to hear reactions, thoughts, or any other feedback from the group members, and of course we want to hear from you as well, Tina.

The counselor continues to facilitate a discussion with feedback from the group and with reactions and feelings from Tina.

USEFULNESS AND EVALUATION OF THE ROLE PLAY TECHNIQUE

Role play—a technique used by reality (Wubbolding & Brickell, 2004), rational-emotive, behavior (James & Gilliland, 2003), cognitive, Gestalt (Seligman & Reichenberg, 2013), and social learning (Young, 2017) counselors—is commonly used with clients who would like to change something about themselves. The role play technique is effective when working with individuals, groups, and families (Hackney & Cormier, 2017). Role-playing a particular family type allows recognition of the importance of issues common to structurally similar families (Browning, Collins, & Nelson, 2008). It also allows students to develop and expand their understanding of family emotions, dilemmas, dynamics, and diversity. Through role play, clients can learn new skills, explore different behaviors, and observe how these behaviors affect others. If a client has trouble setting goals for the counseling sessions, the professional counselor can have the client role-play to figure out why the client is having difficulty coming up with a goal.

In counselor education training, the role play technique has been used to help counselors-in-training to gain multicultural counseling experiences (Rapisarda, Jencius, & McGlothlin, 2011). Role play has been shown to improve overall counseling skills development (Osborn & Costas, 2013; Paladino, Barrio Minton, & Kern, 2011).

The technique of role play also can be used to help prepare teachers for parent–teacher conferences (Johns, 1992). This is particularly useful for beginning teachers who may be nervous about this type of conference. Teachers are given a list of situations, and they role-play either the part of the teacher or the part of the parent. Each situation deals with a different type of difficult parent with whom the teacher may have contact. The practice that the teachers get by role playing may help them feel more comfortable once it is time for the meetings with the parents.

Role play is a technique that is also useful when working with adolescents in school. Students can learn more about the beliefs and values that they hold and can gain a further understanding of the beliefs and values held by others (Kottman, 1999). According to Papadopoulou (2012), role play has many benefits for children's cognitive, emotional, social, and language development. Role play allows people to develop abilities critical for their successful cultural adjustment. Role play becomes the method of expression of the children's current understandings, existential fears, and evolutionary concerns. Role plays can help enhance a child's social skills, promote higher levels of thinking, and lead to better listening skills and more assertiveness (Thompson & Bundy, 1996). Role play is exceptionally useful with adolescents because it is an active technique requiring the students to participate.

This technique also can be used to teach empathy to elementary school children. By being introduced to moral dilemmas, the students may begin to understand a perspective different from their own. Upright (2002) described how a teacher could conduct a role play in the classroom. There are nine steps in the process:

1. The teacher needs to observe the students and evaluate their moral developmental level.
2. An appropriate story needs to be chosen; an obvious problem must exist in the story.
3. The teacher describes the background of the story to the children and should make sure that the students understand any terms found in the story.
4. While the teacher reads the story and presents the moral dilemma, she can have the children role-play different parts of the story.
5. The teacher should ask questions to make sure the students understand the situation, including the conflict.

6. The students work in groups and discuss the moral dilemma, role-playing the different sides of it.
7. If needed, the teacher can add details to the story that could alter students' opinions.
8. To encourage students to think about the moral dilemma, the teacher can have them create alternate endings to the story.
9. By recording the responses of students, the teacher can "look for growth in both empathy and decision-making ability" throughout the school year (p. 19).

To increase the efficacy of this technique, it is important for clients to feel comfortable exposing their weaknesses in front of professional counselors and for professional counselors to be honest with their clients. Professional counselors need to remind themselves and their clients that this technique takes time to work; it is not a quick fix (Wubbolding & Brickell, 2004). Some theorists consider role play more effective if it is paired with cognitive restructuring (Corey, 2016).

Although role play is considered an effective technique, some problems may arise. Clients sometimes get stage fright and do not want to reenact the scenarios. Professional counselors need to make sure that they are allowing clients to have control over the direction of the role play. Sometimes, such strong emotion is expressed that it makes the client and professional counselor uncomfortable (Young, 2017). Ivey, Ivey, and Zalaquett (2018) point out that role playing should not be used with a client until the client's problem is clearly understood. In addition, client performance should be examined after implementation of the role play to bolster client efficacy.

APPLICATION OF THE ROLE PLAY TECHNIQUE

Now apply the role play technique to a current client or student you are working with or revisit the brief case studies presented at the beginning of this book. How can you use the role play technique to address concerns and create movement in the counseling session?

Techniques Based on Behavioral Approaches Using Positive Reinforcement

This section begins with a brief introduction to behavior modification and the general classification of behavioral techniques based on positive reinforcement, negative reinforcement, and punishment. Although no specific techniques based on negative reinforcement will be covered in this text, a number of techniques based on positive reinforcement strategies are presented to help clients increase display of the target behavior. These techniques include the Premack principle, behavior charts, token economy, and behavioral contracting. Several techniques based on punishment will be presented in the next section (Section 10).

A BRIEF INTRODUCTION TO PRINCIPLES UNDERLYING BEHAVIOR MODIFICATION

Behavior modification is the application of B. F. Skinner's theory of operant conditioning. The overriding tenet of operant conditioning theory is that true learning depends on which behaviors are accompanied by reinforcement. Behavior that is rewarded increases in frequency, whereas behavior that is not rewarded decreases in frequency, and behavior that is actively punished ordinarily decreases in frequency as well. Applications of

operant conditioning are defined by a juxtaposition of two dichotomous continua: operation (i.e., whether a stimulus is added to or removed from the environment) and effect (i.e., whether the goal is to increase or decrease the display of a behavior). This juxtaposition is presented in Figure 1 and yields four categories of behavioral intervention: positive reinforcement, negative reinforcement, punishment by stimulus application, and punishment by reinforcement removal.

POSITIVE REINFORCEMENT AND NEGATIVE REINFORCEMENT

Operant conditioning proposes three key terms that are helpful in categorizing applied interventions stemming from the theory: positive reinforcement, negative reinforcement, and punishment. (See Section 10 for a discussion of punishment.) Positive reinforcement is anything that strengthens and increases the likelihood that a behavior will reoccur. A frequently used synonym for positive reinforcement is reward. Examples of positive reinforcers are favorite foods or snacks, preferred activities, stickers, money, attention, social praise, or other treats—almost anything that a person is willing to work to earn (see Figure 1).

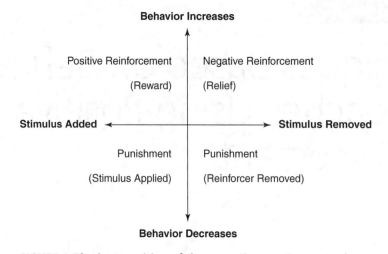

FIGURE 1 The juxtaposition of the operation continuum and the effect continuum in operant conditioning, and the resultant categories of behavioral intervention.

It is important to understand from the outset two essential points about applying positive reinforcement. First, the target behavior must be framed in a manner that indicates a desirable behavior to be increased. Clients, students, parents, and teachers frequently have no problem telling the professional counselor what they would like the client to stop doing (e.g., stop getting out of the seat, calling out, cussing, talking back, arguing as a couple, refusing to do homework), but they sometimes struggle with describing the positive behavior they wish the client to start doing or increase. In such circumstances, it is helpful to ask the client or other stakeholder (e.g., parent, teacher, spouse) "What would you like the client to do more of?" This helps the stakeholder or client to craft a positively framed target behavior that identifies the behavior to be increased—for example, "Stop getting out of the seat" becomes "Stay in the seat until permission is granted to get up," "Stop calling out" becomes "Raise her hand and wait to be called on before speaking," "Stop cussing" becomes "Verbally express himself using appropriate language," "Stop talking back" becomes "Verbally address adults and peers appropriately," "Stop arguing as a couple" becomes "Engage in productive or pleasant conversation," "Stop refusing to do homework" becomes

"Complete homework 95% of the time." (Note that the terms *appropriate* and *appropriately* used in two of the preceding examples may require further defining and clarification.)

The second essential point related to positive reinforcement is that the reward must come just after the behavior. If the client gets the reward before displaying the behavior or in spite of failing to perform the required behavior to the agreed-upon level, the contingency-linking behavior and reward will not occur. Clients need to learn that rewards follow appropriate behaviors; otherwise, the system will not produce the desired results. Also, be sure not to wait too long after the client displays the behavior before providing the reward. One wants the client to make the connection between the behavior and the reward in order to strengthen the display of the behavior. A long delay may weaken the association. Rewards serve as motivators of desirable behaviors, and rewards must follow the occurrence of the behavior for initial learning to occur and for strengthening of previous learned connections to continue.

Negative reinforcement is anything that increases a desirable behavior by reducing or eliminating an aversive stimulus. Negative reinforcement is synonymous with relief.

Negative reinforcement is often confused with the term *punishment*, although it is true that many negative reinforcers are also viewed as punishing by clients. However, there is an essential difference between the two: The goal of negative reinforcement is always to increase a desirable behavior, whereas the goal of punishment is always to decrease an undesirable behavior. This distinction is critical to understanding the differences between these two important concepts. Negative reinforcement is a difficult concept to grasp and apply, and this text does not incorporate a chapter on its application. An example of negative reinforcement would be to increase verbalizations within group counseling interaction by removing a noxious noise (e.g., an annoying hum or buzz) when clients engage in verbal discussion, then reintroducing the noxious noise during periods of silence. A second example would be to increase a child's in-seat behavior (i.e., keeping Billy's bottom on the chair) by removing his chair for a 10-minute interval each time he leaves his seat without permission, forcing him to stand rather than to sit at his desk. Again, having to listen to an annoying hum or stand rather than sit may appear to be punishments, but in these examples they are not punishments as long as the counseling objectives are meant to increase the frequency of a desirable behavior.

ASSESSING PROBLEM BEHAVIORS

One final topic of importance before moving on to the individual behavioral techniques involves a brief discussion of problem behavior assessment. Ordinarily the assessment of problem behaviors is relatively quick, especially when the professional counselor focuses on the frequency, magnitude, and duration of the behavior. Frequency refers to how often a behavior occurs. Determining a behavior's frequency is important for at least two reasons. First, it is important to grasp how problematic a behavior really is and whether the display of a behavior is normal or not. Sometimes, clients and stakeholders expect perfection or have little context for understanding what a normal behavioral display might be, and professional counselors may help provide this context. Second, if professional counselors are going to help modify a problematic behavior, it is

critical to gather baseline data so that the client, counselor, and other stakeholders will be able to determine what a reasonable counseling objective might be and when progress is being made toward meeting that objective.

Magnitude refers to how problematic the behavior has become for the client and other stakeholders. If the magnitude is not substantial, perhaps intervention is unnecessary. After all, if clients or stakeholders are unrealistically expecting perfection or lack context for understanding whether the behavior is normal, professional counselors can be of help contextualizing or reframing the issue. The technique of scaling, discussed in Chapter 1, is frequently helpful in determining the magnitude of a problem behavior.

Duration refers to two facets of assessing problem behaviors. First, professional counselors are interested in knowing how long the behavior has been occurring. The answer to this question, coupled with the response to the question of magnitude, often gives clients and counselors an idea of the seriousness of the problem, the likely resistance to treating the problem, and some impetus for building motivation to address and resolve the problem behaviors. The second facet of duration addresses the question "How long does the behavior last after it begins?" A behavior that lasts only a few seconds will require a different approach than the same behavior lasting hours.

Once the behavior frequency, magnitude, and duration have been assessed and the counseling goals and objectives have been developed, the client and professional counselor using a behavioral approach are ready to implement strategies and techniques to address the issue. The remainder of this section reviews techniques professional counselors will find helpful when dealing with behavioral concerns. If the counseling objective aims to increase the frequency of a desirable behavior, the professional counselor may want to implement one of the techniques based on positive reinforcement: the Premack principle, behavior charts, token economy, or behavioral contracting. If the counseling objective aims to decrease or suppress the frequency of a behavior, the professional counselor may want to implement one of the strategies based on punishment: extinction, time-out, response cost, or overcorrection (positive practice). (See Section 10 for behavioral approaches using punishment.)

MULTICULTURAL IMPLICATIONS OF BEHAVIORAL APPROACHES USING POSITIVE REINFORCEMENT

Clients from some cultures appreciate the directness and the problem-centered and action-oriented nature of behavioral approaches to counseling (Hays & Erford, 2018). For example, clients of Arab and Asian descent frequently expect advice and pursuit of concrete goals within the counseling relationship. Men, in general, may appreciate the action-oriented, goal-focused directedness of behavioral approaches. Latinos often prefer directive approaches, and parents of African descent frequently appreciate how behavioral approaches help them achieve obedience from children, an important intergenerational cultural value.

Behavioral counseling does not emphasize emotional expression and catharsis, or the sharing of personal difficulties or concerns, making it a more comfortable fit in certain cases for individuals from some cultures (e.g., men, Asian Americans). Tanaka-Matsumi, Higginbotham, and Chang (2007) pointed out that behavioral approaches value and focus on the client's cultural and social dimensions by analyzing an individual's specific environmental situation and honing the interventions to address specific therapeutic goals and personalized outcomes. In the process, counselors help clients understand how personal life circumstances have contributed to the difficulties and whether desired changes are possible or how best to accomplish those changes in a way that helps the client adjust to the sociocultural, developmental, and environmental contexts. Behavioral counselors conduct a culturally sensitive functional behavioral analysis (Spiegler, 2016) to help the client understand cultural norms and client-based perceptions of the problem.

Counselors using behavioral approaches sometimes devalue the importance of the therapeutic relationship, and this would be a mistake with individuals of diverse races, ethnicities, genders, and sexual orientations. Rapport and strength of the therapeutic alliance influence the therapeutic process and outcomes of counseling, so professional counselors using behavioral approaches with clients are well advised to attend to rapport and alliance issues throughout the counseling relationship. For example, it is well documented (Hays & Erford, 2018) that clients from some cultures are slow to trust European American counselors. Culturally sensitive counselors recognize and address these issues in the relationship early and often.

Behavioral change affects not only the individual client but also those the client interacts with in the sociocultural environment. Counselors and clients need to discuss and anticipate the cultural as well as personal ramifications of behavioral changes desired by the client in order to predict each change's effect not only on the life of the client but also on the relationships between the client and other important people in the client's life. Changes in an individual often require adjustments by others in the individual's environment; sometimes the changes, although viewed beforehand as positive, can lead to serious difficulties down the road. While all possible consequences cannot be predicted with certainty, discussion ahead of time can often lead to a heightened awareness of the possible ramifications of the considered changes. For example, if a man desires greater independence from his wife and family (e.g., more socializing time with friends, trips to get away), such behavioral changes can strain a relationship and create even more difficulties in the future (e.g., divorce, jealousy/suspicion, lower-quality relationships with children). Behaviors have their consequences; sometimes the consequences lead to positive outcomes, but sometimes they lead to undesirable, unanticipated, or mixed outcomes.

CHAPTER 35

Premack Principle

ORIGINS OF THE PREMACK PRINCIPLE TECHNIQUE

The Premack principle is based on the operant conditioning theory concept of positive reinforcement, which states that higher probability behaviors may act as reinforcers for lower probability behaviors (Brown, Spencer, & Swift, 2002). In other words, individuals will be motivated to do an undesired task if it is followed by a desired one. The Premack principle is used often in everyday life. For instance, a parent might allow a child to watch TV only after he finishes his homework. In lay terms, this technique has been known informally as Grandma's rules because Grandma made sure you finished your vegetables before you got a cookie.

The Premack principle was named after David Premack and was first used with laboratory animals, then applied to human situations. The Premack principle contradicted the traditional theories of that time. Traditional reinforcement theories stated that activities are positive, negative, or neutral. Only neutral activities can serve as instrumental responses, and only positive activities function as reinforcers. Therefore, reinforcement occurs when a positive activity is made contingent on the performance of a neutral activity. In contrast, Premack declared that the positive-neutral-negative trichotomy was irrelevant to reinforcement. Instead, he proposed that all activities are ordered on a preference or probability continuum and that only a difference in preference is necessary for reinforcement. For reinforcement to occur, the instrumental response must simply be less preferential than the reinforcing activity. To validate his theory, Premack (1962) set up a laboratory experiment with rats to show not only that running could be reinforced by drinking, as evident in other earlier experiments, but also that if a situation were created in which running was more preferable than drinking, drinking could be reinforced by running.

To measure the probability of two or more behaviors, these behaviors should be compared in a paired-operant baseline, in which both behaviors are simultaneously and freely available to the client. However, sometimes strict probability is difficult to measure. Therefore, other, more readily available measures have often been used in place of probability. Preference may be measured simply by asking the individual what he would like to do in a given situation or by observing which activities seem to bring the individual pleasure. Preference seems to be quite compatible with Premack's original measure of probability. On the other hand, the use of frequency is somewhat problematic because it often relies on extrinsically maintained responses instead of allowing the participant free choice of activity. Similarly, imminent performance, or the likelihood that the activity will be done next, tends to measure merely a colloquial version of probability rather than the empirical probability that Premack intended. A good rule of thumb to follow when attempting to measure probability is to ensure that preference or relative value is being measured rather than frequency or imminent performance.

HOW TO IMPLEMENT THE PREMACK PRINCIPLE TECHNIQUE

To use the Premack principle technique, one must first assess the preferred activities of the client (Brown et al., 2002). Based on this assessment, a more preferred activity may be chosen to reinforce the target behavior. The client should be informed of the parameters of the Premack conditions. The client should be told that, in order to perform the preferred activity, the client must first complete the target behavior. Once the target behavior is completed, the client may begin the preferred activity. It is essential to remember that if the target behavior is not finished in its entirety, then the preferred activity is not allowed. There is no "partial credit"!

VARIATIONS OF THE PREMACK PRINCIPLE TECHNIQUE

The Premack principle technique can easily be accompanied by a token economy (see Chapter 37). Tokens may be issued upon completion of less-preferred activities and then traded in for the opportunity to perform activities that are more preferred. A reinforcement menu, or list of highly preferred activities, may be available for the client to choose from.

EXAMPLE OF THE PREMACK PRINCIPLE TECHNIQUE

Veronica is an 18-year-old freshman psychology major in her second semester of college. In an effort to improve her academic habits, Veronica joined a study skills group near the beginning of the spring semester. This group consisted of her sorority sisters and met in her sorority house. After catching up on much campus gossip but making no improvements in her study skills, Veronica decided to explore the services offered through the university's counseling center instead. She opted to join an open support group offered for students adjusting to college life with the hope that she would encounter others having difficulty with the same stressors she was facing. Still attending, Veronica feels she benefits from this group in that it is helpful to talk about and hear others' similar issues. However, she has not made any changes in her daily life. Veronica describes herself as someone focused only on the moment with little thought to the eventual outcomes of her behavior. She states that in high school, she

had little responsibility and focused most of her attention on her social life. Now in college, she finds her grades suffering, credit card debt soaring, and weight increasing. The following is an excerpt of an individual session Veronica requested with the professional counselor.

Counselor (C): So you describe yourself as lacking self-control . . . rather impulsive . . . interested in instant gratification.

Veronica (V): That would be me.

C: And this is causing you some concern.

V: It really is. I hate this growing up and being responsible thing. It was so much more fun before. I could eat what I wanted without gaining weight. I could stay up on the phone all night and still ace my exams. That's just not the way it is anymore.

C: Things have changed?

V: I'll say. I'm totally getting fat, and my grades are embarrassing. I've got to do something different than what I'm doing before somebody notices!

C: Tell me specifically, Veronica, what you want to be different as a result of us working together.

V: Well, specifically, I want my grades to be different. I would also like to change some of my lifestyle habits, like being a total mouse potato . . .

C: Mouse potato?

V: Yeah, you know, like a couch potato, except someone who zones out in front of the computer and surfs the Internet all the time.

C: Okay, I'm with you now. So, you would like your grades to improve, I suppose . . .

V: Definitely.

C: And your lifestyle habits, like spending too much time on the Internet, to change?

V: Pretty much. Um . . . see . . . I shop online. I don't always buy . . . well, usually I do . . . but I constantly surf for fashion ideas and trends, and I browse online catalogs relentlessly.

C: This doesn't leave much time for studying.

V: Or exercising, which I've also been meaning to do. Pretty much I just want to eat chocolate and shop.

C: Yes, I'm getting that general idea. But part of you also wants something different—something other than eating chocolate and shopping, like studying and exercising, for example.

V: Yes, a big part of me wants something different like that. And the mirror and report card remind me of that. The last thing I want is to be unhealthy or to do poorly in school. I just have trouble sticking to that thought when I'm in that moment. You know? I'm just, like, whatever . . .

At this point, the professional counselor asks Veronica to complete a reinforcement hierarchy, listing the 10 activities she most prefers and least prefers to engage in. The hierarchy that resulted looked as follows:

Least Favorite	Studying/homework
	Exercising
	Cleaning/laundry
	Going to work at the coffee shop
	Going to class
	Watching television
	Talking on the phone
	Hanging out with friends
	Eating chocolate/sweets
Most Favorite	Online shopping

C: Okay. Now that we have a good idea of the activities you most enjoy and least enjoy, I'd like to ask some specific questions concerning a few of these activities.

V: Sure, okay.

C: Okay. So approximately how often would you say you exercise now?

V: Once a week, maybe.

C: And how often would you like to exercise in order to meet the criteria you have for this new and healthy self?

V: Ideally, I would exercise each morning during the week, Monday through Friday, for about 30 minutes. I'd like for it to become part of my morning routine before I do anything else.

C: Very well. And how much time would you say you spend studying?

V: Some nights, not at all. I get on the computer to do schoolwork, and then I decide to look something up, and that's all I do the rest of the night. That's another reason I haven't been exercising. I spend so much time online at night that I'm too tired to get up an extra 30 minutes earlier in the morning.

C: Okay, good. So, how much time do you want to spend studying?

V: Well, again, I'd like to contain it to the week, you know, Monday through Friday again, unless there is a special reason to put more time in, like a big paper or exam or something. But for regular homework assignments and keeping up with reading assignments, I'd like to do that all during the week . . . so I'd say, at the most, about three hours per night for homework and reading assignments. Then I can put in extra time for larger projects if I need to.

C: Okay, so three hours per night then for studying. And 30 minutes per morning for exercise.

V: Sounds simple. But how am I going to make myself do that?

C: Would you work at the coffee shop if your boss stopped paying you?

V: Um . . . no.

C: Well, would you expect your boss to continue paying you if you stopped working?

V: Um . . . no again. That's just wrong.

C: Well, the way you're going about things now is similar to being paid without having worked. On your reinforcement hierarchy that you completed, you listed your favorite activities as eating sweets and shopping. You admit to doing both of these things in abundance on a daily basis. Essentially, you are giving in to these indulgences without doing anything to earn them. Now, I'm going to set up a plan for you to begin incorporating physical activity into your morning routine and studying into your evening. But I'm not going to ask you to make all this effort without setting up a way for you to "pay yourself" because you wouldn't want to work for free. But this payment that you've been giving yourself up until now will have to be earned. And you will only pay or reward yourself with those activities you so enjoy if you've followed through with the activities that you don't prefer but know you need and want to do.

V: Hmm . . . so . . . okay, keep going.

C: Well, from now on, whenever you engage in physical exercise for 30 minutes, you are allowed one sweet treat, such as a small cookie. We don't want to go overboard on the sweets, though, or you'll be defeating the purpose. Now, if you don't exercise, you absolutely do not get the sweet. It is simply off limits because you did not work for that payment.

V: Okay. I like that.

C: Now regarding the studying, you said that you want to study three hours each evening during the week. And you feel this is reasonable and possible.

V: Yes, it really is.

C: Okay then. For every one hour you spend studying, you may reward yourself with 30 minutes of Internet time. But you receive this Internet time only once you are completely finished studying for the night. So, when you put in your three hours of study tonight, you pay yourself with the privilege of 1.5 hours of Internet shopping time, to begin only after study time is complete.

V: That's not a whole lot of time to shop.

C: Much more than that will interfere with your ability to wake on time in the morning, right?

V: Well, that's true.

C: So, just as you said, you would never take payment from your boss if you had not done the work—"That's just wrong," you said—you also cannot allow yourself to engage in the rewarding activity unless you put in the required time.

V: And I just have to be very strict with myself. This is the new rule, and I am agreeing to it, right?

C: That's right. Keep your focus on the payoff that comes with self-discipline. Not to mention how rewarding it will feel just to make these changes that you've known you wanted to make.

USEFULNESS AND EVALUATION OF THE PREMACK PRINCIPLE TECHNIQUE

The Premack principle technique has been employed to abate chronic food refusal. Seiverling, Kokitus, and Williams (2012) used a combination of the Premack principle technique and extinction in selective food treatment with a 3-year-old boy with autism. Brown et al. (2002) used the Premack principle technique with a young boy who frequently refused to try new foods. He was required to eat small amounts of new foods before being allowed to eat his preferred foods. When the intervention began, the boy immediately ate the new foods that were presented to him in increasing quantities and flavors in order to be allowed to eat his preferred foods.

Working with older children with attention-deficit/hyperactivity disorder (ADHD), Azrin, Vinas, and Ehle (2007) used outdoor play activities as the Premack contingency for extended periods of calm, attentional control in structured classroom activities, yielding promise for generalizable usefulness with students with ADHD of all ages. At the college level, Messling and Dermer (2009) applied the Premack principle technique to upper-level students by allowing students who attended class and presented notes on the daily reading assignments to use their notes during examinations. While generally effective in improving lecture attendance and reading note taking, this no-cost intervention proved particularly helpful in increasing attendance during laboratory sessions, which students previously frequently chose not to attend.

The Premack principle technique presents some limitations, however. Existing data have shown that lower-probability behaviors can sometimes act as reinforcers for higher-probability behaviors. For instance, Konarski, Johnson, Crowell, and Whitman (1981) reported that, in an earlier study, under certain conditions, children would increase coloring for access to math, considered a lower probability behavior. And experiments using the Premack principle technique do not always adequately control for the effects of a schedule. Therefore, it is difficult to determine if the reinforcement is the result of a probability difference between the actual responses or is simply due to the unavailability of the reinforcing response for periods of time because of the response schedule. In other words, clients may be increasing the instrumental behavior because it is the only response available rather than because it allows them to perform the contingent, or reinforcing, response.

APPLICATION OF THE PREMACK PRINCIPLE TECHNIQUE

Now apply the Premack principle technique to a current client or student you are working with or revisit the brief case studies presented at the beginning of this book. How can you use the Premack principle technique to address concerns and create movement in the counseling session?

CHAPTER 36

Behavior Chart

ORIGINS OF THE BEHAVIOR CHART TECHNIQUE

Behavior charts target specific behaviors that are then evaluated at set points throughout the day (Henington & Doggett, 2016). The behavior is then reinforced on some sort of schedule. Behavior charts arise from behavioral theories which posit that behavior is shaped by reinforcement and punishment. Behavior charts include several important components, such as specifying the behaviors to be monitored, rating the behaviors on a set schedule, sharing the information with people other than the rater, and using the chart either to monitor an intervention or as the intervention itself (Chafouleas, Riley-Tillman, & McDougal, 2002). However, behavior charts may vary, depending on the behavior to be rated, the type of rating system, the rating frequency, the rater, the consequences used (reinforcers versus punishment), and the setting and schedule of consequence delivery. Behavior charts are useful because they are a simple and flexible way to provide feedback to the individual being monitored as well as others involved with this person, and behavior charts can be easily modified to meet the specific needs of an individual. Also, behavior charts are time efficient, taking as little as 10 seconds to 1 minute to complete each day.

HOW TO IMPLEMENT THE BEHAVIOR CHART TECHNIQUE

Behavior charts are simple to create. First, define the target behaviors in positive and specific terms so that a positive reinforcement approach can be used (e.g., Leroy will follow parent directions the first time given). Next, decide on the frequency and type of rating system to be used. Then design the behavior chart, stating clearly both the behavior desired and when it will be monitored (Henington & Doggett, 2016). Once the chart has been created, decide how the individual will earn consequences (positive or negative) and what these consequences will be.

EXAMPLES OF THE BEHAVIOR CHART TECHNIQUE

EXAMPLE 1: Freddie the Wiggly Wonder

Freddie is a wiggly and distractible youngster whose second-grade teacher is constantly redirecting and refocusing his attention so that he will complete his class work. The professional counselor consulted with his teacher to construct a behavior chart to address the time on task and redirection issue. Figure 36.1 shows the chart constructed for Freddie. Note that it integrates a point system and rating scale, as well as a reward plan.

EXAMPLE 2: Justin the Space Invader

Justin is an aggressive teenager who often calls out without raising his hand and invades others' personal space (e.g., hits or touches others). Justin's teachers chose to implement a checkmark-based chart monitoring system. The professional counselor consulted with Justin's teachers to construct a behavior chart to address the calling out and touching/hitting issues. Figure 36.2 shows the chart constructed for Justin. Note that it integrates a checkmark-based monitoring system broken down

Freddie's Plan

Goal: Freddie will sit quietly during class time, attend to class activities, and complete work.

   The check sheet will be monitored daily and marked by Freddie's classroom teacher every 15 minutes. It will be tabulated at lunch and at 3:00 p.m. Freddie will carry this check sheet with him to each class on a clipboard. He will be responsible for handing it to the teacher in charge and getting it back at the end of each period. Rewards will be started after Freddie has carried the check sheet and has proven he can be responsible for giving it to and getting it back from each teacher.

Scores*	Morning Rewards/ Consequences	Afternoon Rewards/ Consequences
54–60	Coupon	Coupon
42–53	Prize box or pink ticket	Prize box or pink ticket
0–41	No coupon	No coupon

   * Scores reflect the following: 90% compliance = coupon; 70% compliance = prize box or pink ticket for school store; and less than 70% compliance = no coupon.

Progressive Discipline Plan

After 4 zeros (zero scores) in a row, Freddie must come to the office. Freddie will see the assistant principal, who will then determine a course of action.

Bonus: If Freddie obtains the 90% criterion each day for the entire week, he will also earn one food coupon.

Freddie   Week of: _____

Key:

5 points = Used time appropriately. Freddie is quiet, stays on task, and completes work.

3 points = Was redirected to use time appropriately or stay on task 1 or 2 times.

0 points = Not using time appropriately. Did not complete work. Was redirected 3 or more times.

Report to office to pick up clipboard.

	Time	Monday	Tuesday	Wednesday	Thursday	Friday
Morning work	8:45					
	9:00					
Carpet time	9:15					
	9:30					
Reading— Mrs. Lear	9:45					
	10:00					
	10:15					
	10:30					
	10:45					
Special	11:00					
	11:15					
	11:30					

	Time	Monday	Tuesday	Wednesday	Thursday	Friday
Office— morning total						
Writing— Mrs. Lear	11:45 12:00 12:15 12:30					
Lunch	→					
Recess	→					
Math—Mrs. Lear	1:30 1:45 2:00 2:15 2:30 2:45					
Office— afternoon total						
Rewards for each of the morning and afternoon sessions: 54–60 points = coupon 42–53 points = prize box or pink ticket 41 points or fewer = no coupon						

FIGURE 36.1 Freddie's behavior plan.

Justin's Plan

Goal 1: Justin will control his verbal actions (e.g., raise his hand before calling out, maintain appropriate speaking volume).

Goal 2: Justin will keep his hands to himself (e.g., will not hit or touch others).

A checkmark chart will be used to monitor Justin's behavior. Justin will have the chance to earn two checkmarks for each "section" of the day (i.e., including homeroom, lunch, and blocks 1–6). Justin will earn one checkmark for controlling his verbal actions (e.g., raising his hand before speaking, not calling out, not saying inappropriate or silly things during lessons) and another for keeping his hands to himself during that time period (e.g., not hitting, not touching others).

There are 8 sections in the day, so Justin has the chance to earn a total of 16 checkmarks. Justin will earn a reward at the end of the day if he earns 9 out of 16 checkmarks during the day. This number will be increased once Justin has earned a reward every day of one entire week. Prizes will include visits to the principal or assistant principal to share his daily progress and receive praise and encouragement.

Justin's homeroom teacher will communicate Justin's progress to Ms. Jackson (Justin's mother). Justin's homeroom teacher, Ms. Jug, will send home a note daily with the number of checkmarks Justin earned for the day, and at the end of the week, she will send home a copy of the checkmark chart. These daily notes will take the place of the papers that had been coming home with reports of how many inappropriate behavior warnings Justin received during the day. Ms. Jug will try to focus on rewarding Justin's good behavior rather than punishing his bad behavior (although Justin will still receive warnings for hurting other students or continually failing to follow teacher directions). Justin will receive a prize at the end of the day for having 9 out of 16 checkmarks.

	Monday		Tuesday		Wednesday		Thursday		Friday	
	Controls Voice	Hands to Himself	Controls Voice	Hands to Himself	Controls Voice	Hands to Himself	Controls Voice	Hands to Himself	Controls Voice	Hands to Himself
Homeroom										
Block 1										
Block 2										
Block 3										
Lunch										
Block 4										
Block 5										
Block 6										

FIGURE 36.2 Justin's behavior plan.

according to class activities and a reward plan. As Justin meets success with the "9 of 16" criterion, the number of checks required will be raised until the target behavior is eliminated.

USEFULNESS AND EVALUATION OF THE BEHAVIOR CHART TECHNIQUE

Behavior charts can be used for a wide variety of interventions that involve shaping specific behaviors. Target behaviors may include following directions, keeping hands to oneself, or using appropriate language (Henington & Doggett, 2016). Behavior charts have been found to be effective in a number of empirical studies. In one study, behavior charts monitoring students' obedience of classroom rules produced significant decreases in misbehavior and increases in the amount of work students completed (Chafouleas et al., 2002).

Of course, behavior charts are not always effective, primarily because clients are not always motivated to buy into the system. In such cases, counselors should revisit the reward system to find something more motivating for which the client may work. Sometimes clients do not understand the chart system, or the client or adult responsible for overseeing the monitoring system does not follow through with responsibilities. These difficulties are common in behavior therapy, and counselors need to make large and small adjustments to any behavioral system to maximize success.

APPLICATION OF THE BEHAVIOR CHART TECHNIQUE

Now apply the behavior chart technique to a current client or student you are working with or revisit the brief case studies presented at the beginning of this book. How can you use the behavior chart technique to address concerns and create movement in the counseling session?

CHAPTER 37

Token Economy

ORIGINS OF THE TOKEN ECONOMY TECHNIQUE

The token economy is a technique stemming from the work of the operant behavior theorist, B. F. Skinner. Skinner held the view that consequences maintain behavior (Murdock, 2013); reinforcers are consequences that increase the likelihood of the occurrence of a behavior. Token economies are a form of positive reinforcement in which clients receive a token when they display the desired behavior. After clients have accumulated a certain number of tokens, they can turn the tokens in for reinforcers. The tokens serve to reinforce participants' appropriate behavior by rewarding selected behaviors. The receipt of the token is contingent on the display of appropriate behavior (Comaty, Stasio, & Advokat, 2001). Thus, rather than receiving some tangible reinforcement immediately, tokens are issued that can be exchanged later for tangible rewards.

The earliest token economies existed in closed-ward psychiatric hospitals (Liberman, 2000). However, token economies are considered to be successful across a wide variety of populations and target behaviors. Indeed, the issuance of money for working at a job is an application of a token economy: Money serves as a secondary reinforcer that can be exchanged for goods and services that sate primary needs (and wants). Token economies are also quite acceptable to parents and teachers, trailing behind only response cost procedures among commonly implemented behavior modification techniques (Borrego & Pemberton, 2007).

HOW TO IMPLEMENT THE TOKEN ECONOMY TECHNIQUE

Reid (1999) provided the following steps for implementing a token economy. Because one of the main goals of a token economy is to modify behavior, the first step should be to identify the behaviors that warrant change. Reid suggested naming specific behaviors and describing the standards for satisfactory performance. For example, instead of saying that participants should have better hygiene, one should say that the participants should shower or brush their teeth. Likewise, instead of saying a child should "calm down," the professional counselor should specify the child will "remain in his or her seat" or will "raise his or her hand and wait to be called on by the teacher before calling out."

The second step is creating and displaying the rules. It is very important to make sure that all participants understand the rules for dispensing tokens, the quantity of tokens awarded for different behaviors, and when clients can redeem the tokens for rewards. Next, the professional counselor needs to select what will be used as tokens. Tokens should be safe, sturdy, easy to dispense, and difficult to replicate (i.e., forge). Examples might include points on a check sheet, wooden sticks, or plastic game chips. The professional counselor then needs to determine the backup reinforcers, or the reward items that the participants can receive when they exchange their tokens. It is important that the backup reinforcer have some significance or appeal to the client. If the client enjoys watching television or loves candy, these reinforcers can be offered in exchange for tokens. To discourage materialistic consumption and encourage social interaction, the reward menu should include a number of activities the client may engage in with others (e.g., lunch with teacher, 15 minutes of play with a friend, 15 minutes playing a board game with a parent).

The next step is to set up "prices" by selecting how many tokens a participant must have before exchanging them for a backup reinforcer. Before implementing the system, the persons in charge should field-test the system, ensuring that "prices" are accurate: If the participants are not able to earn enough tokens to make a purchase, they will lose the motivation to engage in the desired behaviors. It is good practice to construct a reward menu with wide-ranging values of tokens required for the reward options. This encourages clients to save tokens for big-ticket items (e.g., family pizza night, baseball mitt, sleepover at a friend's house), rather than immediately spend the tokens on quick, consumable items (e.g., candy, toys).

VARIATIONS OF THE TOKEN ECONOMY TECHNIQUE

A variation of the token economy is the addition of a response cost system (see Chapter 41), a strategy based on punishment. In this approach, the client earns tokens for displaying positive behaviors, but in addition when an individual misbehaves (i.e., violates a target behavior or rule), one of the tokens is surrendered in an attempt to decrease the future likelihood of an undesirable behavior and increase the future likelihood of the desired behavior (Murdock, 2013). Goals are set for participants to retain a certain number of tokens in order to be rewarded at the end of a determined time period.

Another variation to the basic token economy is called the mystery motivator. In this variation, instead of the participants being told what the backup reinforcers are, the reward is placed in an envelope and remains a mystery. In some cases, this motivates the participants to earn tokens in order to discover what is in the envelope. In a study of children with acquired brain injury, Mottram and Berger-Gross (2004) placed mystery motivators based on the children's interests in envelopes and marked them with question marks. If the children earned the required number of tokens, they were given their respective

mystery envelope and rewarded with the contents. As the study went on, the number of tokens needed to receive the mystery motivator increased. The mystery motivator variation improved behavioral compliance over the standard token economy procedure.

In another variation of the token economy, self-monitoring is included in an effort to extend the behavioral changes after the rewards are phased out. Along with the basic token economy procedures, the participant is asked to record instances in which he behaves inappropriately. The rules are posted and specific, so participants should be able to tell easily when the rules are broken. In a classroom study of self-monitoring (Zlomke & Zlomke, 2003), several disruptive students were given an index card to record each instance of their own inappropriate behavior. At the end of the class, the teacher and each student compared cards. If the teacher and the student had the same number of incidents written down, the student earned an extra token. Self-monitoring plus the token economy procedure resulted in significantly fewer problematic behaviors than use of the token economy alone.

Yet another variation of the token economy is group versus individual implementation. Using the token economy with the whole group, whether it is a class, a school, or a prison, takes considerably more time, planning, and patience on the part of the implementer. Filcheck, McNeil, Greco, and Bernard (2004) performed a classroom study using the whole-class method. A level system also was used in which each student received a shape with her or his name on it, and every day it was placed on the center of the ladder chart. The shape was moved up the ladder if the child demonstrated appropriate behavior or down the ladder if the child violated classroom rules (i.e., the token economy with the response cost variation). The children were rewarded according to the level their shape had attained at given times throughout the day. At these times, all of the shapes were moved back to the center position on the ladder chart to give the participants a fresh start.

EXAMPLE OF THE TOKEN ECONOMY TECHNIQUE

The following occurred during a counseling session with a student, Charlie, with attention-deficit/

hyperactivity disorder (ADHD). Charlie is an 8-year-old, third-grade student. Charlie's mother and teacher were also present so that the token economy system could be created and understood by all primary participants. The target behaviors identified by Charlie's teacher for the classroom were as follows:

1. Stays in seat.
2. Raises hand and waits to be called on.
3. Keeps hands to himself.
4. Makes comments relevant to the topic.
5. Follows teacher directions the first time he is asked.

The target behaviors identified by Charlie's mother were the following:

1. Keeps room tidy.
2. Follows parent directions the first time.

Note that the target behaviors are written to specify behaviors that can be increased. Thus, a strategy based on positive reinforcement, such as a token economy, can be used. The school day lasts about six hours, so Charlie's teacher chose to award 6 points per target behavior. Each target behavior was deemed of equivalent importance. Thus, the teacher could award up to 1 point (i.e., 0-, ½-, or 1-point increments) for each one-hour time period during the school day for each of the five target behaviors—a possible total of 30 token points during each school day.

Charlie's mother decided that following her directions at home was twice as important as keeping a tidy room. She decided to award up to 3 points to Charlie each day for keeping his room tidy. She also decided that Charlie could earn up to 1 point for following her directions for the hour preceding school in the morning and for each of the five hours after he arrives home in the afternoon and evening. This made it possible for Charlie to earn an additional 9 token points at home on a school night. To extend the token economy to nonschool days (i.e., weekends, holidays), Charlie's mother could award up to 3 points for a tidy room and up to 36 points on these days for compliance with her instructions.

In summary, Charlie could earn a total of 39 points on any given day, or a total of 273 points

Day: _____ Date: _____ Name: <u>Charlie</u>

School	1	2	3	4	5	6	Total
1. Stays in seat.							
2. Raises hand and waits to be called on.							
3. Keeps hands to himself.							
4. Makes comments relevant to the topic.							
5. Follows teacher directions the first time.							

Home

1. Keeps room tidy.   0 1 2 3   Total for
2. Follows parent   0 1 2 3 4 5 6   the day:
   directions the
   first time.   _____

FIGURE 37.1 Charlie's daily progress chart.

per week. A daily chart was constructed to monitor Charlie's progress and allow daily communication between home and school (see Figure 37.1).

Next, a reward menu was constructed and points were attached to each reinforcer to be purchased. It is essential to align the points needed for reinforcers with the total number of points that can be earned daily. For example, it is unlikely that Charlie will be properly motivated if the system requires that 30 points are needed for 15 minutes of playtime with a friend. Likewise, if the same activity requires only 1 point, Charlie will soon learn that he can fail to meet most of the target behaviors most of the time and still receive a good deal of reward for minimal effort. Figure 37.2 contains the reward menu collaboratively agreed on by the group. Charlie had to agree to place each reward on the menu, even though his mother, teacher, and professional counselor could suggest ideas. There is no need to put a reward on the menu that the client does not find motivating.

The group then discussed how the token economy system would be monitored and reinforcements would be managed. It was determined that Charlie, under supervision of his mother at home, would keep a checkbook-style accounting of his token points. At

Item	Number of Points
15 minutes playing with friend	7
15 minutes game with mother/father	7
Family pizza party	125
First-base mitt	1,000
Family movie	75
Sleepover with a friend	250
15 minutes bike riding	7
15 minutes computer/PlayStation	10
Choose what to have for a meal	10
15 minutes of TV	10
Stay up an extra 30 minutes	12
A half-day outing (park, zoo, etc.)	200

FIGURE 37.2 Charlie's reward menu.

the end of each day, Charlie would make a deposit to his token account of the points he earned for that day. When he chose reinforcers from his reward menu, he would enter these transactions as withdrawals.

Finally, the group decided on follow-up and evaluation procedures. Charlie's mother and teacher would use the daily checklist to communicate back and forth as necessary and would inform the professional counselor every Friday of the daily number of points earned, rewards chosen, and any difficulties encountered over the week. The group would modify the system as needed, including deleting target behaviors that are consistently met and adding new target behaviors of interest. The group would begin to thin and fade the token economy system after 1 month of consistently appropriate behavior on all target behaviors.

USEFULNESS AND EVALUATION OF THE TOKEN ECONOMY TECHNIQUE

Of all the techniques presented in this book, the token economy is arguably the procedure that has received the most detailed coverage in the outcome literature. Token economies have been used to change the behavior of groups or individuals in a variety of different settings. It is likely that a token economy could be implemented, with some success, for any population whose behavior warrants modification.

When a token economy is implemented in an educational setting, it is likely that teachers have noticed behavior problems in an individual student or in their classes as a whole. A token economy can be used to improve classroom management, specifically with students who have problems including, but not limited to, disruptive behavior, attention-deficit/hyperactivity disorder (ADHD), and serious emotional problems (Filcheck et al., 2004; McGoey & DuPaul, 2000; Musser, Bray, Kehle, & Jenson, 2001). A token economy also can be used to increase classroom participation (Boniecki & Moore, 2003) or to increase positive behaviors that are incompatible with "school phobia, tantrums, thumb-sucking, encopresis, fighting, and so forth" (Wadsworth, 1970, p. 63). When assessing classroom participation, Boniecki and Moore (2003) reported that the use of a token economy with rewards for correctly answering questions increased the number of students attempting to answer questions correctly, boosted participation in class discussion, and led to an increase in the number of students who posed their own questions. Soares, Harrison, Vannest, and McClelland (2016) conducted a meta-analysis of 28 single-case studies ($n = 88$ AB phase changes) receiving a token economy treatment and derived a weighted mean *ES* of .82 [95% CI, .77, .88] which is a large effect of treatment. They also determined that a token economy was slightly more effective for 6- to 15-year-olds than for 3- to 5-year-olds, as well as for behavioral goals rather than academic goals. Coelho et al. (2015) reported that a 10-week token economy intervention led to significant reductions in impulsiveness, hyperactivity, disorganization, disobeying rules and routine, poor self-care, low frustration tolerance, compulsive behaviors, and antisocial behaviors in children with ADHD.

Mental health professionals have had good success using token economies to treat problem behaviors related to many psychological disorders, including autism (Charlop-Christy & Haymes, 1998; Reinecke, Newman, & Meinberg, 1999), eating disorders (Kahng, Boscoe, & Byrne, 2003; Okamoto et al., 2002), self-injurious skin picking (Toussaint & Tiger, 2012), and addictions (Silverman, Chutuape, Bigelow, & Stitzer, 1999). Behavior management specialists at prisons have also successfully implemented the token economy to help the prisoners learn the skills and behaviors necessary to adapt to society when they return to the outside world (Stolz, Wienckowski, & Brown, 1975).

A major criticism of the token economy is that an external system of reinforcement may decrease intrinsic motivation. Intrinsic motivation is the drive that comes from within the individual to complete a task or set of tasks. Critics of the token economy fear that, because the participants are rewarded extrinsically through the use of tokens, the motivation to act or behave in a certain way will dissipate once the tokens cease to be rewarded. Of course, the counterargument to this criticism is that if clients possessed the intrinsic motivation to perform a task successfully and consistently, there would be no need for external reinforcers. As such, the purpose of a token economy and other positive reinforcement strategies is to create motivation to perform using extrinsic rewards so that the client will experience success, then fade the reinforcement system so that intrinsic desires for continued success will maintain and expand behavioral gains. For example, in a study conducted in an educational setting, McGinnis, Friman, and Carlyon (1999) examined the outcome of using a token economy to enhance students' intrinsic motivation to do math. The study showed continued gains in math even after the treatment stopped, indicating that successes prompted by token economies may actually help create and bolster, not hinder or supplant, intrinsic motivation.

Token economies have been criticized for their use in educational settings because they lead students to develop performance goals rather than learning goals. Self-Brown and Mathews (2003), in a controlled study, found the students in the token economy group developed goals related to their performance and behavior in class rather than goals that had to do with increasing their knowledge and academic understanding. De Martini-Scully, Bray, and Kehle (2000) had previously responded to criticisms of this type by stating that student compliance is a necessary prerequisite in order for learning to occur, and their study suggested that academics do improve following improved behavior changes.

It is probable that some criticisms could stem from a lack of adherence to standardized implementation procedures shown to be effective. Ivy, Meindl, Overley, and Robson (2017) noticed that published research that used a token economy as an intervention varied as to the descriptiveness for replication purposes; in other words, researchers may use variable procedures making aggregation of results analogous to comparing varieties of apples, rather than the same type of apple. They reviewed articles using token economies published between 2000 and 2015 and concluded that essential component descriptions and vague descriptions of terms are commonplace. Indeed, only 19% of the 96 studies included replicable descriptions of program component implementation. Obviously, more attention to standardized description is needed to ensure generalizability of results.

A final criticism of the token economy is that it often fails to generalize to real-world situations after clients are released from an institutional setting. Glowacki, Warner, and White (2016) conducted a systematic review of seven high quality studies using a token economy with adults with mental illness in inpatient settings that were published between 1999 and 2013. They concluded that a token economy was effective in the short term in reducing negative behaviors and symptoms, including violence and aggression, although they found no evidence of long-term effects when the participants were no longer in inpatient care. Despite the criticism surrounding the technique of the token economy, the research provides overwhelming support of its efficacy when employed with various groups or individuals (Boniecki & Moore, 2003; Filcheck et al., 2004; Kahng et al., 2003; Reinecke et al., 1999).

APPLICATION OF THE TOKEN ECONOMY TECHNIQUE

Now apply the token economy technique to a current client or student you are working with or revisit the brief case studies presented at the beginning of this book. How can you use the token economy technique to address concerns and create movement in the counseling session?

CHAPTER 38

Behavioral Contract

ORIGINS OF THE BEHAVIORAL CONTRACT TECHNIQUE

Behavioral contracts, or contingency contracts, are based on the operant conditioning principle of positive reinforcement and can be used as a variation of the Premack principle. Behavioral contracts are written agreements between two or more individuals in which one or both persons agree to engage in a specific target behavior (Miltenberger, 2016). In addition, behavioral contracts involve the administration of positive (or perhaps sometimes negative) consequences contingent on the occurrence or nonoccurrence of the target behavior. Behavioral contracts specify all the details of the target behavior, including where the behavior will occur, how the behavior will be carried out, and when the behavior must be completed. All persons involved in the contract must negotiate the terms so that the contract is acceptable to everyone.

The term *contingency contract* was first used by L. P. Homme in 1966 when he reported using contracts with high school dropouts in order to reinforce academic performance (Cantrell, Cantrell, Huddleston, & Woolridge, 1969). Although they were made popular by behavioral and reality therapists, behavioral contracts are now integrated into many different theoretical approaches (Hackney & Cormier, 2017), including motivational interviewing (Enea & Dafinoiu, 2009).

A major strength of behavioral contracts is that they require people to be consistent. Therefore, contracts tend to be popular with children because they can hold their parents or teachers responsible under the terms of an agreement. Children no longer feel at the mercy of the person in power. Instead, they learn to accept responsibility for their own actions (Gallagher, 2010). Behavioral contracts establish a level of reciprocity between the involved parties, whether it be a married couple, parent(s) and child, or teacher and student. Contracts can be altered or renegotiated over time and eventually phased out once the target behaviors become routine.

HOW TO IMPLEMENT THE BEHAVIORAL CONTRACT TECHNIQUE

Behavioral contracts should be used when simpler and less intrusive techniques, such as praise and reinforcement, have failed and a more powerful procedure is required. When possible, behavioral contracts should be individualized rather than adapted for use with groups. Before writing a behavioral contract, identify the target behavior. Target behaviors may include undesired behaviors to be decreased or desired behaviors to be increased (Miltenberger, 2016). If possible, the target behavior should be phrased in a positive manner—for instance, "Staying on task during seat work time" rather than "Not distracting others during seat work time." Positive phrasing of goals allows for the application of a strategy based on positive reinforcement and obtaining rewards for appropriate behavioral compliance. All concerned parties should meet as a team to decide which behavior will be addressed. Usually this will be the most disruptive or pervasive issue. Baseline data should be gathered to determine where, under what conditions, and how frequently the behavior currently occurs. This information will be used later in determining the starting goal.

A behavioral contract has a number of essential components (see Table 38.1). Once the target behavior is identified, three more steps must be completed before the behavioral contract is written. First, decide how the target behaviors will be measured (Miltenberger, 2016). The behaviors may be directly observed or measured by outcomes. Choose where the contract will be used and who will be involved in measuring the target behavior. Next, using the baseline data of behavior frequency, identify realistic behavioral expectations and goals. Specify how often the target behavior must be performed in order to be considered a success. The contract should be flexible and allow for successive approximations toward the goal—that is, expectations should be increased slowly in order to allow progress toward the target frequency. To change behavior, the client must be observed behaving appropriately and must receive reinforcement. Therefore, it is important that the client experience success in the first week. Once the behavioral goal is set, identify the reinforcements and/or punishments that will be used contingent on success.

Whenever possible, allow the client to help create a menu of reinforcements, especially when working with children, but remember to keep the reinforcements small and manageable. Decide if negative consequences will be used for failure to meet the goal. Also, decide who will implement the contingency plan and determine what schedule the reinforcement will follow. Fixed-ratio or fixed-interval schedules are often best at the beginning, but moving to a variable-ratio or variable-interval schedule once the target behavior has been mastered can assist in maintenance of this behavior. A bonus clause may also be included to reward the client for sustained or exceptional progress.

After solidifying the details of the behavior plan, write the contract. Be sure to include the beginning date, the target behavior, the criteria and deadline for task completion, and the reinforcement that will be used. Discuss the contract with the client and all other parties involved. The contract should be clear to every person included, and the behavioral goals should be specific. Everyone involved should sign the contract and receive a copy. Finally, set up an evaluation meeting after a week or two

TABLE 38.1   Components of a Behavioral Contract

1. Identify the behavior to be modified.
2. Introduce and discuss the idea of a behavioral contract.
3. Develop the contract and present it to all involved. Include the following details:
   a. The client's name
   b. The specific behavior to be changed (start small)
   c. How you will know when the client is successful
   d. The reinforcement for successful performance.
   e. (Optional) A natural consequence for noncompliance
   f. (Optional) A bonus clause
   g. Follow up by _____ (time and date)
   h. Signatures
4. Outline the follow-up procedures.
5. Initiate the program.
6. Record progress and evaluate outcomes.
7. Modify as necessary (start small and expand).

to monitor the progress of the contract. A progress chart, log, or other visible means should be used to show improvement toward goal attainment. I ordinarily keep a template contract that can be edited and printed easily.

When monitoring progress, every aspect of the contract should be examined. Be sure that the target behavior was appropriate, attainable, and understood by the client. Decide whether suitable time was allotted to complete the task. Evaluate the reinforcements: Were they fitting, effective, and delivered in a timely manner? Also, decide whether the expectations of the contract were realistic and clear.

VARIATIONS OF THE BEHAVIORAL CONTRACT TECHNIQUE

There are several types of behavioral contracts. In *one-party contracts*, also referred to as unilateral contracts, one individual desires to change a target behavior (Miltenberger, 2016). She makes arrangements for a contract manager to implement reinforcement or punishment contingencies. One-party contracts may be used to increase desirable behaviors, such as exercise, studying, good eating habits, or school- and/or work-related behaviors, or to decrease undesirable behaviors, such as overeating, nail biting, excessive TV watching, or tardiness. On the other hand, *two-party contracts*, or bilateral contracts, allow both parties to identify target behaviors and contingencies that they will implement for each other. Two-party contracts are usually written between people who have a significant relationship with each other (e.g., spouses, parents and children, siblings, friends, co-workers). *Quid pro quo* contracts involve a relationship between both target behaviors: One thing will be given in return for something else. However, these parallel quid pro quo contracts allow each individual to work on his own target behavior without relying on the performance of the other.

Another type of behavioral contract, *self-contracts*, may be designed in order to help an individual meet a goal (Hackney & Cormier, 2017). Self-contracts are identical to other behavioral contracts, except that the rewards are self-administered by the client. These contracts can be very helpful when working with children or adolescents. The required behaviors should be clearly identified and broken into smaller subtasks that can be rewarded separately. Often, traditional behavioral contracts can be transitioned into self-contracts as the client becomes more successful at performing the target behavior. The contract manager slowly relinquishes control over the contract beginning with the reinforcements, then the task identification, and finally the time or frequency requirements.

EXAMPLE OF THE BEHAVIORAL CONTRACT TECHNIQUE

Patrick is a 16-year-old high school sophomore who was brought to the attention of the professional counselor for truancy. Patrick has no history of reported behavior problems and has maintained above-average grades throughout his school career. However, during the current spring semester, his teachers have become increasingly concerned about his potential to pass successfully to the 11th grade due to skipping classes.

Counselor (C):   So you aren't skipping entire days of school? You are at school . . . you just aren't showing up to particular classes?

Patrick (P):   I guess so.

C: Help me understand your reasons for this. I bet you have good reasons . . .

P: Not really. I don't know why, really. I mean . . . it just kind of started in the beginning as a once or twice kind of thing because my friends are bad about just hanging out in the parking lot or behind the football field instead of going to class. And I just started sitting around with them. Then I'd feel bad about missing, and I'd avoid that teacher 'cause I figured she'd be steamed at me. Or maybe I'd miss that class again 'cause you know, once you miss, you get behind or whatever. I might miss an assignment or material I needed to study with or something. It just kind of snowballed, I guess. You know what I mean?

C: Yes, I believe I do, Patrick. Seems to make a lot of sense to me.

P: Really?

C: Sure. And I really appreciate how you're sitting here being so honest with me. It takes a lot to just lay it out there like that. And it does . . . it does make sense how it started out just as this thing to do, and then it just kind of got out of control.

P: Yeah, exactly.

C: So does it bother you that you might not pass through to the 11th grade if you keep skipping?

P: Nah, not really. I guess it should. But I don't see what the big deal is. My parents are freaking out that I might have to go to summer school. But, I mean, that wouldn't be that big of a deal either. Most of my friends will probably be going. So, I mean, yeah, whatever. Um . . . no . . . I guess it doesn't bother me too much.

The professional counselor now understands the motivation for Patrick's behavior and also that the natural consequence of grade retention is not enough of a motivator for Patrick to improve his class attendance. Finally, the professional counselor has taken notice of Patrick's respectfulness and honesty within the counseling session and feels both he and his situation could benefit from a behavioral contract. Step 1, identify the behavior to be modified, has been accomplished, and the professional counselor moves on to step 2, introduce the idea of the behavioral contract. In doing so, the counselor tries to collect information needed to construct the written contract.

C: And your "parents freaking out" doesn't bother you either?

P: I mean . . . yeah . . . it does. But then I get here, and I'm like "Man, I don't feel like going to English class today" or whatever class it is, and it's just easier to skip because I'm not thinking about my parents freaking or about passing 10th grade. Those things just seem too far off, and my parents chill out pretty easy anyway, and like I already said, summer school's no big deal.

C: Patrick, do you want to do better about attending classes? (Pauses) If there was a reason that was more important to you, would you commit to attending classes more regularly?

P: Sure, I guess. I mean, sure I would want to do better if there was a reason.

C: Okay, so what I'd like to do is to find out what is important to a 16-year-old like you. What are some things that you find yourself trying to negotiate for from time to time, either with your parents, yourself, or your teachers?

The counselor tries to discern a possible positive reinforcement.

P: Sleeping in late on Saturday! Man, it drives me crazy that my parents will *not* let me sleep past 8:30 or 9:00 a.m. on a Saturday morning . . . never have . . . drives me nuts! I would *love* to sleep until like lunch time or something. But they are both freaks about that, and it's like the dang golden rule around my house or something.

C: Lunch time, huh? That would be pretty nice. Good. Anything else?

P: I negotiate all the time for a new car. Is that what you mean?

C: Well, let me tell you what I have in mind here, and then you'll see how your two suggestions fit in. Your parents and your teachers really want you to do well in school. And they know that can't happen if you continue to skip classes. And now I know that you don't really care all that much about what I call the natural consequences . . . those being failing the 10th grade or your parents freaking out as you say . . . at least you don't care at the time that it matters most . . . like when you are sitting in the parking lot or behind the football field with your friends. In fact, some of the natural consequences, like missing assignments and your teacher's perceptions, actually increase your likelihood to skip again. (Pauses for a moment to let this all sink in with Patrick) This presents a dilemma.

P: When you put it that way, yeah. (Pauses while nodding head and reflecting) I guess it does.

C: What would be great is if we could come up with some mutual agreement between you and your teachers, myself, your parents . . . all of us, that would make you more likely to go to class.

P: I don't see that happening.

C: Well, your parents want you to stop cutting class. Cutting class doesn't really bother you all that much. You want to sleep in on Saturday mornings. Your parents don't allow that. See where I'm going?

P: I think so.

C: With that sort of tit for tat in mind, can you think of any other examples or points of negotiation between you and your parents? The sleeping in on Saturdays fits nicely into a possible proposal to your parents. That is something we might actually get them to consider. The new car is probably not, although we can check if you want.

P: Nah—they already told me no way. Curfew is always a big deal. I'm always asking for a later curfew, and they're always turning me down.

C: Okay, good. That gives us a couple of options. What I'd like to do then is sit down with you and your parents and flesh out a contract that will give you a little more incentive to attend class. This contract would be very specific about what is expected of you and what happens if you follow through, as well as what happens if you don't.

P: What do you mean by "what happens if I don't follow through?"

The counselor is trying to discern the natural consequence for noncompliance.

C: Well, something you said earlier got my attention. You said you assumed your teachers were steamed when you cut their classes and that you knew you fell behind when you cut. Right? And that these two things actually made you more likely to cut that class again. Right?

P: Yep.

C: Well, we don't know yet what the positive will be for you if you improve your attendance . . . we still have to negotiate that with your parents . . . but I would like for the negative consequence to be something along the lines of reporting to your teachers at the end of the day, if you skipped their classes, and obtaining the material you missed and any homework assignments. That way, knowing you have to face your teacher that same day will hopefully be a deterrent to you skipping to begin with. If you skip anyway, obtaining the missed material and assignments will make you less likely to skip the same class the next day. What do you think?

P: Wow, that'd be hard. But . . . I think I like the idea anyway . . . I mean, it'd be good for me to have to do that . . . I'll get to see all this and know the specifics before I definitely agree, right?

C: Yes. We'll actually put it in writing, and you'll see it all before I ask you to sign the contract. Let's set up another appointment for later this week with you and your parents. And in the meantime, I'll discuss your options with your teachers. How does that sound?

P: Cool.

Later that week, the following session takes place with Patrick and both his parents.

C: So, Patrick, your teachers are all on board with giving you your missed material and assignments that same day when you come to them and ask them for it. They are also going to each keep a separate attendance sheet for you each day that I will pick up every afternoon after your last class period. That way, I will be keeping a daily record of your attendance in each class and will report that directly to your mom and dad. Sound okay?

P: Sounds fine. So, if I do skip a class, I have to go to that teacher that same day and ask her for my homework and missed material?

C: Yep.

P: So she'll know I'm really here that day.

C: They know anyway, Patrick. You may as well be brave and just go do what you have to do to keep from falling behind . . . keeps it from snowballing, like you said.

P: Yeah, you're right.

C: Okay, so Mom and Dad, what we want to discuss with you today are some ideas that Patrick and I have already mulled over, that may serve to encourage his class attendance, and I know you guys want that!

Mom (M): Okay, we're listening.

C: Patrick, why don't you start? Tell them the two ideas we are considering.

P: Well, the two things that I could come up with that would really help make me more likely to diss the guys in between classes would be if I knew I could sleep in on Saturday or if I could stay out later on Friday or Saturday night.

Dad (D): Really? Sleeping in or later curfew is more important than passing 10th grade? Remarkable.

C: Sometimes, Dad, what seems obviously important to us is not at all what makes a teenager tick.

D: I guess so. (Toward Mom) What do you think?

M: So, we could consider one or the other as a reward for his class attendance?

C: Yes. As I explained on the phone, I would like to use a behavioral contract between all of us that will outline a specific positive that Patrick will gain for attending a set number of classes, and a negative that Patrick will have to face each time he skips a class. Here's what we've got so far. Whenever he skips a class, he knows and agrees to go to that teacher in person before the school day is up, first showing that he was in fact present that day and, second, requesting any missed information and assignments. We know this is something that Patrick wants to avoid, and we also know that doing so will help prevent him from skipping this class the very next day as an avoidance measure.

M: Okay. I like that.

C: Now, what I'd like to do is state in the contract that for every five days, not necessarily five days in a row but an accumulation of five total days, where each and every class was attended, he gets a certain something, he gets your word that you will follow through with whatever it is we decide today . . . something related to curfew or sleeping in preferably. Those are the privileges that mean the most to him.

M: I see, I see. Well, I am willing to budge on the sleeping in on Saturday mornings more so than on the curfew.

D: I prefer extending his curfew.

M: Extending his curfew could lead to more potential problems, not to mention dangers. What harm will come from him sleeping in late?

D: True. I see your point. I'm not against sleeping in then.

P: You have *no* idea how much I am going to go to class!

C: Alright, let's get this all down on paper, with all the specifics, and get everyone's signatures. And remember, we are all giving our word here. We all have an agreement.

The professional counselor outlines all agreed-upon terms in the contract, complete with the expected behavior phrased in positive language, the means for the counselor to keep track of Patrick's attendance, the positive and negative consequences for attendance or truancy, a starting date, and an ending date. Finally, an appointment is scheduled for two weeks later to assess Patrick's compliance with the terms of the contract. The actual contract designed for Patrick is shown in Figure 38.1.

USEFULNESS AND EVALUATION OF THE BEHAVIORAL CONTRACT TECHNIQUE

The successful use of behavioral contracts has been well documented in the literature for more than 40 years. Behavioral contracts may be used to teach new behaviors, decrease unwanted behaviors, or increase desirable behaviors (Downing, 1990). Contracts are very helpful for use with academic and social skills, and they have been used successfully with students in regular classrooms as well as those in special education. Allen, Howard, Sweeney, and McLaughlin (1993) demonstrated that behavioral contracts could increase on-task behavior immediately and significantly in second- and third-grade students. In addition, Kelley and Stokes (1982) reported that behavioral contracts using money as a reward for completing workbook pages in a vocational training program could increase the productivity of older, disadvantaged students. Parent-designed behavioral contracts have also achieved increases in the homework performance of their children (Miltenberger, 2016). Miller and Kelley (1994) reported that when parents and elementary school children negotiated weekly behavioral contracts, three out of four students improved their homework accuracy, and two out of four students significantly improved their on-task behavior.

In addition to the school environment, contracts have been used in prisons, mental hospitals, and halfway houses (Mikulas, 1978). Behavioral contracting has been used in both inpatient and outpatient medical and psychiatric settings. In long-term care, major problems challenging staff members are residents who do not comply with policies, are resistant to care, or are abusive. Behavioral contracting is one way of providing the structure

Behavioral Contract

Student Name: Patrick Daniels   Date: March 2, 20XX

Terms of Agreement

Patrick agrees to attend each class for which he is enrolled Monday through Friday at Payne High School. Patrick understands that exceptions to class attendance include serious illness or a family emergency, which would require leaving campus for the remainder of the day to attend to these matters. Classes scheduled include American History, Anatomy and Physiology, English Literature I, Sociology, and Excel Applications.

When all five classes have been attended for five cumulative days, Patrick's parents, Eileen and Davis Daniels, agree to reward Patrick by allowing him to sleep until noon on the upcoming Saturday morning. This reward will continue throughout the remainder of this contract.

When Patrick skips a class, he agrees to meet with the teacher of that course, that same day, in person, to request missed material and assignments. This course of action will be expected for the duration of this contract.

The professional counselor, Monica Reed, will keep a record of Patrick's class attendance, reporting his progress to Mr. and Mrs. Daniels. This system of tracking attendance will remain in place for the duration of this contract.

The terms of this contract will begin Monday, March 5, and will continue through the spring semester, ending on Friday, May 18.

We agree to the terms of this behavior contract as written.

_____   _____
Patrick Daniels   Date   Eileen Daniels   Date

_____   _____
Monica Reed   Date   Davis Daniels   Date

FIGURE 38.1 Patrick's behavioral contract.

needed in order for residents to cooperate with their care (Hartz, Brennan, Aulakh, & Estrin, 2010). Contracts are also frequently used in marital or couples therapy (Miltenberger, 2016) and in motivational interviewing (Enea & Dafinoiu, 2009). Behavioral contracts have also been used for weight management, drug and alcohol treatment, reduction in cigarette smoking, and monitoring physical fitness (James & Gilliland, 2003).

APPLICATION OF THE BEHAVIORAL CONTRACT TECHNIQUE

Now apply the behavioral contract technique to a current client or student you are working with or revisit the brief case studies presented at the beginning of this book. How can you use the behavioral contract technique to address concerns and create movement in the counseling session?

Techniques Based on Behavioral Approaches Using Punishment

Figure 1 in Section 9 stated that punishment is defined as anything, either applied or removed, that decreases or suppresses the display of an undesirable behavior. When a client's goal is to do less of something, punishment procedures are very effective in helping the client meet that goal. However, professional counselors should realize that punishment frequently does not totally eliminate the undesirable behavior. More often, punishment reduces the display of an undesirable behavior within the environment that the punishment occurred; for example, punishing a teen for smoking in the house will probably reduce smoking in the house but will not necessarily reduce smoking outside the house. It is essential to understand that, in order to totally extinguish a behavior, a combination of punishing the undesirable behavior and reinforcing the incompatible desirable behavior is usually necessary.

Punishment can involve either adding a stimulus to the situation or removing a reinforcer from the situation. Examples of punishment with stimulus added include corporal punishment, assigning extra chores or homework, or requiring additional practice attempts. Examples of punishment while removing a reinforcer would include grounding or restricting a child from going outside to play, not allowing use of something ordinarily allowed

(e.g., car, bike, video gaming system), or any other restriction of privileges ordinarily granted.

Although punishment can be quite effective in reducing undesirable behaviors, its success depends on many factors. When designing a punishment program, one must consider the type of behavior being punished; the type of punishment that will be used; the schedule of punishment; whether warnings will be given before punishment is delivered; and whether other techniques, such as positive reinforcement, should be used in conjunction with the punishment procedures. In addition, those using punishment techniques should ensure that the consequences are delivered immediately, the intensity of the consequences is appropriate, and the punishment procedure is applied consistently.

Punishment is a controversial technique. On the one hand, punishment procedures have been used effectively with a variety of situations and populations. Punishment has been used effectively with persons with intellectual disabilities, clients with autism, children with schizophrenia, psychiatric patients, self-abusive or physically aggressive persons, and children presenting with noncompliant behavior. Applications of punishment, such as response cost, have been successful at reducing excessive crying, hyperactivity, noncompliance in children, and alcoholic drinking (Henington &

Doggett, 2016). Time out has been used effectively to diminish disruptive behaviors in children. On the other hand, some people argue that punishment procedures should be used only in extreme cases and that positive reinforcement procedures should be used whenever possible. But punishment procedures often work more rapidly than reinforcement procedures, so punishment may be useful with life-threatening behaviors, such as rumination or self-injury.

It is important to note that the effects of punishment procedures may be temporary. When punitive consequences are removed, the punished behavior often reappears. Because of this temporary effect, punishment is often called a suppressor of behavior. Punishment may also have a few other negative side effects. Punishment sometimes leads to escape, avoidance, or aggression (Doyle, 1998). It can also be a poor social learning model, teaching children to use punishment on others. Finally, some aversive stimuli can have negative physiological side effects and end up doing more harm than good.

Several techniques based on punishment are presented in Section 10 to help clients decrease display of the target behavior. These techniques include extinction, time out, response cost, and overcorrection (positive practice). Extinction is a classic procedure that basically deprives the client of any positive reinforcer that helps to continue an undesirable behavior. For example, when a child's acting-out behavior in class is reinforced by a teacher's attention, the teacher tries to extinguish the behavior by paying absolutely no attention to the child during the acting-out episodes. When the child is not acting out, the teacher attends to and rewards the child for desirable behavior.

Time out is a punishment technique that removes the client from a reward-rich environment and places the client in a reward-deprived area. In classic time out, a child is placed in a time out chair for a certain amount of time. Time out serves to deter future misbehavior. Response cost is pretty much the opposite of positive reinforcement. In response cost, a client starts with a certain number of tokens, and display of the target behavior results in the loss of one token. At the end of the time period, if the client has any tokens remaining, the client gets the agreed-upon reward. Overcorrection, sometimes called positive practice, is an effective punishment technique that requires the client to perform the correct action repeatedly—usually 10 times—to (1) teach the client the proper way to perform the behavior, and (2) serve as a deterrent to future misbehavior. So if a child normally slams the door when he enters the house, the child practices entering and exiting the house silently 10 times. In the future, the child will likely remember to close the door quietly. It is important for professional counselors to remember that the effectiveness of punishment interventions is enhanced when the punishment procedure is coupled with a positive reinforcement strategy.

MULTICULTURAL IMPLICATIONS OF BEHAVIORAL APPROACHES USING PUNISHMENT

See Section 9 for a review of multicultural implications when using techniques based on behavioral approaches.

CHAPTER 39

Extinction

ORIGINS OF THE EXTINCTION TECHNIQUE

Extinction is a classic behavioral technique based on punishment that involves withholding reinforcements in order to reduce the frequency of a specific behavior. It is commonly used in parent training and classroom management and was developed and validated more than 50 years ago. Extinction can be used to eliminate behaviors that were previously reinforced (sometimes unknowingly) in the environment. For instance, if a student in class is constantly calling out to gain teacher attention, the teacher should ignore that student rather than acknowledge the student's responses. Acknowledgment of the student constitutes a positive reinforcement of the calling-out behavior. Once this reinforcement is withdrawn, the calling-out behavior should cease.

As with other forms of punishment, extinction is often more effective when combined with positive reinforcement of an alternate behavior. The strategy of substituting a more desirable behavior for the undesirable one is sometimes referred to as counterconditioning (George & Christiani, 1995). It is essential to note that extinction often results in a temporary increase in the target behavior before its decline. This increase in negative behavior is called an *extinction burst*. In addition, when used alone, extinction produces a gradual rather than immediate reduction in the behavior. However, combining extinction with consistent positive reinforcement of an alternate (i.e., competing) behavior can lead to more permanent and rapid results.

HOW TO IMPLEMENT THE EXTINCTION TECHNIQUE

Before deciding to use an extinction procedure, the professional counselor must consider the nature of the behavior to be terminated. If the target behavior is extremely disruptive to the point that an increase in the behavior would not be tolerable or if the behavior is likely to be imitated by others when ignored, extinction is not an appropriate technique.

The first step in designing an extinction procedure is to recognize all possible reinforcers of the target behavior. Common reinforcers for disruptive behaviors are adult attention, adult comments, attention of peers, or escape from an activity. To determine the reinforcers of a behavior, a contingency analysis may be conducted. This analysis requires studying the events and conditions that occur before the undesired and desired behaviors and the consequences of each behavior. Once all reinforcers have been identified, a method of withholding these reinforcements must be designed. If all reinforcers cannot be withheld, then extinction will not be successful. The last step before implementing the extinction procedure is to choose an alternative behavior to be positively reinforced along with the extinction procedure.

When applying extinction, the professional counselor should be prepared for an increase in the target behavior (i.e., extinction burst). The professional counselor should withhold all reinforcement when the target behavior occurs and present positive reinforcement whenever the alternate (competing) behavior takes place. The professional counselor can also monitor or graph the client's behavior to determine the success of the extinction and positive reinforcement procedures.

VARIATIONS OF THE EXTINCTION TECHNIQUE

Several classic variations of extinction have been proposed. *Covert extinction* is identical to extinction except that it occurs in the client's imagination (Ascher & Cautela, 1974). Once the target behavior and consequences maintaining that behavior are identified, the client is instructed to imagine a scene in which the reinforcement does *not* occur (Cautela, 1971). The client imagines this scene over and over until the behavior is eliminated in reality. Covert extinction can be especially useful when the reinforcers are hard to control in the real environment. It can also be used in conjunction with traditional extinction or covert reinforcement. In a laboratory study, Ascher and Cautela (1974) found that covert extinction was successful in eliminating a previously reinforced overt response whether or not external conditions supported the extinction procedure.

EXAMPLE OF THE EXTINCTION TECHNIQUE

Craig is a 5-year-old boy with a recent burst of frequent tantrum behavior. It began suddenly, following a weekend trip to his grandmother's house, where Craig's 3-year-old cousin, quite adept at tantrum behavior, was also visiting. Craig's parents were so taken aback at their son's new reaction to disappointment that they've yet to devise a consistent and effective plan to handle it.

Counselor (C):   Okay, Mom and Dad, tell me in a little bit more detail about this new skill your son has developed.

Mom (M):   (With Craig in her lap) Well, it has been happening daily for some time now, usually several times in one day. He begins to cry very loudly and hides his face on the floor. He seems more distraught than angry, unless you don't give in immediately, and then it becomes more of an angry fit. Um . . . the crying will turn more to yelling or screaming . . . not directly at me or my husband, just in general. It's so nerve-wracking. I can feel my blood pressure rise. I just want it to stop.

C: So it really gets to you, huh?

M: Yeah. I mean it's so hard to see him on the floor crying, like he's really devastated. I'm his mother. I don't want him to feel so upset. And then I think to myself "Is it really worth all this?" You know? Is it that big of a deal for him to go to bed right now, or to put his toys away, or brush his teeth right at this moment? It just doesn't seem worth it. So I just give in.

C: So you might let him stay up a little later or leave his toys out or avoid brushing his teeth?

M: Yes.

C: And how does he respond when you give in?

M: Oh, he returns to normal very quickly, sometimes even happier than before the tantrum began.

C: Which reinforces you to keep giving in! Okay, I'm getting the idea. And does he ever do anything to hurt himself or others during these tantrums?

M: No, never. Even though it really gets to me, part of me knows it's very contrived. Sometimes he even stops long enough to look up to see if we're paying attention.

C: Oh, I see. Okay. Well, Dad, can you tell me your take on all this?

Dad (D):   I just feel like maybe it's a phase he's going through. Or I thought it was at first. But it seems to be getting worse lately, and that bothers me. I feel like we've tried everything but nothing works, and it's getting worse instead of better.

C: Right. Right. Can you tell me how you respond to these tantrums?

D: Um . . . well, usually I just let my wife deal with it, but if she's not around then I usually try to talk to him to calm him down. I've tried being very soothing, and I've tried being very stern. Neither seems to work really. (Craig gets down from Mom's lap and goes to the paper and crayons in the bookcase. He sits down at the other end of the office and begins coloring.)

C: Okay. Let me make sure I've got this right. Craig probably picked up this new behavior from his cousin. He saw this cousin use tantrums when he didn't get his way, and then probably saw him get his way as a result of the tantrum. At the very least, he probably saw his cousin receive an awful lot of attention from all the commotion. So Craig decided this seemed to be a very effective behavior and he should try it out himself. So he gets home from Grandma's, and the first time he doesn't get what he wants, he gives it a try. Both of you were probably so surprised that you thought something was terribly wrong. Imagine his delight when you rushed to him, gave in to his demands, and soothed him.

M: (Laughs) Kids are so smart, aren't they?

C: They do learn quickly—which will work to our advantage. Okay. So Craig continues this behavior, it is working more and more effectively, and he is fine-tuning his emotional displays. Dad may not always give in to him, but he does give him attention, which is nice, and Mom almost always gives in, which is even better. I'd say you have a pretty smart kid on your hands!

D: He takes after me.

M: That's true!

C: (Laughs) All right. So let me ask just one or two more questions to make certain I have a clear idea of the situation. It seems to me so far that Craig uses tantrums to get attention and to get his way, either by avoiding something he does not want to do or getting something he does want. Thinking on the most recent instances, can you see anything that occurs before the tantrum or after that would indicate any other reason for the tantrums?

M: (Both parents think for several moments. Mom speaks first.) Every example I'm coming up

with in my mind is exactly for those reasons. Exactly those.

D: (Nods head in agreement.) Yeah, me too. I agree.

The counselor is now going to introduce the concept of extinction, also called planned ignoring.

C: What I'd like to suggest is the use of a technique known as extinction. The general rule behind this principle is that if you want a behavior to continue and increase, you attend to it. If you don't want to see it anymore, you do not attend to it. Now, the more the child wants the reinforcer, which, in Craig's case, is the attention and getting his way, the more he will resist your attempts at extinction.

D: Oh boy.

C: Yeah. It is very important for you to know this going in, though, so that you'll be prepared. In fact, you should know that he may actually throw tantrums much more intensely in the beginning.

Recall that this is known as an extinction burst.

C: Does either of you watch television?

D: I do when I get home from work and on Saturdays during college football season.

C: Okay. Um . . . imagine that you settle into your seat with a drink and a snack to watch a football game one Saturday afternoon. You make yourself comfortable, prop your feet up perhaps, have your drink in your hand, and reach for the remote control. You push the power button to turn the television on and nothing happens. What do you do?

D: Push it again!

C: And probably again and again and again. Anytime you've pushed this button on the remote in the past, the television has come on. You think that if you keep pushing it, maybe a little more forcefully, maybe holding it up and at a different angle, the television will work. Why not just put the remote down, walk to the television set, and turn it on manually?

D: Because I know that remote will eventually work—and I'm comfy!

C: Exactly my point. This is exactly what Craig will be thinking when you first begin to extinguish his tantrums. He'll try even harder because he is certain it will eventually work as it has in the past. Now, will you eventually give up on the remote?

D: Yes.

C: And so will Craig. There are a few things, though, that you can do to speed up that process. First, be consistent. If sometimes you use extinction and sometimes you don't, you will actually increase his tantrums because your consequences are unpredictable. Second, giving in later is worse than giving him what he wants to begin with. So decide up front that if you are going to refuse a request of Craig's, you are certain you are going to stick with it and see it through. If you know you are going to eventually give in to it, just give in before the tantrum behavior ever begins. The last thing is to, immediately, as soon as he begins to calm down and displays appropriate behavior, immediately give him attention and praise. You want there to be a marked difference between your reactions to him while he is in a tantrum and your reactions to him while he is calm. Remember: Ignore behavior you do not want to continue, and attend to behavior you want to see more of.

M: This is going to be hard, isn't it?

C: It will not be easy. But it will be worth it. And it will work if we are right in assuming the reasons for the tantrums and if you are consistent and don't give up. (Pause) I tell you what, why don't we give it a try now? (Up to this point, Craig has been coloring while sitting on the floor and off to the side in the counselor's office.)

D: You mean right now? Here? How?

M: All we'd have to do is take away the crayons.

C: Good idea, Mom. We could ask him to put them up and come join us. What do you think?

M: And then what will we do?

C: We will do exactly what you will be doing when you leave here today. We will carry on as if nothing is happening. We will not look at him, raise our eyebrows, or address him in any way. And when he calms himself, we will be overjoyed at how good he is being.

M: This could really help. Okay. Let's try it.

C: Dad?

D: Sure, why not? Nothing else we've tried has worked.

C: Mom, why don't you do the honors?

M: Okay. (Turns toward Craig) Craig, I would like for you to put the crayons back in the bookcase and come sit with us for a moment.

Craig: I'm not done yet.

M: You may finish after we talk to you. I would like for you to place the crayons back in the bookcase and come sit with us for a moment.

Craig: *Mom!* I'm not done yet! (Pause.) Nooooooo! (Wailing begins) I don't want tooooo! (Craig's wailing gets louder, and he places his face in his hands, bends at the knees, and buries his face in his hands. Craig's mother becomes visibly nervous.)

C: Okay, Mom, look at me and talk to me about anything as normally as possible. Nothing is happening. We are still three adults having a conversation. Everything is fine. Why don't you talk to me about how anxious you seem right now? Tell me how this is for you.

M: (A long pause as Mom looks at the floor, possibly to prevent herself from looking over at Craig) He seems so disappointed. (Looks over to Craig, who is still wailing)

C: Look this way. Remember, no eye contact, no body language, no reaction at all.

M: Okay. (Deep breath) Part of me just wants to let him keep the c-r-a-y-o-n-s so he won't be upset.

C: (Looks out of the corner of an eye to see that Craig has looked up to see if he is being attended to. Then the crying gets louder and, just as his parents stated, begins to sound less devastated and more angry.) Wow, you predicted that exactly. So part of you wants to just make it all better for him. Keep talking. It will help you get through this.

M: (Looks at Craig's dad, who then takes her hand) Yeah, but you know it's funny . . . the fact that right now was so predictable is actually helping me feel better. If it's that routine, then surely it can't be that real. Don't you think? (Craig has just taken the intensity level up another notch.) Do you think the people in the hall can hear?

C: (Before the counselor has a chance to respond, Craig very suddenly stops and becomes quiet.) Oh, Craig, I like the way you just calmed right down. That was very good. We'd like for you to join us now. (Crying and yelling begins again, with even more enthusiasm.)

C: It's okay. Don't attend to it. Remember? It isn't happening.

M: But why did it happen again? Usually once he stops, he's done.

C: That's because, in the past, he stops because he gets what he wants. This time is different. I actually made the same request as the one that initially set him off. This is the extinction burst we discussed. (This time, after a more intense, though shorter tantrum, Craig stops again.) Mom, you go ahead this time.

M: Very good, Craig! We'd like you to come over here now. (Craig complies, gets in Mom's lap, and Mom gives him a big hug. Dad pats him on the back.)

C: Mom, Dad, Craig, you all did great. Notice how our reactions did not change no matter how loud or upset he became, nor when he stopped and began again. Notice that he still does not have the c-r-a-y-o-n-s, yet he is fine. Also notice the difference in our reactions to him while having a tantrum: We ignored him, and after he calmed himself, we praised and hugged him.

M: He does seem just fine now.

C: Yes, he certainly does.

D: I think we can do this. It really helped to try it out here. We would have been stuck with the second wave of it and wouldn't have known how to react.

C: Good. I'm glad it helped. Do you have any questions before you venture out on your own?

M: It's okay to give in to some things, right? Just make sure I do it to begin with?

C: Of course. But once you make a choice, stand your ground.

M: Okay.

C: It would help for you to keep a record each day of how frequent the tantrums are and how long they last. This will help you gauge the effectiveness of the extinction.

M: All right. Just write down when they occur and when they stop?

C: Yes, that should do it. You can be more detailed if you like. The important thing, though, is that you get an idea over the next few weeks of the progress that is being made. Oh, and one other thing. If anyone else is going to be at your home or with you, explain to them ahead of time that you are working on eliminating Craig's tantrum behavior. Stress to them the importance of following your lead and ignoring Craig's behavior.

D: Wish us luck!

USEFULNESS AND EVALUATION OF THE EXTINCTION TECHNIQUE

Much of the outcome research on the extinction technique was conducted almost 50 years ago and is considered classic. Extinction can be used in a variety of situations, as long as the target behavior is not too disruptive or prone to imitation by others (Benoit & Mayer, 1974). It is important that the professional counselor have control over all possible reinforcers of the target behavior before using extinction. When combined with positive reinforcement of an alternate behavior, extinction has been used successfully with child noncompliance and aggression (Groden & Cautela, 1981). Williams (1959) found that extinction was effective in eliminating tantrum behavior in a child. When the parents no longer reinforced the child's tantrums by reentering the child's bedroom after putting him to sleep, the tantrum behavior was completely eliminated within 10 occasions. In contrast, Scheveneels, Boddez, Vervliet, and Hermans (2016) studied the use of extinction as a laboratory model for clinical exposure therapy and concluded that the efficacy of the extinction model may be overstated. A major challenge to successful implementation of the extinction technique may be parental motivation: Borrego and Pemberton's (2007) survey of parents indicated extinction was the least favorite technique of the six behavioral strategies listed (after response cost [most acceptable], token economy, time-out, overcorrection, and differential attention).

APPLICATION OF THE EXTINCTION TECHNIQUE

Now apply the extinction technique to a current client or student you are working with or revisit the brief case studies presented at the beginning of this book. How can you use the extinction technique to address concerns and create movement in the counseling session?

CHAPTER 40

Time Out

ORIGINS OF THE TIME OUT TECHNIQUE

The widely used time out technique is a form of behavioral treatment based on the operant conditioning principle of punishment. Those who espouse behavioral therapy hold that all behavior, maladaptive and adaptive, is learned through operant processes and modeling. Negative punishment involves removing a stimulus to reduce the probability that a behavior will recur. Due to the positive effects of time out, the technique has become an important part of addressing the behavior of children in a school setting (Knoff, 2009). Time out is one of the most frequently employed behavioral interventions used to reduce behavior problems in children (Evere, Hupp, & Olmi, 2010) and was ranked third most acceptable to parents of the six behavior management strategies listed (Borrego & Pemberton, 2007). Time out is both a frequent component of parent-training procedures (Eaves, Sheperis, Blanchard, Baylot, & Doggett, 2005) and an intervention with wide popular appeal.

Time out is a type of negative punishment in which any form of positive reinforcement is removed from the child after a display of maladaptive behavior. This is done with the hope that the child will not continue to engage in the maladaptive behaviors in the future because the child wants to keep the positive reinforcers. Time out is used to decrease inappropriate behavior (i.e., punishment) and increase appropriate (i.e., reinforcing) behavior. Therefore, time out is a technique designed to educate children about what to do and what not to do (Knoff, 2009). Time out serves as punishment for current misbehavior and a deterrent to future misbehavior.

HOW TO IMPLEMENT THE TIME OUT TECHNIQUE

Time out is used most frequently with children. Before implementing time out, professional counselors should be familiar with the three different types. *Seclusionary time out* occurs when a child is sent to a different room, referred to as a time out room. *Exclusionary time out* occurs when the child is removed from the environment where the activity is happening. The child is sent to another location such as the steps or the hallway. *Nonseclusionary time out* occurs when a child remains in the environment but is not allowed to participate in the reinforcing activity.

When implementing time out, the adult needs to make sure to tell the child, in a clear and concise manner, why she is being sent to time out. Time out should be used only after the child has been given redirection and a warning. Depending on the type of maladaptive behavior displayed, the adult should choose which type of time out to use. The adult should attempt to have the child go to time out without having to physically constrain the child but at times may need to use some force to get the child to comply. Physical restraint requires specialized training and should be used only if the child is endangering herself or another person. The amount of time the child stays in time out varies, but it is typically around 5 minutes. With younger children, less time may be needed, and with older children, more time may be necessary to serve as an effective deterrent to future misbehavior. It is important for the adult to monitor the child when the child is in time out, and when her time is up, the child needs to rejoin the activity. When a child comes back from time out, the adult should make sure to treat the child with respect and update the child on what to do to rejoin the activity in progress. The child should not be reprimanded or forced to apologize, although if the child offers to apologize voluntarily, such behavior should be encouraged. Forcing a child to apologize is seldom productive. You can make a child apologize, but you cannot make a child feel sorry for engaging in some misbehavior.

When one chooses to implement the time out technique, it is a good idea to gather baseline data to support its use. The record should include a description of the child's behavior before implementing time out, the time of day the behavior occurred, the duration of time out, the type of time out used, and a description of how the child behaved while in time out. After a 2-week period of time, the adult can examine the data to evaluate whether or not time out appears to be effective. Typically, this technique can be used with children as young as 2 or 3 years (Spencer, 2000) or as old as the early teenage years. Time out has even been used effectively with adults with intellectual disabilities.

When a child is in time out, Erford (1999, p. 208) suggested having the child follow these seven rules to enhance behavioral compliance: (1) feet on the floor, (2) chair legs on the floor, (3) hands in lap, (4) bottom on chair, (5) eyes open and on the wall, (6) not a sound, and (7) sit up straight with back against the chair. Although it is fine to discuss implementation of time out procedures in front of the child, there may be advantages to allowing for some private time with the parent(s), teacher(s), or caretaker(s) to answer questions and predict circumstances where some modifications and troubleshooting may be necessary. It is also essential that the child comply with the behavior the adult required the child to perform before the child is released from the chair (e.g., "Are you ready to do what I asked, or would you like to remain in the chair for another time out? You decide.").

VARIATIONS OF THE TIME OUT TECHNIQUE

Erford (1999) described a contingent delay variation of time out. After the client is sent to time out and understands the seven rules described above, the client is expected to follow the rules for the entire time spent in time out. The client is informed that any time she violates one of the rules, 1 minute will be added to the amount of time spent in time out (e.g., 5 minutes plus any penalty minutes). It is important that whoever is implementing the technique with the child is strict about adding the extra minute, or the child will not view the time out as a punishment.

The "sit and watch" variation of this technique is for use in the classroom setting. If the student is sent to "sit and watch," the student picks up an hourglass (filled with enough sand to last 3 minutes), moves to an area away from the rest of the class, sits down, and watches the timer. Once the sand flows through the timer, the student can rejoin the activity. Teachers may find it useful to develop contingencies when using "sit and watch." Examples include:

> Go to Sit and Watch once, lose daily computer time. Go to Sit and Watch more than once, lose a free play period every 2 weeks. Engage in disruptive behavior while in Sit and Watch, lose free play time later in the day. Talk to someone in Sit and Watch or tattle on others, go to Sit and Watch. (White & Bailey, 1990, p. 356)

EXAMPLE OF THE TIME OUT TECHNIQUE

The following transcript illustrates the teaching and use of contingent delay time out with 8-year-old Kevin and his mother. The professional counselor first assesses Kevin's behavior and determines time out to be an appropriate intervention for his mother to use to reduce problematic behavior. Then the counselor works with Kevin's mother to teach and train her in the use of time out. During this session, the professional counselor first role-plays the time out procedure briefly with Kevin and then assists the mother as she does the same.

Counselor (C):   Okay, Mom, Kevin, what I'd like for us to do now is go through all the steps and specifics of the time out procedure with contingent delay. So, Mom, you can watch as I role-play, and we will keep it short, just long enough to give you and Kevin the general feel for it, and then I will ask you to do the same. Sound okay?

Mom (M):   Okay.

Kevin (K):   Yeah, all right.

C: Here we go then. "Kevin, it's time to turn off the television and come get dressed for bed." Now, Kevin, just for the sake of role-playing, it's okay not to follow through with my directions. Remember, Mom, he gets 5 seconds to comply. If he says no or chooses not to comply by the end of that time, you give a warning.

K: Okay, then . . . No! I ain't gonna!

C: "Kevin, you may choose to come get dressed for bed or go to time out. You decide." This way, Mom, you are letting Kevin make the choice—to either get dressed for bed or punish himself. It is *his* decision!

M: Yes, I like that it feels like it's of his own making.

K: (Sticks out his tongue at the counselor and crosses his arms)

C: Right, and again, he has 5 seconds. "Okay, Kevin. Go and sit in the time out chair until I say you can get up." (Kevin grumbles on his way to the chair but complies.) Remember, Mom, once he is in the chair, you should remind him of the seven rules of time out. Or you can post them on the wall at home in front of the chair as a reminder for him.

M: Yes, the seven rules.

C: "Kevin, remember to follow the seven rules of the time out chair: keep your feet on the floor, the chair legs on the floor, your hands stay in your lap, all of your bottom is on the chair, your back is against the back of the chair, do not make any sounds, and look at the wall in front of you with your eyes open. If you break a rule, 1 minute will be added to your stay in time out."

M: Is it okay if he breaks a rule now so I can see how you handle it?

C: Sure, Kevin, just so we can demonstrate for Mom, go ahead and break one of the time out rules just this once.

K: Okay. (Kevin begins swinging and tapping his feet loudly on the floor.)

C: (In a firm but calm voice) "I said to keep your feet on the floor. One minute has been added, Kevin." (Pauses for a few moments) Now, Mom, ordinarily Kevin would need to stay in the time out chair for the minimum 5 minutes plus any penalty minutes for violating any of the seven rules. And then you will conduct the interaction at the end of that time to be sure he is ready to comply with your original request. "Kevin, your time is up. Are you ready to turn off the TV and get ready for bed, or do you want to stay in time out? You decide."

K: I'll do it.

C: Okay, Kevin, we have completed our role play of time out. You did a very good job, and I appreciate your help.

K: Sure. Is that what it will be like?

C: Yes, but it will feel different when it is the real thing because you may be upset, probably won't like it, and you'll want to do other things instead of sit in the corner. Okay, Mom, your turn. Kevin, Mom is now going to practice with you.

Thus far, the professional counselor has assessed Kevin's problem behaviors, educated the mother about the contingent delay time out procedure, and modeled the procedure for Mom. It is only at this point that Mom tries it with Kevin, first through role play in the professional counselor's office and then under realistic circumstances at home.

K: I'll be in the chair.

M: Okay, why don't you come sit in the chair then? Can he do that?

C: That's okay. Now go over the seven rules of the time out chair.

M: "Now remember, feet on the floor, sit back, eyes on the wall, no talking, no sounds or anything for 5 minutes."

C: "Also, chair legs on the floor, hands in lap, and your entire bottom on the chair, Kevin." Once you feel he has gotten to know the rules, you won't have to repeat them each time. But it is fair that we teach him the rules so he knows why penalty minutes are added. And also, as I mentioned earlier, some parents have actually written the rules down and placed them on the wall in front of the chair so that they're up there in writing, kind of as your contract . . . So, Mom, how's he doing sitting for his 5 minutes?

M: He has his eyes closed.

C: Go ahead and attend to that.

M: "Kevin, keep your eyes open."

C: Remember that if he is violating one of the rules, then go ahead and put an extra minute on as a contingency.

M: "Your eyes are closed, Kevin, I'll have to add a minute, okay?"

C: One of the things that I notice in the way you give your directives, and I don't know if this is what you notice at home also, but I notice that when you give the directive, you seem to put it like it is a question. Don't ask it as a question. Don't add an "okay" at the end of it.

M: Okay. Ugg . . . there I go again.

C: It's not important that he agree with your directive, it's important that he do it. So that questioning tone at the end often leads to . . . leads Kevin to think . . . "Well, I might have a choice here." Or another thought it could lead to . . . it could lead to kind of thinking in response "No, actually, Mom, it's not okay." You asking "okay" can lead him to think he is allowed to actually disagree or even argue with you, and that is not okay. You want a directive to be a directive, so to help with that, it's a good idea to always take your voice down at the end of the statement as opposed to up.

M: Okay, that makes sense. I am bad about that. Gosh, if I could just improve that, it would probably help tremendously.

C: I agree with you. It will be interesting to see. So, he's been doing pretty good, and it looks like his time is up . . .

M: "Kevin, can you come here, please?"

C: (Modeling for Mom) "Kevin, come here please."

M: Right. "Kevin, come here, please. Now, you are going to go with me now and create no problems when you go to Grandma's, correct?" I can say "correct," right?

C: That's okay, or "Do you understand?" would work well also.

M: "Do you understand that you have to come with me when we go grocery shopping and behave? And no whining or complaining."

K: "I guess so."

C: I wouldn't accept "I guess so."

M: Okay.

C: I would accept "Yes" or "No."

M: What do you do then?

C: Well, I would say to him, at that point, I would say, "Kevin, I need for you to answer me yes or no. 'I guess so' is not an acceptable answer."

K: "No."

M: Hmm . . .

C: "You can either go shopping with me, or you can go and sit in the time out chair for another 5 minutes. You decide."

K: "I'll go with you."

M: Well, that was magical.

C: Not so much. The chair is serving as a deterrent. He would rather do what he was asked than go to time out. It is working already. Very nice, Mom! The chair is, at this point, not something that he wants. Okay. Mom, how do you feel about using this at home? Do you feel ready?

M: I believe so. I'm sure I'll have questions and challenges, though.

C: Good. We can handle those as they arise. And remember to continue to use the noncompliance chart I gave you last time we met, and continue to chart Kevin's behavior over this coming week, so that when we meet next, we can look at this chart together, and we will have a good idea of how well the time out is working.

Kevin and his mom return approximately one week later to evaluate the effectiveness of the time out procedure and discuss any areas that may need elaboration. Now that Mom has had the opportunity to use the method at home in real situations with Kevin, complete with his reactions and her emotions, there will surely be some questions or areas that need fine-tuning. It is imperative that the professional counselor be available for this type of consultation; all too often the reason time out procedures are not effective is because they are not implemented consistently or as intended. Below is a short excerpt from this session.

C: Alright, this is what I call a troubleshooting session so we can monitor changes in Kevin's behaviors and talk about how the time out has been going for you.

M: Well, I charted Kevin's behavior over the course of the last week and compared it to the week before. He has certainly improved, and we had fewer problems, but not as much as . . .

C: Not as much as you thought or would like?

M: Well, yes. And maybe it will just be this way . . .

C: You believe the time out method should be working better than it is?

M: I thought that it would, yes. I also find it more difficult to do than I thought I would.

C: Okay. Well, what we know is that time out is very effective for reducing noncompliant behaviors like those that Kevin displays. What we also know is that, when it is not as effective as it could be, it's usually simply a matter of tweaking a few things. So let me hear more about any specific difficulties you've had implementing it. You said it's harder than you thought it would be?

M: Yes . . . well, first let me start with what I don't find difficult and then I can tell you the other.

C: Good idea. Yes, let me hear the parts that are going well for you first.

M: I remember you stressing that it should be very boring and not stimulating . . . and I feel I do a good job of making certain that there is a big difference between when he's in time out and when he's not. Um, I mean, I make sure that as soon as he comes from time out and complies with my original request, I make sure that I praise him immediately for his appropriate behavior, and I make certain that there is no positive reinforcement while he is in time out.

C: Okay, great. Sounds like you really are intentional about that.

M: I try. And I also feel like I've been able to stress that he is making a choice to enter time out and therefore is choosing to punish himself, so I don't feel badly about it.

C: Very important, yes. Good.

M: What I seem to have trouble with, though, is not getting irritated while he's in time out and not following all of the rules.

C: So when Kevin doesn't sit still or quietly, you find your emotions getting involved.

M: Yes. And then I feel like we end up in this power struggle while he's in time out.

C: What do you mean? Tell me more.

M: Well, say he won't keep his feet on the floor and keep quiet. I'll remind him to, and then he doesn't, and then I tell him I'm going to have to add another minute, and he still doesn't follow the rule, and then I say, "Okay, that's another minute you've added, Kevin, for not keeping your feet still," and then he begins to argue with me and whine. Then I get more irritated and add another minute, and then I feel like I've added too many too quickly and so I try to explain it to him and it's just this cycle. I feel like time out lasts too long because of it, and it feels like too much work.

C: Yes, I think I understand. Well, what I see as the biggest issue here is that as long as you are engaging Kevin, and emotionally at that, time out isn't nearly as boring as it should or could be. In fact, Kevin is being entertained quite nicely. Some parents actually have this same trouble when using contingent delay time out, so know that you are in good company. I know it is so difficult to do, but it is very important that you do your very best to keep your dialogue with him to a minimum. Could you and Kevin demonstrate for me what a typical dialogue has been like for you this week during time out? Kevin?

K: Okay. Can this be the time out chair that I'm in now? It's plushy!

C: (Smiles) Sure.

M: Okay. So he's in time out, and it isn't long before he begins tapping his toes or squirming around, sometimes even closing his eyes on purpose.

C: Okay, Kevin, go ahead and do one of those things. (Kevin closes his eyes tightly with a grin on his face.)

M: Kevin, you should have your eyes open and on the wall. Kevin, open your eyes or I'll have to add a minute . . . okay, Kevin, you have another minute in time out now because you didn't open your eyes.

C: Okay, I see. And then Kevin might begin to argue or whine, you say? And then you try to explain?

M: Yes.

C: All right, thank you, Kevin. (Turning back to Mom) Again, let me say that what seems to be happening is that you are engaging him in conversation in a way that both is stimulating to him and leads him to believe he has choices while in time out. Let me offer you a few options to remedy this and see which one you might be most comfortable with.

M: All right.

C: If you'll recall from last week, when I modeled adding 1 minute, I simply stated, "I said to keep your feet on the floor. That's an extra minute, Kevin." Stating it very firmly and precisely like this does not encourage him to bargain or negotiate back. It also does not issue a warning, as I heard you do. There are no warnings while in time out. A warning is used

before going to time out, but once he is there, he knows the seven rules and there is no need for a warning. If he breaks a rule, he gets an extra minute added to his time. If he breaks another rule, he gets yet another minute added.

M: Would it be okay if I talked even less than you just did and simply state that he has a minute added?

C: Why do you ask?

M: Well, because he probably already knows why the 1 minute was added because, like you said, he knows what the rules are.

C: That may be true. And if he is confused about why, this can be discussed when he is released from time out. Well, because it is difficult for you to refrain from a full-blown conversation with Kevin while he is in time out, thus reducing its effectiveness, perhaps another suggestion will be helpful. One way to bypass any talking whatsoever while Kevin is in time out, which could make a very big difference for both of you, is to simply use an egg timer or some other timing device that Kevin can clearly see. When he breaks a time out rule, you simply, without saying a word, add 1 minute to the timer. He sees this, and he knows what has happened and why. The other option is called a finger method. All this means is that each time a rule is broken during time out, you simply, and again without saying a word, hold up a finger to let him know 1 minute has been added to his time. This way, there is no conversation, no explanation, and no warning while in time out.

M: Okay. I like the idea of just holding up one finger each time a minute is added.

C: I believe this will also help prevent any power struggles and will reduce your feelings of frustration. Why don't we role-play this one more time?

Kevin and his mom once again return in two weeks for the professional counselor to assess their progress and offer any additional assistance that may be needed.

C: It's been about two weeks since I saw you last, and we sent you home with the time out procedure, but this time having tweaked it a bit to make it easier on you, Mom, and more effective for Kevin. How did that go?

M: Kevin, do you want to tell or do you want me to talk first?

K: I've been good!

M: He has been.

C: Tell me what "good" means, Kevin.

K: I only went to time out two times!

C: In two weeks? You've only been in time out two times in the last two weeks? You're kidding me. You went twice in two weeks? Really?

M: It's incredible. It was incredible.

C: Tell me about it.

M: Well, the first thing is that it is no longer this emotional battle with us. I give a directive, and he has a choice to follow through with it or not. Once in time out, he follows the rules. If he does not, I hold up one finger to show him that I have added one minute because he has broken a rule. I'm not upset. He understands the procedure. And when his time is up, it's like everything is back to normal, and he then complies with the original request. You can really tell that he wants to avoid being in time out now. It really is boring for him, and he prefers to just comply.

C: So it's kind of become this deterrent that we talked about?

M: Yes. The only two times we've used it, in both cases he was extremely tired and there was a lot going on. He was more irritable than anything, and he is more stubborn and defiant when he's irritable and tired. But you know, we used it and it worked.

C: So, Kevin, you would say that time out is something that you would not want to do? Tell me, specifically, what's not so good about it that you want to stay away from time out.

K: You have to sit still, and then when it's over you still have to do whatever it was she asks you to do in the first place.

C: Kevin, do you feel proud of yourself for behaving so well these past two weeks?

K: It's been a lot more fun not being in trouble so much.

M: Things have been running so much more smoothly, and it is just much more peaceful than before. I've got to say, too, that as a parent, it feels nice to feel in control.

USEFULNESS AND EVALUATION OF THE TIME OUT TECHNIQUE

Time out has been used to reduce a variety of behaviors including tantrums, thumb sucking, and aggression. Historically, time out also has been used with a number of different populations, including children with intellectual disabilities who had disruptive behaviors (Foxx & Shapiro, 1978), children in special education classrooms (Cuenin & Harris, 1986), adults with intellectual disabilities who had undesirable behavior during meals (Spindler Barton, Guess, Garcia, & Baer, 1970) or were self-injurious and aggressive (Matson & Keyes, 1990), children with attention-deficit/hyperactivity disorder (ADHD; Reid, 1999), children who are noncompliant (Erford, 1999; Reitman & Drabman, 1999), and children who are violent and aggressive (Sherburne, Utley, McConnell, & Gannon, 1988). In schools, time out has been employed successfully with a variety of child behavior problems across multiple educational settings. Although certainly used in regular education programming, its application in special education settings is equally beneficial (Ryan, Peterson, & Rozalski, 2007). Time out also has been implemented as a smaller element of larger parent-training programs. These programs, often referred to as parent management training, allow parents to progress from less intrusive interventions to more restrictive ones (Kazdin, 2008).

Several factors influence the efficacy of this technique. Many of the factors that contribute toward the success of this technique fall to the person implementing the time out procedures. In addition, Erford (1999) discerned that nearly all children dislike being bored and will go to great lengths to avoid this deterrent. Thus, the time out environment needs to be devoid of visual and auditory stimulation so that the child is not receiving any sort of positive reinforcement for being sent to time out. Donaldson, Vollmer, Yakich, and Van Camp (2013) recommended reducing the time-out punishment interval for compliance with verbal instructions to go to time out and, in a sample of six pre-school students, found this strategy to further reduce problem behavior.

A significant amount of empirical research lends support to the effectiveness of time out for children with self-control issues. One researcher found that using time out as part of a treatment plan for students with emotional disturbances positively affected the students' behaviors and work efforts (Ruth, 1994). Barton, Brulle, and Repp (1987) found time out effective in helping students with intellectual disabilities to develop more self-control. Another study found time out to be effective in reducing the amount of inappropriate, noncompliant behavior of a 4-year-old child (Olmi, Sevier, & Nastasi, 1997). Time out also has been used effectively in reducing the amount of aggression between siblings (Olson & Roberts, 1987). Because time out assists children in emotional regulation by allowing the child a chance to calm down and to learn to manage difficult and frustrating situations, not only does the child's behavior improve, but so does the parent–child relationship (Kazdin, 2008). Therefore, time out has become an effective parental discipline practice (Morawska & Sanders, 2010). Tingstrom (1990) investigated behaviors for which teachers found time out procedures useful and discovered that time out was more acceptable for severe problem behaviors. To increase the usefulness of time out, Erford (1999) suggested using time out in combination with positive reinforcement to teach children desirable behaviors.

Stary, Hupp, Jewell, and Everett (2016) surveyed parents and determined that time out (60%) was a less popular intervention than response cost (71%) and positive reinforcement (73%), but it was more popular than spanking (18%). In spite of its effectiveness, parents often rate time out as less useful than other child disciplinary techniques, perhaps due to actual implementation variations. Drayton et al. (2017) asked 55 mothers to analyze time out procedures and found that their conceptions of time out often differed markedly from empirically defined and effective time out procedures. One of the major problems of the time out technique is that it is often misused (Betz, 1994). Betz suggested using time out for serious matters and as a last resort. Others who do not support time out criticized that "it is not an appropriate way to deal with misbehavior . . . it may create subsequent childhood problems that can affect a child's well-being and severely strain the parent–child relationship" (Haimann, 2005, p. 1). When using time out appears to be ineffective, the implementer should check to make sure the placement of the time out chair or space is not more interesting than the environment from which the child was removed. If it is, some children may act out to be sent to time out (Bacon, 1990).

Time out is often unsuccessful for low-functioning children with autism spectrum disorder, who, by definition, do not mind reduced social contact. Factors that decrease the likelihood that time out will be effective include overusing it for every rule broken, postponing the time out, not following through, and yelling at the child. It is important for those implementing time out to be realistic and to remember that this technique is not a cure-all. It is most effective when it is not used frequently (Spencer, 2000). Time out is meant to serve as a deterrent to future misbehavior.

When using time out, it is important to know that there could be legal and ethical implications. Yell (1994, p. 295) provided the following guidelines for use by those in schools who choose to employ this technique: Be aware of local or state policies regarding time out; have written procedures on the use of time out; obtain permission prior to using time out; involve the individualized educational plan (IEP) team in making decisions concerning the behavior reduction procedures, such as time out, with children in special education services; ensure that time out serves a legitimate educational function and that it is used in a reasonable manner; and keep thorough records.

APPLICATION OF THE TIME OUT TECHNIQUE

Now apply the time out technique to a current client or student you are working with or revisit the brief case studies presented at the beginning of this book. How can you use the time out technique to address concerns and create movement in the counseling session?

CHAPTER 41

Response Cost

ORIGINS OF THE RESPONSE COST TECHNIQUE

Response cost is a method of operant conditioning based on punishment principles and involves removing a positive stimulus in order to decrease a specific behavior (Henington & Doggett, 2016). Response cost, also called cost contingency, is the basis for fines, traffic tickets, and yardage penalties in football. Response cost often takes the form of a point or token system where the individual loses points or tokens for performing some undesired behavior. A child earns points for exhibiting specific positive behaviors and loses points for exhibiting negative behaviors. At a predetermined time, the child can redeem his or her points for rewards (Curtis, Pisecco, Hamilton, & Moore, 2006). Response cost may be externally or internally managed. In externally managed programs, teachers, parents, or some other trained individual is responsible for removing the positive stimulus. In self-managed programs, the individual is responsible for removing the stimulus.

Response cost can be extremely effective in reducing unwanted behaviors, especially when used in combination with praise, a point (token) system, and time out as a backup procedure. Response cost can be used at home, in the classroom, or on the playground and is easy to implement (Keeney, Fisher, Adelinis, & Wilder, 2000). Borrego and Pemberton (2007) found that response cost was the most popular and acceptable behavior management strategy among surveyed parents from among the list of six commonly used behavior management techniques in U.S. society. Response cost can be monitored by a single person and requires little extra time or money.

HOW TO IMPLEMENT THE RESPONSE COST TECHNIQUE

Response cost is typically used with school-age students. Before implementing response cost, three important steps must be completed. First, identify the specific behaviors that will be targeted and try to focus only on one or two behaviors at a time. Next, decide what the penalty or cost will be for each of the above-mentioned behaviors. If possible, costs should be natural or logical consequences, although tokens are frequently used to represent chances or reminders. Sometimes clients may be able to help determine the costs. Third, inform the client of the costs before beginning the program. Reminder lists or behavior contracts may be used.

VARIATIONS OF THE RESPONSE COST TECHNIQUE

A response cost program can be constructed in many ways. The important component is that the individual is losing a specified positive stimulus for performing the behavior targeted for extinction. To begin, a baseline count of the target behavior should be observed. The professional counselor should then decide whether the individual will start with a set number of points at the beginning of the day, tokens will be earned through a positive reinforcement procedure, or the system will rely on some other form of stimulus removal, such as minutes taken off recess time. Next, implement the response cost program by removing the stimulus, whatever it may be, every time the individual performs the target behavior. Finally, a reward should be built in at the end of the time period, day, or week if the program is based on a point or token system. If the client has any tokens left at the end of the time period, the reward is given; if all of the tokens have been removed, the reward is not given.

Several guidelines help make the response cost program more effective (Walker, Colvin, & Ramsey, 1995). Response cost systems should be linked to a reinforcement system in order to strengthen desired behaviors. The individual's positive behavior should be praised frequently. Also, the response cost must be employed immediately after the target behavior occurs, every time it occurs. Individuals should not be able to accumulate negative points, and the ratio of points earned to those lost should be controlled.

The number of remaining tokens should be monitored. After 3 to 5 consecutive days of the client receiving the reward, the criterion can be lowered. For example, if 15 tokens per day comprise the beginning level, and the client has 5 tokens left on day 1, 7 on day 2, and 8 on day 3, the professional counselor should begin the next day by presenting the client with only 6 or 7 tokens. The process repeats in this manner until only 1 token remains. This represents a modified fading procedure and serves as an outcome measure to determine the effectiveness of the response cost procedure. Once the client goes 1 week without losing the sole token (i.e., no display of the inappropriate target behavior), the system is ended.

EXAMPLE OF THE RESPONSE COST TECHNIQUE

Nine-year-old Samantha has already made much improvement in her behavior with the help of her parents and professional counselor. Thus far, Samantha's mother and father have incorporated a strong and consistent system of positive reinforcement through praise and rewards for behaviors such as making the bed, completing homework, and displaying good table manners. They have also successfully implemented the use of contingent delay time out as a punishment technique for Samantha's inappropriate behaviors, usually related to refusal to follow Mom or Dad's directives and rules. During the following session, Samantha and her parents discuss a behavior that does not seem as easily suited to either of the behavior modification plans already in place.

Counselor (C): So when you called to set up the appointment, Mom, you said there was a specific behavior that Samantha was displaying that you really wanted to work on with her, but that it didn't really fit well with time out or positive reinforcement.

Mom (M): Yes. And I just knew you'd have a suggestion for us. I hope you do.

C: I bet we can come up with something helpful if we put our heads together!

M: I was hoping you would say that! So, Samantha has done really well. I just want to start with that. But there is this little issue of . . . whining . . . that's really hard to overlook.

C: Ahh . . . the whining . . . yes, whining is hard to overlook. And we shouldn't necessarily overlook it. Whining doesn't go over well in life inside or outside the home, so I agree that it is important to attend to it or we wouldn't be doing young Samantha here any favors.

Samantha (S): And the screaming.

M: You don't really scream like you whine. You're not a real screamer, screamer.

S: (In a whining voice) But I want to work on the screaming. (Smiles.)

M: See what I mean?

C: I do, I do. Yep, that's whining. Dad? What about you? Is the whining a difficulty that you'd like to have her work on?

S: Yeah, ask Dad.

C: Dad?

Dad (D): I would say whining or talking back.

C: Okay. Now we can treat those as one, but it's often better if we, or better to—

M: Separate.

C: Separate them, yes. It's probably best to just start simple, work on one behavior at a time, the one you're most interested in. So, Mom, Dad, the whining or the talking back?

D: Is the whining really more of a response to requests, or is it whining in general? I mean I'm trying to figure it out.

M: To requests. She whines when we make requests . . . yeah.

D: It's a reaction to requests. So that makes it a form of talking back, right?

C: Now you can choose to specify only when she's given a directive or a request is made of her. You can say that is specifically what we will work on and that is the definition of the behavior we want to eliminate. But what that does is it limits you to only use this new behavior modification plan when she whines in response to a request, making all other whining fair game . . . and I don't know that you want that. It might be more effective and less confusing for us to include whining in general, any whining, whining that is in response to a request or any other form of whining. What do you think?

M: Why specify it to just whining about requests? As soon as she whines for some other reason, we'll wish we had defined it more globally.

C: Dad? Don't feel pressured to agree. Give us your thoughts on this.

D: I'm sorting it out in my mind and trying to think back on specific examples with Samantha . . . it seems that all talking back is whining, but not all whining is talking back, so, yeah, I'm on board. Whining in general is the way to go.

C: Okay, whining in general then! Now, the next very important thing we must do is to define what we mean by whining. Of course, it seems obvious in some ways, but it is important to specify it out loud because what we don't want is for you, Mom, to have one definition of whining in your mind and Dad to have another image and Samantha to have yet another. We want everyone to be on the same page with their idea of what constitutes whining.

M: Right.

C: So what we'll do right now is just have Mom give us an example of what Samantha sounds like whenever she whines. Now pay close attention to this everyone. All right, let's hear it, Mom.

M: Okay. I might say, "Samantha, we're all going on a trip" . . . just for an example. "You're going to go with us; we're going to take a trip." And she would immediately start with (in a great Samantha whining imitation) "I don't wanna go, I'm not gonna go, I don't wanna, I don't want you to take meeeeee!" Her facial expressions change, her voice changes, even the way she is standing or sitting . . . it's an all-out production.

D: (Laughing) You did pretty well there. You even got the little high-pitch thing right.

C: That really was pretty good, Mom. And Dad, based on your comment, I assume that was a good example of how you define the whining also?

D: Definitely.

C: Okay, then, Samantha? I'd like you to demonstrate responding to Mom's request to go on a trip in a way that defines whining for you. I want to hear you whining, Samantha.

S: That's easy. "*Mom!* But, but, but, I don't wanna go on a trip . . . I don't like trips . . . (Pokes lip out, slumps over, even fakes a crying sound)

C: Wow. Mom was right on the facial expressions and body language changing too. (Mom is nodding her head in agreement.) Okay. Now then, Samantha, I would like to hear you give me an example of a response to your mom, still protesting the trip but without whining.

S: I don't know how to do that.

C: Um . . okay . . . well, how about you pretend you are me. Act as if you are Dr. Erford. Pretend you are me when you respond to Mom saying you are all going on a trip. If you were all grown up, how might you sound?

S: (Giggles. Sits straight up in her chair and places her hands in her lap. Giggles again. Clears throat.) "I prefer for you to take the trip without me. I prefer not to go. I have homework, I mean, a book to write . . . " (Samantha smiles broadly at Dr. Erford.)

D: Cute, Samantha. Now could you do that all the time?

C: That tells me, Samantha, that you do have a clear idea of what whining is and what whining is not . . . and that you know after all how to respond to Mom and Dad's requests without whining.

S: Oops. Busted!

C: Okay, so it seems we all agree that whining involves a pleading, pouting type of dialogue with a different tone of voice than regular conversation. The words also get drawn out when whining. Everybody have a clear definition of what is and is not whining?

M: You know, Samantha, if you would actually respond like you did just now to our requests, we might actually talk about it.

D: Or if you had an alternative suggestion, and you approached it in a less childish way, instead of whining about it . . .

S: (Takes a deep breath, groans, and bounces the back of her head against the back of her chair) I am, I'm not, I will, I won't, I do, I don't . . .

C: Okay, Samantha, are you understanding this? You just demonstrated that you do understand when you were able to respond to Mom in a responsible and respectful way and then the other way with the little whining, immature way.

S: (Making whining noises)

C: Exactly. Thank you for making my point. (Samantha and Dr. Erford exchange smiles.) So, what we're trying to do is to get you from being disrespectful and whiny to being more respectful and mature.

The professional counselor has now assisted Samantha's parents in selecting one specific behavior to target. They have also worked together to define this behavior in a very specific fashion that everyone agrees on.

C: We are all in agreement that whining is the focus, and we all agree on what whining is and is not. The method I want to talk to you about today, that I believe will be very appropriate

for eliminating the whining, is response cost, and response cost is simply the opposite of positive reinforcement. As you know, positive reinforcement is giving a positive reward when you get a specific good or appropriate behavior from Samantha. Now, the good news is I am going to provide you with the information and tools you will need to begin using the response cost method. You will leave here today with a plan to implement; however, before beginning, you will first need to document her episodes of whining for a few days. This is very important for reasons I will explain in a few moments.

M: You mean document her whining like we have when we charted other behavior in the past?

C: I mean exactly that. You will want to mainly get a frequency count of how many episodes of whining there are a day and at what times they are occurring.

M: We can't just say infinity, and go from there? Okay, okay. Got it.

C: All right. So, let's see . . . where to start. Okay, so response cost is akin to the teacher who, on the first day of class, tells students "You all start out with an A+ in my class. Now you have to work to keep it."

S: I like that teacher!

C: Exactly. This is very motivating for students. It makes them feel good to have such a positive start, and this motivates them to work extra hard to keep that average as high as possible.

M: So I start Samantha with an A+.

C: Well, not exactly. But it's a similar idea. Let's say after you keep a tally of Samantha's whining episodes for a couple of days, you discover that on average, she has about . . . well, off the top of your head, Mom and Dad, how many episodes would you say she has a day?

D: Twenty!

S: Do not!

M: Around three to five.

D: Yeah, okay, probably more like around five. It just seems like more. (Samantha lightly punches Dad in the arm and smiles.)

C: Okay, so we'll know for sure after you write it down for a few days, but let's just assume for now that it is around three to five. Okay then. The response cost system means that instead of giving a positive for a positive, or giving a negative for a negative, you take away a positive for every time there is a negative. Now the negative is going to be the whining. Every time there is a whining episode, a positive will be taken away. Now, just for now, let's call the positive a marker. We'll decide what that will be specifically in a moment. But for now, the markers are the positive that you will be taking away each time Samantha whines. Make sense so far?

M: I'm with you.

C: Dad?

D: I'm good.

C: Okay. Now the reason determining the average number of whining episodes is important prior to implementing response cost is because you sort of want to rig the system in favor of Samantha in the beginning so that Samantha has a good chance of being successful. You also do not want to have more negative occurrences than you have markers or a child will have no incentive to refrain from the negative behavior and will give up, perhaps even get worse. Makes sense, right? Oh, and one other thing, you do not want to have too many markers left over each day either, because the feeling of really having to work hard to earn that reward will lessen and she may not try as hard. I mean, if it's too easy to get, then what's the big deal, right? You want there to be a good fit between markers and occurrences throughout the process.

M: Throughout the process?

C: Yes, you'll actually decrease the number of markers she begins with every few days as her behavior improves. So if she goes, oh, say, three to five days without losing all her markers, you'll want to decrease the number of markers accordingly.

M: Oh, okay.

C: Okay, so assuming Samantha has an average of three to five episodes of whining a day, you'll want to begin your first day of response cost with, oh, say, four markers. That morning, remind Samantha that she has four markers and that the fewer whining episodes she has throughout the day, the more markers she'll get to keep for herself at the end of the evening. So her goal, her incentive for the day, is to retain as many markers as possible. So she starts with this clean slate each morning, but each time she whines, she loses a marker. You simply remove one of the markers.

M: And we'll decide what those are in a bit?

C: Yep. Or now if you'd like. We can . . .

M: I've actually been thinking about it and already have an idea. But first, could you give us a few examples of what others usually use as markers?

C: Certainly. Markers can themselves be rewards, or they can stand for a reward. What I mean is that you can use quarters, for example. And you might start the day off with, what did we say? Oh, yes, four . . . let's just say four to make the point. And say Samantha had three episodes of whining that day, so that by the end of the day, she has one quarter left over. The quarters themselves are the prize or reward, and the incentive is to whine less to keep more quarters. Some parents use a snack or candy item, like jelly beans or sticks of gum. Either way, in these examples, the marker is, in and of itself, a prize. The other way you can go about it is to use markers that are representative of some other prize . . . like a token economy. You could use pennies, or tokens, or popsicle sticks . . . and these items don't hold much value to Samantha by themselves, but we decide what X number of tokens means, and we build that reward into the system. Am I making sense?

D: It always sounds a little complicated at first, and then it seems perfectly sensible.

M: It's making sense to me.

C: Alright. So, Mom, you said you had an idea for a marker?

M: Yes. I was thinking about stickers.

C: Oh, yes, stickers could make very appropriate markers. It's important that markers are both safe to use and impossible for Samantha to reproduce or counterfeit, and I believe stickers meet both of these standards.

M: Well, Samantha does keep a sticker collection, so we could use them as the rewards themselves, like in the first example you gave. Only, they would need to be the really nice stickers that she enjoys collecting, not just stars or smiley face stickers.

C: Alright.

M: Or they could just be the little star stickers, and we could use them as tokens for a reward. (Pauses and is thinking) Samantha, do you have a preference?

S: Sometimes you don't get the stickers I like.

M: That's true. I can just hear it now . . . her whining that the stickers I have for the reward are not the good ones. Yes, let's use simple stickers as tokens. I could even set up a chart for her to put them on at the end of each day, and she can trade that sheet in for a reward when she has enough. Isn't that how it works?

C: Exactly. So let's talk about the reward we want to build in.

D: I prefer not having to buy something every time she turns in a full sticker sheet.

M: I agree.

C: What about activities or special privileges?

M: Yes, that could work! We could make a list to choose from, like, maybe a picnic in the park, or a slumber party, or a popcorn and movie rental of your choice. What do you think, Samantha?

S: (Excitedly) Yeah! And a spa night!

C: What's a spa night?

S: It's when me and Mom do our toenails and fingernails, and we give each other facials and stuff. It's my favorite!

C: These all sound wonderful, and Samantha looks motivated to stop whining already . . . and that is the most important point . . . that the positive reinforcer that is being taken away each time she whines is something she values and wants to work hard to keep. So you'll make an official activity list, and each time Samantha collects a certain number of stickers on her sticker sheet, she can trade it in for an activity.

M: I think we're set!

C: One more important component of response cost that I want us to cover is the specifics of taking away the token or sticker. Earlier I said to remind Samantha each morning "Samantha, remember you start today with four new stickers, and each time you whine, you lose a sticker. I want you to work very hard today to keep as many of them as you can!" And so whenever you hear her voice do the whining thing, you would immediately remove a sticker and say "Samantha, you just violated the whining rule. You just lost one of your stickers. You have three left," and you take a sticker off the sheet and place it back with your supply. Remember to keep this brief, without emotion, and without a discussion. Continue to chart her whining episodes and how many stickers she has left over each day, and remember that as she becomes successful in keeping more and more stickers, the trick then is to calibrate the system back down. So then the next time she only gets four of them, and the next time she only gets three of them, until eventually she only gets one sticker a day, which means she only has one shot at the misbehavior. Once you have an entire week without losing that one and only sticker each day, meaning no whining episodes have occurred for an entire week, the system can end. Then you can use it with another behavior if you'd like, and you would start from the beginning, with first charting and defining the behavior specifically. Remember, though, to rig it for success in the beginning. A lot of people make the mistake with behavior modification of making the system so difficult that, from the very beginning, the person doesn't experience the success, never gets the rewards, so he or she thinks that it's hopeless. That person is thinking "Why should I even try because I'm never going to get it anyway?" So, if you think even five episodes or fewer of whining is going to be impossible for her, then just do five times in the morning, between the time that she gets up and the time that she has lunch, and if she's good there, then you have another five in the afternoon. And then a few days later just make it four until eventually she's able to be successful without even having to have the system because the goal of any behavior modification is not to need it. We all want people to be successful every day with just the minimum amount of supervision. We want them to see that they can behave appropriately without intervention and to have that personal responsibility for themselves eventually. That's the goal.

USEFULNESS AND EVALUATION OF THE RESPONSE COST TECHNIQUE

The response cost technique has been used successfully for decades to manage individual, small-group, and classroom behavior. Proctor and Morgan (1991) studied the use of a response cost raffle on the disruptive behavior of adolescents. Students were given five tickets at the beginning of class, and the students lost tickets for displays of disruptive behavior. All tickets remaining at the end of class were placed in a raffle for a prize. This procedure was effective in increasing appropriate behaviors and decreasing disruptive behaviors. Salend and Allen (1985) found that externally managed and self-managed response cost systems were equally effective in reducing the inappropriate classroom behavior of learning disabled students. Both response cost programs greatly reduced the number of out-of-seat behaviors and inappropriate verbalizations from the students.

Response cost has also been used with children with hyperactive and antisocial behaviors. Carlson, Mann, and Alexander (2000) tested the effectiveness of rewards and response cost on the arithmetic performance of children with attention-deficit/hyperactivity disorder (ADHD). Although they found that children with ADHD completed fewer problems correctly than control children regardless of whether they were in the reward, response cost, or control condition, they also observed that response cost was more effective than reward in improving the performance of children with ADHD. Walker et al. (1995) compared the effectiveness of praise, token reinforcement, and response cost in reducing aggression among antisocial elementary school boys. Neither praise alone nor praise combined with token reinforcement was able to control negative-aggressive behavior or increase positive social interactions among these boys. However, once negative-aggressive behavior was countered with a response cost procedure, the boys' social interactive behavior began to increase substantially.

Response cost has been used with persons with intellectual disabilities. Keeney et al. (2000) studied the effects of a response cost procedure on the aggressive outbursts of an adult woman with an intellectual disability; they compared noncontingent reinforcement, removal of attention, and removal of music against baseline behaviors. They found that the response cost removal of music was extremely effective in reducing the destructive behavior.

Stary, Hupp, Jewell, and Everett (2016) surveyed parents and determined that response cost (71%) was as popular as positive reinforcement (73%), but more popular than time out (60%) and spanking (18%). Partly, this may be due to the prominent use of a single "go-to" approach to discipline. It is a good idea for parents to use several disciplinary techniques, and better yet to use them in combination. I often combine response cost with token economy to extinguish the undesirable behavior (with response cost) while reinforcing the incompatible positive behavior (with a token economy or some other technique based on positive reinforcement). Fiksdal (2017) combined response cost with token economy to reduce classroom-based disruptive behavior and found that both were highly effective on their own, whereas a synergistic effect of combining the two approaches may hold an advantage over either approach alone. In addition, Jowett Hirst, Dozier, and Payne (2016) compared response cost to differential reinforcement procedures and found both to be equally effective in both group and individualized settings. Thus, it is not an either/or. When using a technique based on punishment, it is best practice to couple the punishment with a technique based on positive reinforcement.

APPLICATION OF THE RESPONSE COST TECHNIQUE

Now apply the response cost technique to a current client or student you are working with or revisit the brief case studies presented at the beginning of this book. How can you use the response cost technique to address concerns and create movement in the counseling session?

CHAPTER 42

Overcorrection

ORIGINS OF THE OVERCORRECTION TECHNIQUE

Overcorrection was originally developed by Foxx and Azrin (1972) in the early 1970s as a technique to eliminate maladaptive behaviors while also reeducating the individual; thus, much of the classic literature on the technique and outcome research is quite old. Overcorrection involves two components: restitution and positive practice. Restitution requires the individual to restore the situation that was disrupted to the same or an even better condition than existed previously, and positive practice entails repeated practice of an appropriate behavior for that same situation (Henington & Doggett, 2016). For example, if a child slams a door, the parent may be encouraged to have the child apologize and then practice silently opening and closing the door while entering and exiting ten times or for a specified period of time such as 5 minutes. Such repeated positive practice has the effect of making the punishment "worse than the crime" and leads frequently to one-trial learning, in which the person remembers never to slam the door again.

Overcorrection is a form of punishment, but it does not follow a single theory; rather, it incorporates aspects of many different techniques, including feedback, time out, compliance training, extinction, and punishment (Henington & Doggett, 2016). Unlike other forms of punishment, however, overcorrection is not arbitrary; instead, it teaches individuals to take responsibility for their actions and recognize the impact their actions have on others. Restitution is designed to teach natural consequences of misbehavior, and positive practice teaches appropriate behavior, thus acting as a preventive measure.

HOW TO IMPLEMENT THE OVERCORRECTION TECHNIQUE

Before using overcorrection, positive reinforcement methods should be tried in an attempt to shape the individual's behavior. If positive reinforcement is unsuccessful, however, overcorrection may be implemented. There are four steps to using overcorrection. First, the professional counselor must identify the target behavior as well as the alternate behavior to be taught through positive practice. When the target behavior is performed, the professional counselor should immediately tell the client that the behavior is inappropriate and should instruct the client to stop. Then the professional counselor should verbally guide the client through the overcorrection procedure, instructing the client to complete restitution and then to undergo positive practice for a set time or number of repetitions. If necessary, the professional counselor may manually guide the client through the overcorrection procedure using the minimum force necessary. Finally, the individual is allowed to return to her previous activity.

In their classic study, Foxx and Azrin (1972) made several recommendations for the effective use of overcorrection. Restitution should be directly related to the misbehavior. In addition, restitution should be performed immediately after the misbehavior in order to achieve two outcomes. First, the misbehavior should eventually reach extinction because the client will have no time to enjoy the effects of the misbehavior. Second, future acts of misbehavior should be discouraged because immediate negative consequences are more effective than nonimmediate consequences. Also, restitution should be extended in duration. Finally, the individual should be actively involved in performing restitution and should not pause during the restitution process.

VARIATIONS OF THE OVERCORRECTION TECHNIQUE

Foxx and Azrin's (1972) recommendations are not set in stone; later research suggested that successful overcorrection results may be achieved without following some of their recommendations. Overcorrection has been accomplished even when the overcorrection behaviors are unrelated to the target misbehavior. Similar results can be achieved with immediate and delayed positive practice overcorrection. In addition, overcorrection has been successful in short, intermediate, and long durations.

Although most overcorrection procedures involved both restitution and positive practice, some research suggests that these two procedures are effective when used alone, and it may not be necessary to use both (Matson, Horne, Ollendick, & Ollendick, 1979). In a study of school-age children, Matson et al. found that restitution reduced target behavior by 89%, and positive practice reduced these behaviors by 84%, suggesting that the two procedures are equally effective in treating childhood classroom misbehaviors. Indeed, some situations may involve a simple apology, although one can never really be sure that an apology is heartfelt restitution leading to positive behavior change. In such instances, the repeated positive practice becomes the active intervention.

EXAMPLE OF THE OVERCORRECTION TECHNIQUE

Ken is an 8-year-old boy consistently displaying moderate oppositional behavior toward his parents. This session was attended by Ken, his mother, and his father with the goal of decreasing noncompliant episodes and increasing his compliance with parental requests. One request Ken consistently chooses not to comply with is to clean up after himself: his coat, shoes, clothing, school books, dishes, and so on. As his father stated at the outset of counseling,

"Ken has taken the 'Stop, Drop, and Roll' technique to heart—he *never* cleans up after himself!" Note also that this example uses positive practice without restitution, although a suggestion for restitution is made at the end of this example.

Counselor (C):   This procedure is called overcorrection, which is the one that will help to get Ken to stop leaving his towel lying on the floor, his coat, shoes, and everything else as he comes into the house, strips down, and goes on his merry way. Sometimes we call it positive practice because it is a punishment procedure, and positive practice sounds so much nicer than talking about punishment. Overcorrection has him do what he should have done the first time but repeating it a great number of times so that, in the future, he realizes before it happens that he was punished for not just doing it the first time. So basically I use, under most circumstances, the 10 practices rule. If he comes in and drops his coat, then what he needs to do is go over, pick up his coat, put it on the hanger, and hang it in the closet. That's one practice. Then he takes it out, throws it on the floor, replaces the hanger, and starts over. You have him do that 10 times. Okay? So, what can we do in here today to practice? Of course, you've got your shoes with you, and that has been a problem in the past. (Parents nod yes, Ken nods no.) So, Ken, take your shoes off . . .

Ken (K):   My socks too?

C: Those are cute little socks.

K: They're too small.

C: Leave the socks on this time. All right, now where are you supposed to put your shoes whenever you come into the house?

K: In the shoe basket, which I *always* do. (Ken gives a big smile and a chuckle. Mom and Dad both grunt and roll their eyes at each other.)

C: Okay, so you're pretty good about putting your shoes in the shoe basket when you enter the house, but let's pretend that you're not (everyone laughs) so that Mom and Dad can practice the overcorrection procedure. So you're supposed to come in the house, take your shoes off, and put them . . .

K: The shoe thing. In the basket.

C: The shoe basket. Now let's pretend that you just came home and you tossed your shoes off to the side. (Ken does this with some flair.) Mom, you role-play with Ken about what it is that he should do.

Mom (M):   Ken, you didn't put your shoes away where they belong the first time, so you have to practice doing it the right way 10 times. So please go put your shoes back where they belong 10 times.

C: Okay. Now you have to pick them up and put them back on your feet . . . (Ken does this as the counselor directs his actions.) . . . tie them . . . take them back off . . . and put them in the basket. That's one.

M: Okay. Let's do the second practice—put them back on.

K: 10 times?!

M: Yeah.

K: Arrghhhh! (Ken begins again.)

C: Yep, practicing is hard; makes you realize that it is just easier to do it right the first time. (To parents) As we've already discussed, that's what a deterrent is.

M: (Mom encourages.) That's a good one, Ken.

C: Now I usually have them count while they're doing it. Now, how many times is that?

K: Five.

M: No, it's two.

K: Okay, two. (Ken continues to do 10 practices.)

C: Very good. Now you can see how this can be kind of annoying to a young lad.

M: (Ken finishes his final practice.) Okay, that's 10.

K: That was hard—and boring!

Father (F):   It can't be that hard, Ken. I've seen you play outside a lot harder than that.

C: Beautiful, okay. Now, Ken, how does that make you feel whenever you have to do that 10 times?

K: Tired.

C: Is it something you would like to repeat?

K: No way! It would take me all day!

C: Now this can be used with just about any kind of annoying behavior that he does that involves an action or behavior that he did not perform correctly but could and should, particularly one that involves responsible behavior, any kind of clothing. You know . . . if he leaves a towel on the floor, dropping the coat, slamming the door. It has a very powerful effect on kids, sometimes even what we call one-trial learning—that is, he does it the first time, and he remembers from then on whenever he comes into the house where his shoes are supposed to go.

F: If you want some exercise, you can drop your clothes on the floor, then pick them up and put your clothes down the laundry chute and fetch them from the basement 10 times. That would be real exercise!

K: (Ken offers his patented "death stare.")

Note that restitution was not used in this example, but if it were, an appropriate additional behavior would have been required to return the environment to a condition as good as or better than before the infraction. For example, for restitution, Kevin could have been asked to clean up the floor in the area in which his shoes were hurled, or take the basket outside, remove the shoes, clean out the basket, replace the shoes, and return the basket to its place.

USEFULNESS AND EVALUATION OF THE OVERCORRECTION TECHNIQUE

Overcorrection has been around for many decades and the related outcome literature is dated. Overcorrection began as a procedure used to help persons with intellectual disabilities reduce property destruction, physical attacks, and self-stimulating behaviors, as well as to teach toileting and correct eating behaviors (Axelrod, Brantner, & Meddock, 1978), and there is extensive research attesting to the success of overcorrection procedures in this regard. For instance, Foxx and Azrin (1972) found that restitution training was effective in eliminating disruptive-aggressive behaviors, such as throwing objects, attacking others, and screaming fits. The results were immediate and endured over several months. Azrin and Wesolowski (1974) found that overcorrection reduced thefts among institutionalized persons with intellectual disabilities by 90% in only three days.

However, overcorrection has since been used with a variety of populations ranging from the non-handicapped to the severely handicapped, including persons with schizophrenia (Axelrod et al., 1978). Overcorrection has been used to treat nervous habits and out-of-seat behaviors. It has also been used by teachers as a classroom management technique (Smith & Misra, 1992). Overcorrection is a procedure that can easily be used by those without formal counseling training.

Overcorrection has several drawbacks. It can require considerable time on the part of both the professional counselor and the client (Smith & Misra, 1992). The results of overcorrection do not tend to generalize to other behaviors displayed by the individual or to other individuals observing the procedure. Instead the results tend to be specific to the behaviors treated, the setting in which they were treated, and the person who experienced the treatment. Therefore, some generalization can be encouraged by varying the setting in which the treatment occurs and by varying the person who administers the treatment. Borrego and Pemberton (2007) indicated that parental motivation to implement overcorrection may be only moderate because it was ranked fourth of six common behavior management strategies in terms of parent acceptability.

APPLICATION OF THE OVERCORRECTION TECHNIQUE

Now apply the overcorrection technique to a current client or student you are working with or revisit the brief case studies presented at the beginning of this book. How can you use the overcorrection technique to address concerns and create movement in the counseling session?

Techniques Not Better Categorized Elsewhere

The purpose of this final section is to introduce three new techniques that are not better categorized elsewhere in the array of counseling paradigms and theories. Erford (2019b) referred to a fifth counseling paradigm as "emerging," and the following three techniques and approaches certainly fall within this fifth paradigm: narrative therapy, strengths-based counseling, and advocacy counseling. Counseling is continually developing and the approaches that emerge are not necessarily easy to categorize from the paradigmatic perspective. Nonetheless, these three approaches to counseling have earned a presence in the professional counselor's repertoire of effective counseling interventions.

Narrative therapy (White & Epston, 1990) assumes that clients are the "experts" on their own lives. Counseling is a collaborative process with a client who is competent, resourceful, and capable of resolving personal problems, with some help from the counselor, of course. Narrative therapy helps clients to externalize the presenting problems, then analyze and understand the effects of the problems on their lives. Clients are then guided to create a new, more positive narrative by which to live, thus reframing how they will deal with important life issues. No matter how we arrived at our current state, the rest of the story of our lives is still unwritten.

In a strengths-based approach, counselors help clients understand their strengths and wells of resilience to access during challenging times. Thus, clients can exhibit protective factors and use available resources to weather rough patches, create hope, and develop the motivation to change. Several models of strengths-based approaches will be explored, as well as several variations on these models.

Finally, client advocacy is more of an approach than a technique, and it is composed of numerous concepts, strategies, and techniques across a number of philosophical and theoretical perspectives. Client advocacy occurs when counselors act with or for clients to empower clients and remove barriers to the clients' personal growth and development and is very much in keeping with the Ratts et al. (2015) Multicultural and Social Justice Counseling Competencies. Counselors must reflect upon and help address the life circumstances and experiences of clients—particularly clients of color, women, gender nonconforming individuals, or affectional minorities—that lead to prejudice, discrimination, or other types of societal and interpersonal oppression, and these problems should be addressed on multiple levels. Creating this multisystemic understanding of clients' social, political, and environmental barriers promotes self- and other-acceptance and helps to reframe problematic behaviors in pro-developmental and proactive terms.

MULTICULTURAL IMPLICATIONS OF TECHNIQUES NOT BETTER CATEGORIZED ELSEWHERE

Emerging approaches are diverse in perspectives so cannot be grouped according to multicultural similarities. However, this specific group of newcomers do all emphasize the importance of rapport and the therapeutic alliance, and ordinarily appeal to clients from a wide array of cultural backgrounds. Narrative therapy is a culturally sensitive, nonjudgmental, empowerment approach that respects the client's story and helps to adapt the client's personal narrative in a pro-developmental manner. Narrative therapy is applicable to numerous counseling settings and approaches, including school, substance use, and marriage and family counseling, and group work, and it is very amenable to cross-cultural adaptations. Techniques such as narrative therapy may be particularly accepted by cultures with storytelling traditions (Hays & Erford, 2018). For example, Native American cultures have a very strong oral storytelling tradition, and *cuento* therapy was designed for use with Latinos and Latinas.

These three approaches are nonjudgmental, nonthreatening, and accepting of clients from diverse backgrounds and worldviews because they do not view clients or client issues and behaviors as problematic, pathological, bad, or inferior. They are strengths based, rather than pathology based. Such approaches strengthen the therapeutic bond and empower clients to take control of their lives in a positive, proactive, and productive manner.

CHAPTER 43

Narrative Therapy

ORIGINS OF THE NARRATIVE THERAPY TECHNIQUE

White and Epston (1990) developed the postmodern approach known as narrative therapy based on the belief that clients are the "experts" on their lives. Counseling is viewed as a collaboration with a client who is competent, resourceful, and capable of resolving personal problems, with a bit of guidance from the counselor. Narrative therapy is a culturally sensitive, nonjudgmental, empowerment approach that respects the client's story and helps to adapt the client's personal narrative in a pro-developmental manner. Narrative therapy is applicable to numerous counseling settings and approaches, including school, substance use, and marriage and family counseling, as well as group work, and it is very amenable to cross-cultural adaptations.

HOW TO IMPLEMENT THE NARRATIVE THERAPY TECHNIQUE

Narrative therapy helps clients to externalize the presenting problems (i.e., separate the person from the problem), then analyze and understand the effects of the problems on their lives. Clients are then guided to create a new, more positive story (narrative) by which to live. As such, clients reframe their life journeys and rewrite how they will deal with the various problems that arise (Blanton, 2007).

Human beings are constructivists, perpetually trying to make sense of their lives, often unknowingly creating a narrative or story to explain their experiences and existences (German, 2013). Clients begin the counseling process in a traditional manner by talking about their problems and how the problems are affecting their life, while the counselor listens nonjudgmentally, helping the client clarify the narrative and make sense of it all. Next, the counselor helps the client to externalize the problem by pointing out that people are not their problems; the problem is the problem. Clients are helped to understand that the problems have their own identities and do not define them as people.

As the problem is externalized, a counselor may use a technique called *mapping the effects*, wherein the client discusses various thoughts and feelings experienced whenever the problem occurs. The counselor then challenges the client to think of how he or she might handle the problem in the future. Finally, the client and counselor collaborate to create a new narrative to recontextualize the problem. This new story or narrative paints the client in a positive light, absent the negativity of the problem so the client can address the problem, or perhaps learn to live more effectively with the problem as part of life.

Narrative therapy becomes an instrument of empowerment (Duba, Kindsvatter, & Priddy, 2010). Through projects and feedback, clients reframe their problems and are motivated to enact changes in thoughts, feelings, and behaviors. Duba et al. proposed that two phases (i.e., deconstruction and construction) helped clients break down the dilemma, overcome the problem, and create the "new normal." Deconstruction is composed of "externalizing the problem" and "mapping the relative influence of the problem over time." To facilitate problem externalization, clients separate the problem from the person by assigning an identity (i.e., name) to the problem on which clients agree, followed by a project showing "the ideals that support the problem and who profits, benefits from, or agrees with these ideals" (p. 111). Next, clients are encouraged to analyze how they confronted the problem in the past, which helps universalize the concerns and empower the clients and others to stand up to the problem in the future. In so doing, clients identify the times they are most vulnerable or struggle most with the problems, thus learning to overcome the influences.

Construction involves creation of an alternative story (i.e., *thickening*) that specifies the "skills, abilities, preferences and desires of persons to live in a preferred manner that contradicts the ends to which problems lead" (Duba et al., 2010, p. 113). Thickening creates a clear path forward to promote change and *unique outcomes* by using memories of when the client stood up to the problem. The thought and feeling memories associated with these unique outcomes bolster the alternative narrative or story. Finally, a project that shows the client living a life free of the problem helps to motivate the client to change and solidify the thoughts, feelings, behaviors, and attitudes that establish and support those change structures.

Journaling is commonly used in narrative therapy to help clients share perceptions, actions, and feelings toward presenting problems. Clients also journal about strategies they can use to address unhealthy thoughts, feelings, and actions. *Speaking back* is another strategy implemented to confront those (e.g., family, friends) who perpetuate the problem, and it can be accomplished indirectly (e.g., letter writing [whether sent or not sent], creating dialogue for what to say in different situations) or directly.

VARIATIONS OF THE NARRATIVE THERAPY TECHNIQUE

Of course, narrative therapy requires some variation when embedded in other approaches, like group work and family counseling, and numerous variations on the primary process have been developed. For example, in family counseling family collaboration is required to deconstruct the family's problematic, nonfunctional stories and construct new narratives that do work for the family (Waters, 2011). Having each family member give their account of the problem is crucial to the deconstruction process. In collaboration with the counselor,

families deconstruct the problem, describe unique outcomes, and then create an agreeable alternative story that encompasses the diverse family member viewpoints. Then the counselor and family develop strategies and techniques to address the problem at home. The FOCUS program (Saltzman, Pynoos, Lester, Layne, & Beardslee, 2013) is a more specific family model that promotes resilience within military families.

Journals and e-journals (Haberstroh, Trepal, & Parr, 2005) complement narrative therapy by enhancing self-reflection and continued introspection between sessions, thereby developing deeper connections and support mechanisms. Of course, counselors must be sensitive to the needs or limitations of clients who have a learning disability in writing or prefer not to journal or e-journal and should strive to keep all journal-related content confidential.

According to German (2013), the Tree of Life (ToL) is a "flexible tool that uses different parts of a tree as metaphors to represent the different aspects of our lives" (p. 78). The *roots* represent clients' important, supportive, and influential people; *ground* demonstrates safety and support structures; *trunk* represents client abilities and strengths; *branches* display current and future aspirations; *fruits* indicate positive accomplishments related to the narrative. Clients are encouraged to share stories about why various items were chosen as they create their trees. Use of the ToL in a group context can be used to construct a community forest (i.e., *Forest of Life*) to promote the idea that "we are all standing together." This is followed by the *Storm of Life* to get clients thinking about what to do when they experience difficulties. Finally, a celebration is often conducted in which an award is given by the counselor (or group members).

EXAMPLE OF THE NARRATIVE THERAPY TECHNIQUE

Maria is a 32-year-old woman seeking help for a long-term battle with depression that gets worse from time to time depending on life stressors, especially work and interpersonal relationships. This lead to bouts of overeating, obsessive thoughts and visualizations, and insomnia. We pick up this case in session four with the therapeutic alliance strengthening and Maria making good progress after learning and applying the "Big Four" (i.e., deep breathing, progressive muscle relaxation training [PMRT], visual imagery, and cognitive self-talk). But the counselor is concerned that Maria still internalizes the depression, referring to herself as depressed, a depressed woman, "sad case," and "gloomy girl." The counselor enacts a narrative therapy approach to help Maria externalize the problem ("The Darkness"), map the problem's effects, challenge Maria to think how she might handle the problem in the future, and create a new narrative to recontextualize the problem. The counselor also assigns journaling for homework and, as a supplemental activity, asks Maria to write a letter to "The Darkness" to let it know that it no longer has control over her.

Counselor (C):   Wow! Those are powerful images! I can see how you are feeling trapped. The way you tell that story, that narrative, you are doomed to travel the Earth with this unbearable burden for the rest of your days.

Maria (M):   Better, but it still seems to envelop me in its grasp. It is so hard to break out of this funk, especially when life gets stressful at work and, well, don't even get me started about men! Ugh! I am just resigned to always being depressed, this all-encompassing darkness or gloom. At times I feel like a cursed, gloomy girl, sinking in quicksand with no hope of escape.

M: I know. I sound like a cursed drama queen, right. Well I do feel that way sometimes. Cursed in a land of darkness.

C: And yet you have said that many days are actually good days and only some are not—and that life has been better over the past month since you started counseling.

M: It is. But every time I think deeply about my problems, really deeply, I feel like I *am* the problem, and I can't fix it . . . that it will never really get any better.

C: Maria, you are not the problem. The problem is the problem. Let's think back to some of the images you brought up a minute ago:

quicksand, darkness, cursed, gloom, among others we have discussed. If you had to give a name to the problem, what would you call it.

M: My depression? Oh, definitely "The Darkness" because it just descends upon me like a dark cloud, a funk that makes it difficult to shake. It rules my life!

C: The Darkness. I like that name—it certainly describes the thing that affects your mood, that great sadness you feel.

M: It sure does. The Darkness is like some evil movie persona—the bad guy in the movie.

C: Exactly! That's a great way to frame The Darkness. It is some villain or force that descends upon you and tries to influence you. Okay. When you feel The Darkness descend, how do you feel?

M: Well . . . sad, obviously, like nothing I do matters, like I am in its grip. I hate feeling that way . . . hopeless . . . helpless. And that makes me angry, also. I'm mad that it makes me feel that way.

Notice how Maria is beginning to externalize the problem using terms like "it" and "The Darkness." The counselor now starts to access internal dialogue from that externalized voice.

C: What does The Darkness say when it comes?

M: Oh, Lord! "Maria, you are a hopeless twit, a helpless damsel in distress." I wish it would go away and leave me alone. "Maria, you are an idiot, no one can like you or care about you let alone *love* you because you are so pathetic." I just want to eat comfort food, which is so counterproductive—I'm 32 and won't keep this body much longer if I keep bingeing! Of course, it picks up on that thread immediately. "Keep stuffing your face, Maria. When you get fat and old no one will ever love you!" This stupid Darkness makes me hate myself. It sucks! Why can't I be happy like all of my friends? How much longer will they let Gloomy Girl hang out with them? I am such a downer! I just want to be happy, but The Darkness . . . it seems so long since I was truly happy.

C: Those are very powerful messages from The Darkness. And you are influenced by letting him control your feelings, your thoughts, your behaviors.

M: I am. That hateful, spiteful, sucky dark cloud just takes over my life! And my stomach and muscles knot up and I say "Here we go again!"

C: When you feel The Darkness descending, what are some things you can do to stop him from taking control?

M: Stop him? Hmm . . . I never . . . hmm . . . oh, I get it. I could use the Big Four . . . you know, take myself to my calming and relaxing place in my mind, repeat my calming and relaxing self-talk messages, do my deep breathing and muscle relaxation. I should stand up to him, but he is sooooo strong!

C: You can be stronger! Those are excellent strategies, and you can see how using visual imagery to take yourself to your calm, relaxing place can help to block any negative visualizations by The Darkness, how your positive self-messages will block his intrusive thoughts, and how the breathing and muscle relaxation will help you regain control of the body symptoms. Good. Very good. Now, we have talked about several instances in which The Darkness is present—especially when you are stressed at work and in interpersonal relationships. Tell me, have you ever stood up to The Darkness, ever not let him win?

M: Hmm . . . I never really thought about it that way, but yes, yes there have been times I just couldn't . . . wouldn't give in. Like last year on my birthday.

At this point, The Darkness is truly personified as an external force, and Maria shares a few examples of times she stood up to him. The counselor continues to guide Maria through these iterations of when she stood up to the descending Darkness, and they developed even more coping strategies to enact in the future. For homework, the counselor assigned a journaling activity. Maria was to record all instances of The Darkness rearing its cloudy head and how she responded to keep him at bay. After a successful week, the counselor instructed Maria to write a letter to The Darkness to inform him that he is done controlling her thoughts, feelings, and behaviors. Indeed, Maria's letter introduced "The Sunshine" to represent her new positive attitudes and their effects on her life. Maria continued to refine her new narrative under the theme that she had the power to write the rest of her life's story from this day onward, and that no force controlled her destiny; she was now in control of her future.

USEFULNESS AND EVALUATION OF THE NARRATIVE THERAPY TECHNIQUE

Very little outcome research was available on the narrative approach. Lopes et al. (2014) evaluated the efficacy of narrative therapy and cognitive-behavioral therapy (CBT) in a clinical trial for moderate depression among 63 adult clients and determined that both approaches were superior to the waitlist (no treatment) control condition. They determined that CBT was more effective than narrative therapy in reducing symptoms of depression as measured by the Beck Depression Inventory (BDI-II), but both approaches were equivalent on other clinical outcome variables. Farzadfard, Abdekhodaee, and Chaman Abadi (2015) randomly assigned 60 kindergarteners with normal-range IQs to four treatment conditions: play therapy, narrative therapy, combined purposeful play therapy and narrative therapy, and control group. The 12-session intervention helped the children in the combination group to display increased levels of attentional control. Finally, Sequeira and Alarcão (2013) created the *Assessment System of Narrative Change* (ASNC) for use with narrative therapies, although no literature was located that used this resource.

APPLICATION OF THE NARRATIVE THERAPY TECHNIQUE

Now apply the narrative therapy technique to a current client or student you are working with or revisit the brief case studies presented at the beginning of this book. How can you use the narrative therapy technique to address concerns and create movement in the counseling session?

CHAPTER 44

Strengths-Based Counseling

ORIGINS OF THE STRENGTHS-BASED COUNSELING TECHNIQUE

Clinical treatment of mental disorders is pathology based. Insurance companies demand to know what is wrong with clients and patients, so they can decide whether to pay to fix it! As such, patients and clients are viewed as revealing some deficit in need of remediation. The other side of the coin, which historically has gotten far less attention, is a resilience-based, positive psychology, wellness-oriented, or strengths-based approach to counseling. In a strengths-based approach, counselors help clients understand strengths and sources of resilience that can be tapped when the going gets rough (Davidson, 2014; Wilding & Griffey, 2014). Thus, clients can exhibit protective factors and use available resources to weather rough patches and tough times, thereby creating hope and the motivation to change (Scheel, Davis, & Henderson, 2013). Prominent in strengths-based approaches is the view that each individual is unique within a personal context (Grothaus, McAuliffe, & Craigen, 2012; Wilding & Griffey, 2014), and therefore this approach may be particularly appropriate for minority clients with divergent cultural values and contexts.

The origins of strengths-based counseling are difficult to pinpoint because it appears to be commensurate with numerous counseling approaches and traditions, including multicultural counseling, social work, school counseling, solution-focused counseling, and narrative therapy, among others. Multicultural counseling views clients as embedded within their own systemic context (Grothaus et al., 2012; Hays & Erford, 2018) with unique strengths, assets, and resources that should be celebrated rather than viewed as deficits when compared to dominant cultural values and beliefs. School and career counselors have played a key role in implementation of strengths-based approaches as each discipline shares the goal of helping clients and students identify what they are good at to match interests, skills, and abilities to potential careers and higher education pathways. Social work has a tradition of strengths-based client advocacy, believing that focusing on problems and deficits sets up an artificial power dynamic that hurts the therapeutic alliance. Thus, focusing on strengths reduces the focus on deficits and improves the counseling relationship (Smith, 2006). As revealed in Section 1 of this book, solution-focused approaches deemphasize problems and focus on solutions—or what the client is already doing right to solve the problem (George, 2008; Scheel et al., 2013). And narrative therapy (Chapter 43) uses client experiences to first externalize the problem, and then reframe or retell the client's story in a more positive manner. In addition, positive psychology focuses on client strengths to help clients self-actualize, hope, love, and maintain the motivation to persevere (Gable & Haidt, 2005; Seligman & Csikszentmihalyi, 2000). Importantly, positive psychology does not propose that negative elements do not exist, just that the positive qualities of a person's life are more important in sustaining successes into the future. This is also the case in the strengths-based approach.

HOW TO IMPLEMENT THE STRENGTHS-BASED COUNSELING TECHNIQUE

At least three models of strengths-based counseling have appeared in the literature, as have many more specific techniques and assessments. The three strengths-based models covered here include Smith (2006), Davidson (2014), and Whitmarsh and Mullette (2011), and each source should be consulted for expansions of their models. The ten stages of Smith's (2006) strengths-based model include the following:

1. Creating the therapeutic alliance (rapport)
2. Identifying client strengths (biological, psychological, social, cultural, environmental, economic, material, political, etc.) through client retelling of life
3. Assessing presenting problems
4. Instilling hope and future orientation
5. Framing solutions using the exception question
6. Building strength and competence through helping clients understand their immense power to effect change
7. Giving the client permission and power to find solutions within
8. Using the client's foundational strengths to create change
9. Building resilience and future capacity through improvement of personal problem-solving skills
10. Evaluating and terminating, focusing on the growth experienced by the client

Davidson's (2014) STRENGTH model draws upon other counseling models (solution focused, Adlerian, person centered, narrative) and techniques. The STRENGTH acronym stands for the following:

1. **S**olution focus
2. **T**rajectory preview—clients are encouraged to think about how changes could affect the future
3. **R**esource development—collaboration to identify and expand resources
4. **E**xceptions analysis—discover successes and figure out successful solutions
5. **N**oticing positives
6. **G**oal setting
7. **T**enacity review
8. **H**uman capacity development—the counselor uses positive affirmations to help clients achieve a sense of mastery using three types of compliments: direct, indirect and self-compliments (Davidson, 2014)

The SEARCH model (Whitmarsh & Mullette, 2011) focuses specifically on counseling adolescents from a strengths-based perspective and includes three stages:

1. Exploring the SEARCH model domains: **S**elf-domain; **E**ducation, work and career domain; **A**ctivities domain; **R**elationships domain; **C**ommunity and culture domain; and **H**ome domain
2. Goal setting building on previously identified strengths
3. Termination and integration of these strengths into life

Assessments are easy ways to focus client attention on the positive aspects of life. Numerous formal assessments of client strengths are available, and each of the following can be used to identify strengths, create goals, document progress, and identify areas for intervention (Tedeschi & Kilmer, 2005):

1. The *Clinical Assessment Package for Client Risks and Strengths* (CAPCRS; Gilgun, 1999) assesses the strengths and weaknesses with which the client presents.
2. The *Child and Adolescent Strengths Assessment* (CASA; Lyons, Uziel-Miller, Reys, & Sokol, 2000) measures strengths, family, school, psychological, peer, moral/spiritual, and extracurricular.
3. The *Behavioral and Emotional Rating Scale-2* (BERS-2; Buckley & Epstein, 2004) assesses interpersonal strength, family involvement, intrapersonal strength, school functioning, and affective strengths.
4. The *Assets Interview* (Morrison, Brown, D'incau, O'Farrell, & Furlong, 2006) is used with children.

5. The *40 Developmental Assets* by the Search Institute (Scales, Benson, Roehlkepartain, Sesma, & van Dulmen, 2006) external assets (support, empowerment, boundaries and expectations, and constructive use of time) and internal assets (values, skills, commitment to learning, social competencies, and self-perceptions).

6. *Strengths Use Scale* (Govindji & Linley, 2007).

VARIATIONS OF THE STRENGTHS-BASED COUNSELING TECHNIQUE

Strengths-based approaches can be applied across settings and client populations but appear especially applicable to youth in school settings where pathological designations are especially avoided (Bozic, 2013). The counseling relationship with school-age youth (and their parents) is particularly critical because school referrals are often deficit based (Bozic, 2013; Climie & Mastoras, 2015; Gardner & Toope, 2011). Strengths-based approaches view students in a positive light and empower them to take responsibility for their actions by creating hope and motivation.

EXAMPLE OF THE STRENGTHS-BASED COUNSELING TECHNIQUE

Gerry is a 16-year-old who is at risk for academic failure. His grades have been slipping and, rather than reaching out for help and support, he has been pulling inside himself. He has also been getting into a bit of trouble with the neighborhood kids, which is gaining him a reputation as someone slipping toward a life of crime. Because Gerry is internalizing his problems and hearing from everyone in his life about how he is becoming a failure, troublemaker, and "loser," the counselor decided to use a strengths-based approach to demonstrate to Gerry that he has a lot that is positive about his life and can address these problematic issues if he chooses. The counselor has known Gerry for about two years, and they already have a pretty good working rapport, so this session is aimed at identifying some of Gerry's sources of resilience and support. Using Smith's (2006) 10-step strengths-based model, Gerry completed the Strengths Use Scale and reviewed the 40 Developmental Assets produced by the Search Institute. The counselor is using these instruments as the basis for strength identification: the pools or wells of resiliency that Gerry can draw upon when things get challenging. Talking about what Gerry is good at and what support systems he has in place has also deepened and solidified the client–counselor therapeutic relationship and given Gerry new insights into who he can become.

Counselor (C): I notice the look on your face, and your overall mood is very different when we talk about these strengths you possess, as opposed to the problems.

Gerry (G): Well, yeah, talking about what's wrong with me gets me all defensive and angry. These things are the things that I'm good at. Sure beats being dissed for all the stuff wrong with me. That just gets me frustrated. Taking about the positives . . . well, that actually gives me hope that this all might work out.

C: Fair point. Well, you certainly have a long list of assets and strengths, everything from home support and high parent expectations to several supportive teachers and community resources—church, rec league. You also have a number of personal responsibility strengths and an honest streak.

G: Yeah . . . that honest streak has been getting me into trouble recently. I just can't lie to my mom!

C: Understood. So tell me about some times when the problem is not a problem. When you are completing schoolwork . . . when you are keeping your behavior in line with expectations when out with your friends.

This is similar to the exceptions technique from Section 1 of this book: solution-focused counseling. The counselor walks Gerry through several iterations of when problems do not exist, giving Gerry all the credit for his choices that lead to those exceptions. The counselor then helps Gerry apply some of his strengths and resources to problem resolution, thereby increasing the percentage of instances when the problem is not a problem.

G: Well, okay, I see how that could work. Mr. Jackson did say that he is available to tutor me if I need extra help, but I think if I just buckled down and did my schoolwork first before setting out into the neighborhood, that would solve most of the problems right there. And if I head to the rec center instead of the hood, well . . .

C: Right. Tapping into the systems that you draw strength from gives you an incredible amount of control over your life. It affects the decisions you make and how successful you are in accomplishing your goals. You just need to free yourself to use your strengths to find the solutions. And what you will eventually find is that the decisions you make will make your life either better and easier, or worse and harder.

G: Yeah. I see that. It is tough with all those temptations on the street . . .

Gerry and the counselor continue through several more iterations of this process, spliced with encouragement and personal responsibility, encouraging Gerry to find the solutions to his difficulties within himself by applying his strengths, and using these foundational strengths to enact positive changes in his life. In doing so, Gerry builds on his resilience, builds his future capacity to solve personal problems, and realizes the power he has over his own positive growth and well-being.

USEFULNESS AND EVALUATION OF THE STRENGTHS-BASED COUNSELING TECHNIQUE

Preliminary, summative research indicates that strengths-based counseling improves overall client happiness, life satisfaction (Proyer, Gander,

Wellenzohn, & Rush, 2015) and well-being over the course of their lives (Wood, Linley, Maltby, Kashdan, & Hurling, 2011). Still, only a couple of outcome research studies were located that specifically addressed the effectiveness of the approach.

Ibrahim, Michail, and Callaghan (2014) conducted a meta-analysis of RCTs and quasi-experimental studies of the strengths-based service model for adults with severe mental illness (primarily psychotic disorders) and found some significant benefits compared to other approaches, although they caution that power was low because only a few studies were included. In one of the largest studies, Gelkopf et al. (2016) studied the effectiveness of a new strengths-based case management (SBCM) service by randomly assigning 1,276 Israeli adults with serious psychiatric illness to treatment as usual (TAU) or TAU plus SBCM. After 20 months, the SBCM group participants showed significantly better progress related to self-efficacy, unmet needs, and general quality of life, and they also consumed fewer services at follow-up.

APPLICATION OF THE STRENGTHS-BASED APPROACH

Now apply the strengths-based approach to a current client or student you are working with or revisit the brief case studies presented at the beginning of this book. How can you use the strengths-based approach to address concerns and create movement in the counseling session?

CHAPTER 45

Client Advocacy

ORIGINS OF THE CLIENT ADVOCACY TECHNIQUE

Client advocacy is more of an approach than a technique, and it is composed of numerous concepts, strategies, and techniques across a number of philosophical and theoretical perspectives. Client advocacy occurs when counselors act with or for clients to empower clients and remove barriers to the clients' personal growth and development (Ratts, Singh, Nassar-McMillan, Butler, & McCullough, 2015). Thus, it is not a surprise that the origins of client advocacy are diverse and multidisciplinary. Clifford Beers, Frank Parsons, and Carl Rogers are all early historic figures in the application of advocacy to counseling, whereas the more current conceptualizations of advocacy counseling stem from feminist and multicultural counseling movements (Astramovich & Harris, 2007; Ratts & Hutchins, 2009). These more recent approaches were from a growing societal dissatisfaction in the United States with the inequitable life situations of persons of color and women. Most recently, comprehensive counseling advocacy competencies have been developed (Ratts et al., 2015) that extend to all clients experiencing discrimination or oppression across individual, community, and systemic contexts.

IMPLEMENTATION OF THE CLIENT ADVOCACY TECHNIQUE

Multiculturally competent counselors constantly reflect upon and are self-aware of personal values, attitudes and beliefs (Dowden, 2009, Hays & Erford, 2018). Counselors must also reflect upon and help address the life circumstances and experiences of clients—particularly clients of color, women, gender nonconforming individuals, or affectional minorities—that lead to prejudice, discrimination, or other types of societal and interpersonal oppression. This reflection and action should be multisystemic as multiple contextual levels envelop the client (Gerhart, 2007) so these problems should be addressed on multiple levels. Creating this multisystemic understanding of clients' social, political, and environmental barriers promotes self- and other-acceptance and helps to reframe problematic behavior (Goodman et al., 2004; Ratts et al., 2015). For example, instead of viewing a client's behavior from a deficit perspective, the problematic behavior could be viewed as an adaptation to the client's social and political lived experiences

Building on facets of the strengths-based approach discussed in Chapter 44, the first step in advocacy counseling is to identify how clients' strengths help build positive client self-identities (Savage, Harley, & Nowak, 2005) by empowering clients to understand their skill and attitudinal mastery in new ways that are simply at odds with majority social and political conventions (Dowden, 2009; Goodman et al., 2004).

Co-construction of this new understanding of the "problem behavior" as "adaptive behavior" next leads to collaborative construction of an action plan, further enhancing client self-advocacy and empowerment (Ratts et al., 2015). This may involve the feminist strategy of "giving voice" so that clients can create a personal (or community) narrative of the current situation. Narrative techniques (see Chapter 43) may help clients develop this more empowering story, although sometimes the counselor may need to model and even speak for clients who may not be native English language speakers and therefore cannot access necessary resources. Action plans need to be refined to access needed resources but also must address (social, political, and environmental) challenges and barriers that may impede progress, usually through brainstorming and problem solving. This is similar to "flagging the minefield" (see Chapter 5) and can help reinforce the action plan.

Step three is to take action (Savage et al., 2005), which entails true empowerment. Preferably, the client takes action during this phase, but sometimes the counselor needs to take action on behalf of the client by collaborating with allies and support clients in developing the partnerships that allow goals to be accomplished (Astramovich & Harris, 2007; Dowden, 2009; Hatch, Shelton, & Monk, 2009; Ratts et al., 2015). Often counselors can help connect clients to other people needing self-advocacy training through group work or through alliance or political advocacy groups aimed at systemic change on the macro level (Ratts et al., 2015).

VARIATIONS OF THE CLIENT ADVOCACY TECHNIQUE

Counselors can implement the advocacy counseling technique in numerous ways. In general, it is preferable that clients learn to self-advocate and act for themselves. In such cases, counselors can collaborate with and train clients to carry out the process so that it can generalize to future problem events in the client's life. In contrast, some clients are not always able to self-advocate effectively, such as when a client has an intellectual disability or has not developed effective language skills in the primary language of a society. In such instances, counselors can collaborate and train caregivers or assistants. In some cases, however, counselors may need to take the lead and advocate on behalf of the client. In short, a range of counselor actions is available on a continuum from acting with to acting on behalf of the client.

The promotion of self-advocacy includes many training needs applied differentially according to the developmental level of the client. Skills training may involve assertiveness, mediation, and

communication (Astramovich & Harris, 2007; Hatch et al., 2009). Training is often accomplished using modeling, behavioral rehearsal, and role play. Finally, clients can be helped to build self-awareness of their own and others' cultural backgrounds and identities, understand social and political power dynamics, and take on support and leadership roles in community organizations.

EXAMPLE OF THE CLIENT ADVOCACY TECHNIQUE

Shanique is an 18-year-old with a learning disability who is transitioning to college for her freshman year and concerned that she will get off to a rough start with the social and academic transitions ahead.

Shanique (S):   I am mostly concerned that the supports and accommodations I get here at school won't be available. And I heard I need a new evaluation since my last one was over a year ago.

Counselor (C):   So this transition worries you. You want to keep getting the help you need to be successful.

S: Sure. I worked so hard here, and I'm scared that it will all come apart. That no one will know me at college, and I won't know who to get help from. That I will fail.

C: This sounds like an excellent opportunity to use your self-advocacy skills to learn about what resources and services are available. Interested in exploring what might be available at your new university?

S: Absolutely, I just don't know where to start. And the university is so big. . . . I admit that I'm kinda scared . . .

At this point, Shanique and the counselor used the office computer to search for available resources at the university. Doing a search for disability support services, they found the Office of Disability Services Web page and read through the policies and procedures. In the process, Shanique's awareness of her responsibilities grew, and she and the counselor developed an action plan for Shanique to enact. It was composed of a phone call between Shanique and the office personnel to be sure her paperwork was in order and to better understand what accommodations she could receive. At this point, the counselor prepared Shanique for the phone call by constructing and ordering a list of possible questions and then using modeling and role play to practice the conversation. The list included questions related to disability documentation/report, potential accommodations, counseling services, clubs and activities, and how to best approach her social and academic transitions to college. The discussion also reviewed Shanique's rights under Section 504 of the U.S. Rehabilitation Act of 1973. This activity lasted about 40 minutes, and Shanique's efficacy and knowledge level were high by the end of the activity. Shanique then sent a message to the university disability office asking for a phone call/interview related to her transition issues. The phone call happened the following afternoon, and Shanique and the counselor met the next morning.

S: I feel so much better emotionally and so much better prepared for college now.

C: Outstanding. Summarize the call, please.

S: Well, I talked to this really nice lady who has been there a long time, and she said it is natural to worry about the transition to college but that there will be thousands of new freshmen going through the same thing and everyone is nervous. I asked her about documentation, and she said that because I just had an evaluation a year ago they can use that one for their eligibility determination. She said that they consider any report up to 3 years old as recent. Whew . . . what a relief. I was freaking out about how I was going to pay for one—we're not at all rich, you know. On top of that, she said the university has a clinic, and in about two years I can get a new evaluation report there for almost nothing to continue services if I still need them. What a relief!

C: Sounds like a productive phone call. You asked some important questions, and the university had some helpful answers. What else did you discuss?

S: It was very helpful. And she even complimented me on how informed and prepared I was! Well

I need to send a copy of the report to the disability services office and discuss with them the accommodations I am eligible for. She took my list over the phone of what I am getting now and said the accommodations should not be a problem. There are a lot of students with those same accommodations. When I asked her about counseling services, I couldn't believe it. She said the university counseling center has groups for both students with transition issues *and* students with disabilities.

C: That's wonderful.

S: Yep. So I'm gonna contact the counseling center and talk more with them over the next few weeks. Looks like things might work out after all. I was so worried, but the preparation we went through really helped. I also asked about extracurricular clubs and stuff.

C: Excellent. What did they say?

S: Well they had all kinds of stuff, some of it sounded interesting. But ya know what?

C: What?

S: I was thinking, why not start a club or student organization focused on people with disabilities *and* their allies. You know, kind of like what we do here with safe zones and LGBT students. I mean, people with disabilities have rights and feel oppressed and discriminated against too. What do you think? Does that sound crazy?

C: Not at all, Shanique! It sounds like you are moving from self-advocacy to community and societal advocacy—caring about other people is very noble and greatly needed. You want to help others with disabilities navigate the college transition process. Who knows? Even other students in other universities might have similar needs.

S: Yay. I could start a chain reaction! Wow. All these grand ideas from a simple phone call.

Shanique is understanding that others can benefit from her experiences and advocacy. She is starting to think about community action goals. Before the session ended and as part of termination, we

"flagged the minefield." (See Chapter 5.) We usu-
ally look for three to five additional examples the
client might encounter in the future and attempt to
address how the client could handle those situations
effectively by applying the self-advocacy counseling
technique and other strategies.

C: Now that you have learned how effective self-
     advocacy can be, I want you to think about
     your future . . . near term and a few years
     down the road. When do you anticipate other
     times you will need to stand up for yourself—
     self-advocate—and what have we learned
     about this self-advocacy experience with your
     college transition that we can generalize to
     those future occasions?

USEFULNESS AND EVALUATION OF THE CLIENT ADVOCACY TECHNIQUE

Interestingly, only three outcome research studies were located using advocacy counseling, and
each involved school-age students in a school environment. More and broader outcome research is
needed in this area of the counseling literature. In
a psychoeducational group for six "at-risk" high
school students, Dowden (2009) focused on interpersonal communication skills, application, and
reinforcement. Advocacy-based topics included
self-empowerment, self-determination, and social
justice competencies. Activities included self-
reflection, journaling, and constructing action
plans to address perceived injustices in the school
environment. Four of the six participants passed all
coursework in the spring semester, and five of the
six participants demonstrated lower rates of truancy.
     Two outcome studies involved preparing high
school students with disabilities to self-advocate and
take a more active role in their IEP (individual education plan) meetings. Bos and Van Reusen (1994)
helped one group of high school students with disabilities prepare for IEP conferences, whereas a
control group was not helped. The prepared (treatment) group participants learned to identify interests, goals, strengths, and weaknesses; summarize
goals; and how to communicate and answer questions that were likely to occur in the conferences.
As observed and analyzed in the actual IEP conferences, students in the treatment group were rated
with more positive attitudes, made greater contributions to the conversation, and identified and
discussed more IEP goals than participants in the
control condition. In a second school-based study
with 25 ninth-grade students with learning disabilities, Hatch et al. (2009) also provided self-advocacy
training to help students prepare for IEP meetings.
Students learned the differences among passive,
aggressive, and assertive behaviors and used narrative, modeling, role play, and solution-focused
strategies to learn to ask for appropriate accommodations. Treatment group participants attended more
IEP meetings, contributed more to the conversation,
experienced greater levels of interpersonal comfort,
and were more informed of the outcomes of their
IEP than comparison group students who received
no training.

APPLICATION OF THE ADVOCACY COUNSELING TECHNIQUE

Now apply the advocacy counseling technique to
a current client or student you are working with or
revisit the brief case studies presented at the beginning of this book. How can you use the advocacy
counseling technique to address concerns and create
movement in the counseling session?

Concluding Remarks

Successful counseling involves moving clients from situation or problem identification to successful attainment of their goals and objectives. The operational word in the previous sentence is *moving*. All professional counselors know how to establish counseling objectives and how to tell when those objectives have been met. All professional counselors are skilled in implementation of a counseling process, whether it stems from a single theoretical orientation or from an integrative approach. But what happens when the counseling process stagnates, the client becomes frustrated with little or no progress, and the counseling relationship is in danger of premature termination?

In this text, we have advocated for a flexible approach to counseling that allows professional counselors to choose techniques shown in the outcome literature to address specific counseling objectives effectively and create the movement in counseling that is vital to success. I have *not* advocated for the nonjudicious or haphazard application of the techniques contained herein; such an approach is unprofessional and unethical. But when you are in session with a client whose progress has halted, I hope you will recall enough of the knowledge and procedures contained within this text to help move that client forward in the counseling process and ever closer to the counseling objective that both you and the client committed to reaching. Counseling is indeed an art, but technical know-how allows the artist to create an exceptional work.

References

Abdullah, M. (2002). *Bibliotherapy* (Report No. EDO-CS-02-08). Washington, DC: Office of Educational Research and Improvement. (ERIC Document Reproduction Service No. ED00036)

Abramowitz, J. S., Moore, E. L., Braddock, A. E., & Harrington, D. L. (2009). Self-help cognitive-behavioral therapy with minimal therapist contact for social phobia: A controlled trial. *Journal of Behavior Therapy and Experimental Psychiatry*, *40*(1), 98–105. doi:10.1016/j.jbtep.2008.04.004

Abrams, M., & Ellis, A. (1994). Rational emotive behavior therapy in the treatment of stress. *British Journal of Guidance and Counseling*, *22*(1), 39–51. doi:10.1080/03069889408253664

Ahmed, S. (2017). An attitude of gratitude: A randomized controlled pilot study of gratitude journaling among parents of young children. *Dissertation Abstracts International: Section B: The Sciences and Engineering*, *77*(11-B)(E).

Akerblad, A., Bengtsson, F., von Knorring, L., & Ekselius, L. (2006). Response, remission and relapse in relation to adherence in primary care treatment of depression: A 2-year study. *International Clinical Psychopharmacology*, *21*, 117–124.

Allanson, S. (2002). Jeffrey the dog: A search for shared meaning. In A. Cattanach (Ed.), *The story so far: Play therapy narratives* (pp. 59–81). Philadelphia, PA: Jessica Kingsley Publishers.

Allen, L. J., Howard, V. F., Sweeney, W. J., & McLaughlin, T. F. (1993). Use of contingency contracting to increase on-task behavior with primary students. *Psychological Reports*, *72*, 905–906.

Alvord, M. K., & Grados, J. J. (2005). Enhancing resilience in children: A proactive approach. *Professional Psychology: Research and Practice*, *36*, 238–245. doi:10.1037/07357028.36.3.238

Ameli, M., & Dattilio, F. M. (2013). Enhancing cognitive behavior therapy with logotherapy: Techniques for clinical practice. *Psychotherapy*, *50*, 387–391. doi:10.1037/a0033394

American Academy of Sleep Medicine (AASM). (2014). Psychological and behavioral treatments for insomnia. *Focus: The Journal of Lifelong Learning*, *12*(1), 31–37. doi:10.1176/appi.focus.12.1.31

Anderson, N. D., Lau, M. A., Segal, Z. V., & Bishop, S. R. (2007). Mindfulness-based stress reduction and attentional control. *Clinical Psychology & Psychotherapy*, *14*, 449–463. doi:10.1002/cpp.544

Ansari, F., Molavi, H., & Neshatdoost, H. T. (2010). Effect of stress inoculation training on general health of hypertensive patients. *Psychological Research*, *12*, 81–96.

Ansbacher, H. L., & Ansbacher, R. R. (1956). *The individual psychology of Alfred Adler: A systematic presentation in selections from his writings.* New York, NY: Basic Books.

Apadoca, T. R., Magill, M., Longabaugh, R., Jackson, K. M., & Monti, P. M. (2013). Effect of a significant other on client change talk in motivational interviewing. *Journal of Counseling and Clinical Psychology*, *81*, 35–46. doi:10.1037/a0030881

Arad, D. (2004). If your mother were an animal, what animal would she be? Creating play stories in family therapy: The animal attribution story-telling technique (AASTT). *Family Process*, *43*, 249–263. doi:10.1111/j.1545-5300.2004.04302009.x

Arbuthnott, K. D., Arbuthnott, D. W., & Rossiter, L. (2001). Guided imagery and memory: Implications for psychotherapists. *Journal of Counseling Psychology*, *48*, 123–132. doi:10.1037/0022-0167.48.2.123

Arenofsky, J. (2001). Control your anger before it controls you! *Current Health 1*, *24*(7), 6.

Armitage, C. J. (2012). Evidence that self-affirmation reduces body dissatisfaction by basing self-esteem on domains other than body weight and shape. *Journal of Child Psychology and Psychiatry*, *53*(1), 81–88. doi:10.1111/j.1469-7610.2011.02442.x

Aron, L. (2001). *A meeting of minds: Mutuality in psychoanalysis.* Hillsdale, NJ: Analytic Press.

Ascher, L. M., & Cautela, J. R. (1974). An experimental study of covert extinction. *Journal of Behavior Therapy and Experimental Psychiatry*, *5*, 233–238. doi:10.1016/0005-7916(74)90069-X

Astramovich, R. L., & Harris, K. R. (2007). Promoting self-advocacy among minority students in school counseling. *Journal of Counseling & Development*, *85*, 269–276. doi:10.1002/j.1556-6678.2007.tb00474.x

Ataoglu, A., Ozcetin, A., Icmeli, C., & Ozbulut, O. (2003). Paradoxical therapy in conversion reaction. *Journal of Korean Medical Science*, *18*, 581–584. doi:10.3346/jkms.2003.18.4.581

Atkinson, C. (2007). Using solution-focused approaches in motivational interviewing with young people. *Pastoral Care in Education*, *25*(2), 31–37. doi:10.1111/j.1468-0122.2007.00405.x

Audet, C. T., & Everall, R. D. (2010). Therapist self-disclosure and the therapeutic relationship: A phenomenological study from the client perspective. *British Journal of Guidance & Counselling*, *38*, 327–342. doi:10.1080/03069885.2010-.482450

Austin, S. J., & Partridge, E. (1995). Prevent school failure: Treat test anxiety. *Preventing School Failure*, *40*, 10–14. doi:10.1080/1045988X.1995.9944644

Axelrod, S., Brantner, J. P., & Meddock, T. D. (1978). Overcorrection: A review and critical analysis. *The Journal of Special Education, 12,* 367–391. doi:10.1177/002246697801200404

Azrin, N. H., Vinas, V., & Ehle, C. T. (2007). Physical activity as reinforcement for classroom calmness of ADHD children: A preliminary study. *Child & Family Behavior Therapy, 29*(2), 1–8. doi:10.1300/J019v29n02_01

Azrin, N. H., & Wesolowski, M. D. (1974). Theft reversal: An overcorrection procedure for eliminating stealing by retarded persons. *Journal of Applied Behavior Analysis, 7,* 577–581. doi:10.1901/jaba.1974.7-577

Bacon, E. H. (1990). Using negative consequences effectively. *Academic Therapy, 25,* 599–610.

Bakker, G. M. (2009). In defense of thought stopping. *Clinical Psychologist, 13*(2), 59–68.

Bandura, A. (2006). *Psychological modeling: Conflicting theories.* Piscataway, NJ: Aldine Transaction.

Banks, T. (2006). Teaching rational emotive behavior therapy to adolescents in an alternative urban educational setting. Unpublished doctoral dissertation, Kent State University, OH.

Barber, J., Liese, B., & Abrams, M. (2003). Development of cognitive therapy adherence and competence scale. *Psychotherapy Research, 13,* 205–221. doi:10.1093/ptr/kpg019

Barnett, J. E. (2011). Psychotherapist self-disclosure: Ethical and clinical considerations. *Psychotherapy, 48,* 315–321. doi:10.1037/a0026056

Baspinar Can, P., Dereboy, Ç., & Eskin, M. (2012). Comparison of the effectiveness of cognitive restructuring and systematic desensitization in reducing high-stakes test anxiety. *Türk Psikiyatri Dergisi, 23*(1), 9–17.

Beamish, P. M., Granello, D. H., & Belcastro, A. L. (2002). Treatment of panic disorder: Practical guidelines. *Journal of Mental Health Counseling, 24,* 224–246.

Beck, A., Berchick, R., Clark, D., Solkol, L., & Wright, F. (1992). A crossover study of focused cognitive therapy for panic disorder. *The American Journal of Psychiatry, 149,* 778–783. doi:10.1176/ajp.149.6.778

Beck, A. T., & Weishaar, M. (2013). Cognitive therapy. In D. Wedding & R. J. Corsini (Eds.), *Current psychotherapies* (10th ed., pp. 231–261). Belmont, CA: Brooks-Cole.

Becvar, D. S., & Becvar, R. J. (2012). *Family therapy: A systemic integration* (8th ed.). Needham Heights, MA: Allyn & Bacon.

Benoit, R. B., & Mayer, G. R. (1974). Extinction: Guidelines for its selection and use. *The Personnel and Guidance Journal, 52,* 290–295. doi:10.1002/j.2164-4918.1974.tb04027.x

Betz, C. (1994). Beyond time-out: Tips from a teacher. *Young Children, 49*(3), 10–14.

Beyebach, M. (2014). Change factors in solution-focused brief therapy: A review of Salamanca studies. *Journal of Systemic Therapies, 33,* 62–77. doi:10.1521/jsyt.2014.33.1.62

Beyebach, M., Rodríguez, M. S., Arribas de Miguel, J., Herrero de Vega, M., Hernández, C., & Rodríguez-Morejón, A. (2000). Outcome of solution-focused therapy at a university family therapy center. *Journal of Systemic Therapies, 19,* 116–128. doi:10.1521/jsyt.2000.19.1.116

Black, D. S., O'Reilly, G. A., Olmstead, R., Breen, E. C., & Irwin, M. R. (2015). Mindfulness meditation and improvement in sleep quality and daytime impairment among older adults with sleep disturbances: A randomized clinical trial. *JAMA Internal Medicine, 175,* 494–501. doi:10.1001/jamainternmed.2014.8081

Blanton, P. (2007). Adding silence to stories: Narrative therapy and contemplation. *Contemporary Family Therapy: An International Journal, 29,* 211–221. doi:10.1007/s10591-007-9047-x

Boardman, T., Catley, D., Grobe, J. E., Little, T. D., & Ahluwalia, J. S. (2006). Using motivational interviewing with smokers: Do therapist behaviors relate to engagement and therapeutic alliance? *Journal of Substance Abuse Treatment, 31,* 329–339. doi:10.1016/j.jsat.2006.05.006

Boelen, P., Kip, H., Voorsluijs, J., & van den Bout, J. (2004). Irrational beliefs and basic assumptions in bereaved students: A comparison study. *Journal of Rational-Emotive & Cognitive-Behavior Therapy, 22,* 111–129. doi:10.1023/B:JORE.0000025441.39310.49

Bombardier, C. H., Ehde, D. M., Gibbons, L. E., Wadhwani, R., Sullivan, M. D., Rosenberg, D. E., & Kraft, G. H. (2013). Telephone-based physical activity counseling for major depression in people with multiple sclerosis. *Journal of Consulting and Clinical Psychology, 81,* 89–99. doi:10.1037/a0031242

Boniecki, K. A., & Moore, S. (2003). Breaking the silence: Using a token economy to reinforce classroom participation. *Teaching of Psychology, 30,* 224–227. doi:10.1207/S15328023TOP3003_05

Bootzin, R. R. (1975). *Behavior modification and therapy: An introduction.* Cambridge, MA: Winthrop Publishers.

Borders, S., & Paisley, P. (1992). Children's literature as a resource for classroom guidance. *Elementary School Guidance and Counseling, 27,* 131–139.

Borge, C. R., Mengshoel, A. M., Omenaas, E., Moum, T., Ekman, I., Lein, M. P., … Wahl, A. K. (2015). Effects of guided deep breathing on breathlessness and the breathing pattern in chronic obstructive pulmonary disease: A double-blind randomized control study. *Patient Education and Counseling, 98,* 182–190. http://dx.doi.org/10.1016/j.pec.2014.10.017

Bornmann, B. A., Mitelman, S. A., & Beer, D. A. (2007). Psychotherapeutic relaxation: How it relates to levels of aggression in a school within inpatient child psychiatry: A pilot study. *The Arts in Psychotherapy, 34,* 216–222. doi:10.1016/j.aip.2007.01.004

Borrego, J., Jr., & Pemberton, J. R. (2007). Increasing acceptance of behavioral child management techniques: What do parents say? *Child & Family Behavior Therapy, 29*(2), 27–45. doi:10.1300/J019v29n02_03

Borton, J., Markowitz, L., & Dieterich, J. (2005). Effects of suppressing negative self-referent thoughts on mood and self-esteem. *Journal of Social and Clinical Psychology, 24,* 172–190. doi:10.1521/jscp.24.2.172.62269

Bos, C. S., & Van Reusen, A. K. (1994). Facilitating student participation in individualized education programs through motivation strategy instruction. *Exceptional Children, 60,* 466–476. doi:10.1177/001440299406000510

Bowles, N., Mackintosh, C., & Torn, A. (2001). Nurses' communication skills: An evaluation of the impact of solution-focused communication training. *Journal of Advanced Nursing, 36,* 347–354. doi:10.1046/j.1365-2648.2001.01979.x

Bozic, N. (2013). Developing a strength-based approach to educational psychology practice: A multiple case study. *Educational and Child Psychology, 30,* 18–29.

Bratter, T. E., Esparat, D., Kaufman, A., & Sinsheimer, L. (2008). Confrontational psychotherapy: A compassionate and potent psychotherapeutic orientation for gifted adolescents who are self-destructive and engage in dangerous behavior. *International Journal of Reality Therapy, 27*(2), 13–25.

Brewster, L. (2008). The reading remedy: Bibliotherapy in practice. *Aplis, 21(4),* 172–176.

Brown, J. F., Spencer, K., & Swift, S. (2002). A parent training programme for chronic food refusal: A case study. *British Journal of Learning Disabilities, 30,* 118–121. doi:10.1046/j.1468-3156.2002.00128.x

Brown, Z. A., & Uehara, D. L. (1999, November). Coping with teacher stress: A research synthesis for Pacific educators. *Pacific Resources for Education and Learning, 2*–22.

Browning, S., Collins, J. S., & Nelson, B. (2008). Creating families. *Marriage & Family Review, 38*(4), 1–19.

Bryant, R. A., Moulds, M. L., Guthrie, R. M., Dang, S. T., Mastrodomenico, J. N., Reginald, D. V., … Creamer, M. (2008). A randomized controlled trial of exposure therapy and cognitive restructuring for posttraumatic stress disorder. *Journal of Consulting and Clinical Psychology, 76,* 695–703. doi:10.1037/a0012616

Buckley, J. A., & Epstein, M. H. (2004). The Behavioral and Emotional Rating Scale-2 (BERS-2): Providing a comprehensive approach to strength-based assessment. *The California School Psychologist, 9*(1), 21–27.

Bucknell, D. (2000). Practice teaching: Problem to solution. *Social Work Education, 19,* 125–144. doi:10.1080/02615470050003511

Buggey, T. (2005). Video self-modeling application with students with autism spectrum disorder in a small private school setting. *Focus on Autism and Other Developmental Disabilities, 20*(1), 52–63. doi:10.1177/10883576050200010501

Burwell, R., & Chen, C. P. (2006). Applying the principles and techniques of solution-focused therapy to career counseling. *Counseling Psychology Quarterly, 19,* 189–203. doi:10.1080/09515070600917761

Byrne, N., Regan, C., & Livingston, G. (2006). Adherence to treatment in mood disorders. *Current Opinion in Psychiatry, 19,* 44–49. doi:10.1097/01.yco.0000191501.54034.7c

Campbell, J. C., & Christopher, J. C. (2012). Teaching mindfulness to create effective counselors. *Journal of Mental Health Counseling, 34,* 213.

Carmody, J., Baer, R. A., Lykins, E. L. B., & Olendzki, N. (2009). An empirical study of the mechanisms of mindfulness in a mindfulness-based stress reduction program. *Journal of Clinical Psychology, 65*(6), 613–626. doi:10.1002/jclp.20579

Cantrell, R. P., Cantrell, M. L., Huddleston, C. M., & Woolridge, R. L. (1969). Contingency contracting with school problems. *Journal of Applied Behavior Analysis, 2,* 215–220. doi:10.1901/jaba.1969.2-215

Carlbring, P., Maurin, T., Sjömark, J., Maurin, L., Westling, B. E., Ekselius, L., Cuijpers, P., & Andersson, G. (2011). All at once or one at a time? A randomized controlled trial comparing two ways to deliver bibliotherapy for panic disorder. *Cognitive Behaviour Therapy, 40,* 228–235. doi:10.1080/16506073.2011.553629

Carlson, C., & Hoyle, R. (1993). Efficacy of abbreviated progressive muscle relaxation training: A quantitative review of behavioral medicine research. *Journal of Consulting and Clinical Psychology, 61,* 1059–1067. doi:10.1037/0022-006X.61.6.1059

Carlson, C. L., Mann, M., & Alexander, D. K. (2000). Effects of reward and response cost on the performance and motivation of children with ADHD. *Cognitive Therapy and Research, 24,* 87–98. doi:10.1023/A:1005455009154

Carlson, J., Watts, R. E., & Maniacci, M. (2006). *Adlerian therapy: Theory and practice.* Washington, DC: American Psychological Association.

Carr, A. (1997). Positive practice in family therapy. *Journal of Marital and Family Therapy, 23,* 271–293. doi:10.1111/j.1752-0606.1997.tb01036.x

Carroll, M., Bates, M., & Johnson, C. (2003). *Group leadership: Strategies for group counseling leaders* (4th ed.). Denver, CO: Love Publishing.

Cash, E., Salmon, P., Weissbecker, I., Rebholz, W. N., Bayley-Veloso, R., Zimmaro, L. A., … Sephton, S. E. (2015). Mindfulness meditation alleviates fibromyalgia symptoms in women: Results of a randomized clinical trial. *Annals of Behavioral Medicine, 49,* 319–330. doi:10.1007/s12160-014-9665-0

Cautela, J. R. (1971). Covert extinction. *Behavior Therapy, 2,* 192–200. doi:10.1016/S0005-7894(71)80005-9

Chafouleas, S. M., Riley-Tillman, T. C., & McDougal, J. L. (2002). Good, bad, or in-between: How does the daily behavior report card rate? *Psychology in the Schools, 39,* 157–169. doi:10.1002/pits.10027

Chan, K. M., & Horneffer, K. (2006). Emotional expression and psychological symptoms: A comparison of writing and drawing. *The Arts in Psychotherapy, 33*(1), 26–36. doi:10.1016/j.aip.2005.06.001

Charlop-Christy, M. H., & Haymes, L. K. (1998). Using objects of obsession as token reinforcers for children with autism. *Journal of Autism and Developmental Disorders, 28,* 189–199. doi:10.1023/A:1026061220171

Chaves, J. (1994). Recent advances in the application of hypnosis to pain management. *American Journal of Clinical Hypnosis, 37,* 117–129. doi:10.1080/00029157.1994.10403124

Cheung, M., & Nguyen, P. V. (2013). Connecting the strengths of Gestalt chairs to Asian clients. *Smith College Studies in Social Work, 82*(1), 51–62. doi:10.1080/00377317.2012.638895

Cheung, S., & Kwok, S. Y. C. (2003). How do Hong Kong children react to maternal I-messages and inductive reasoning? *The Hong Kong Journal of Social Work, 37,* 3–14.

Chien, H-C., Chung, Y-C., Yeh, M-L., & Lee, J-F. (2015). Breathing exercise combined with cognitive behavioural intervention improves sleep quality and heart rate variability in major depression. *Journal of Clinical Nursing, 24,* (21/22), 3206–3214. doi:10.1111/jocn.12972

Christenbury, L., & Beale, A. (1996). Interactive bibliocounseling: Recent fiction and nonfiction for adolescents and their counselors. *School Counselor, 44,* 133–145.

Clance, P. R., Thompson, M. B., Simerly, D. E., & Weiss, A. (1993). The effects of the Gestalt approach on body image. *The Gestalt Journal, 17,* 95–114.

Climie, E. A., & Mastoras, S. M. (2015). ADHD in schools: Adopting a strengths-based perspective. *Canadian Psychological Association, 56,* 295–300. doi:10.1037/cap0000030

Coelho, L. F., Barbosa, D. L. F., Rizzutti, S., Muszkat, M., Bueno, O. F. A., & Miranda, M. C. (2015). Use of cognitive behavioral therapy and token economy to alleviate dysfunctional behavior in children with attention-deficit hyperactivity disorder. *Frontiers in Psychiatry, 6.* https://doi.org/10.3389/fpsyt.2015.00167

Coker, J. K. (2010). Using Gestalt counseling in a school setting. In B. T. Erford (Ed.), *Professional school counseling: A handbook of theories, programs, and practices* (2nd ed., pp. 381–390). Austin, TX: Pro-Ed.

Comaty, J. E., Stasio, M., & Advokat, C. (2001). Analysis of outcome variables of a token economy system in a state psychiatric hospital: A program evaluation. *Research in Developmental Disabilities, 22,* 233–253. doi:10.1016/S0891-4222(01)00070-1

Cook-Vienot, R., & Taylor, R. J. (2012). Comparison of eye movement desensitization and reprocessing and biofeedback/stress inoculation training in treating test anxiety. *Journal of EMDR Practice & Research, 6,* 62–72. doi:10.1891/1933-3196.6.2.62

Cooley, K., Szczurko, O., Perri, D., Mills, E. J., Bernhardt, B., Zhou, Q., & Seely, D. (2009). Naturopathic care for anxiety: A randomized controlled Trial ISRCTN78958974. *Plos Clinical Trials, 6*(8), 1–10. doi:10.1371/journal.pone.0006628

Corcoran, J. (1997). A solution-oriented approach to working with juvenile offenders. *Child and Adolescent Social Work Journal, 14,* 277–288. doi:10.1023/A:1024546425621

Corcoran, J. (1998). Solution-focused practice with middle and high school at-risk youths. *Social Work in Education, 20,* 232–244. doi:10.1093/cs/20.4.232

Corcoran, J. (1999). Solution-focused interviewing with child protective services clients. *Child Welfare, 78,* 461–479.

Corey, G. (2016). *Theory and practice of counseling and psychotherapy* (10th ed.). Belmont, CA: Cengage.

Corey, M. S., Corey, G., & Corey, C. (2018). *Groups: Process and practice* (9th ed.). Belmont, CA: Cengage.

Corsini, R. J. (1982). The relapse technique in counseling and psychotherapy. *Individual Psychology, 38,* 380–386.

Cortés, B., Peralta, A., & Machado, M. C. (2007, September). *What makes for good outcomes in solution-focused therapy? A follow-up study.* Paper presented at European Brief Therapy Association Conference, Brugges, Belgium.

Courtney, E. A. (2015). Effect of cognitive restructuring, worry exposure, and contrast exposure on worry. *Dissertation Abstracts International: Section B: The Sciences and Engineering, 74*(6-B)(E).

Couser, G. (2008). Challenges and opportunities for preventing depression in the workplace: A review of the evidence supporting workplace factors and interventions. *Journal of Occupational and Environmental Medicine, 50,* 411–427. doi:10.1097/JOM.0b013e318168efe2

Crawford, R. M. (1998). Facilitating a reading anxiety treatment program for preservice teachers. *Reading Improvement, 35,* 11–14.

Crose, R. (1990). Reviewing the past in the here and now: Using Gestalt therapy techniques with life review. *Journal of Mental Health Counseling, 12,* 279–287.

Cuenin, L. H., & Harris, K. R. (1986). Planning, implementing, and evaluating timeout interventions with exceptional students. *Teaching Exceptional Children, 18,* 272–276. doi:10.1177/004005998601800408

Cupal, D., & Brewer, B. (2001). Effects of relaxation and guided imagery on knee strength, re-injury anxiety, and pain following anterior cruciate ligament reconstruction. *Rehabilitation Psychology, 46,* 28–43. doi:10.1037/0090-5550.46.1.28

Curtis, D. F., Pisecco, S., Hamilton, R. J., & Moore, D. W. (2006). Teacher perceptions of classroom interventions for children with ADHD: A cross-cultural comparison of teachers in the United States and New Zealand. *School Psychology Quarterly, 21,* 171–196. doi:10.1521/scpq.2006.21.2.171

D'Amico, E. J., Houck, J. M., Hunter, S. B., Miles, J. N. V., Osilla, K. C., & Ewing, B. A. (2015). Group motivational interviewing for adolescents: Change talk and alcohol and marijuana outcomes. *Journal of Consulting and Clinical Psychology, 83*(1), 68–80. doi:10.1037/a0038155

Dattilio, F. M. (2013). *Cognitive behavior therapy with couples and families.* New York, NY: Guilford Press.

Davidson, A., & Horvath, O. (1997). Three sessions of brief couples therapy: A clinical trial. *Journal of Family Psychology, 11,* 435–442. doi:10.1037/0893-3200.11.4.422-435

Davidson, K., & Fristad, M. (2006). The Treatment Beliefs Questionnaire (TBQ): An instrument to assess beliefs about children's mood disorders and concomitant treatment needs. *Psychological Services, 31,* 1–15. doi:10.1037/1541-1559.3.1.1

Davidson, T. (2014). STRENGTH: A system of integration of solution-oriented and strength-based principles. *Journal of Mental Health Counseling, 36,* 1–17. doi:10.17744/mehc.36.1.p0034451n14k4818

Davies, M. F. (2006). Irrational beliefs and unconditional self-acceptance. Correlational evidence linking two key features of REBT. *Journal of Rational-Emotive & Cognitive Behavior Therapy, 2,* 113–126. doi:10.1007/s10942-006-0027-0

Davis, M., Robbins-Eshelman, E., & McKay, M. (2009). *The relaxation and stress reduction workbook* (6th ed.). Oakland, CA: New Harbinger Publications.

Dawood, S., & Jehan, F. (2013). Efficacy of behavior therapy in the treatment of obsessive compulsive disorder. *Pakistan Journal of Clinical Psychology, 12*(1), 35–42.

Deacon, B. J., Fawzy, T. I., Lickel, J. J., & Wolitzky-Taylor, K. B. (2011). Cognitive defusion versus cognitive restructuring in the treatment of negative self-referential thoughts: An investigation of process and outcome. *Journal of Cognitive Psychotherapy, 25*, 218–232. doi:10.1891/0889-8391.25.3.218

Dean, S., Britt, E., Bell, E., Stanley, J., & Collings, S. (2016). Motivational interviewing to enhance adolescent mental health treatment engagement: A randomized clinical trial. *Psychological Medicine, 46*, 1961–1969. https://doi.org/10.1017/S0033291716000568

Deane, F. P., Mercer, J., Talyarkhan, A. I., Lambert, G., & Pickard, J. (2012). Group cohesion and homework adherence in multi-family group therapy for schizophrenia. *The Australian and New Zealand Journal of Family Therapy, 33*, 128–141. doi:10.1017/aft.2012.15

DeBord, J. B. (1989). Paradoxical interventions: A review of the recent literature. *Journal of Counseling & Development, 67*, 394–398. doi:10.1002/j.1556-6676.1989.tb02099.x

De Jong, P., & Hopwood, L. E. (1996). Outcome research on treatment conducted at the Brief Family Therapy Center, 1992–1993. In S. D. Miller, M. A. Hubble, & B. Duncan (Eds.), *Handbook of solution-focused brief therapy: Foundations, applications, and research* (pp. 272–298). San Francisco, CA: Jossey-Bass.

De Jong, P., & Miller, S. D. (1995). How to interview for client strengths. *Social Work, 40*, 729–736. doi:10.1093/sw/40.6.729

Dekker, R. (2015). Cognitive therapy for the treatment of depressive symptoms in patients with heart failure. *Dissertation Abstracts International: Section B: The Sciences and Engineering, 75*(9-B)(E).

De Martini-Scully, D., Bray, M. A., & Kehle, T. J. (2000). A packaged intervention to reduce disruptive behaviors in general education students. *Psychology in the Schools, 37*, 149–156. doi:10.1002/(SICI)1520-6807(200003)37:2<149::AID-PITS6>3.0.CO;2-K

de Shazer, S. (1988). *Clues: Investigating solutions in brief therapy.* New York, NY: W. W. Norton.

de Shazer, S. (1991). *Putting difference to work.* New York: W. W. Norton.

de Shazer, S., Dolan, Y., Korman, H., Trepper, T., McCollum, E., & Berg, I. K. (2007). *More than miracles: The state of the art of solution-focused brief therapy.* New York, NY: Haworth.

Diamond, G. M., Rochman, D., & Amir, O. (2010). Arousing primary vulnerable emotions in the context of unresolved anger: "Speaking about" versus "speaking to." *Journal of Counseling Psychology, 57*, 402–410. doi:10.1037/a0021115

Dixon, C., Mansell, W., Rawlinson, E., & Gibson, A. (2011). A transdiagnostic self-help guide for anxiety: Two preliminary controlled trials in subclinical student samples. *The Cognitive Behaviour Therapist, 4*(1), 1–15. doi:10.1017/S1754470X10000176

Donaldson, J. M., Vollmer, T. R., Yakich, T. M., & Van Camp, C. (2013). Effects of a reduced time-out interval on compliance with the time-out instruction. *Journal of Applied Behavior Analysis, 46*(2), 369–378. doi:10.1002/jaba.40

Dowden, A. R. (2009). Implementing self-advocacy training within a brief psychoeducational group to improve the academic motivation of black adolescents. *The Journal for Specialists in Group Work, 34*, 118–136. doi:10.1080/01933920902791937

Downing, J. A. (1990). Contingency contracts: A step-by-step format. *Intervention in School & Clinic, 26*, 111–113.

Doyle, J. S., & Bauer, S. K. (1989). Post-traumatic stress disorder in children: Its identification and treatment in a residential setting for emotionally disturbed youth. *Journal of Traumatic Stress, 2*, 275–288. doi:10.1002/jts.2490020304

Doyle, R. E. (1998). *Essential skills and strategies in the helping process* (2nd ed.). Pacific Grove, CA: Brooks/Cole.

Drayton, A. K., Byrd, M. R., Albright, J. J., Nelson, E. M., Andersen, M. N., & Morris, N. K. (2017). Deconstructing the time-out: What do mothers understand about a common disciplinary procedure? *Child & Family Behavior Therapy, 39*, 91–107. https://doi.org/10.1080/07317107.2017.1307677

Dryden, W. (1995). *Brief rational emotive behaviour therapy.* New York, NY: John Wiley & Sons.

Dryden, W., & Branch, R. (2008). *Fundamentals of rational emotive behavior therapy: A training handbook* (2nd ed.). New York, NY: Wiley.

Dryden, W., & David, D. (2008). Rational emotive behavior therapy: Current status. *Journal of Cognitive Psychotherapy: An International Quarterly, 22*, 195–209. doi:10.1891/08898391.22.3.195

Dryden, W., David, D., & Ellis, A. (2010). Rational emotive behavior therapy. In K. Dobson (Ed.), *Handbook of cognitive-behavioral therapies* (pp. 226–276). New York, NY: Guilford Press.

Duba, J. D., Kindsvatter, A., & Priddy, C. J. (2010). Deconstructing the mirror's reflection: Narrative therapy groups for women dissatisfied with their body. *Adultspan Journal, 9*, 103–116. https://doi.org/10.1002/j.21610029.2010.tb00075.x

Dwyer, S. C., Piquette, N., Buckle, J. L., & McCaslin, E. (2013). Women gamblers write a voice: Exploring journaling as an effective counseling and research tool. *Journal of Groups in Addiction & Recovery, 8*(1), 36–50. doi:10.1080/15560 35X.2013.727735

Eaves, S. H., Sheperis, C. J., Blanchard, T., Baylot, L., & Doggett, R. A. (2005). Teaching time out and job card grounding to parents: A primer for family counselors. *The Family Journal: Counseling and Therapy for Couples and Families, 13*, 252–258. doi:10.1177/1066480704273638

Eckstein, D. (1997). Reframing as a specific interpretive counseling technique. *Individual Psychology, 53*, 418–428.

Edelman, R. E., & Chambless, D. L. (1993). Compliance during sessions and homework in exposure-based treatment of agoraphobia. *Behaviour Research and Therapy, 31*, 767–773.

Egan, G. (2013). *The skilled helper* (10th ed.). Belmont, CA: Cengage.

Egbochukuand, E. O., & Obodo, B. O. (2005). Effects of systematic desensitisation (SD) therapy on the reduction of test anxiety among adolescents in Nigerian schools. *Journal of Instructional Psychology, 32*, 298–304.

Elias, M. J. (1983). Improving coping skills of emotionally disturbed boys through television-based social problem solving. *American Journal of Orthopsychiatry, 53*, 61–71. doi:10.1111/j.1939-0025.1983.tb03350.x

Ellis, A. (1969). A weekend of rational encounter. In A. Burton (Ed.), *Encounter* (pp. 112–127). San Francisco, CA: Jossey-Bass.

Ellis, A. (1971). An experiment in emotional education. *Educational Technology, 11*(7), 61–63.

Ellis, A. (1993). Reflections on rational-emotive therapy. *Journal of Consulting and Clinical Psychology, 61*, 199–201.

Ellis, A. (1997a). Must musterbation and demandingness lead to emotional disorders? *Psychotherapy: Theory, Research, Practice, Training, 34*, 95–98. doi:10.1037/h0087779

Ellis, A. (1997b). Using rational emotive behavior therapy techniques to cope with disability. *Professional Psychology: Research and Practice, 28*, 17–22. doi:10.1037/0735-7028.28.1.17

Ellis, A. (1999). Why rational-emotive therapy to rational emotive behavior therapy? *Psychotherapy: Theory, Research, Practice, Training, 36*, 154–159. doi:10.1037/h0087680

Ellis, A. (2001). *Overcoming destructive beliefs, feelings and behaviors: New directions for rational emotive behavior therapy.* New York, NY: Prometheus Books.

Ellis, A. (2003). Reasons why rational emotive behavior therapy is relatively neglected in the professional and scientific literature. *Journal of Rational-Emotive & Cognitive-Behavior Therapy, 21*, 245–252. doi:10.1023/A:1025842229157

Ellis, A. (2015). *Better, deeper, and more enduring brief therapy: The rational emotive behavior therapy approach.* New York, NY: Brunner/Mazel Inc.

Ellis, A., & Dryden, W. (2007). *The practice of rational emotive behavior therapy* (2nd ed.). New York, NY: Springer Publishing Company.

Ellis, A., Shaughnessy, M., & Mahan, V. (2002). An interview with Albert Ellis about rational emotive behavior therapy. *North American Journal of Psychology, 4*, 355–362.

Ellis, A., & Wilde, J. (2002). *Case studies in rational emotive behavior therapy with children and adolescents.* Upper Saddle River, NJ: Merrill Prentice Hall.

Emlyn-Jones, R. (2007). Think about it till it hurts: Targeting intensive services to facilitate behavior change—two examples from the field of substance misuse. *Criminal Behavior & Mental Health, 17*, 234–241. doi:10.1002/cbm.667

Enea, V., & Dafinoiu, I. (2009). Motivational/solution-focused intervention for reducing school truancy among adolescents. *Journal of Cognitive & Behavioral Psychotherapies, 9*, 185–198.

Eonta, A. M., Christon, L. M., Hourigan, S. E., Ravindran, N., Vrana, S. R., & Southam-Gerow, M. A. (2011). Using everyday technology to enhance evidence-based treatments. *Professional Psychology: Research and Practice, 42*, 513–520. doi:10.1037/a0025825

Erford, B. T. (1999). A modified time-out procedure for children with noncompliant or defiant behaviors. *Professional School Counseling, 2*, 205–210.

Erford, B. T. (2000). *The mutual storytelling game CD-ROM.* Alexandria, VA: American Counseling Association.

Erford, B. T. (2001). *Stressbuster relaxation exercises.* Alexandria, VA: American Counseling Association.

Erford, B. T. (Ed.). (2018). *Orientation to the counseling profession* (3rd ed.). Columbus, OH: Pearson.

Evans, J. R., Velsor, P. V., & Schumacher, J. E. (2002). Addressing adolescent depression: A role for school counselors. *Professional School Counseling, 5*, 211–219.

Evere, G. E., Hupp, S. D., & Olmi, D. J. (2010). Time-out with parents: A descriptive analysis of 30 years of research. *Education and Treatment of Children, 33*, 235–259. doi:10.1353/etc.0.0091

Faelton, S., & Diamond, D. (1990). *Tension turnaround.* Emmaus, PA: Rodale Press.

Farber, B. A. (2003). Self-disclosure in psychotherapy practice and supervision: An introduction. *Journal of Clinical Psychology, 59*, 525–528. doi:10.1002/jclp.10156

Farber, B. A. (2006). *Self-disclosure in psychotherapy.* New York, NY: Guilford Press.

Farzadfard, S. A., Abdekhodaee, M. S., & Chaman Abadi, A. G. (2015). Effectiveness of combined purposeful play therapy and narrative therapy on pre-school children's attention and concentration. *Journal of Fundamentals of Mental Health, 17*, 222–228.

Fearrington, J. Y., McCallum, R., & Skinner, C. H. (2011). Increasing math assignment completion using solution-focused brief counseling. *Education and Treatment of Children, 34*(1), 61–80. doi:10.1353/etc.2011.0005

Fernández-Marcos, T., & Calero-Elvira, A. (2015). Effects of thought stopping and cognitive defusion on discomfort and the ability to deal with negative thoughts. *Psicología Conductual: Revista Internacional Clínica y de la Salud, 23*(1), 107–126.

Fiksdal, B. L. (2017). A comparison of the effectiveness of a token economy system, a response cost condition, and a combination condition in reducing problem behaviors and increasing student academic engagement and performance in two first grade classrooms. *Dissertation Abstracts International: Section B: The Sciences and Engineering, Vol 75*(11-B)(E).

Filcheck, H. A., McNeil, C. B., Greco, L. A., & Bernard, R. S. (2004). Using a whole-class token economy and coaching of teacher skills in a preschool classroom to manage disruptive behavior. *Psychology in the Schools, 41*, 351–361. doi:10.1002/pits.10168

Fisher, G., & Harrison, T. (2013). *Substance abuse: Information for school counselors, social workers, therapists and counselors* (5th ed.). Upper Saddle River, NJ: Pearson.

Flaxman, A. E., & Bond, F. W. (2010). A randomized worksite comparison of acceptance and commitment therapy and stress inoculation training. *Behaviour Research and Therapy, 48*, 816–820. doi:10.1016/j.brat.2010.05.004

Fleming, M. F., Balousek, S. L., Grossberg, P. M., Mundt, M. P., Brown, D., Wiegel, J. R., … Saewyc, E. M. (2010). Brief physician advice for heavy drinking college students: A randomized controlled trial in college health clinics. *Journal of Studies on Alcohol and Drugs, 71*, 23–31.

Foa, E. B., Dancu, C. V., Hembree, E. A., Jaycox, L. H., Meadows, E. A., & Street, G. P. (1999). A comparison of exposure therapy, stress inoculation training, and their combination in reducing posttraumatic stress disorder in female assault victims. *Journal of Consulting and Clinical Psychology, 67*, 194–200. doi:10.1037/0022-006X.67.2.194

Fontaine, K. L. (2014). *Complementary and alternative therapies for nursing practice* (4th ed.). Upper Saddle River, NJ: Pearson.

Foxx, R. M., & Azrin, N. H. (1972). Restitution: A method of eliminating aggressive-disruptive behavior of retarded and brain damaged patients. *Behaviour Research & Therapy, 10*, 15–27. doi:10.1016/0005-7967(72)90003-4

Foxx, R. M., & Shapiro, S. T. (1978). The timeout ribbon: A non-exclusionary timeout procedure. *Journal of Applied Behavior Analysis, 11*, 125–136. doi:10.1901/jaba.1978.11-125

Frain, M. P., Berven, N. L., Tschopp, M. K., Lee, G. K., Tansey, T., & Chronister, J. (2007). Use of the resiliency model of family stress, adjustment and adaptation by rehabilitation counselors. *Journal of Rehabilitation, 73*(3), 18–25.

Frankl, V. E. (2004). *On the theory and therapy of mental disorders*. New York, NY: Runner-Routledge.

Frankl, V. E. (2006). *Man's search for meaning*. Boston, MA: Beacon Press.

Franklin, C., Biever, J., Moore, K., Demons, D., & Scamardo, M. (2001). The effectiveness of solution focused therapy with children in a school setting. *Research on Social Work Practice, 11*, 411–434. doi:10.1177/104973150101100401

Franklin, C., Streeter, C. L., Kim, J. S., & Tripodi, S. J. (2007). The effectiveness of a solution-focused, public alternative school for dropout prevention and retrieval. *Children & Schools, 29*, 133–144. doi:10.1093/cs/29.3.133

Freeman, A., & Rosenfield, B. (2002). Modifying therapeutic homework for patients with personality disorders. *Psychotherapy in Practice, 58*, 513–524. doi:10.1002/jclp.10029

Frey, A. J., & Doyle, H. D. (2001). Classroom meetings: A program model. *Children & Schools, 23*, 212–223. doi:10.1093/cs/23.4.212

Furmark, T., Carlbring, P., Hedman, E., Sonnenstein, A., Clevberger, P., Bohman, B., ... Andersson, G. (2009). Guided and unguided self-help for social anxiety disorder: Randomised controlled trial. *The British Journal of Psychiatry, 195*, 440–447. doi:10.1192/bjp.bp.108.060996

Gable, S. L., & Haidt, J. (2005). What (and why) is positive psychology? *Review of General Psychology, 9*, 103–110. doi:10.1037/1089-2680.9.2.103

Gallagher, P. A. (2010). *Teaching students with behavior disorders: Techniques and activities for classroom instruction* (3rd ed.). Denver, CO: Love.

Gardner, M., & Toope, D. (2011). A social justice perspective on strengths-based approaches: Exploring educators' perspectives and practices. *Canadian Journal of Education, 34*, 86–102.

Gardner, R. A. (1974). The mutual storytelling technique in the treatment of psychogenic problems secondary to minimal brain dysfunction. *Journal of Learning Disabilities, 7*, 135–143. doi:10.1177/002221947400700303

Gardner, R. A. (1986). *The psychotherapeutic techniques of Richard A. Gardner*. Cresskill, NJ: Creative Therapeutics.

Gelkopf, M., Lapid, L., Werbeloff, N., Levine, S. Z., Telem, A., Zisman-Ilani, Y., & Roe, D. (2016). A strengths-based case management service for people with serious mental illness in Israel: A randomized controlled trial. *Psychiatry Research, 241*, 182–189. doi:10.1016/j.psychres.2016.04.106

George, C. M. (2008). Solution-focused therapy: Strength-based counseling for children with social phobia. *Journal of Humanistic Counseling, Education and Development, 47*, 144–156. https://doi.org/10.1002/j.2161-1939.2008.tb00054.x

George, E., Iveson, C., & Ratner, H. (1999). *Problem to solution: Brief therapy with individuals and families* (rev. ed.). London, UK: BT Press.

George, R. L., & Christiani, T. S. (1995). *Counseling: Theory and practice* (4th ed.). Boston, MA: Allyn & Bacon.

Gerhart, D. R. (2007). Client advocacy in marriage and family therapy: A qualitative case study. *Journal of Family Psychotherapy, 18*, 39–56. doi:10.1300/J085v18n01_04

German, M. (2013). Developing our cultural strengths: Using the 'Tree of Life' strength-based, narrative therapy intervention in schools, to enhance self-esteem, cultural understanding and to challenge racism. *Educational & Child Psychology, 30*(4), 75–99.

Gilgun, J. F. (1999). CASPARS: New tools for assessing client risks and strengths. *Families in Society: The Journal of Contemporary Human Services, 80*, 450–459. doi:10.1606/1044-3894.1474

Gitlin-Weiner, K., Sandgrund, A., & Schaefer, C. (Eds.). (2000). *Play diagnosis and assessment* (2nd ed.). New York, NY: John Wiley & Sons.

Gladding, S., & Gladding, C. (1991). The ABCs of bibliotherapy for school counselors. *School Counselor, 39*, 7–11.

Glowacki, K., Warner, G., & White, C. (2016). The use of a token economy for behaviour and symptom management in adult psychiatric inpatients: A critical review of the literature. *Journal of Psychiatric Intensive Care, 12*, 119–127. https://doi.org/10.20299/jpi.2016.009

Gold, J. M., & Hartnett, L. (2004). Confronting the hierarchy of a child-focused family: Implications for family counselors. *The Family Journal, 12*, 271–274. doi:10.1177/1066480704264429

Gong, H., Ni, C-X., Liu, Y-Z., Zhang, Y., Su, W-J., Lian, Y-J., ... Jiang, C-L. (2016). Mindfulness meditation fo insomnia: A meta-analysis of randomized controlled trials. *Journal of Psychosomatic Research, 89*, 1–6. doi:10.1016/j.jpsychores.2016.07.016

Gonsalkorale, W. (1996). The use of hypnosis in medicine: The possible pathways involved. *European Journal of Gastroenterology & Hepatology, 8*, 520–524.

Gonzalez, J., Nelson, J., Gutkin, T., Saunders, A., Galloway, A., & Shwery, C. (2004). Rational emotive therapy with children and adolescents: A meta-analysis. *Journal of Emotional and*

Behavioral Disorders, 12, 222–235. doi:10.1177/10634266040120040301

Goodman, L. A., Llang, B., Helms, J. E., Latta, R. E., Sparks, E., & Weintraub, S. R. (2004). Training counseling psychologists as social justice agents: Feminist and multicultural principles in action. *The Counseling Psychologist, 32*, 793–837. doi:10.1177/0011000004268802

Gordon, T. (1975). *P.E.T., Parent effectiveness training: The tested new way to raise responsible children.* New York, NY: Plume.

Govindji, R., & Linley, P. A. (2007). Strengths use, self-concordance and well-being: Implications for strengths coaching and coaching psychologists. *International Coaching Psychology Review, 2*, 143–153.

Goyal, M., Singh, S., Sibinga, E. M. S., Gould, N. F., Rowland-Seymour, A., Sharma, R., … Haythornthwaite, J. A. (2014). Meditation programs for psychological stress and well-being: A systematic review and meta-analysis. *JAMA Internal Medicine, 174*, 357–368. doi:10.1001/jamainternmed.2013.13018

Grainger, R. (1991). The use and abuse of negative thinking. *American Journal of Nursing, 8*, 13–14.

Graziano, A. M., DeGiovanni, I. S., & Garcia, K. A. (1979). Behavioral treatment of children's fears: A review. *Psychological Bulletin, 86*, 804–830. doi:10.1037/0033-2909.86.4.804

Green, V. A., Drysdale, H., Boelema, T., Smart, E., Van der Meer, L., Achmadi, D., … Lancioni, G. (2013). Use of video modeling to increase positive peer interactions of four preschool children with social skills difficulties. *Education and Treatment of Children, 36*(2), 59–85. doi:10.1353/etc.2013.0016

Greenberg, L. J., Warwar, S. H., & Malcolm, W. M. (2008). Differential effects of emotion-focused therapy and psychoeducation in facilitating forgiveness and letting go of emotional injuries. *Journal of Counseling Psychology, 55*, 185–196. doi:10.1037/0022-0167.55.2.185

Greenberg, L. S., & Higgins, H. M. (1980). Effects of two-chair dialogue and focusing on conflict resolution. *Journal of Counseling Psychology, 27*, 221–224. doi:10.1037/0022-0167.27.3.221

Gregory, R., Canning, S., Lee, T., & Wise, J. (2004). Cognitive bibliotherapy for depression: A meta-analysis. *Professional Psychology: Research and Practice, 35*, 275–280. doi:10.1037/0735-7028.35.3.275

Groden, G., & Cautela, J. R. (1981). Behavior therapy: A survey of procedures for counselors. *The Personnel and Guidance Journal, 60*, 175–180. doi:10.1002/j.2164-4918.1981.tb00774.x

Groeneveld, I. F., Proper, K. I., van der Beek, A. J., & van Mechelen, W. (2010). Sustained body weight reduction by an individual-based lifestyle intervention for workers in the construction industry at risk for cardiovascular disease: Results of a randomized controlled trial. *Preventive Medicine: An International Journal Devoted to Practice and Theory, 51*, 240–246. doi:10.1016/j.ypmed.2010.07.021

Grothaus, T., McAuliffe, G., & Craigen, L. (2012). Infusing cultural competence and advocacy into strength-based counseling. *Journal of Humanistic Counseling, 51*, 51–65. https://doi.org/10.1002/j.2161-1939.2012.00005.x

Guardino, C. M., Dunkel Schetter, C., Bower, J. E., Lu, M. C., & Smalley, S. L. (2014). Randomised controlled pilot trial of mindfulness training for stress reduction during pregnancy. *Psychology & Health, 29*, 334–349. doi:10.1080/08870446.2013.852670

Haberstroh, S., Trepal, H., & Parr, G. (2005). The confluence of technology and narrative approaches in group work: Techniques and suggestions for using interactive e-journals. *Journal of Creativity in Mental Health, 1*(2), 29–44. https://doi.org/10.1300/J456v01n02_04

Hackney, H., & Cormier, L. (2017). *The professional counselor: A process guide to helping* (8th ed.). Upper Saddle River, NJ: Pearson.

Haimann, P. E. (2005). Time out to correct misbehavior may aggravate it instead. *Brown University Child & Adolescent Behavior, 14*, 1–5.

Hains, A. A., & Szyjakowski, M. (1990). A cognitive stress-reduction intervention program for adolescents. *Journal of Counseling Psychology, 37*, 79–84. doi:10.1037/0022-0167.37.1.79

Hajzler, D. J., & Bernard, M. E. (1991). A review of rational-emotive education outcome studies. *School Psychology Quarterly, 6*, 27–49. doi:10.1037/h0088242

Hallenbeck, B. A., & Kauffman, J. M. (1995). How does observational learning affect the behavior of students with emotional or behavioral disorders? A review of research. *Journal of Special Education, 29*, 45–71. doi:10.1177/002246699502900103

Hammond, J. M. (1981). *When my dad died.* Ann Arbor, MI: Cranbrook Publishing.

Han, H-Y., Yao, S-M., Li, Z-J., Guo, M., Fu, Z-Y., Xu, Z-Y., … Liu, J. (2013). Cognitive-behavioral therapy components for generalized anxiety disorder: A Delphi poll study. *Chinese Mental Health Journal, 27*(1), 4–10.

Hardcastle, S. J., Taylor, A. H., Bailey, M. P., Harley, R. A., & Haggar, M. S. (2013). Effectiveness of a motivational interviewing intervention on weight loss, physical activity and cardiovascular disease risk factors: A randomised controlled trial with a 12-month post-intervention follow-up. *The International Journal of Behavioral Nutrition and Physical Activity, 10*, 40. doi:10.1186/1479-5868-10-40

Hardy, J., Oliver, E., & Tod, D. (2008). A framework for the study and application of self-talk in sport. In S. D. Mellalieu & S. Hanton (Eds.), *Advances in applied sport psychology: A review* (pp. 37–74). London, UK: Routledge.

Harman, R. L. (1974). Techniques of Gestalt therapy. *Professional Psychology, 12*, 257–263. doi:10.1037/h0037289

Harrison, R. (2001). Application of Adlerian principles in counseling survivors of sexual abuse. *The Journal of Individual Psychology, 57*(1), 91–101.

Hartz, G. W., Brennan, P. L., Aulakh, J. S., & Estrin, M. T. (2010). Behavioral contracting with psychiatric residents in long-term care: An exploratory study. *The Journal of Aging and Mental Health, 33*, 347–362. doi:10.1080/07317115.2010.502466

Hatch, T., Shelton, T., & Monk, G. (2009). Making the invisible visible: School counselors empowering students with disabilities through self-advocacy training. *Journal of School Counseling, 7*(14). Retrieved from http://www.jsc.montana.edu/articles/v7n14.pdf

Hay, C. E., & Kinnier, R. T. (1998). Homework in counseling. *Journal of Mental Health Counseling, 20*, 122–133.

Hayes, S. C., Strosahl, K. D., & Wilson, K. G. (2003). *Acceptance and commitment therapy: An experiential approach to behavior change.* New York, NY: Guilford Press.

Hays, D. G., & Erford, B. T. (Eds.). (2018). *Developing multicultural counseling competency: A systems approach* (3rd ed.). Columbus, OH: Pearson.

Hayward, M., Overton, J., Dorey, T., & Denney, J. (2009). Relating therapy for people who hear voices: A case series. *Clinical Psychology & Psychotherapy, 16*, 216–227. doi:10.1002/cpp.615

Healy, C. C. (1974). Furthering career education through counseling. *Personnel and Guidance Journal, 52*, 653–658. doi:10.1002/j.2164-4918.1974.tb03955.x

Heaton, L. J., Leroux, B. G., Ruff, P. A., & Coldwell, S. E. (2013). Computerized dental injection fear treatment: A randomized clinical trial. *Journal of Dental Research, 92*(7 Suppl), 37S-42S. doi:10.1177/0022034513484330

Hebert, T., & Furner, J. (1997). Helping high ability students overcome math anxiety through bibliotherapy. *Journal of Secondary Gifted Education, 8*, 164–178.

Henington, C., & Doggett, R. A. (2016). Setting up and managing a classroom. In B. T. Erford (Ed.), *Professional school counseling: A handbook of theories, programs, & practices* (3rd ed., pp. 233–250). Austin, TX: Pro-Ed.

Hensel-Dittmann, D., Schauer, M., Ruf, M., Catani, C., Odenwald, M., Elbert, T., & Neuner, F. (2011). Treatment of traumatized victims of war and torture: A randomized controlled comparison of narrative exposure therapy and stress inoculation training. *Psychotherapy and Psychosomatics, 80*, 345–352. doi:10.1159/000327253

Herring, R. D., & Runion, K. B. (1994). Counseling ethnic children and youth from an Adlerian perspective. *Journal of Multicultural Counseling & Development, 22*, 215–226. doi:10.1002/j.2161-1912.1994.tb00255.x

Hofmann, S. G., & Asmundson, G. J. (2008). Acceptance and mindfulness-based therapy: New wave or old hat? *Clinical Psychology Review, 28*(1), 1–16. doi:10.1016/j.cpr.2007.09.003

Hoge, E. A., Guidos, B. M., Mete, M., Bui, E., Pollack, M. H., Simon, N. M., & Dutton, M. A. (2017). Effects of mindfulness meditation on occupational functioning and health care utilization in individuals with anxiety. *Journal of Psychosomatic Research, 95*, 7–11. https://doi.org/10.1016/j.jpsychores.2017.01.011

Hogg, V., & Wheeler, J. (2004). Miracles R them: Solution-focused practice in a social services duty team. *Practice, 16*, 299–314.

Hollandsworth, J. G., Jr. (1977). Differentiating assertion and aggression: Some behavioral guidelines. *Behavior Therapy, 8*, 347–352. doi:10.1016/S0005-7894(77)80067-1

Hopp, M. A., Horn, C. L., McGraw, K., & Meyer, J. (2000). *Improving students' ability to problem solve through social skills instruction.* Chicago, IL: St. Xavier University.

Horan, J. J. (1996). Effects of computer-based cognitive restructuring on rationally mediated self-esteem. *Journal of Counseling Psychology, 43*, 371–375. doi:10.1037/0022-0167.43.4.371

Horton, A. M., Jr., & Johnson, C. H. (1977). The treatment of homicidal obsessional ruminations by thought-stopping and covert assertion. *Journal of Behavioral Therapy & Experimental Psychiatry, 8*, 339–340. doi:10.1016/0005-7916(77)90084-2

Houlding, C., Schmidt, F., & Walker, D. (2010). Youth therapist strategies to enhance homework completion. *Child and Adolescent Mental Health, 15*, 103–109. doi:10.1111/j.1475-3588.2009.00533

Houram, L. L., Kizakevich, P. N., Hubal, R., Spira, J., Strange, L. B., Holiday, D. B., Bryant, S., & McLean, A. N. (2011). Predeployment stress inoculation training for primary prevention of combat-related stress disorders. *Journal of CyberTherapy and Rehabilitation, 4*(1), 101–116.

Hubbard, K. K., & Blyler, D. (2016). Improving academic performance and working memory in health science graduate students using progressive muscle relaxation training. *The American Journal of Occupational Therapy, 70*. doi:10.5014/ajot.2016.020644

Ibrahim, N., Michail, M., & Callaghan, P. (2014). The strengths-based approach as a service delivery model for severe mental illness: A meta-analysis of clinical trials. *BMC Psychiatry, 14*, 243. https://doi.org/10.1186/s12888-014-0243-6

Iftene, F., Predescu, E., Stefan, S., & David, D. (2015). Rational-emotive and cognitive-behavior therapy (REBT/CBT) versus pharmacotherapy versus REBT/CBT plus pharmacotherapy in the treatment of major depressive disorder in youth: A randomized clinical trial. *Psychiatry Research, 225*, 687–694. https://doi.org/10.1016/j.psychres.2014.11.021

Iskander, J. M., & Rosales, R. (2013). An evaluation of the components of a Social Stories™ intervention package. *Research in Autism Spectrum Disorders, 7*(1), 1–8. doi:10.1016/j.rasd.2012.06.004

Ivey, A. E., Ivey, M. B., & Zalaquett, C. P. (2018). *Intentional interviewing and counseling: Facilitating client development in a multicultural society* (9th ed.). Boston, MA: Cengage.

Ivy, J. W., Meindl, J. N., Overley, E., & Robson, K. M. (2017). Token economy: A systematic review of procedural descriptions. *Behavior Modification, 41*, 708–737.

Jackson, S. (2001). Using bibliotherapy with clients. *Journal of Individual Psychology, 57*, 289–297.

Jacobson, E. (1977). The origins and development of progressive relaxation. *Journal of Behavior Therapy & Experimental Psychiatry, 8*, 119–123. doi:10.1016/0005-7916(77)90031-3

Jacobson, E. (1987). Progressive relaxation. *American Journal of Psychology, 100*, 522–537.

Jallo, N., Bourguignon, C., Taylor, A., & Utz, S. W. (2008). Stress management during pregnancy: Designing and evaluating a mind-body intervention. *Family & Community Health: The Journal of Health Promotion & Maintenance, 31*, 190–203. doi:10.1097/01.FCH.0000324476.48083.41

James, R. K., & Gilliland, B. E. (2003). *Theories and strategies in counseling and psychotherapy* (5th ed.). Boston, MA: Allyn & Bacon.

Jeffcoat, T., & Hayes, S. C. (2012). A randomized trial of ACT bibliotherapy on the mental health of K–12 teachers and staff. *Behaviour Research and Therapy, 50,* 571–579. doi:10.1016/j.brat.2012.05.008

Jessee, E. H., Jurkovic, G. J., Wilkie, J., & Chiglinsky, M. (1982). Positive reframing with children: Conceptual and clinical considerations. *American Journal of Orthopsychiatry, 52,* 314–322. doi:10.1111/j.1939-0025.1982.tb02692.x

Jewell, J. D., & Elliff, S. J. (2013). An investigation of the effectiveness of the Relaxation Skills Violence Prevention (RSVP) program with juvenile detainees. *Criminal Justice and Behavior, 40,* 203–213. doi:10.1177/0093854812464221

Jiang, S., Wu, L., & Gao, X. (2017). Beyond face-to-face individual counseling: A systematic review on alternative modes of motivational interviewing in substance abuse treatment and prevention. *Addictive Behaviors, 73,* 216–235. https://doi.org/10.1016/j.addbeh.2017.05.023

Johnco, C., Wuthrich, V. M., & Rapee, R. M. (2012). The role of cognitive flexibility in cognitive restructuring skill acquisition among older adults. *Journal of Anxiety Disorders, 27(6), 576–584.* doi:10.1016/j.janxdis.2012.10.004

Johns, K. (1992). Lowering beginning teacher anxiety about parent-teacher conferences through role-playing. *School Counselor, 40,* 146–153.

Johnson, C., Wan, G., Templeton, R., Graham, L., & Sattler, J. (2000). *"Booking it" to peace: Bibliotherapy guidelines for teachers.* (ERIC Document Reproduction Service No. ED451622)

Jokar, E., & Rahmati, A. (2015). The effect of stress inoculation training on anxiety and quality of sleep of pregnant women in third trimester. *Journal of Fundamentals of Mental Health, 17(2),* 103–109. http://doi.org/jfmh.mums.ac.ir/article_3985.html

Joling, K. J., van Hout, H. P. J., van't Veer-Tazelaar, P. J., van der Horst, H. E., Cuijpers, P., van de Ven, P. M., & van Marwijk, H. W. J. (2011). How effective is bibliotherapy for very old adults with subthreshold depression? A randomized controlled trial. *The American Journal of Geriatric Psychiatry, 19,* 256–265. doi:10.1097/JGP.0b013e3181ec8859

Jung, K., & Steil, R. (2012). The feeling of being contaminated in adult survivors of childhood sexual abuse and its treatment via a two-session program of cognitive restructuring and imagery modification: A case study. *Behavior Modification, 36(1),* 67–86. doi:10.1177/0145445511421436

Jungbluth, N. J., & Shirk, S. R. (2013). Promoting homework adherence in cognitive-behavioral therapy for adolescent depression. *Journal of Clinical Child and Adolescent Psychology, 42,* 545–553.

Kabat-Zinn, J. (2006). *Coming to our senses: Healing ourselves and the world through mindfulness.* New York, NY: Hyperion.

Kabat-Zinn, J. (2016). *Wherever you go, there you are: Mindfulness meditation for everyday life* (new ed.). London, UK: Piatkus Books.

Kahng, S. W., Boscoe, J. H., & Byrne, S. (2003, Fall). The use of an escape contingency and a token economy to increase food acceptance. *Journal of Applied Behavior Analysis, 36,* 249–353. doi:10.1901/jaba.2003.36-349

Kammerer, A. (1998). *Conflict management: Action research.* Greensboro, NC: ERIC-CASS (ERIC Document Reproduction Services No. ED422100).

Kantor, L., & Shomer, H. (1997). Lifestyle changes following a stress management programme: An evaluation. *South African Journal of Psychology, 27,* 81–246.

Kaplan, D. M., & Smith, T. (1995). A validity study of Subjective Unit of Discomfort (SUD) score. *Measurement & Evaluation in Counseling & Development, 27,* 195–199.

Kaplan, S., Engle, B., Austin, A., & Wagner, E. F. (2011). Applications in schools. In S. Naar-King & M. Suarez (Eds.) *Motivational interviewing with adolescents and young adults* (pp. 158–164). New York, NY: Guilford Press.

Kapoor, V., Bray, M. A., & Kehle, T. J. (2010). School-based intervention: Relaxation and guided imagery for students with asthma and anxiety disorder. *Canadian Journal of School Psychology, 25,* 311–327. doi:10.1177/0829573510375551

Kashani, F., Kashani, P., Moghimian, M., & Shakour, M. (2015). Effect of stress inoculation training on the levels of stress, anxiety, and depression in cancer patients. *Iranian Journal of Nursing & Midwifery Research, 20,* 359–364.

Katofsky, I., Backhaus, J., Junghanns, K., Rumpf, H. J., Hüppe, M., von Eitzen, U., & Hohagen, F. (2012). Effectiveness of a cognitive behavioral self-help program for patients with primary insomnia in general practice—a pilot study. *Sleep Medicine, 13,* 463–468. doi:10.1016/j.sleep.2011.12.008

Kazantzis, N., Deane, F. P., & Ronan, K. R. (2000). Homework assignments in cognitive and behavioral therapy: A meta-analysis. *Clinical Psychology: Science and Practice, 7,* 189–202.

Kazantzis, N., & Lampropoulos, G. K. (2002). Reflecting on homework in psychotherapy: What can we conclude from research and experience? *Journal of Clinical Psychology, 58,* 577–585. doi:10.1002/jclp.10034

Kazdin, A. E. (2008). *Parent management training: Treatment for oppositional, aggressive, and antisocial behavior in children and adolescents.* New York, NY: Oxford University Press.

Keeling, M. L., & Bermudez, M. (2006). Externalizing problems through art and writing: Experiences of process and helpfulness. *Journal of Marital and Family Therapy, 32,* 405–419. doi:10.1111/j.1752-0606.2006.tb01617.x

Keeney, K. M., Fisher, W. W., Adelinis, J. D., & Wilder, D. A. (2000). The effects of response cost in the treatment of aberrant behavior maintained by negative reinforcement. *Journal of Applied Behavior Analysis, 33,* 255–258. doi:10.1901/jaba.2000.33-255

Kehle-Forbes, S. M., Polusny, M. A., MacDonald, R., Murdoch, M., Meis, L. A., & Wilt, T. J. (2013). A systematic review of the efficacy of adding nonexposure components to exposure therapy for posttraumatic stress disorder. *Psychological Trauma: Theory, Research, Practice, and Policy, 5,* 317–322. doi:10.1037/a0030040

Kelley, M. L., & Stokes, T. F. (1982). Contingency contracting with disadvantaged youths: Improving classroom performance. *Journal of Applied Behavior Analysis, 15,* 447–454. doi:10.1901/jaba.1982.15-447

Keng, S., Smoski, M. J., & Robins, C. J. (2011). Effects of mindfulness on psychological health: A review of empirical studies. *Clinical Psychology Review, 31,* 1041–1056. doi:10.1016/j.cpr.2011.04.006

Kerner, E. A., & Fitzpatrick, M. R. (2007). Integrating writing into psychotherapy practice: A matrix of change processes and structural dimensions. *Psychotherapy: Theory, Research, Practice, and Training, 44,* 333–346. doi:10.1037/0033-3204.44.3.333

Kilfedder, C., Power, K., Karatzias, T., McCafferty, A., Niven, K., Chouliara, Z., Galloway, L., & Sharp, S. (2010). A randomized trial of face-to-face counselling versus telephone counselling versus bibliotherapy for occupational stress. *Psychology and Psychotherapy: Theory, Research and Practice, 83,* 223–242. doi:10.1348/147608309X476348

Kim, B. K., Hill, C. E., Gelso, C. J., Goates, M. K., Asay, P. A., & Harbin, J. M. (2003). Counselor self-disclosure, East Asian American client adherence to Asian cultural values, and counseling process. *Journal of Counseling Psychology, 50,* 324–332. doi:10.1037/0022-0167.50.3.324

Kiselica, M., & Baker, S. (1992). Progressive muscle relaxation and cognitive restructuring: Potential problems and proposed solutions. *Journal of Mental Health Counseling, 14,* 149–165.

Klainin-Yobas, P., Oo, W. N., Yew, P. Y. S., & Lau, Y. (2015). Effects of relaxation interventions on depression and anxiety among older adults: A systematic review. *Aging & Mental Health, 19*(12). https://doi.org/10.1080/13607863.2014.997191

Kleinpeter, C. B., Brocato, J., Fischer, R., & Ireland, C. (2009). Specialty groups for drug court participants. *Journal of Groups in Addiction & Recovery, 4,* 265–287. doi:10.1080/15560350903340486

Knoff, H. M. (2009). Time-out in the schools: Punitive or educative? Evidence based or poorly conceived? *Communiqué, 37,* 6.

Koken, J., Outlaw, A., & Green-Jones, M. (2011). Sexual risk reduction. In S. Naar-King & M. Suarez (Eds.), *Motivational interviewing with adolescents and young adults* (pp. 106–111). New York, NY: Guilford Press.

Konarski, E. A., Jr., Johnson, M. R., Crowell, C. R., & Whitman, T. L. (1981). An alternative approach to reinforcement for applied researchers: Response deprivation. *Behavior Therapy, 12,* 653–666. doi:10.1016/S0005-7894(81)80137-2

Kottler, J. A., & Chen, D. D. (2011). *Stress management and prevention* (2nd ed.). New York, NY: Routledge.

Kottman, T. (1990). Counseling middle school students: Techniques that work. *Elementary School Guidance & Counseling, 25,* 216–224.

Kottman, T. (1999). Integrating the crucial C's into Adlerian play therapy. *The Journal of Individual Psychology, 55,* 288–297.

Kotz, D., Huibers, M. H., West, R. J., Wesseling, G., & van Schayck, O. P. (2009). What mediates the effect of confrontational counselling on smoking cessation in smokers with COPD? *Patient Education and Counseling, 76*(1), 16–24. doi:10.1016/j.pec.2008.11.017

Koziey, P. W., & Andersen, T. (1990). Phenomenal patterning and guided imagery in counseling: A methodological pilot. *Journal of Counseling & Development, 68,* 664–667. doi:10.1002/j.1556-6676.1990.tb01433.x

Kraft, R. G., Claiborn, C. D., & Dowd, T. E. (1985). Effects of positive reframing and paradoxical directives in counseling for negative emotions. *Journal of Counseling Psychology, 32,* 617–621. doi:10.1037/0022-0167.32.4.617

Kress, V. E., Adamson, N., DeMarco, C., Paylo, M. J., & Zoldan, C. A. (2013). The use of guided imagery as an intervention in addressing nonsuicidal self-injury. *Journal of Creativity in Mental Health, 8*(1), 35–47. doi:10.1080/15401383.2013.763683

Kronner, H. W. (2013). Use of self-disclosure for the gay male therapist: The impact on gay males in therapy. *Journal of Social Service Research, 39*(1), 78–94. doi:10.1080/01488376.2012.686732

Kropp, P., Meyer, B., Dresler, T., Fritsche, G., Gaul, C., Niederberger, U., … Straube, A. (2017, October). Relaxation techniques and behavioural therapy for the treatment of migraine: Guidelines from the German Migraine and Headache Society. *Schmerz, 31*(5), 433–447. doi:10.1007/s00482-017-0214-1

Kubany, E. S., & Richard, D. C. (1992). Verbalized anger and accusatory "you" messages as cues for anger and antagonism among adolescents. *Adolescence, 27,* 505–516.

Kubany, E. S., Richard, D. C., Bauer, G. B., & Muraoka, M. Y. (1992). Impact of assertive and accusatory communication of distress and anger: A verbal component analysis. *Aggressive Behavior, 18,* 337–347. doi:10.1002/1098-2337(1992)18:5<337::AID-AB2480180503>3.0.CO;2-K

Lamb, C. S. (1980). The use of paradoxical intention: Self-management through laughter. *The Personnel and Guidance Journal, 59,* 217–219.

Lannin, D. G., Guyll, M., Vogel, D. L., & Madon, S. (2013). Reducing the stigma associated with seeking psychotherapy through self-affirmation. *Journal of Counseling Psychology, 60,* 508–519. doi:10.1037/a0033789

Laselle, K. M., & Russell, T. T. (1993). To what extent are school counselors using meditation and relaxation techniques? *School Counselor, 40,* 178–184.

Lazarus, A. A. (1989). *The practice of multimodal therapy: Systematic, comprehensive, and effective psychotherapy.* Baltimore, MD: Johns Hopkins University Press.

Lee, D. J., Schnitzlein, C. W., Wolf, J. P., Vythilingam, M., Rasmusson, A. M., & Hoge, C. W. (2016). Psychotherapy versus pharmacotherapy for posttraumatic stress disorder: Systematic review and meta-analysis to determine first-line treatments. *Depression and Anxiety, 33,* 72–806, doi:10.1002/da.22511

Lee, M. (1997). A study of solution-focused brief family therapy: Outcomes and issues. *The American Journal of Family Therapy, 25,* 3–17. doi:10.1080/01926189708251050

Lega, L., & Ellis, A. (2001). Rational emotive behavior therapy in the new millennium: A cross-cultural approach. *Journal of Rational-Emotive & Cognitive-Behavior Therapy, 19,* 201–222. doi:10.1023/A:1012537814117

Lent, J. (2009). Journaling enters the 21st century: The use of therapeutic blogs in counseling. *Journal of Creativity in Mental Health, 4*, 68–73. doi:10.1080/15401380802705391

Lerma, A., Pérez-Grovas, H., Bermudez, L., Peralta-Pedrero, M. L., Robles-García, R., & Lerma, C. (2017). Brief cognitive behavioural intervention for depression and anxiety symptoms improves quality of life in chronic haemodialysis patients. *Psychology and Psychotherapy: Theory, Research and Practice, 90*(1), 105–123.

Lethem, J. (2002). Brief solution-focused therapy. *Child and Adolescent Mental Health, 7*, 189–192. doi:10.1111/1475-3588.00033

Leucht, C. A., & Tan, S. Y. (1996). "Homework" and psychotherapy: Making between-session assignments more effective. *Journal of Psychology and Christianity, 15*, 258–269.

Leung, A. W., & Heimberg, R. G. (1996). Homework compliance, perceptions of control, and outcome of cognitive-behavioral treatment of social phobia. *Behaviour Research and Therapy, 34*, 423–432.

Lewis, T. (2014). *Substance abuse and addiction treatment: Practical application of counseling theory.* Upper Saddle River, NJ: Pearson.

Liberman, R. P. (2000, September). Images in psychiatry: The token economy. *The American Journal of Psychiatry, 157*, 1398. doi:10.1176/appi.ajp.157.9.1398

Lindforss, L., & Magnusson, D. (1997). Solution-focused therapy in prison. *Contemporary Family Therapy, 19*, 89–104. doi:10.1023/A:1026114501186

Linehan, M. M. (1993). *Cognitive behavioral therapy for borderline personality disorder.* New York, NY: Guilford Press.

Linton, J. M. (2005). Mental health counselors and substance abuse treatment: Advantages, difficulties, and practical issues to solution-focused interventions. *Journal of Mental Health Counseling, 27*, 297–310. doi:10.17744/mehc.27.4.qpj656h044442370

Littrell, J. M., Malia, J. A., & Vanderwood, M. (1995). Single-session brief counseling in a high school. *Journal of Counseling & Development, 13*, 451–458. doi:10.1002/j.1556-6676.1995.tb01779.x

Lopes, R. T., Gonçalves, M. M., Machado, P. P. P., Sinai, D., Bento, T., & Salgado, J. (2014). Narrative therapy vs. cognitive-behavioral therapy for moderate depression: Empirical evidence from a controlled clinical trial. *Psychotherapy Research, 24*(6), 662–674. https://doi.org/10.1080/10503307.2013.874052

Lowe, R. (2004). *Family therapy: A constructive framework.* Thousand Oaks, CA: Sage Publications.

Lundahl, B., Moleni, T., Burke, B. L., Butters, R., Tollefson, D., Butler, C., & Rollnick, S. (2013). Motivational interviewing in medical care settings: A systematic review and meta-analysis of randomized controlled trials. *Patient Education and Counseling, 93*, 157–168. https://doi.org/10.1016/j.pec.2013.07.012

Luskin, F., & Pelletier, K. R. (2005). *Stress free for good.* San Francisco, CA: Harper Collins.

Lynch, R. (2006). Coercion and social exclusion: The case of motivating change in drug-using offenders. *British Journal of Community Justice, 4*(1), 33–48.

Lyons, J. S., Uziel-Miller, N. D, Reys, F., & Sokol, P. T. (2000). Strengths of children and adolescents in residential settings: Prevalence and associations with psychopathology discharge placement. *American Academy of Child and Adolescent Psychiatry, 39*, 176–181. https://doi.org/10.1097/00004583-200002000-00017

MacCluskie, K. (2010). *Acquiring counseling skills: Integrating theory, multiculturalism, and self-awareness.* Columbus, OH: Merrill.

Macrae, C. N., Bodenhasen, G. V., Milne, A. B., & Jetten, J. (1994). Out of mind but back in sight: Stereotypes on the rebound. *Journal of Personality and Social Psychology, 67*, 808–817. doi:10.1037/0022-3514.67.5.808

Madu, V. N., & Adadu, P. M. A. (2011). Counseling students with depressive tendencies for better educational and personal-social adjustment: The cognitive restructuring approach. *Global Journal of Educational Research, 10*(1), 29–33.

Mahalik, J., & Kivlighan, D. (1988). Self-help treatment for depression: Who succeeds? *Journal of Counseling Psychology, 35*, 237–242. doi:10.1037/0022-0167.35.3.237

Martinez, C. R. (1986). *Classroom observations of three behavior management programs.* Greensboro, NC: ERIC-CASS (EDRS No. ED269164).

Matson, J. L., Horne, A. M., Ollendick, D. G., & Ollendick, T. H. (1979). Overcorrection: A further evaluation of restitution and positive practice. *Journal of Behavior Therapy & Experimental Psychiatry, 10*, 295–298. doi:10.1016/0005-7916(79)90006-5

Matson, J. L., & Keyes, J. B. (1990). A comparison of DRO to movement suppression time-out and DRO with two self-injurious and aggressive mentally retarded adults. *Research in Developmental Disabilities, 11*, 111–120. doi:10.1016/0891-4222(90)90008-V

Maultsby, M., Jr. (1990). *Rational behavior therapy.* Martindale, TX: Seaton Foundation.

McDonald, B. R., & Morgan, R. D. (2013). Enhancing homework compliance in correctional psychotherapy. *Criminal Justice and Behavior, 40*, 814–828. doi:10.1177/0093854813480781

McGinnis, J. C., Friman, P. C., & Carlyon, W. D. (1999, Fall). The effect of token rewards on "intrinsic" motivation for doing math. *Journal of Applied Behavior Analysis, 32*, 375–379. doi:10.1901/jaba.1999.32-375

McGoey, K. E., & DuPaul, G. J. (2000, Fall). Token reinforcement and response cost procedures: Reducing the disruptive behavior of preschool children with attention-deficit/hyperactivity disorder. *School Psychology Quarterly, 15*, 330–343. doi:10.1037/h0088790

McManus, F., Van Doorn, K., & Yiend, J. (2012). Examining the effects of thought records and behavioral experiments in instigating belief change. *Journal of Behavior Therapy and Experimental Psychiatry, 43*, 540–547. doi:10.1016/j.jbtep.2011.07.003

Meichenbaum, D. (2003). *A clinical handbook/practical therapist manual for assessing and treating adults with post-traumatic stress disorder.* Toronto, Ontario, Canada: Institute Press.

Meichenbaum, D. H., & Deffenbacher, J. L. (1988). Stress inoculation training. *The Counseling Psychologist, 16*, 69–90. doi:10.1177/0011000088161005

Menzies, V., & Kim, S. (2008). Relaxation and guided imagery in Hispanic persons diagnosed with fibromyalgia: A pilot study. *Family & Community Health: The Journal of Health Promotion & Maintenance, 31*, 204–212. doi:10.1097/01.FCH.0000324477.48083.08

Messling, P. A., III, & Dermer, M. L. (2009). Increasing students' attendance at lecture and preparation for lecture by allowing students to use their notes during tests. *Behavior Analyst Today, 10*, 381–390. doi:10.1037/h0100678

Meyer, D. D., & Cottone, R. (2013). Solution-focused therapy as a culturally acknowledging approach with American Indians. *Journal of Multicultural Counseling and Development, 41*(1), 47–55. doi:10.1002/j.2161-1912.2013.00026.x

Michalopoulou, E., Tzamalouka, G., Chrousos, G., P., & Darviri, C. (2015). Stress management and intimate partner violence: A randomized controlled trial. *Journal of Family Violence, 30*, 795–802. doi:10.1007/s10896-015-9740-8

Mikulas, W. L. (1978). *Behavior modification.* New York, NY: Harper & Row.

Miller, D. L., & Kelley, M. L. (1994). The use of goal setting and contingency contracting for improving children's homework performance. *Journal of Applied Behavior Analysis, 27*, 73–84. doi:10.1901/jaba.1994.27-73

Miller, M., Kelly, W., Tobacyk, J., Thomas, A., & Cowger, E. (2001). A review of client compliancy with suggestions for counselors. *College Student Journal, 35*, 504–513.

Miller, W. R., & Rollnick, S. (1992). *Motivational interviewing: Preparing people to change addictive behavior.* New York, NY: Guilford Press.

Miller, W. R., & Rollnick, S. (2013). *Motivational interviewing: Helping people change* (3rd ed.). New York, NY: Guilford Press.

Miltenberger, R. G. (2016). *Behavior modification: Principles and procedures* (6th ed.). Boston, MA: Cengage.

Moldovan, R., Cobeanu, O., & David, D. (2013). Cognitive bibliotherapy for mild depressive symptomatology: Randomized clinical trial of efficacy and mechanisms of change. *Clinical Psychology & Psychotherapy, 20*, 482–493. doi:10.1002/cpp.1814

Morawska, A., & Sanders, M. (2010). Parental use of time out revisited: A useful or harmful parenting strategy? *Journal of Child Family Studies 20*, 1–8. doi:10.1007/s10826-010-9371-x

Morgenstern, J., Amrhein, P., Kuerbis, A., Hail, L., Lynch, K., & McKay, J. R. (2012). Motivational interviewing: A pilot test of active ingredients and mechanisms of change. *Psychology of Addictive Behaviors, 26*, 859–869. doi:10.1037/a0029674

Moritz, S., Schröder, J., Klein, J. P., Lincoln, T. M., Andreou, C., Fischer, A., & Arlt, S. (2016). Effects of online intervention for depression on mood and positive symptoms in schizophrenia. *Schizophrenia Research, 175*, 216–222. https://doi.org/10.1016/j.schres.2016.04.033

Morrison, G. M., Brown, M., D'incau, B., O'Farrell, S., & Furlong, M. J. (2006). *Psychology in Schools, 43*, 19–31. doi:10.1002/pits.20126

Mottram, L., & Berger-Gross, P. (2004). An intervention to reduce disruptive behaviours in children with brain injury. *Pediatric Rehabilitation, 7*, 133–143. doi:10.1080/1363849042000202286

Muller, A., & Hammill, H. (2015). The effect of Pilates and progressive muscle relaxation therapy (Mrt) on stress and anxiety during pregnancy: A literature review. *South African Journal of Sports Medicine, 27*(Suppl.), 53.

Murdoch, J. W., & Connor-Greene, P. A. (2000). Enhancing therapeutic impact and therapeutic alliance through electronic mail homework assignments. *The Journal of Psychotherapy Practice and Research, 9*, 232–237.

Murdock, N. L. (2013). *Theories of counseling and psychotherapy* (3rd ed.). Upper Saddle River, NJ: Pearson Education.

Murphy, J. J. (2015). *Solution-focused counseling in schools* (3rd ed.). Alexandria, VA: American Counseling Association.

Musser, E. H., Bray, M. A., Kehle, T. J., & Jenson, W. R. (2001). Reducing disruptive behaviors in students with serious emotional disturbance. *School Psychology Review, 30*, 294–305.

Myers, D., & Hayes, J. A. (2006). Effects of therapist general self-disclosure and countertransference disclosure on ratings of the therapist and session. *Psychotherapy: Theory, Research, Practice, Training, 43*, 173–185. doi:10.1037/0033-3204-.43.2.173

Myrick, R. D., & Myrick, L. S. (1993). Guided imagery: From mystical to practical. *Elementary School Guidance & Counseling, 28*, 62–70.

Naar-King, S., & Suarez, M. (Eds). (2011). *Motivational interviewing with adolescents and young adults.* New York, NY: Guilford Press.

Naugle, A. E., & Maher, S. (2008). Modeling and behavioral rehearsal. In W. O'Donohue, J. E. Fisher, & S. C. Hayes (Eds.), *Cognitive behavior therapy: Applying empirically supported techniques in your practice* (2nd ed.). New York, NY: John Wiley & Sons.

Neimeyer, R. A., Kazantzis, N., Kassler, D. M., Baker, K. D., & Fletcher, R. (2008). Group cognitive behavioural therapy for depression outcomes predicted by willingness to engage in homework, compliance with homework, and cognitive restructuring skill acquisition. *Cognitive Behavioural Therapy, 37*, 199–215. doi:10.1080/16506070801981240

Newman, M. G., & Fisher, A. J. (2010). Expectancy/credibility change as a mediator for cognitive behavioral therapy for generalized anxiety disorder: Mechanism of action or proxy for symptom change? *International Journal of Cognitive Therapy, 3*, 245–261.

Newsome, W. S. (2004). Solution-focused brief therapy (SFBT) groupwork with at-risk junior high school students: Enhancing the bottom-line. *Research on Social Work Practice, 14*, 336–343. doi:10.1177/1049731503262134

Nock, M., & Kazdin, A. (2005). Randomized control trial of a brief intervention for increasing participation in parent management training. *Journal of Consulting and Clinical Psychology, 73,* 872–879. doi:10.1037/0022-006X.73.5.872

Noggle, J. J., Steiner, N. J., Minami, T., & Khalsa, S. B. S. (2012). Benefits of yoga for psychosocial well-being in a U.S. high school curriculum: A preliminary randomized controlled trial. *Journal of Developmental and Behavioral Pediatrics, 33,* 193–201. doi:10.1097/DBP.0b013e31824afdc4

Nordin, S., Carlbring, P., Cuijpers, P., & Andersson, G. (2010). Expanding the limits of bibliotherapy for panic disorder: Randomized trial of self-help without support but with a clear deadline. *Behavior Therapy, 41,* 267–276. doi:10.1016/j.beth.2009.06.001

Nuernberger, P. (2007). *Freedom from stress: A holistic approach.* Honesdale, PA: Himalayan International Institute.

Oberst, E., & Stewart, A. E. (2003). *Adlerian psychotherapy: An advanced approach to individual psychology.* New York, NY: Brunner-Routledge.

O'Brien, J. D. (2000). Children with ADHD and their parents. In J. D. O'Brien & D. J. Pilowsky (Eds.), *Psychotherapies with children and adolescents: Adapting the psychodynamic process* (pp. 109–124). Washington, DC: American Psychiatric Press.

Ockene, J. K. (2001). Strategies to increase adherence to treatment. In L. E. Burke & I. S. Ockene (Eds.), *Monograph series. Compliance in Healthcare and Research* (pp. 43–55). Armonk, NY: Futura Publishing Co.

O'Hanlon, W. H., & Weiner-Davis, M. (2004). *In search of solutions: A new direction in psychotherapy* (rev. ed.). New York, NY: Norton.

Okamoto, A., Yamashita, T., Nagohshi, Y., Masui, Y., Wada, Y., & Kashima, A. (2002). A behavior therapy program combined with liquid nutrition designed for anorexia nervosa. *Psychiatry and Clinical Neurosciences, 56,* 515–520. doi:10.1046/j.1440-1819.2002.01047.x

Olmi, D. J., Sevier, R. C., & Nastasi, D. F. (1997). Time in/time-out as a response to noncompliance and inappropriate behavior with children with developmental disabilities: Two case studies. *Psychology in the Schools, 34,* 31–39. doi:10.1002/(SICI)1520-6807(199701)34:1<31::AID-PITS4>3.0.CO;2-Y

Olson, R. L., & Roberts, M. W. (1987). Alternative treatments for sibling aggression. *Behavior Therapy, 18,* 243–250. doi:10.1016/S0005-7894(87)80018-7

Orr, J. (2018). Counseling theories: Traditional and alternative approaches. In D. G. Hays & B. T. Erford (Eds.), *Developing multicultural counseling competency: A systems approach* (3rd ed., pp. 476–498). Columbus, OH: Pearson.

Osborn, D., & Costas, L. (2013). Role-playing in counselor student development. *Journal of Creativity in Mental Health, 8,* 92–103. doi:10.1080/15401383.2013.763689

Ost, L.-G. (1989). One-session treatment for specific phobias. *Behavior Research and Therapy, 27,* 1–7. doi:10.1016/0005-7967(89)90113-7

Overholser, J. (2000). Cognitive-behavioral treatment of panic disorder. *Psychotherapy: Theory, Research, Practice & Training, 37,* 247–256. doi:10.1037/h0087692

Oxman, E. B., & Chambliss, C. (2003). *Reducing psychiatric inpatient violence through solution-focused group therapy.* Retrieved from http://files.eric.ed.gov/fulltext/ED475586.pdf

Pagoto, S. L., Kozak, A. T., Spates, C. R., & Spring, B. (2006). Systematic desensitization for an older woman with a severe specific phobia: An application of evidenced-based practice. *Clinical Gerontologist: The Journal of Aging and Mental Health, 30*(1), 89–98. doi:10.1300/J018v30n01_07

Paivio, S. C., & Greenberg, L. S. (1995). Resolving "unfinished business": Efficacy of experimental therapy using empty chair dialogue. *Journal of Consulting and Clinical Psychology, 63,* 419–425. doi:10.1037/0022-006X.63.3.419

Paladino, D. A., Barrio Minton, C. A., & Kern, C. W. (2011). Interactive training model: Enhancing beginning counseling student development. *Counselor Education & Supervision, 50,* 189–206. doi:10.1002/j.1556-6978.2011.tb00119.x

Papadopoulou, M. (2012). The ecology of role play: Intentionality and cultural evolution. *British Educational Research Journal, 28,* 575–592. doi:10.1080/01411926.2011.569005

Park, J. M., Small, B. J., Geller, D. A., Murphy, T. K., Lewin, A. B., & Storch, E. A. (2013). Does D-cycloserine augmentation of CBT improve therapeutic homework compliance for pediatric obsessive–compulsive disorder? *Journal of Child and Family Studies, 23,* 863–871. doi:10.1007/s10826-013-9742-1

Patton, M., & Kivlighan, D. (1997). Relevance of the supervisory alliance to the counseling alliance and to treatment adherence in counselor training. *Journal of Counseling Psychology, 44,* 108–115. doi:10.1037/0022-0167.44.1.108

Paul, N. A., Stanton, S. J., Greeson, J. M., Smoski, M. J., & Wang, L. (2013). Psychological and neural mechanisms of trait mindfulness in reducing depression vulnerability. *Social Cognitive and Affective Neuroscience, 8,* 56–64. doi:10.1093/scan/nss070

Pearlman, M. Y., D'Angelo Schwalbe, K., & Cloltre, M. (2010). *Grief in childhood: Fundamentals of treatment in clinical practice.* Washington, DC: American Psychological Association.

Pearson, Q. M. (1994). Treatment techniques for adult female survivors of childhood sexual abuse. *Journal of Counseling & Development, 73,* 32–37. doi:10.1002/j.1556-6676.1994.tb01706.x

Peck, H. L., Bray, M. A., & Kehle, T. J. (2003). Relaxation and guided imagery: A school-based intervention for children with asthma. *Psychology in the Schools, 40,* 657–675. doi:10.1002/pits.10127

Peden, A. R., Rayens, M. K., Hall, L. A., & Beebe, L. H. (2001). Preventing depression in high-risk college women: A report of an 18-month follow-up. *Journal of American College Health, 49,* 299–306. doi:10.1080/07448480109596316

Pelekasis, P., Matsouka, I., & Koumarianou, A. (2017, August). Progressive muscle relaxation as a supportive intervention for cancer patients undergoing chemotherapy: A systematic review. *Palliative & Supportive Care, 15*(4), 475–473. https://doi.org/10.1017/S1478951516000870

Penzien, D., & Holroyd, K. (1994). Psychological interventions in the management of recurrent headache disorders 2: Description of treatment techniques. *Behavioral Medicine, 20,* 64–74. doi:10.1080/08964289.1994.9934618

Perciavalle, V., Blandini, M., Fecarotta, P., Buscemi, A., Di Corrado, D., Bertolo, L., ... Coco, M. (2017). The role of deep breathing on stress. *Neurological Sciences, 38,* 451–458. doi:10.1007/s10072-016-2790-8

Peterson, R. F., Loveless, S. E., Knapp, T. J., Loveless, B. W., Basta, S. M., & Anderson, S. (1979). The effects of teacher use of I-messages on student disruptive and study behavior. *Psychological Record, 29,* 187–199.

Phillips-Hershey, E., & Kanagy, B. (1996). Teaching students to manage personal anger constructively. *Elementary School Guidance & Counseling, 30,* 229–234.

Piccinin, S. (1992). Impact of treatment adherence intervention on a social skills program targeting criticism behaviours. *Canadian Journal of Counseling, 26,* 107–121.

Plummer, D. L., & Tukufu, D. S. (2001). Enlarging the field: African-American adolescents in a Gestalt context. In M. McConville & G. Wheeler (Eds.), *The heart of development: Vol II. Adolescence: Gestalt approaches to working with children, adolescents and their worlds* (pp. 54–71). New York, NY: Analytic Press/Taylor & Francis Group.

Polcin, D. L., Galloway, G. P., Bond, J., Korcha, R., & Greenfield, T. K. (2010). How do residents of recovery homes experience confrontation between entry and 12-month follow-up? *Journal of Psychoactive Drugs, 42*(1), 49–62. doi:10.1080/0 2791072.2010.10399785

Ponniah, K., & Hollon, S. D. (2009). Empirically supported psychological treatments for adult acute stress disorder and posttraumatic stress disorder: A review. *Depression & Anxiety, 26,* 1086–1109. doi:10.1002/da.20635

Popadiuk, N., Young, R. A., & Valach, L. (2008). Clinician perspectives on the therapeutic use of the self-confrontation procedure with suicidal clients. *Journal of Mental Health Counseling, 30*(1), 14–30. doi:10.17744/ mehc.30.1.h37l81l71u4986n0

Powell, S., Rosner, R., & Butollo, W. (2015). Dialogical exposure with traumatically bereaved Bosnian women: Findings from a controlled trial. *Clinical Psychology & Psychotherapy, 22,* 604–618. doi:10.1002/cpp.1921

Premack, D. (1962). Reversibility of the reinforcement relation. *Science, 136,* 255–257.

Presbury, J. H., Echterling, L. G., & McKee, J. E. (2002). *Ideas and tools for brief counseling.* Upper Saddle River, NJ: Pearson Education.

Prins, P., & Hanewald, G. (1999). Coping self-talk and cognitive interference in anxious children. *Journal of Consulting and Clinical Psychology, 67,* 435–439. doi:10.1037/0022-006X.67.3.435

Proctor, M. A., & Morgan, D. (1991). Effectiveness of a response cost raffle procedure on the disruptive classroom behavior of adolescents with behavior problems. *School Psychology Review, 20,* 97–109.

Proyer, R. T., Gander, F., Wellenzohn, S., & Rush, W. (2015). Strengths-based positive psychology interventions: A randomized placebo-controlled online trial on long-term effects for a signature strengths vs. a lesser strengths intervention. *Frontiers in Psychology, 6,* 456, 1–16. doi:10.3389/ fpsyg.2015.00456.

Purdon, C., & Clark, D. A. (2001). Suppression of obsession-like thoughts in nonclinical individuals: Impact on thought frequency, appraisal and mood state. *Behaviour Research and Therapy, 39,* 1163–1181. doi:10.1016/ S0005-7967(00)00092-9

Quigney, T. A., & Studer, J. R. (1999). Using solution-focused intervention for behavioral problems in an inclusive classroom. *American Secondary Education, 28*(1), 10–18.

Rapee, R. M., Abbott, M. J., & Lyneham, H. J. (2006). Bibliotherapy for children with anxiety disorders using written materials for parents: A randomized controlled trial. *Journal of Consulting & Clinical Psychology, 74,* 436–444. doi:10.1037/0022-006X.74.3.436

Rapisarda, C., Jencius, M., & McGlothlin, J. (2011). Master's students' experiences in a multicultural counseling role-play. *International Journal for the Advancement of Counselling, 33,* 361–375. doi:10.1007/s10447-011-9139-z

Rasmussen, P. R. (2002). Resistance: The fear behind it and tactics for reducing it. *The Journal of Individual Psychology, 58,* 148–159.

Rasmussen, P. R., & Dover, G. J. (2006). The purposefulness of anxiety and depression: Adlerian and evolutionary views. *The Journal of Individual Psychology, 62,* 366–396.

Ratts, M. J., & Hutchins, A. M. (2009). ACA advocacy competencies: Social justice advocacy at the client/student level. *Journal of Counseling and Development, 87,* 269–275. doi:10.1002/j.1566-6678.2009.tb00106.x

Ratts, M. J., Singh, A. A., Nassar-McMillan, S., Butler, S. K., & McCullough, J. R. (2015). *Multicultural and social justice counseling competencies.* Retrieved from http:// www.multiculturalcounseling.org/index.php?option=com_ content&view=article&id=205:amcd-endorses-multicultural- and-social-justice-counseling-competencies&catid=1:latest &Itemid=123

Reid, R. (1999). Attention deficit hyperactivity disorder: Effective methods for the classroom. *Focus on Exceptional Children, 32*(4), 1–20.

Reinecke, D. R., Newman, B., & Meinberg, D. L. (1999, Spring). Self-management of sharing in three pre-schoolers with autism. *Education and Training in Mental Retardation and Developmental Disabilities, 34,* 312–317.

Reiter, M. D. (2004). The surprise task: A solution-focused formula task for families. *Journal of Family Psychotherapy, 14*(3), 37–45. doi:10.1300/J085v15n03_03

Reitman, D., & Drabman, R. S. (1999). Multifaceted uses of a simple timeout record in the treatment of a noncompliant 8-year-old boy. *Education & Treatment of Children, 22,* 136–146.

Remer, R. (1984). The effects of interpersonal confrontation on males. *American Mental Health Counselors Association Journal, 6,* 56–70.

Richmond, C. J., Jordan, S. S., Bischof, G. H., & Sauer, E. M. (2014). Effects of solution-focused versus problem-focused intake questions on pre-treatment change. *Journal of Systemic Therapies, 33,* 33–47. doi:10.1521/jsyt.2014.33.1.33

Richmond, R. L. (2017). *Systematic desensitization.* Retrieved from http://www.guidetopsychology.com/sysden.htm

Riley, B. J. (2015). The role of homework in exposure-based CBT outcome for problem gambling. *International Gambling Studies, 15,* 394–407.

Riordan, R., & Wilson, L. (1989). Bibliotherapy: Does it work? *Journal of Counseling & Development, 67,* 506–508. doi:10.1002/j.1556-6676.1989.tb02131.x

Robbins, M. S., Alexander, J. F., & Turner, C. W. (2000). Disrupting defensive family interactions in family therapy with delinquent youth. *Journal of Family Psychology, 14,* 688–701. doi:10.1037/0893-3200.14.4.688

Roemer, L., & Burkovec, T. D. (1994). Effect of suppressing thoughts about emotional material. *Journal of Abnormal Psychology, 103,* 467–474. doi:10.1037/0021-843X.103.3.467

Rogers, C. (1995). *Client-centered therapy: Its current practice, implications, and theory (reprint edition).* London, UK: Constable.

Roome, J., & Romney, D. (1985). Reducing anxiety in gifted children by inducing relaxation. *Roeper Review, 7,* 177–179. doi:10.1080/02783198509552888

Rosenberg, H. J., Jankowski, M. K., Fortuna, L. R., Rosenberg, S. D., & Mueser, K. T. (2011). A pilot study of a cognitive restructuring program for treating posttraumatic disorders in adolescents. *Psychological Trauma: Theory, Research, Practice, and Policy, 3,* 94–99. doi:10.1037/a0019889

Ross, M., & Berger, R. (1996). Effects of stress inoculation training on athletes' post-surgical pain and rehabilitation after orthopedic injury. *Journal of Consulting and Clinical Psychology, 64,* 406–410. doi:10.1037/0022-006X.64.2.406

Ruth, W. J. (1994). Goal setting, responsibility training, and fixed ratio reinforcement: Ten-month application to students with emotional disturbance in a public school setting. *Psychology in the Schools, 31,* 146–154. doi:10.1002/1520-6807(199404)31:2<146::AID-PITS2310310209>3.0.CO;2-3

Rutledge, P. C. (1998). Obsessionality and the attempted suppression of unpleasant personal intrusive thoughts. *Behaviour Research and Therapy, 36,* 403–416. doi:10.1016/S0005-7967(98)00018-7

Ruwaard, J., Lange, A., Broeksteeg, J., Renteria-Agirre, A., Schrieken, B., Dolan, C. V., & Emmelkamp, P. (2013). Online cognitive-behavioural treatment of bulimic symptoms: A randomized controlled trial. *Clinical Psychology & Psychotherapy, 20,* 308–318. doi:10.1002/cpp.1767

Ryan, J. B., Peterson, R. L., & Rozalski, M. (2007). State policies concerning the use of seclusion timeout in schools. *Education and Treatment of Children, 30,* 215–239.

Sajadi, M., Goudarzi, K., Khosravi, S., Farahani, M. F., & Mohammadbeig, A. (2017). Benson's relaxation effect in comparing to systematic desensitization on anxiety of female nurses: A randomized clinical trial. *Indian Journal of Medical & Paediatric Oncology, 38,* 111–115.

Salend, S. J., & Allen, E. M. (1985). Comparative effects of externally managed and self-managed response-cost systems on inappropriate classroom behavior. *Journal of School Psychology, 23,* 59–67. doi:10.1016/0022-4405(85)90035-4

Saltzberg, J., & Dattilio, F. (1996). Cognitive techniques in clinical practice. *Guidance & Counseling, 11,* 27–31.

Saltzman, W., Pynoos, R., Lester, P., Layne, C., & Beardslee, W. (2013). Enhancing family resilience through family narrative co-construction. *Clinical Child and Family Psychology Review, 16,* 294–310. doi:10.1007/s10567-013-0142-2

Samaan, M. (1975). Thought-stopping and flooding in a case of hallucinations, obsessions, and homicidal-suicidal behavior. *Journal of Behavioral Therapy & Experimental Psychiatry, 6,* 65–67. doi:10.1016/0005-7916(75)90016-6

Sam Houston State University Counseling Center. (2018). *Breathing techniques.* Retrieved from http://www.shsu.edu/dept/counseling/breathing-techniques.html

Savage, T. A., Harley, D. A., & Nowak, T. M. (2005). Applying social empowerment strategies as tools for self-advocacy in counseling lesbian and gay male clients. *Journal of Counseling and Development, 83,* 131–137. doi:10.1002/j.1556-6678.2005.tb00589.x

Scales, P. C., Benson, P. L., Roehlkepartain, E. C., Sesma, A., & van Dulmen, M. (2006). *Journal of Adolescence, 29,* 691–708. doi:10.1016/j.adolescence.2005.09.001

Schaefer, C. E. (2011). *Foundations of play therapy* (2nd ed.). New York, NY: John Wiley & Sons.

Schafer, W. (1999). *Stress management for wellness* (4th ed.). Fort Worth, TX: Harcourt Brace Jovanovich College Publishers.

Scheel, M. J., Davis, C. K., & Henderson, J. D. (2013). Therapist use of client strengths: A qualitative study of positive processes. *The Counseling Psychologist, 41,* 392–427. doi:10.1177/0011000012439427

Scheel, M. J., Hanson, W. E., & Razzhavaikina, T. I. (2004). The process of recommending homework in psychotherapy: A review of therapist delivery methods, client acceptability, and factors that affect compliance. *Psychotherapy: Theory, Research, Practice, Training, 41,* 38–55. doi:10.1037/0033-3204.41.1.38

Scheveneels, S., Boddez, Y., Vervliet, B., & Hermans, D. (2016). The validity of laboratory-based treatment research: Bridging the gap between fear extinction and exposure treatment. *Behaviour Research & Therapy, 86,* 87–94. doi:10.1016/j.brat.2016.08.015

Schoettle, U. C. (1980). Guided imagery: A tool in child psychotherapy. *American Journal of Psychotherapy, 34,* 220–227.

Schuler, K., Gilner, F., Austrin, H., & Davenport, G. (1982). Contribution of the education phase to stress-inoculation training. *Psychological Reports, 51,* 611–617.

Schumacher, R., & Wantz, R. (1995). Constructing and using interactive workbooks to promote therapeutic goals. *Elementary School Guidance and Counseling, 29,* 303–310.

Schure, M. B., Christopher, J., & Christopher, S. (2008). Mind-body medicine and the art of self-care: Teaching mindfulness to counseling students through yoga, meditation, and

Qigong. *Journal of Counseling & Development*, *86*, 47–56. doi:10.1002/j.1556-6678.2008.tb00625.x

Scorzelli, J. F., & Gold, J. (1999). The mutual storytelling writing game. *Journal of Mental Health Counseling*, *21*, 113–123.

Scott, J. L., Brown, A. C., Phair, J. K., Westland, J. N., & Schüz, B. (2013). Self-affirmation, intentions and alcohol consumption in students: A randomized exploratory trial. *Alcohol & Alcoholism*, *48*, 458–463. doi:10.1093/alcalc/agt027

Seal, K. H., Abadjian, L., McCamish, N., Shi, Y., Tarasovsky, G., & Weingardt, K. (2012). A randomized controlled trial of telephone motivational interviewing to enhance mental health treatment engagement in Iraq and Afghanistan veterans. *General Hospital Psychiatry*, *34*, 450–459. doi:10.1016/j.genhosppsych.2012.04.007

Segal, Z. V., Williams, J. M. G., & Teasdale, J. D. (2002). *Mindfulness-based cognitive therapy for depression: A new approach to preventing relapse*. New York, NY: Guilford.

Seiverling, L., Kokitus, A., & Williams, K. (2012). A clinical demonstration of a treatment package for food selectivity. *Behavior Analyst Today*, *13*(2), 11–16. doi:10.1037/h0100719

Self-Brown, S. R., & Mathews, S. (2003, November/December). Effects of classroom structure on student achievement goal orientation. *The Journal of Educational Research*, *97*, 106–111. doi:10.1080/00220670309597513

Seligman, L., & Reichenberg, L. R. (2013). *Theories of counseling and psychotherapy: Systems, strategies, and skills of counseling and psychotherapy* (4th ed.). Upper Saddle River, NJ: Pearson.

Seligman, M. E., & Csikszentmihalyi, M. (2000). Positive psychology: An introduction. *American Psychologist*, *55*, 5–14. doi:10.1037//0003-066X.55.1.5

Sequeira, J., & Alarcão, M. (2013). Assessment system of narrative change. *Journal of Systemic Therapies*, *32*(4), 33–51. doi:10.1521/jsyt.2013.32.4.33

Shapiro, F. (2001). *Eye movement desensitization and reprocessing: Basic principles, protocols, and procedures* (2nd ed.). New York, NY: Guilford Press.

Shapiro, L. (1994). *101 tricks of the trade*. Plainview, NY: Childswork/Childsplay.

Shapiro, S. L., Astin, J. A., Bishop, S. R., & Cordova, M. (2005). Mindfulness-based stress reduction for health care professionals: Results from a randomized trial. *International Journal of Stress Management*, *12*, 164–176. doi:10.1037/1072-5245.12.2.164

Sharry, J. (2004). *Counseling children, adolescents and families. A strengths-based approach*. Thousand Oaks, CA: Sage Publications.

Shechtman, Z. (2000). An innovative intervention for treatment of child and adolescent aggression: An outcome study. *Psychology in the Schools*, *37*, 157–167. doi:10.1002/(SICI)1520-6807(200003)37:2<157::AID-PITS7>3.0.CO;2-G

Shechtman, Z., & Yanov, H. (2001). Interpretives (confrontation, interpretation, and feedback) in preadolescent counseling groups. *Group Dynamics: Theory, Research, and Practice*, *5*, 124–135. doi:10.1037/1089-2699.5.2.124

Sheely, R., & Horan, J. J. (2004). Effects of stress inoculation training for 1st-year law students. *International Journal of Stress Management*, *11*, 41–55. doi:10.1037/1072-5245.11.1.41

Sherburne, S., Utley, B., McConnell, S., & Gannon, J. (1988). Decreasing violent or aggressive theme play among preschool children with behavior disorders. *Exceptional Children*, *55*, 166–173. doi:10.1177/001440298805500208

Sherman, D. K., Hartson, K. A., Binning, K. R., Purdie-Vaughns, V., Garcia, J., Taborsky-Barba, S., … Cohen, G. L. (2013). Deflecting the trajectory and changing the narrative: How self-affirmation affects academic performance and motivation under identity threat. *Journal of Personality and Social Psychology*, *104*, 591–618. doi:10.1037/a0031495

Shurick, A. A., Hamilton, J. R., Harris, L. T., Roy, A. K., Gross, J. J., & Phelps, E. A. (2012). Durable effects of cognitive restructuring on conditioned fear. *Emotion*, *12*, 1393–1397. doi:10.1037/a0029143

Sidhu, P. (2014). The efficacy of mindfulness meditation in increasing the attention span in children with ADHD. *Dissertation Abstracts International: Section B: The Sciences and Engineering*, *75*(7-B)(E).

Silverman, K., Chutuape, M. A., Bigelow, G. E., & Stitzer, M. L. (1999). Voucher-based reinforcement of cocaine abstinence in treatment-resistant methadone patients: Effects of reinforcement magnitude. *Psychopharmacology*, *146*, 128–138. doi:10.1007/s002130051098

Simi, N. L., & Mahalik, J. R. (1997). Comparison of feminist versus psychoanalytic/dynamic and other therapists on self-disclosure. *Psychology of Women Quarterly*, *21*, 465–483. doi:10.1111/j.1471-6402.1997.tb00125.x

Sklare, G. B. (2014). *Brief counseling that works: A solution-focused approach for school counselors* (3rd ed.). Thousand Oaks, CA: Corwin Press.

Slomski, A. (2015). Meditation promotes better sleep in older adults. *Journal of the American Medical Association*, *313*(16), 1609. doi:10.1001/jama.2015.2943

Smith, E. J. (2006). The strength-based counseling model. *The Counseling Psychologist*, *34*, 13–79. doi:10.1177/0011000005277018

Smith, G., & Celano, M. (2000). Revenge of the mutant cockroach: Culturally adapted storytelling in the treatment of a low-income African-American boy. *Cultural Diversity and Ethnic Minority Psychology*, *6*, 220–227.

Smith, I. C. (2005). Solution-focused brief therapy with people with learning disabilities: A case study. *British Journal of Learning Disabilities*, *33*, 102–105. doi:10.1111/j.1468-3156.2005.00293.x

Smith, J. E., Richardson, J., Hoffman, C., & Pilkington, K. (2005). Mindfulness-based stress reduction as supportive therapy in cancer care: Systematic review. *Journal of Advanced Nursing*, *52*, 315–327. doi:10.1111/j.1365-2648.2005.03592.x

Smith, M. A., & Misra, A. (1992). A comprehensive management system for students in regular classrooms. *The Elementary School Journal*, *92*, 353–371. doi:10.1086/461697

Smith, S. (2002). *Applying cognitive-behavioral techniques to social skills instruction* (Report No. EDO-EC-02-08).

Arlington, VA: ERIC Clearinghouse on Disabilities and Gifted Education. (ERIC Document Reproduction Service No. ED469279).

Smokowski, P. R. (2003). Beyond role-playing: Using technology to enhance modeling and behavioral rehearsal in group work practice. *Journal for Specialists in Group Work, 28,* 9–22. doi:10.1080/714860206

Smyth, J. M., Hockemeyer, J. R., & Tulloch, H. (2008). Expressive writing and post-traumatic stress disorder: Effects on trauma symptoms, mood states, and cortisol reactivity. *British Journal of Health Psychology, 13,* 85–93. doi:10.1348/13591070 8X250866

Soares, D. A., Harrison, J. R., Vannest, K. J., & McClelland, S. S. (2016). Effect size for token economy use in contemporary classroom settings: A meta-analysis of single-case research. *School Psychology Review, 45,* 379–399. https://doi.org/10.17105/SPR45-4.379-399

Songprakun, W., & McCann, T. V. (2012). Evaluation of a bibliotherapy manual for reducing psychological distress in people with depression: A randomized controlled trial. *Journal of Advanced Nursing, 68,* 2674–2684. doi:10.1111/j.1365-2648.2012.05966.x

Southam-Gerow, M. A., & Kendall, P. C. (2000). Cognitive behavior therapy with youth: Advances, challenges, and future directions. *Clinical Psychology and Psychotherapy, 7,* 343–366. doi:10.1002/1099-0879(200011)7:5<343::AID-CPP244>3.0.CO;2-9

Spencer, P. (2000). The truth about time-outs. *Parenting, 14*(8), 116–121.

Spiegler, M. D. (2016). *Contemporary behavior therapy* (6th ed.). Boston, MA: Cengage.

Spindler Barton, E., Guess, D., Garcia, E., & Baer, D. (1970). Improvement of retardates' mealtime behaviors by time-out procedures using multiple baseline techniques. *Journal of Applied Behavior Analysis, 3,* 77–84. doi:10.1901/jaba.1970.3-77

Springer, D., Lynch, C., & Rubin, A. (2000). Effects of a solution-focused mutual aid group for Hispanic children of incarcerated parents. *Child & Adolescent Social Work Journal, 17,* 431–442. doi:10.1023/A:1026479727159

Stary, A. K., Hupp, S. D. A., Jewell, J. D., & Everett, G. E. (2016). Parent acceptability of time-out, spanking, response cost, and positive reinforcement. *The Behavior Therapist, 39*(4), 112–117.

Steele, C. M. (1988). The psychology of self-affirmation: Sustaining the integrity of the self. In L. Berkowitz (Ed.), *Advances in experimental social psychology, Vol. 21: Social psychological studies of the self: Perspectives and programs* (pp. 261–302). San Diego, CA: Academic Press.

Stevens, S. E., Hynan, M. T., Allen, M., Beaun, M. M., & McCart, M. R. (2007). Are complex psychotherapies more effective than biofeedback, progressive muscle relaxation, or both? A meta-analysis. *Psychological Reports, 100,* 303–324. doi:10.2466/PR0.100.1.303-324

Stice, E., Rohde, P., Gau, J. M., & Wade, E. (2010). Efficacy trial of a brief cognitive–behavioral depression prevention program for high-risk adolescents: Effects at 1- and 2-year follow-up. *Journal of Consulting and Clinical Psychology, 78,* 856–867. doi:10.1037/a0012645

Stice, E., Rohde, P., Seeley, J. R., & Gau, J. M. (2008). Brief cognitive-behavioral depression prevention program for high-risk adolescents outperforms two alternative interventions: A randomized efficacy trial. *Journal of Consulting and Clinical Psychology, 76,* 595–606. doi:10.1037/a0012645

Stiles, K., & Kottman, T. (1990). Mutual storytelling: An intervention for depressed and suicidal children. *School Counselor, 37,* 337–342.

Stith, S. M., Miller, M., Boyle, J., Swinton, J., Ratcliffe, G., & McCollum, E. (2012). Making a difference in making miracles: Common roadblocks to miracle question effectiveness. *Journal of Marital and Family Therapy, 38,* 380–393. doi:10.1111/j.1752-0606.2010.00207.x

Stolz, S. B., Wienckowski, L. A., & Brown, B. S. (1975, November). Behavior modification: A perspective on critical issues. *American Psychologist, 30,* 1027–1048. doi:10.1037/0003-066X.30.11.1027

Strumpfel, U., & Goldman, R. (2002). Contacting Gestalt therapy. In D. J. Cain & J. Seeman (Eds.), *Humanistic psychotherapies: Handbook of research and practice* (pp. 189–219). Washington, DC: American Psychological Association.

Sukhodolsky, D. G., Gorman, B. S., Scahill, L., Findley, D., & McGuire, J. (2013). Exposure and response prevention with or without parent management training for children with obsessive-compulsive disorder complicated by disruptive behavior: A multiple-baseline across-responses design study. *Journal of Anxiety Disorders, 27,* 298–305. doi:10.1016/j.janxdis.2013.01.005

Sundram, B. M., & Dahlui, M., & Chinna, K. (2016). Effectiveness of progressive muscle relaxation therapy as a worksite health promotion program in the automobile assembly line. *Industrial Health, 54,* 204–214.

Surilena, S., Ismail, R. I., Irwanto, I., Djoerban, Z., Utomo, B., Sabarinah, S., … Akip, A. A. P. (2014). The effect of rational emotive behavior therapy (REBT) on antiretroviral therapeutic adherence and mental health in women infected with HIV/AIDS. *Acta Medica Indonesiana, 46,* 283–291.

Sussman, S., Sun, P., Rohrbach, L. A., & Spruijt-Metz, D. (2011). One-year outcomes of a drug abuse prevention program for older teens and emerging adults: Evaluating a motivational interviewing booster component. *Health Psychology, 31,* 476–485. doi:10.1037/a0025756

Swoboda, J. S., Dowd, E. T., & Wise, S. L. (1990). Reframing and restraining directives in the treatment of clinical depression. *Journal of Counseling Psychology, 37,* 254–260. doi:10.1037/0022-0167.37.3.254

Szabo, Z., & Marian, M. (2012). Stress inoculation training in adolescents: Classroom intervention benefits. *Journal of Cognitive & Behavioral Psychotherapies, 12,* 175–188.

Tahan, H., & Sminkey, P. (2012). Motivational interviewing: Building rapport with clients to encourage desirable behavioral and lifestyle changes. *Professional Case Management, 17,* 164–172. doi:10.1097/NCM.0b013e3182 53f029

Tanaka-Matsumi, J., Higginbotham, H. N., & Chang, R. (2007). Cognitive-behavioral approaches to counseling across cultures: A functional analytic approach for clinical applications. In P. B. Pedersen, J. G. Draguns, W. J. Lonner, & J. E. Trimble (Eds.), *Counseling across cultures* (6th ed., pp. 337–379). Thousand Oaks, CA: Sage.

Taylor, P. J., Russ-Eft, D. F., & Chan, D. W. (2005). A meta-analytic review of behavior modeling training. *Journal of Applied Psychology, 90*, 692–709. doi:10.1037/0021-9010.90.4.692

Tedeschi, R. G., & Kilmer, R. P. (2005). Assessing strengths, resilience, and growth to guide clinical interventions. *Professional Psychology: Research and Practice, 36*, 230–237. doi:10.1037/0735-7028.36.3.230

Thompson, K., & Bundy, K. (1996). Social skill training for young adolescents: Cognitive and performance components. *Adolescence, 31*, 505–521.

Thompson, S., Sobolew-Shubin, A., Galbraith, M., Schwankovsky, L., & Cruzen, D. (1993). Maintaining perceptions of control: Finding perceived control in low-control circumstances. *Journal of Personality and Social Psychology, 64*, 293–304. doi:10.1037/0022-3514.64.2.293

Thorpe, G. L., & Olson, S. L. (1997). *Behavior therapy: Concepts, procedures, and applications* (2nd ed.). Boston, MA: Allyn & Bacon.

Toth, M., Wolsko, P. M., Foreman, J., Davis, R. B., Delbanco, T., Phillips, R. S., & Huddleston, P. (2007). A pilot study for a randomized, controlled trial on the effect of guided imagery in hospitalized medical patients. *The Journal of Alternative and Complementary Medicine, 13*, 194–197. doi:10.1089/acm.2006.6117

Toussaint, K. A., & Tiger, J. H. (2012). Reducing covert self-injurious behavior maintained by automatic reinforcement through a variable momentary DRO procedure. *Journal of Applied Behavior Analysis, 45*, 179–184. doi:10.1901/jaba.2012.45-179

Town, J. M., Hardy, G. E., McCullough, L., & Stride, C. (2012). Patient affect experiencing following therapist interventions in short-term dynamic psychotherapy. *Psychotherapy Research, 22*, 208–219. doi:10.1080/10503307.2011.637243

Treadwell, K., & Kendall, P. (1996). Self-talk in youth with anxiety disorders: States of mind, content specificity, and treatment outcome. *Journal of Consulting and Clinical Psychology, 64*, 941–950. doi:10.1037/0022-006X.64.5.941

Treyger, S., Ehlers, N., Zajicek, L., & Trepper, T. (2008). Helping spouses cope with partners coming out: A solution-focused approach. *American Journal of Family Therapy, 36*(3), 30–47. doi:10.1080/01926180601057549

Triscari, M. T., Faraci, P., D'Angelo, V., Urso, V., & Catalisano, D. (2011). Two treatments for fear of flying compared: Cognitive behavioral therapy combined with systematic desensitization or eye movement desensitization and reprocessing (EMDR). *Aviation Psychology and Applied Human Factors, 1*, 9–14. doi:10.1027/2192-0923/a00003

Turner, M. J., Slater, M. J., & Barker, J. B. (2014). Not the end of the world: The effects of rational-emotive behavior therapy (REBT) on irrational beliefs in elite soccer academy athletes. *Journal of Applied Sport Psychology, 26*, 144–156. doi:10.1080/10413200.2013.812159

Turner, S. M., Calhoun, K. S., & Adams, H. E. (1992). *Handbook of clinical behavior therapy* (2nd ed.). New York, NY: John Wiley & Sons.

Upright, R. (2002). To tell a tale: Use of moral dilemmas to increase empathy in the elementary school child. *Early Childhood Education Journal, 30*, 15–20. doi:10.1023/A:1016585713774

Utley, A., & Garza, Y. (2011). The therapeutic use of journaling with adolescents. *Journal of Creativity in Mental Health, 6*, 29–41. doi:10.1080/15401383.2011.557312

Van Dixhorn, J. (1988). Breathing awareness as a relaxation method in cardiac rehabilitation. In F. J. McGuigan, W. E. Sime, & J. M. Wallace (Eds.), *Stress and tension control 3: Stress management* (pp. 19–36). New York, NY: Plenum Press.

Vare, J., & Norton, T. (2004). Bibliotherapy for gay and lesbian youth overcoming the structure of silence. *Clearing House, 77*, 190–194. doi:10.3200/TCHS.77.5.190-195

Velting, O. N., Setzer, N. J., & Albano, A. M. (2004). Update on advances in assessment and cognitive-behavioral treatment of anxiety disorders in children and adolescents. *Professional Psychology: Research and Practice, 35*, 42–54. doi:10.1037/0735-7028.35.1.42

Vernon, A., & Clemente, R. (2004). *Assessment and intervention with children and adolescents: Developmental and cultural considerations*. Alexandria, VA: American Counseling Association.

Vickerman, K. A., & Margolin, G. (2009). Rape treatment outcome research: Empirical findings and state of the literature. *Clinical Psychology Review, 29*, 431–448. doi:10.1016/j.cpr.2009.04.004

Wadsworth, H. G. (1970, July). Initiating a preventive-corrective approach in an elementary school system. *Social Work, 15*(3), 54–59. doi:10.1093/sw/15.3.60

Waelde, L. C., Feinstein, A. B., Bhandari, R., Griffin, A., Yoon, I. A., & Golianu, B. (2017). A pilot study of mindfulness meditation for pediatric chronic pain. *Children, 4*(5), 32. doi:10.3390/children4050032

Walker, H. M., Colvin, G., & Ramsey, E. (1995). *Antisocial behavior in school: Strategies and best practices*. Pacific Grove, CA: Brooks/Cole.

Walsh, J. (2002). Shyness and social phobia. *Health & Social Work, 27*, 137–144.

Walter, J. L., & Peller, J. E. (1992). *Becoming solution-focused in brief therapy*. New York, NY: Brunner/Mazel.

Warnemuende, C. (2000). The art of working with parents. *Montessori Life, 12*, 20–21.

Waters, K. R. (2011). The hungry-for-attention metaphor: Integrating narrative and behavioural therapy for families with attention seeking children. *Australian & New Zealand Journal of Family Therapy, 32*, 208–219.

Watson, J. (2011). Resistance is futile? Exploring the potential of motivational interviewing. *Journal of Social Work Practice, 25*, 465–479. doi:10.1080/02650533.2011.626653

Watts, R. E. (2003). Reflecting "as if": An integrative process in couples counseling. *The Family Journal: Counseling and Therapy for Couples and Families, 11*, 73–75. doi:10.1177/1066480702238817

Watts, R. E., & Garza, Y. (2008). Using children's drawings to facilitate the acting "as if" technique. *The Journal of Individual Psychology, 64*, 113–118.

Watts, R. E., Peluso, P. R., & Lewis, T. F. (2005). Expanding the acting as if technique: An Adlerian/constructive integration. *The Journal of Individual Psychology, 61*, 380–387.

Watts, R. E., & Trusty, J. (2003). Using imaginary team members in reflecting "as if." *Journal of Constructivist Psychology, 16*, 335–340. doi:10.1080/10720530390227676

Webb, N. B. (Ed.). (2007). *Play therapy with children in crisis: A casebook for practitioners* (3rd ed.). New York, NY: Guilford Press.

Wegner, D. M., Schneider, D. J., Carter, S. R., & White, T. L. (1987). Paradoxical effects of thought suppression. *Journal of Personality and Social Psychology, 53*, 5–13. doi:10.1037/0022-3514.53.1.5

Weikle, J. (1993). *Self-talk and self-health* (Report No. EDO CS-93-07). Bloomington, IN: ERIC Clearinghouse on Reading, English, and Communication. (ERIC Document Reproduction Service No. ED361814).

Weinrach, S., Ellis, A., MacLaren, C., Di Giuseppe, R., Vernon, A., Wolfe, J., … Backx, W. (2001). Rational emotive behavior therapy successes and failures: Eight personal perspectives. *Journal of Counseling & Development, 79*, 259–269. doi:10.1002/j.1556-6676.2001.tb01970.x

Wenzlaff, R. M., Wegner, D. M., & Roper, D. W. (1988). Depression and mental control: The resurgence of unwanted negative thoughts. *Journal of Personality and Social Psychology, 55*, 882–892. doi:10.1037/0022-3514.55.6.882

Westra, H. A., Constantino, M. J., & Antony, M. M. (2016). Integrating motivational interviewing with cognitive-behavioral therapy for severe generalized anxiety disorder: An allegiance-controlled randomized clinical trial. *Journal of Consulting and Clinical Psychology, 84*, 768–782. http://dx.doi.org/10.1037/ccp000009

White, A. G., & Bailey, J. S. (1990). Reducing disruptive behaviors of elementary physical education students with sit and watch. *Journal of Applied Behavior Analysis, 23*, 353–359. doi:10.1901/jaba.1990.23-353

Whitmarsh, L., & Mullette, J. (2011). SEARCH: An integrated model for counseling adolescents. Journal of Humanistic Counseling, Education, and Development, 48(2), 144–159. https://doi.org/10.1002/j.2161-1939.2009.tb00075.x

Wicks, R. J., & Buck, T. C. (2011). Reframing for change: The use of cognitive behavioral therapy and native psychology in pastoral ministry and formation. *Human Development, 32*(3), 8–14.

Wilding, L., & Griffey S. (2014). The strength-based approach to educational psychology practice: A critique from social constructionist and systemic perspectives. *Educational Psychology in Practice, 31*, 43–55. https://doi.org/10.1080/02667363.2014.981631

Williams, C. D. (1959). Case report: The elimination of tantrum behavior by extinction procedures. *Journal of Abnormal & Social Psychology, 59*, 269. doi:10.1037/h0046688

Williams, M. H. (1997). Boundary violations: Do some contended standards of care fail to encompass commonplace procedures of humanistic, behavioral, and eclectic psychotherapies? *Psychotherapy, 34*, 238–249. doi:10.1037/h0087717

Williams, M. H. (2009). How self-disclosure got a bad name. *Professional Psychology: Research and Practice, 40*, 26–28. doi:10.1037/a0014745

Wolfert, R., & Cook, C. A. (1999). Gestalt therapy in action. In D. J. Wener (Ed.), *Beyond talk therapy: Using movement and expressive techniques in clinical practices* (pp. 3–27). Washington, DC: American Psychological Association.

Wolpe, J. (1958). *Psychotherapy by reciprocal inhibition*. Stanford, CA: Stanford University Press.

Wolpe, J. (1991). *The practice of behavior therapy* (4th ed.). New York, NY: Pergamon Press.

Wolters, C. (1999). The relation between high school students' motivational regulation and their use of learning strategies, effort, and classroom performance. *Journal of Learning & Individual Differences, 11*, 281–293. doi:10.1016/S1041-6080(99)80004-1

Wood, A. M., Linley P. A., Maltby, J., Kashdan T. B., & Hurling, R. (2011). Using personal and psychological strengths leads to increases in well-being over time: A longitudinal study and the development of the strengths use questionnaire. *Personality and Individual Differences, 50*, 15–19. doi:10.1016/j.paid.2010.08.004

Worling, J. (2012). The assessment and treatment of deviant sexual arousal with adolescents who have offended sexually. *Journal of Sexual Aggression, 18*, 36–63. doi:10.1080/13552600.2011.630152

Wu, J. Q., Appleman, E. R., Salazar, R. D., & Ong, J. C. (2015). Cognitive behavioral therapy for insomnia comorbid with psychiatric and medical conditions: A meta-analysis. *JAMA Internal Medicine, 175*, 1461–1472.

Wubbolding, R., & Brickell, J. (2004). Role play and the art of teaching choice theory, reality therapy, and lead management. *International Journal of Reality Therapy, 23*, 41–43.

Wynd, C. A. (2005). Guided health imagery for smoking cessation and long-term abstinence. *Journal of Nursing Scholarship, 37*, 245–250. doi:10.1111/j.1547-5069.2005.00042.x

Yalom, I. D. (2009). *The gift of therapy: An open letter to a new generation of therapists and their patients*. New York, NY: HarperCollins.

Yankura, J., & Dryden, W. (Ed.). (1997). *Special applications of REBT: A therapist's casebook*. New York, NY: Springer.

Yauman, B. (1991). School-based group counseling for children of divorce: A review of the literature. *Elementary School Guidance and Counseling, 26*, 130–138.

Yell, M. L. (1994). Timeout and students with behavior disorders: A legal analysis. *Education and Treatment of Children, 17*, 257–271.

Young, M. E. (2017). *Learning the art of helping: Building blocks and techniques* (6th ed.). Columbus, OH: Pearson.

Young, T. (2013). Using motivational interviewing within the early stages of group development. *The Journal for Specialists in Group Work, 38,* 169–181. doi:10.1080/01933922.2013.764369

Zenner, C., Herrnleben-Kurz, S., & Walach, H. (2014). Mindfulness-based interventions in schools—a systematic review and meta-analysis. *Frontiers in Psychology, 5,* 1–20. doi:10.3389/fpsyg.2014.00603

Zimmerman, T. S., Prest, L. A., & Wetzel, B. E. (1997). Solution-focused couples therapy groups: An empirical study. *Journal of Family Therapy, 19,* 125–144. doi:10.1111/1467-6427.00044

Zinbarg, R. E., Barlow, D. H., Brown, T. A., & Hertz, R. M. (1992). Cognitive-behavioral approaches to the nature and treatment of anxiety disorders. *Annual Review of Psychology, 43,* 235–267. doi:10.1146/annurev.ps.43.020192.001315

Ziv-Beiman, S. (2013). Therapist self-disclosure as an integrative intervention. *Journal of Psychotherapy Integration, 23*(1), 59–74. doi:10.1037/a0031783

Ziv-Beiman, S., Keinan, G., Livneh, E., Malone, P. S., & Shahar, G. (2017). Immediate therapist self-disclosure bolsters the effect of brief integrative psychotherapy on psychiatric symptoms and the perceptions of therapists: A randomized clinical trial. *Psychotherapy Research, 27,* 558–570. doi:10.1080/10503307.2016.1138334

Zlomke, K., & Zlomke, L. (2003). Token economy plus self-monitoring to reduce disruptive classroom behaviors. *The Behavior Analyst Today, 4,* 177–182. doi:10.1037/h0100117

Zourbanos, N., Hatzigeorgiadis, A., & Theodorakis, Y. (2007). A preliminary investigation of the relationship between athletes' self-talk and coaches' behavior and statements. *International Journal of Sports Science and Coaching, 2,* 57–66. doi:10.1260/174795407780367195

Zourbanos, N., Theodorakis, Y., & Hatzigeorgiadis, A. (2006). Coaches' behaviour, social support and athletes' self-talk. *Hellenic Journal of Psychology, 3,* 150–163.

Index